Ending
Homelessness

POINTS OF VIEW

Series editor: Alex Holzman

So much of what passes for debate on contemporary social, political, and economic issues focuses more on "winning" than on making sense. The books in the Points of View series are designed to elevate the discussion—with reasoned arguments and lively writing bent on encouraging real problem solving.

Ending Homelessness

Why We Haven't, How We Can

edited by
Donald W. Burnes
David L. DiLeo

LYNNE
RIENNER
PUBLISHERS

BOULDER
LONDON

Paperback published in the United States of America in 2019 by
Lynne Rienner Publishers, Inc.
1800 30th Street, Boulder, Colorado 80301
www.rienner.com

and in the United Kingdom by
Lynne Rienner Publishers, Inc.
Gray's Inn House, 127 Clerkenwell Road, London EC1 5DB

ISBN 978-1-62637-839-1 (pb: alk. paper)

The Library of Congress cataloged the hardcover edition of this book as follows:
Names: Burnes, Donald W., editor. ǀ DiLeo, David L., editor.
Title: Ending homelessness : why we haven't, how we can /
  edited by Donald W. Burnes and David DiLeo.
Description: Boulder, CO : Lynne Rienner Publishers, Inc., 2016.
  ǀ Includes bibliographical references and index.
Identifiers: LCCN 2015043541 ǀ ISBN 9781626375079 (hc: alk. paper)
Subjects: LCSH: Homelessness. ǀ Housing. ǀ Social policy.
Classification: LCC HV4493 .E535 2016 ǀ DDC 362.5/926--dc23
LC record available at http://lccn.loc.gov/2015043541

British Cataloguing in Publication Data
A Cataloguing in Publication record for the hardcover edition
of this book is available from the British Library.

Printed and bound in the United States of America

∞   The paper used in this publication meets the requirements
     of the American National Standard for Permanence of
     Paper for Printed Library Materials Z39.48-1992.

5 4 3

Contents

List of Tables and Figures   vii
Acknowledgments   ix

1   Are We There Yet?   1
    Donald W. Burnes

2   An Individual Experiences Homelessness   11
    Michelle McHenry-Edrington

Part 1: Where Are We Now?

3   The New Demographics of Homelessness   29
    Kerri Tobin and Joseph Murphy

4   Three Decades of Homelessness   47
    Martha R. Burt

Part 2: What Have We Done (Or Not Done)?

5   A Housing First Approach   67
    Sam Tsemberis and Benjamin F. Henwood

6   Special Needs Housing   83
    Richard L. Harris

7   Systems for Homelessness and Housing Assistance   101
    Jill Khadduri

8   Controversies in the Provision of Services   121
    Jason Adam Wasserman and Jeffrey Michael Clair

Part 3: Why Aren't We Further?

9   How We've Learned to Embrace Homelessness   141
     David L. DiLeo

10   Homelessness Is About Housing   159
     Sheila Crowley

11   Work, Wages, Wealth, and the Roots of Homelessness   177
     Bristow Hardin

12   Rights, Responsibilities, and Homelessness   197
     Collin Jaquet Whelley and Kate Whelley McCabe

Part 4: What Do We Do?

13   In Pursuit of Quality Data and Programs   215
     Tracey O'Brien

14   Public Opinion, Politics, and the Media   231
     Paul A. Toro and Corissa Carlson

15   Community Planning and the End of Homelessness   245
     Samantha Batko

16   The Role of Funders   261
     Anne Miskey

17   Where Do We Go from Here?   277
     Donald W. Burnes

References   291
The Contributors   323
Index   325
About the Book   341

Tables and Figures

Tables

11.1 Unemployment and Underemployment, 1979–2014   180
11.2 US Poverty Rate by Race and Ethnicity, 1979–2013   187
15.1 Community Adoption of the Ten Year Plan Elements and
      Ten Essentials for Ending Homelessness   250

Figures

1.1   Housing Costs as a Percentage of Income, 2011   3
4.1   Factors Affecting Homelessness   50
8.1   *Los Angeles Herald* Cartoon, December 8, 1907   123
8.2   *Washington Times* Cartoon, October 27, 1907   124
11.1 Changes in Wage/Salary Workers' Median Weekly Earnings
      by Sex, 1979–2014   181
11.2 Changes in Wage/Salary Workers' Median Weekly Earnings
      by Race, 1979–2014   181
11.3 Changes in Real Wages of Workers at Selected Percentiles,
      1979–2013   182
11.4 Growth in Real After-tax Income from 1979 to 2007 by
      Income Group   183
11.5 Changes in Percentage Shares of Income by Quintile,
      1979–2007   183
11.6 Distribution of Total US Financial Wealth Among Wealthy
      Classes, 1983–2010   185
11.7 Changes in Union Membership and Top 10% Share of
      Income, 1979–2013   189

11.8   Top 1% of Households' Percentage Share of Federal Taxes,
       1979–2007   190
11.9   Percentage Share of Federal Transfers by Income Group,
       1979–2007   190
13.1   Outputs Versus Outcomes: Frequency of References   219
14.1   Trends in the Volume of Newspaper and Professional
       Coverage on Homelessness, 1974–2013, and McKinney
       Act Federal Funding, 1987–2013   235
15.1   Percentage of Plans Completed by Year   253

Acknowledgments

Over the past 30 years of working on the issue of homelessness, my journey has included: running a direct services program in Washington, DC; writing *A Nation in Denial: The Truth About Homelessness* with my late wife, Alice Baum; serving on various boards and commissions in the Denver metro area; and listening to people experiencing homelessness, service providers, policymakers, and other stakeholders. In 2013, Tracey O'Brien, Gilana Rivkin, and I created the Burnes Institute on Poverty and Homelessness, and that same year, the dean of the Graduate School of Social Work at the University of Denver invited me to be a scholar in residence and teach a seminar about homelessness.

Because of these experiences, I felt a strong need to share my expanded understanding of the problem, and to let people know that my own thinking had been significantly transformed and that I had developed much broader and more nuanced perspectives on the topic than was evidenced in the first book. Despite my years of involvement, it was also evident that I still had much to learn.

This is not *my* book. It is the culmination of the efforts of many people, without whom the book would have remained only a fantasy. I can't begin to express my deep appreciation for all the thinking and hard work that my coeditor, David DiLeo, has given the project. He is such a thoughtful and insightful individual, and his chapter is a must read. He is also a great editor, and I really looked forward to our early-morning phone calls to scrutinize and amplify the submissions from our talented authors. His considerable effort during the course of this project has surpassed my wildest expectations.

Let me also express my deep appreciation to all the authors for their signature contributions. I am grateful to Samantha Batko, Marti Burt, Corissa Carlson, Jeffrey Michael Clair, Sheila Crowley, David DiLeo, Bristow

Hardin, Richard L. Harris, Benjamin F. Henwood, Jill Khadduri, Kate Whelley McCabe, Michelle McHenry-Edrington, Anne Miskey, Joseph Murphy, Tracey O'Brien, Kerri Tobin, Paul Toro, Sam Tsemberis, Jason Adam Wasserman, and Collin Whelley for adding so much to our understanding of this inexcusable tragedy. The author descriptions in The Contributors section at the end of the book attest to the considerable expertise each has brought to this volume. Initially, I knew most of them only by their well-deserved reputations, and I felt a bit awkward even asking them to participate in this venture. I am thankful that they all agreed, and I have personally learned a great deal from each of them. They all have my deepest thanks.

Our project director, Virginia McCarver, has been superb. She wrote much of the initial book proposal, contacted and worked with each of the authors, helped ensure timely delivery of chapters, and dotted and crossed all the logistical i's and t's in truly remarkable fashion. She also occasionally did double duty as a copyeditor. This volume would not have materialized without her constant and excellent support, and she accomplished all this with much grace, humor, and aplomb.

I couldn't be more grateful to our publisher. Lynne Rienner, head of Lynne Rienner Publishers, has been most helpful and gracious throughout the entire process. It has also been a pleasure to work with Andrew Berzanskis. Steve Barr, director of production at LRP, has been a magnificent manuscript shepherd, and the remaining staff at LPR have been unfailingly efficient and pleasant. Thank you all.

Let me also thank others who have reviewed parts of the manuscript and offered valuable suggestions. Courtney Brown provided very helpful insights on the final chapter. Burnes Institute interns Elizabeth Johnson, Anne Olson, Sallie Strueby, Kyle Ingram, Monika Schneider, Genevieve Flynn, and Rachael Sheaffer proved invaluable in helping me think through some tough issues. Chris Conner, Jeff Hirota, Michelle McHenry-Edrington, and Tracey O'Brien helped to shape very early iterations of the emerging book. Nancy Deyo, our own copyeditor, improved the manuscript immensely.

Not least, I want to thank my wife, Lynn, for her incredible patience during the entire process and for her valuable contributions to various chapters. I have been able to maintain my sanity throughout the development of the book only because of her constant encouragement and support. The book wouldn't have happened without her. Many thanks, Love.

I hope that reading this book will expand your horizons about this very important issue. We still have a long way to go to successfully address this national nightmare, and it is my hope that this volume will help move the needle.

—*Donald W. Burnes*

1

Are We There Yet?

Donald W. Burnes

I have spent most of the past thirty years working to address homelessness. In 1993 my late wife, Alice Baum, and I wrote *A Nation in Denial: The Truth About Homelessness*, a book that represented the culmination of academic research and direct service. Twenty years later and still absorbed by the issue, I helped create the nonprofit Burnes Institute on Poverty and Homelessness, which is dedicated to policy research and program evaluation.

While puzzling over the possibility of a second book, I found myself asking these questions: Why aren't we closer to the goal of ending homelessness? What are the political, cultural, and programmatic barriers? Despite the billions of dollars spent by the private and public sectors, the hundreds of millions of paid and volunteer person-hours, and the countless words uttered and published imploring us to do better, the number of persons experiencing homelessness has not changed significantly in the past thirty-five years. Why? These fundamental questions are addressed in this volume and, with the help of nationally known experts in the field, I hope it will provide some compelling answers.

The United States has always struggled with its attitudes about those experiencing homelessness. Endless debates, repeated by successive generations, have been fueled by cycles of pity, distaste, fear, anger, and apathy felt by all, rich and poor, when there is destitution in our midst. Over time, homelessness has given rise to important policy questions. Should we provide direct financial assistance, or should we provide shelter? Should the help be compassionate and generous, or should it exercise social control by rewarding work and industry while punishing idleness and intemperance? Should assistance be an entitlement paid for by the general public through taxes, or should it be available only when it has been earned by work? Should helping those experiencing homelessness be the responsibility of government, or should the primary source of help be private charitable organizations? Answers to these questions have often depended on the definition of who is worthy of assistance and who is not.

As Joel John Roberts, chief executive officer of PATH Partners, recently reported, between 2000 and 2013 we reduced the number of people experiencing homelessness by 90,000, from 700,000 to 610,000. At that rate, he calculates, it will take eighty-eight years to eliminate it (Roberts, 2014). Waiting that long is an abdication of our social responsibility and a forfeiture of an opportunity to leave a stronger, smarter, and more compassionate society to future generations.

Simple numbers about the magnitude of the problem are staggering. The National Low Income Housing Coalition (NLIHC, 2015, p.1) has declared that the current shortage of affordable rental units has now risen to 7.1 million for extremely low-income renters. This number does not include persons who are homeless. If we add the 400,000 homeless households, who by definition do not rent, the shortage of units climbs to about 7.5 million (National Alliance to End Homelessness, 2015).

Every state, on average, would have to produce 150,000 units over the next ten years for us to eliminate the shortage of affordable housing units, and every one of those units would have to be specifically designated for those experiencing homelessness or households on the brink. This also assumes that there is no increase in the number of homeless and near-homeless households over that period of time. (Given the present political climate and our cultural tolerance for homelessness, there is no realistic chance of every state reaching this goal.)

The general rule of thumb according to the US Department of Housing and Urban Development (HUD) is that a household should spend no more that 30 percent of its total annual income on housing. Any household that does so is considered "housing challenged." Furthermore, if a household spends more that 50 percent of its income on housing, that household is considered "severely housing challenged" (NLIHC, 2015, p.1). If we now add the 6.6 million people that are severely housing challenged to the 7.5 million homeless and at risk of homelessness, we have roughly 14.2 million people who are either homeless, at significant risk of becoming homeless, or are severely housing challenged. That represents about 5 percent of our national population. A recent poll conducted in Denver indicated that almost half of the respondents knew a family member or friend who had experienced homelessness at some point in their life (Metz and Weigel, 2015). If this poll is at all representative of the country as a whole, that means that as many as 150,000,000 Americans have been homeless at some point in their lives.

In its report on the state of homelessness, the National Alliance to End Homelessness (NAEH, 2013b) calculated the average amount of money spent on housing as a percentage of average annual income and arrayed these calculations on a continuum. For the top 20 percent of housing consumers (i.e., families that either own or rent their homes), the average annual income was about $153,300, and they spent on average approximately 19 percent on housing. For the bottom quintile, the average annual income was approximately $10,100, and those households spent 87 percent of their income on housing, leaving them about $1,000 per year for everything else, including food, health care, and clothing (see Figure 1.1). Talk about being severely housing challenged! What is more, since people experiencing homelessness and those staying with friends or family are not actual consumers of housing, they are not even included in these calculations.

These stark figures describe the current situation in the United States. The level of human and financial effort to end homelessness may well be at its highest level in the past thirty years, but we have made little real progress. Unless we change our level of effort by several orders of magnitude, we will not realize even our most conservative goals. It is not as though federal subsidies for housing are lacking. A recent working paper by the National Bureau of Economic Research suggests that federal support for low-income rental housing is less than 25 percent of the subsidies provided by the federal government to US homeowners, a whopping $195 billion (NBER, 2015, p.1). A major portion of this amount is derived from the mortgage interest deduction for homeowning taxpayers. In short, homeowners, especially wealthier homeowners, receive four times as much in federal housing subsidies as do those who rent, especially those in poverty, and those experiencing homelessness are on the bottom rung of that ladder. Those who need the least help get four times as much as those who need it most.

More important than the numbers is the human dimension of homelessness, the personal stories documenting the circumstances and the tragedy of life without reliable shelter. Many of us have never had to live through such

Figure 1.1 Housing Costs as a Percentage of Income, 2011

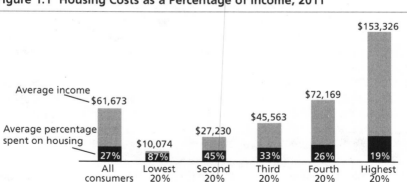

an experience. We have no concept of what being homeless means, no concept of the hardships and the tribulations of such an existence. Our only direct contact with persons experiencing homelessness is with the panhandlers on street corners. Even there, the vast majority of us do everything we can to avoid engaging the panhandler when the light turns red. We stare at our dashboard or glance over at the car on our right; in fact, we try our best to ignore the panhandler. We look at but don't see them on the street corners waving cardboard signs, nor do we acknowledge them asleep on sidewalks or huddled in doorways. We may read about them in newspapers or watch stories about them on the TV news, but we have no direct connection with any of them. It's almost as though they don't exist.

It is not surprising that the street corner high flier represents our stereotype of the person experiencing homelessness. But the fact is that most of those experiencing homelessness are not panhandlers; many are women with families, some are runaway or throwaway youth, some are veterans suffering from the ravages of post-traumatic stress disorder (PTSD), some have cognitive or physical disabilities, and all are sons and daughters of parents who love them. We as a nation marginalize them and do them and ourselves a terrible disservice by stereotyping them as drunken or mentally ill street people who are invading our public space.

Unfortunately, most of us think that people become homeless as a result of addictions, mental illness, or bad decisions. Our judgments may not include the fact that many of us housed citizens also have addictions, mental illness, or made bad decisions. What is the difference? The difference for the homeless is a lack of resources. Others of us think that those experiencing homelessness are on the streets because they choose to be there. In fact, few individuals with options choose life on the streets, and most of those who make that choice do so because their only alternative is the crowded and dangerous environment so typical of many of the emergency shelters that currently exist.

For reasons explored throughout this volume, we need a comprehensive cultural change in how we, as Americans and as members of a human family, feel about the systemic conditions that give rise to homelessness generally and about those persons actually experiencing homelessness. The civil rights movement changed how we felt about race, the disability movement altered how we perceived those with physical and cognitive challenges, and recent cultural forces have revolutionized how we feel about gay marriage. We need a similar kind of cultural tsunami to change our attitudes about homelessness. All of us need to interact directly with persons experiencing homelessness to learn about the hardships, disappointments, and tragedies that they endure on a daily basis.

While it is certainly the intent of this book to highlight important policy issues, it is also our intent to connect policy with practice and academic research with boots on the ground. Although there is evidence about the effectiveness of some practices, there are still major holes in our understanding of the best ways to provide for the needs of everyone experiencing homelessness. Top-down policy pronouncements from Washington, DC, tend to maximize a one-size-fits-all approach, when local understanding negates this premise. If we are to develop sound policies, the hard-won knowledge about local complexities has to filter upward to national, state, and local policymakers.

Current homelessness services buzzwords include "best practices," "evidence-based practice," and "evidence-based policy" (EBPol). Although it may be only a semantic argument, the concept of best practice is unfortunate, since "best" is a superlative adjective that can never be guaranteed simply because the number of comparable practices is, in theory, infinite. EBPol, while an attractive option in the abstract, "has also been critiqued for being inherently undemocratic and disempowering" (Stanhope and Dunn, 2011, p. 277). Critics of social science tinkering charge that shaping programs based on empirical evidence is an exercise in power. Stanhope and Dunn add that "the claim to objectivity rests on technical skills, methods, information, and professional networks that historically have excluded those groups most vulnerable to poverty" (p. 277).

In our desire to bridge the chasm between policy and practice, we provide a range of intellectual perspectives from those who have experienced homelessness and those whose backgrounds and experience are quite removed from the social science expertise so often found in a volume like this. For this reason, we have included a first-person account from an individual who has experienced homelessness as well as chapters by noted researchers in the field, chapters by authors whose primary experience has been in on-the-ground programs, and an analysis of homelessness by a professor of history and the humanities. The addition of these perspectives enhances the value of this book and its ability to transcend the separation often found between theory and practice.

Unfortunately, evaluations done at most service agencies compound the separation between policy and practice. At a point where good solid outcome evaluations could amplify our understanding of homelessness and lead to good policies, service agencies collect only output data (i.e., numbers of persons served, numbers of units of service). For example, at Denver's Road Home (DRH), the name given to the ten-year plan to end homelessness in the Mile High City (DRH, 2013), staff members have assiduously collected data on numbers of housing units built, numbers of outreach contacts, numbers of shelter and transitional housing beds, and now the number of permanent supported housing units available and filled. Clearly, these numbers are important and useful. But none of them illuminates the actual impact of any of these service units on the lives of those who are supposed to be benefiting from the services. Part of the problem is that there is no consensus about exactly what the indicators of successful impacts are, and there is considerable disagreement about how best to collect and analyze the data. And in those relatively rare instances where good impact data are available, they seldom reach the hands of individuals who could put them to good use.

Finally, I call your attention to the work of the Burnes Center on Poverty and Homelessness, where we are committed to infusing the realities of everyday circumstances into the evaluation work and the policy research that we do. The research that our staff undertakes is intended to inform both policy and practice and is based on our understanding of local practices. As results of this work become available, we make every effort to disseminate them to policymakers and researchers.

About the Book

In conceptualizing the book and in discussing the book with my coeditor, I was cognizant that most of the earlier edited volumes about homelessness deal exclusively with policy issues, or with agency and stakeholder practices, without much reflection on the actual lives of those experiencing homelessness. I strongly felt the need to include a chapter by a formerly homeless woman who could write about and reflect on her experiences as a way of bringing the whole issue into a sharper focus.

In Chapter 2, Michelle McHenry-Edrington provides an engagingly written account of a person who lost her home and experienced homelessness, "An Individual Experiences Homelessness." Her narrative illustrates what homelessness often looks like and provides an example of the frustration and futility often felt by those experiencing homelessness when faced with systems that have accomplished little to address the issue over the past three decades. Her story also helps to contradict the commonly held stereotypes of the street corner bum and the panhandler.

Part 1, "Where Are We Now?" presents a picture of homelessness today — one that is significantly different from thirty years ago — and analyzes how the new demographic complexities might be addressed.

In Chapter 3, "The New Demographics of Homelessness," Kerri Tobin and Joseph Murphy describe how the face of homelessness has changed dramatically over the past several decades. Once predominantly a problem of single men, homelessness has been perceptibly feminized, and Tobin and Murphy attempt to understand some basics about the new homeless, especially those who have suffered the ravages of the Great Recession. Although the characteristics of the population may have changed, the numbers have not been significantly reduced, and those at risk have increased substantially. In short, we as a nation have barely put a dent in the problem.

In Chapter 4, "Three Decades of American Homelessness," Martha R. Burt examines the size and characteristics of homeless populations in the

United States over the past thirty-five years, when homelessness became a major public issue for the first time since the Great Depression. She discusses the intricacies of how we count those experiencing homelessness and provides an important perspective on Point-in-Time (PIT), annual, and lifetime prevalence counts. Because we have yet to substantially reduce homelessness, she suggests that every household with a worst case housing need be provided a rent subsidy for as long as necessary. According to Burt, "There can be little doubt that we would reduce homelessness substantially" (p. 65) if we made that a policy decision. All that is required is renewed political will.

Part 2, "What Have We Done (or Not Done)?" analyzes two important programmatic approaches to addressing homelessness, based on the experiences of two longtime and successful practitioners. The chapters in this section discuss the current efforts to provide housing and services across the country, and examine the accomplishments and the shortcomings in both arenas.

In Chapter 5, "A Housing First Approach," Sam Tsemberis and Benjamin F. Henwood describe Pathways' Housing First (PHF) as an effective, evidence-based, permanent housing program that also supports recovery for individuals with psychiatric disabilities and co-occurring addiction diagnoses. The program, based on the belief that housing is a basic human right, emphasizes self-determination, harm reduction, and recovery. Tsemberis and Henwood describe the challenges faced in implementing PHF at the individual, agency, community, and policy level as well as the opportunities missed in utilizing the program for wider impact.

In Chapter 6, "Special Needs Housing," Richard L. Harris recounts his experiences at Central City Concern (CCC), a social service agency dedicated to helping those struggling with homelessness and poverty and one of the largest nonprofits in Portland, Oregon. He describes the development of the CCC housing and service model, especially the Alcohol and Drug Free Community (ADFC) concept, and some of the challenges that this model has experienced and addressed in the past. Harris also discusses the ten basic issues that agencies must face as they try to develop special needs housing. The ADFC concept is in direct opposition to the Housing First model, and the two programs stand in interesting juxtaposition to each other.

In Chapter 7, "Systems for Homelessness and Housing Assistance," Jill Khadduri reviews the models for providing shelter and housing that have evolved since 1980. Specifically, she considers the extent to which housing subsidy programs are playing a role in ending homelessness and the opportunities that are available to do more. She is particularly troubled by the consequences of the failure to combine mainstream housing programs with those intended for people experiencing homelessness.

In Chapter 8, "Controversies in the Provision of Services," Jason Adam Wasserman and Jeffrey Michael Clair describe various attempts to provide social services to homeless individuals and the shift from housing ready to housing first programs. They detail the evolution of homeless services, examining how a diverse set of religious philosophies and values underpins many approaches to addressing homelessness. They conclude by highlighting several key contemporary social conflicts related to homeless service provision and discuss how efforts to provide services may also work to obviate the potential positive effects that many services could have.

Part 3, "Why Aren't We Further?" identifies cultural and political impediments to addressing homelessness. The chapters in this section analyze various pieces of the homelessness puzzle—housing, employment, the law, and the social fabric—and describe how, as a nation, we have failed to understand the complexities of the issues and the magnitude of the problem, resulting in our failure to remedy the situation.

In Chapter 9, "How We've Learned to Embrace Homelessness," David L. DiLeo explores the roots and evolution of the ethical and political norms that foster a popular ambivalence toward persons experiencing homelessness. He argues that there are powerful ideological foundations—many subconscious and unexamined—that explain the persistence of poverty and homelessness throughout US history. He asserts that the general public's perception of homelessness as a benign, intractable, and, even providentially ordained, phenomenon diminishes the ability of advocates to compete for resources. Finally, he offers a strategy, which he terms "a conceptual reengagement," to facilitate the expansion of homelessness coalitions (p. 154).

In Chapter 10, "Homelessness Is About Housing," Sheila Crowley documents the major shortfall in the number of available units of low-income housing for those experiencing homelessness, thus creating a major barrier to our efforts. In addition, large numbers of residents spend substantially more of their income on housing than the recommended 30 percent. She describes the major federal housing initiatives and several of the most substantial housing tax breaks that benefit the wealthiest Americans, further exacerbating the economic inequality of our housing system.

In Chapter 11, "Work, Wages, Wealth, and the Roots of Homelessness," Bristow Hardin identifies one of the significant impediments for people trying to move out of homelessness: the lack of income and wealth. Although an estimated 40 percent of the homeless work, it is most often at low-skilled, part-time, or day labor jobs with minimal paychecks and no benefits—wages that are far from sufficient to afford housing. Furthermore, over the past thirty years, we have seen a growing concentration of wealth among the richest Americans while the bottom 80 percent of all Americans hold only 5 percent of the nation's wealth. Those experiencing homelessness, being on the lowest rung of the financial ladder, are hardest hit by this inequality and, as Hardin points out, this is directly related to a host of educational, health, and criminal justice issues.

Collin Jaquet Whelley and Kate Whelley McCabe discuss the rights and responsibilities of society to address and regulate homelessness in Chapter 12, "Rights, Responsibilities, and Homelessness." They examine antihomeless laws and the political priorities that result from them; theoretical conceptions of homelessness that influence priorities and policy; political arguments in support of, and in opposition to, antihomeless laws; legal understandings of antihomeless laws; and ways to reorient government policies. They confidently suggest that a judicial approach to the rights of those experiencing homelessness may be the next frontier in the battle to end this social tragedy.

Part 4, "What Do We Do?" approaches the question—What next?—from the perspective of data and evaluation, public will and the media, coordinated planning, and collaborative funding. Without improvements in each of these areas, we are not likely to make much real progress.

In Chapter 13, "In Pursuit of Quality Data and Programs," Tracey O'Brien argues that, to end homelessness, we will need to know much more about good programs and good practices. Our failure to generate reliable data often means that programmatic approaches continue to exist, virtually indefinitely, even when they are not particularly successful. She also discusses various federal data reporting requirements, their necessity, and the cost of meeting them. As she suggests, to have a real chance at accomplishing an end to homelessness, we need a vastly improved system of information and evaluation.

In Chapter 14, "Public Opinion, Politics, and the Media," Paul A. Toro and Corissa Carlson discuss the interaction of public opinion, policy, the media, and professional research interests in homelessness over the past forty years. In their conclusion, Toro and Carlson state that "the extent of homelessness over the past four decades has been surprisingly robust and has shown little hope of a dramatic reduction anytime soon" (p. 243). In light of comparatively low-level coverage of the issue by the media and a relatively sympathetic public, they argue that we will successfully address the problem only if professionals and citizen advocates coordinate their efforts.

In Chapter 15, "Community Planning and the End of Homelessness," Samantha Batko describes the movement to create ten-year plans to end homelessness, starting with the release of *A Plan, Not a Dream: How to End Homelessness in Ten Years* by the National Alliance to End Homelessness in 2000 (NAEH, 2000a). The effectiveness and impact of ten-year plans have varied greatly, but the process has paved the way for a new focus on measuring progress across a community, creating time lines, and developing benchmarks as central elements of a systems approach to addressing homelessness on both a federal and local level. Batko explores the efficacy of ten-year plans as tools to address homelessness, the expectations such plans produce, and the barriers that plans often encounter in mobilizing funding and political support.

In Chapter 16, "The Role of Funders," Anne Miskey examines funding strategies to end homelessness, particularly the role that philanthropy has played. Unfortunately, according to Miskey, many funders focus on short-term, one-year grants, and they are reluctant to fund evaluation, research, and organizational capacity, to the real detriment of sustained comprehensive efforts to address homelessness. Further, she urges us to consider total service delivery systems, rather than individual agencies. Only when we do this, will we be able to mount the necessary effort to have a substantial impact on the issue.

In Chapter 17, "Where Do We Go from Here?" I revisit questions posed throughout the book. I draw heavily on the expertise provided by the chapter authors as well as my own experiences and observations. Readers are called on to consider individual and programmatic efforts to address homelessness, and to reflect on the broader cultural and political landscapes that will require much attention in the years ahead.

2

An Individual Experiences Homelessness

Michelle McHenry-Edrington

I am a black woman; how could I be invisible? It is a tale to tell but, before I tell this tale of what I will call my "two years at the spa" (two years of being homeless), I have to acknowledge some folks. Also, I am not a professional writer; my chapter is not what the editors will say is smooth or flowing because that is not the way I think . . . sorry. This chapter is some of my recollections of my two years at the spa, and I don't recommend that you go there. I can now say it was a gift because I can serve people better with the knowledge that I gained but, while I was in it, it was hell and, at times, I was a hot mess.

To my mom, Margie McHenry, I give thanks for her everlasting love and for instilling in me the idea to never, never give up on anything and, to my dad, Elroy McHenry, who instilled in me the idea that every day is the opportunity for a new beginning. My dear, dear stepmother, Azale, who has passed away, made me promise to pursue my dreams and do something that I really wanted to do just for myself because life was short. She told me to ignore all of the negative things that everyone would say and always follow my heart, and so I did; I packed up and moved to pursue my education. To my children, Stacey, Tracey, and Zachary: they gave me the strength, love, and desire to keep moving forward for them when I had no energy or strength to do it for myself. To my friend Gino: not being family, he loved me and didn't have to. When a person loves you and they don't have to, it means a great deal; he was my lifeline, he listened to all of my fears and kept them safely locked away from others and always made me feel protected from the monsters in the world. To Don and Lynn Burnes, and Tracey O'Brien: well, I can never thank them enough for helping me to begin to fulfill my dreams of being of service to my community. They listened to my ideas and my dreams of doing work in the community with the attitude that anything is possible,

11

and they proceeded to help me accomplish those dreams. To Rhiannon McGaw, my friend at the Burnes Institute, who worked by my side and suffered through my thinking out loud, yet always wore a smile: she will be part of my life until the end. Lastly, my friend Toni Slade and former soldier, also my blood sister through an act of self-mutilation of our thumbs one night after a party on base, has been my friend for over thirty years. She has loved me without seeing me, and I know I can count on her no matter what. We are like Lucy and Ethel.

I kept the fact that I became homeless from my mother, father, children, Toni, Gino, and most people that knew me because I felt ashamed. In doing this, I was privy to the thoughts and attitudes of what many of those around me felt about those that were homeless or living in poverty.

The rest of this book will give facts and stats about homelessness and poverty; I want to tell you a little of what it was like through my eyes, a veteran, a black woman, a person with a career, a degree, a volunteer in the community, a mentor, and a leader who lost her home and became homeless, a person without a roof. I was the person that people used to count on for help, the one that took people in, served those experiencing homelessness and then, almost in the blink of an eye, I lost my home. I never thought I was immune to becoming homeless; I just never thought about becoming homeless because I was always working and doing for others. I was too busy to become homeless; God needed me to keep taking care of others. Yes, I thought I didn't have time to become homeless. In my chapter, I use the term "being at the spa," which took the edge off of saying I was homeless. If you think being homeless is difficult, consider being homeless, being a student, working in the Capitol, serving on boards of directors around town, and keeping your homelessness a secret. Well, hold on—here we go.

In 2011, I was living in Houston, working as a paralegal part time, going to night school at the University of Houston full time, and teaching a legal secretary program at a technical college during the day. During the fall of 2011, my school was purchased by a corporation that wanted to exclusively offer medical programs; therefore, my legal program was phased out. I was given a severance package, and my job was over. I decided I could finally do something for myself since my three children were adults, and my twenty-eight-year marriage had ended. I thought about moving to Chicago, New York, or Colorado to finish my degree. I was accepted at the University of Colorado Denver (UCD) on the Auraria Campus, so I was moving to Denver. I had money in the bank, investments, an apartment, my severance, qualification for financial aid, excellent letters of reference, a paralegal degree, experience; I had everything I needed to make a successful move.

On December 19, I arrived in Castle Rock, Colorado, after a long drive. My brother helped me to move. I settled into my apartment and, on Christmas Day, I delivered meals for Meals on Wheels in Denver. It was my first time driving in snow and ice; it was a treacherous adventure, but very satisfying.

After the holidays, I went to register for school but, due to a glitch at UCD, I was not allowed to begin school in the spring of 2012 as planned; therefore, I was not able to get the financial aid that I had calculated into my budget to supplement my income. I applied for unemployment, which was granted, so I did have some income. I began searching for a job until I could begin school.

Not being in school, I was at my apartment a great deal. Castle Rock is such a beautiful place, but I never saw anyone that looked like me; it was what I would call very sterile. I was in a restaurant one day and a woman came to my table and put her hands on my face and said, "You are so pretty." I was so startled. How could a person come up to me and do that? Where I come from, that falls under assault and battery.

Anyway, moving on, work was not coming, and was I getting nervous! I was applying everywhere. I learned that there were no jobs in Castle Rock. I started looking north to Denver, thinking that with my experience, I would be a good catch. WRONG! Some employers thought I was overqualified and that I would not stay, and some thought I was of the wrong aesthetic. For example, one company phoned me after seeing my resume online and said I was perfect for their office and could I come in right away. I rushed to their office, walked in and told them who I was, and the look on the receptionist's face was a Kodak moment. She went to her boss's office and came back and told me they had filled the position. I asked her, "You just phoned me and told me to come right away and that I was a perfect fit. How could you have filled it?" She had no reply. Things like this happened to me over and over, and it is very difficult to stay positive when you are getting rejected at the same time. I used to think, "Who could not like me, even if I am black, even in Denver, Colorado." I guess some people just didn't get it, even in 2012.

Well, my depression began to set in when I could not find a job, and my bank account was getting smaller. One good thing was happening and that was: as my bank account was getting smaller, so was my waistline. Going to the gym was my sanctuary; the endorphins made me feel better, if not good. I felt powerful and in control while exercising. I was in control of everything while at the gym but, in my life, everything seemed to be out of control. I always went to the gym at about 3:30 or 4:00 in the morning, because I didn't and still don't care to be around a lot of people. Oh, I forgot to mention that I have PTSD, left over from the military. I now have a service dog, Edgar, but I didn't get him until May 17, 2014. For some reason, I lost interest in eating. I just wanted to sleep. I felt no one would hire me because I was not going to stop being black; my future was uncertain. I continued going to therapy at the center in Denver, but once I left their office, I felt isolated out in Castle Rock. I was too proud to tell my family what I was going through, I couldn't tell my friend Gino because I didn't want to seem help-less or sound needy, and Toni, well, I had been so happy and sure of myself about the move to Colorado that I didn't want to sound like a failure. I felt my only choice was to keep getting up every morning and trying another day. I just knew God would not have played a joke on me and brought me this far and left me hanging. Well, it was August of 2012 and things were spiraling downhill for me, and my hope was teetering like the Weeble people; you know, leaning all of the way over, but not quite falling down.

On an off day while teetering a little too much, I was hospitalized at the Veterans Affairs (VA) facility; I guess I blinked, and I lost faith for a moment. I felt that I was all alone even though I had and have a family that loves me; Gino loves me, Toni loves me, but I guess I didn't love me. Maybe I felt that I had failed in some way and that I was doing something incor-rectly, and that is why I couldn't get a job or maybe people really didn't like me for who I was. I would look back over everything that I had done, trying to remember if I had done some terrible thing to deserve this misfortune. Once in the hospital, I would not talk to anyone; I just wanted to sleep, to escape the reality of feeling nonproductive and unlikeable. It was just my luck that I had a roommate in the hospital who, God bless her, was on her way out from this world. I turned my back to her and all of the equipment attached to her. Initially, I thought, "Is this a hint that I will move into her bed once she is gone and the equipment will already be here for me. Oh shit!" I also refused to eat; I slept all day and continued to not speak to any-one. I lost track of time. I didn't even know what day it was, but I was told that I had a visitor. "Oh, my gosh," I thought, "I have no friends here but, could it be, no, it couldn't be." I rushed to the bathroom and looked in the mirror and ohhhh yuk: I was a mess. I had not showered or combed my hair or cared about these things, and I had a visitor. Yes, it was Gino. So I put a little water on my hands to rub through my hair; I rinsed out my mouth, a pinch on my brown cheeks (which resulted in nothing but pain), and a strug-gle to adjust my clothing that I had been sleeping in for a couple of days. (Let's not mention my smell.) I took some deep breaths and searched my soul for a smile and went out into the hallway and watched as he came through the door. Oh my God, I hugged him like I would never see him again; I felt like he came to save me. I could not let go of him; we sat down and he told me that, when I looked at him, he felt as though I was looking into his soul. I have known Gino since he was seventeen and I was twenty-three. I am now fifty-seven. Our conversation was like putting life back into me. Right then, I knew I would not be moving to the deathbed in my room; I would be escaping. God had not abandoned me; it was like I said, I was the one who blinked and stumbled. My eyes were now opened. *The lesson was to know that, on this overcrowded earth, we are not alone unless we isolate ourselves in our minds.* When Gino had to leave, my heart didn't break; I embraced the thought that he came. A nurse that I had seen earlier came to me and for the first time said, "You do not need to be here. Tell them whatever they want to hear, even if you don't believe it, and get out of here." I looked at her and smiled and thought to myself, I have rested enough; I am ready to face whatever awaits me. I did just what she said; I told the doctors just what they needed to hear to make them feel they had accomplished their goal, and I busted out. I got in my car, smelled the fresh air, turned the radio on loud and, get this: I hadn't eaten in four or five days so I stopped at the first Ross store and ran in, found a black pencil skirt, tried on a size 10 and it fit perfectly. Yea, I had lost a couple of pounds. I had gone through all this shit, but I was in a size 10. I don't recommend this to anyone as a way to lose weight!

The drive out to Castle Rock was nice; freedom was nice, my head was clear. However, during the previous few months, I had not spent all my money, including my investments; by investments, I mean the small amount of money that I had put into an IRA, which totaled less than $7,000. So I made my mind up to give up my apartment, liquidate my investments, put my furniture in storage, and move into a shelter where there were other female veterans. I am a planner so I thought ahead about my car payments, my life insurance, car insurance, and my phone. My thought was if I lost my roof, I could have enough money to take care of my essentials until I could start school and get my financial aid. If I were to lose my car, that would have been a terrible situation with my PTSD and dealing with public transportation. On some days, my hypervigilance is very bad and I have triggers that can cripple me. Also, the thought of something happening to me and having my family being responsible for getting my body home and cremating me was a terrifying thought; I had to have my life insurance. I had to be responsible for myself. I figured out the amount of financial funds it would take to take care of my essentials. I barely had enough to last until school started but, thanks to an act of God, my unemployment benefits were extended.

My therapist helped me to locate a place that was near the university and close to a secure storage facility. By doing this, I felt that I was in control. I would receive my unemployment, put all of my funds in the bank and only use what I needed. I made plans to visit the shelter to see if I would feel safe before committing. I have to feel safe; that is a real issue for me. I arranged for movers and everything was set. I was so busy, I did not have time to be afraid, plus Joyce Meyer (minister) always says you can do things while you are afraid; so onward.

The shelter had a large room downstairs where only female vets stayed. It had a nice bathroom and six beds. It was very clean, but I was scared and there was no room for my STUFF. I need to be near my stuff and, of course, I have that PTSD thing. It is not that I dislike people; I just don't want to be around them all of the time. The intake consisted of sitting in a room full of many people and being asked a great many personal questions about your life. There is absolutely no privacy so I was very humiliated, but I could not refuse to answer questions or I would have been denied shelter. This was one time that I was happy that someone speaking to me never looked at me. I looked around this room and saw personal information about other women in the shelter written on a board for everyone to see. It was during intake that I first started to notice that there was a caste system in the shelter. By this, I mean that the clients were at the bottom, the staff was above them, the supervisor was above the regular staff, and the director was at the top.

This so-called intake was a joke but I had to keep in mind that I didn't want my car to be my zip code, plus I was so tired from moving out of my apartment and getting my furniture into the storage unit that I was not thinking very clearly. It had been a very long day. The first night, I just passed out from exhaustion. The army, navy and, of course, I represented the air force; we were all there except the navy and she had the bunk next to me. She came back on the second or third night I was there, and she was drunk; I had gotten out of the cuckoo's nest and landed in the damn beehive. I had always tried to ignore drunk people because they don't make for great conversation; well, she didn't like that, and she put her hands on me and I didn't like that. I am a coward; I don't know how to fight. I walked away, but she followed me and kept screaming. I couldn't move; it was like not being able to scream when you open your mouth and nothing comes out. Yes, I was a wimp and reported that she put her hands on me because I just thought in the long run, it would be better for me. I hate violence of any kind. In the next day or so, I had the option to move to a small hotel next to the shelter; I refer to it as the lovely Hanoi Hilton. I would have a room of my own with a kitchenette (small hotel room). They made all kinds about assurances no single males, no loitering, and safety. Ha-ha!!!!! I moved in, got some of my stuff from storage, took a bath, bought some fresh food for the fridge, some sheets, and rabbit ears for the TV. I started to breathe, but they were short breaths. I still hadn't told anyone that I was homeless. I told my family that I was living in a dorm with female vets. I told Gino that too, I think. The family decided to send a delegate here to find out what was really going on with the hospital thing. You see, I had told my neighbors that if there came a time that they didn't see me for two or three days, to either phone Gino or my mother as emergency contacts; God bless them, they phoned both of them when I was in the hospital. That is how Gino found me there. I thought he was so in touch with my feelings that he felt my vibes of distress from the hospital and located me; oh well. I received a phone call from Mom asking, "What's going on? Your neighbor called me." I can't remember what lie I told, but I said I moved into this dorm because I was running out of money and was in the hospital because I was just overwhelmed and stressed out. I don't think she really believed me, but when she flew to Denver and I arrived at her hotel room, we had lunch, and I was able to drive her by the building and it looked nice from the outside. My mom knows that I have a great deal of pride, and I will take care of myself. Of course, Mom said I looked thin, but I was loving it; she watched me eat. I am a grandmother, and she watched me eat. I am beginning to believe that people think that, when a woman gets divorced, her mind leaves along with the husband. Little do they know the woman's mind returns when the husband leaves. Anyway, the visit concluded, I promised I would eat, be careful, and to call her if I needed anything. I put her on the plane so that she could return to the delegation back in Houston and report that her mission was a success and all was well with Mom.

Meanwhile, back at the Hanoi Hilton, I was really beginning to understand the art of being homeless. I learned that the women at the shelter would play any role necessary to get what they needed as far as supplies and privileges at the shelter. I was meeting other female vets, but they were housed at other shelters, not the Hanoi Hilton. I met a lovely army vet, and I told her where I was lodging and she said that she had had the pleasure of staying there, at the Hanoi Hilton. She asked what room, and I told her. The rooms didn't have keys, they had combinations, and it just so happens that she was in the same room that I was in and guess what, she told me what the SECURE combination lock was to my door. They had not changed the combination in weeks. Anyone could have gotten in my room when I was there or when I was gone, taken me or taken my stuff. I went to my case manager and the Hanoi Hilton front desk with the information that I had met a stranger who knew the combination to the door to my room; they said they would get around to changing it when they could—nothing urgent for them. The security that I needed to feel was not falling into place.

I made the room look and feel as nice as I could; I was determined to make the best of it. I bought some dishes, sheets, towels, soaps, rabbit ears for the TV, groceries, and a candle. Yes, I spent some of the money from my unemployment check; just because I was homeless didn't mean that I had lost my desire for nice things. I just purchased them at the dollar store and Walmart instead of the usual places. I would make believe it was better. Trying to sleep in a room on West Colfax is no easy task, and falling asleep acknowledging that you are now a member of the homeless population is hard. You see, people make you think you've left the human population altogether and become a member of a whole new subpopulation when you lose your roof (home); all of my life, I was under the impression that we were all human beings, no matter what your living situation was.

While in Castle Rock, I had begun searching for places to volunteer while I was looking for employment. Looking for volunteer opportunities was a daunting task; Denver was very unwelcoming. I came with over thirty years' experience, and no one had time to talk to me. Then, I found one of the greatest directors in Denver, Shannon Southall at Rocky Mountain Cares. She ran her agency like it was her family and the clients were her relatives. She was so caring. She asked me to be on their board and I am still there as of today. I also began volunteering at a legal nonprofit downtown for a group of female attorneys who did fantastic work. I found a class to audit at night, and life was very busy. Doing for others kept my mind off myself, and I have always felt that we are all our brother's keeper.

Time passed quickly, and the holidays were upon me; my children sent me a ticket to come home. I was very excited to see everyone, but I had lost so much weight that my head looked big. It was very important that my family think that I was doing well and ready to start school and fulfill my dream of finishing this degree. They could never know that I was without a home.

My flight home was nice. When my mom took me to one of my daughters' homes, Stacy took me into a room and asked me, "Mom, do you have cancer?" I said, "No, Stacey, I am fine." I knew Christmas would be all about my weight, but I was happy because no one would be concerned about my living conditions. LOL. My other daughter, Tracey, was of course briefed by her twin Stacey via text so, when she saw me, she was better prepared and was able to pull off not looking shocked when she saw me. My son, Zachary, is always nonexpressive, but I am sure he was briefed by Stacey and Tracey via text as well. You see, there are no secrets in my family, nor discretion.

The holidays went very well; the New Year arrived, and it was time to return to Denver. I was going to begin school at the University of Colorado in a few days. We all said our farewells and everyone was convinced that I was doing fine. After a few days back in Denver, I was very busy getting registered at school. I took a full load of classes and got acquainted with the Veterans Student Center on campus. I would come to find that the Vet Center on campus would be my lifeline. It was at the Vet Center that I would meet Cameron, my marine. I felt he was one of two personal angels that God put in my path to help me along with the fire that I would encounter at school. Every time there was a roadblock at school, Cameron would help me hurdle it and sometimes crawl under it; once or twice we even busted right through them, carrying the banner "Fuck You." You see, Cameron is a man of ethics and equity for everyone, not just sometimes, but all of the time. Like me, he believes what is right is right, and we should always do the right thing at all costs no matter how much money we make or how many times we fall down.

At the Hanoi Hilton, I was assigned other case managers from the VA since I am a veteran. Meetings, meetings, meetings became the rule of the day. The goal was document numbers to turn in to the VA. I told the case managers, I have a plan: finish my degree, get a job, and get on with my life. They had one thought: everyone who was without a roof was an addict, alcoholic, could not manage their money, and had no discipline. "Well," I told them, "I don't abuse alcohol, use or abuse legal or illegal drugs. I have raised three children; they have all gone to college; and I have earned one degree and am working on a second. I took the US Air Force to court and won my case; all that I choose to say about that case is that my enemy wore that same uniform that I wore and I was sent back to the same trainer in the Twenty-sixth Equipment Maintenance Squadron who was my perpetrator. I handled my own divorce case, and you say that I need to go to life management classes. I was mandated to attend all of these meetings and actually leave classes to attend meetings that have nothing to do with me just so you can have numbers to turn in."

I already attended therapy at the Vet Center; I was doing that before I left Texas and had that in place when I arrived in Colorado. I found myself getting very frustrated with case managers who thought the process was more important than the individual. Not all people are the same, so the case managers cannot and should not attempt to apply all of the same variables to everyone.

I found myself falling into depression but while I was able to push it down when I was away from the room, at night when I was alone that was when the demons would come. The tears would fall with such force and I would turn my TV up louder so that the lady downstairs would not hear me crying. My hope was that my fears would leave me in each tear that would fall, and that the crying would exhaust me so that I could sleep and not ponder what would come tomorrow. After a while, sleep would finally come. Every night, it would be the same routine; I would look forward to tears to bring sleep in hopes that I would stop thinking. There is something about the nature of a system of the people saying they are there to help you, and yet they are the very ones caus- ing you agony. How can they help you when they never ask what it is that you need? So many nights, I feared that I would have a stroke or someone would break into that disgusting room and kill me, and I would only be identified by the necklace I always wear that has an M on it. I did not want my family to be notified that I had died in a seedy hotel room. With the help of my therapist at the Vet Center, I had made a list of three people that I could call when I got really depressed or had anxiety attacks and they would come. I went to the director of the shelter with this list so that I could leave their names at the front desk. Her question to me was, "When do you think you will have these anxiety attacks?" I almost laughed. I told her that I don't plan them like a party, I can't give you dates, and therefore she denied me. Thank God for bringing tears to put me to sleep when in that room and giving me the strength to push my agony down inside me when I had to leave that room and function, but I have had years of practice, thanks to Uncle Sam.

Cameron and I discussed my being homeless and the case managers wanting me to leave class to come to meetings that had nothing to do with me. By the way, Cameron is the director of the Veterans Student Center on campus. He was there to run the Vet Center and also to help veterans with any issues that may be roadblocks keeping them from completing their education. He became an invaluable asset for me. Once a vet walked through the doors of the center, they knew that everyone inside had their backs, no matter what. You could study, sleep, eat, sit quietly, you didn't have to talk if you chose not to, and everything was just OK; everyone got it.

Back to the case managers: I could not get them to understand that I only needed shelter until I completed my education and that none of my behavior caused me to lose my home. My leaving class or the campus would have been detrimental to doing my best in school; I thought understanding that was not rocket science. I was told by the case managers that, if I did not comply with the meetings, I would lose my shelter. I asked them, "Just to be clear, if I don't leave school to attend meetings that had nothing to do with me, you would take my shelter away?" They would never say yes; they would always say, "If you do not comply with the meetings, you will have to leave the program." Same thing, right?

When I told Cameron all of this, he decided to go with me to the meeting; of course, I did not tell them he was coming. Imagine the look on their faces when he walked in. He said the very same thing I said; he and I made sure of that but, oh my gosh, the response was totally different when a white male approached the situation. Not only did I not have to attend the meetings but, if they needed me, they would come to his office on the school campus when I was not in class. WTF, the power of a white male never ends, even if it is used for a black homeless female. I pimped him out to get what I needed. You see, they never heard me when I said the very same thing; I was invisible and voiceless because if you are roofless, you have no choice, no sense, and no value. Like I said, I am black; how can I be invisible? Because I had no Internet at the Hanoi Hilton, Cameron arranged for me to have a key to the Veterans Student Center on campus so that I could do my homework. I lived there virtually from the time the school was open at 6:30 A.M. until after midnight. The other students would tease me because I would be there when they arrived in the mornings and I would be there when they left at night. Of course, they did not know that I was without a roof. It was difficult listening to some of the remarks that they would make about some of the roofless people that slept during the day in the Tivoli Center and food court or just made random jokes about roofless people. I didn't dare give myself away. When things got to be too tough, I would always take refuge in Cameron's office. Some of the teachers that I encountered were less than accommodating because I did not have the most up-to-date phone with recorders and taping abilities to do projects. College is difficult if you don't have economic resources. That first semester, I had school seven days a week; I was so tired all of the time and I had my volunteer work on top of everything. For me, helping others is like a hobby, it brings me such joy and peace. But I got through it with the support of others.

My HIV volunteer work led me to attending Colorado Organizations Responding to AIDS (CORA) meetings. There, I met Jeff Thormodsgaard, a lobbyist. I was so impressed with his passion that I wanted to meet him. We had coffee and I asked him to become my mentor. He introduced me to the Capitol and the business of getting things done. Everything moved at the speed of sound; my three-inch heels needed wheels. Jeffery had opened the door to a new world for me and I like it; box it up for me. Through Jeffery, I met Representative Rhonda Fields, and I liked her straightaway. I spent time with her in the chamber and in her office. We would go to events on the weekends and, before long, I became her aide. I had school going on, my board work, and my aide work; I was as happy as a tick on a fat ass. In the summer of 2013, Representative Fields sent me to Atlanta to represent her at a conference—me, this roofless person. Of course, she had no idea that I was roofless; no one knew, not even Jeffrey. I didn't want anyone at the Capitol to know because I didn't want their pity; I wanted them to respect me for my work. Anyway, there I was flying to Atlanta with the bigwigs; the hotel was glorious and, because the hotel screwed up in picking me up, there was a beautiful basket of champagne and strawberries on my big bed.

That weekend, I would forget that I was roofless. I was meeting with President Jimmy Carter again, with whom I had worked in Houston to build 100 houses in a week for Habitat for Humanity; when I asked him if he remembered, he laughed and said he would never forget the heat and humidity. I was able to chat with Patrick Kennedy, President Carter, and several other people that I admired for their work.

Then, I was back to Denver and summer school since the legislative session was over. With the school schedule lighter, I had more time to participate in being homeless. I discovered that, when you are homeless, the VA treats you to more benefits such as dental and vision. The doctors seem to treat you with respect whereas the case managers don't. There was a constant battle between the case managers and me; they seemed to resent that I asked questions and advocated for myself. I have not met a single one that has any knowledge about cultural concerns, age, gender, or the importance of remembering that I am a human being, not a number. Every time that I had to see them, I felt that I had to armor up and get ready like I was going off to war. Even though this is an issue, I never missed a meeting except once; I had a doctor's note and they still wrote me up.

Things at the Hanoi Hilton remained miserable; critters in and out of my room, destroying my possessions. I was in fear every day. My life was miserable every day. One of the worst times was the hotel office sending the police that hunt missing felons who have open warrants up to my room in the middle of the night looking for someone. The rooms are behind a gate that has a combination that is supposed to be secure, and the staff is supposed to be able to see the entrance to every room from their desk, and no one is allowed visitors. No one has ever been to my room, I have never had a violation, and yet they sent these people to my room, pounding on the door, shining lights through the window and scaring me to death, in the middle of the night, and they knew I have PTSD. I will never forget that night, and no one had to answer for it.

I reported that the people in the room next to me were smoking drugs, and nothing was done. When I would leave messages for the case manager at the VA, they wouldn't respond; supervisors told me their phone system probably messed up. How many times can a person leave them a message and they not respond and blame it on the phone system?

Too many things, too much, too much. I was waking up every day wondering what was going to be today. They became the enemy. I could not focus on school. They were now saying I was not in compliance with looking for housing; a meeting was called. I was so tired of being bullied by them and with their talking out of the other side of their mouths, saying they were here to help me. In the meeting with the shelter (Hanoi Hilton), the case manager was to my right, the VA case manager to my left, and I was on the end. Both came at me with accusations, which I can't even remember. I do remember telling them that all they had done for me was give me a roof over my head, and it was not a safe one. Oopsy.

After that comment, I was told I was out; thirty days and I was to vacate my room, right in the middle of finals. November 19 would be my last day at the Hanoi Hilton. I kept my composure, left, and went back to campus where I felt safe. At this time, my support, Marine Cameron, had moved on to Houston to take a better job; I felt lost and alone because, as I have mentioned, I had not told Gino my secret of being without a roof and I was not about to run to him now.

I had another lifeline at school in the Veterans Student Center and that was Izzy (army); he was my Boots to Suits sponsor and adviser. (Boots to Suits is a group for juniors and seniors who are veterans; they can be assigned mentors and internships in their chosen field of study.) Izzy was there for me when Cameron was busy or not available and I needed to vent or needed a shoulder or to just talk. He also connected me to the Veterans of Foreign Wars (VFW) Post. Izzy got busy helping locate a place for me to live; he contacted his connections, and it seemed like I had a team working to help me meet my needs, not to meet the needs of a process. Dana Niemela, homeless veteran reintegration program coordinator, actually asked me what I wanted and needed to reach my goals and then hit the ground running, and in heels. She secured a roof for thirty days; it was the Hanoi Hilton's twin hotel, but it was a roof and I was warm. The VFW Post paid for everything and I was able to get through finals and pass everything; 2014 had to be better.

January came and Izzy was still making things happen. I had very good grades and I was in Boots to Suits, so Izzy asked if I would like to interview to work as an intern in the governor's office in February of 2014; of course, I said, "Okeydokey." I had had such a great time with Representative Fields the year before and I had met so many great people, I could not wait to get back to the Capitol. I had the interview and it was great; I was in and I started right away. Did I mention that this was a paid internship? Having a salary qualified me for a program that helped veterans get housing. Into my life comes Terri the WOLF; that is what I call her because she got things done. She and I found an apartment that was perfect for me, in the perfect location, and it was safe. I am actually still there. All of this happened in February of 2014—the internship, the housing, school, all of it in a matter of weeks. Izzy, Dana, and the Wolf were stepping stones in helping me when I tripped on the road of life. All of the case managers and their processes almost made me blink and take my eyes off the prize and say cheese; damn them. OK, I did great work in the governor's office and the folks at the Capitol remembered me from when I was there before; that made me very happy. While I was there, my boss, Richard Sandrock, had me working on homeless issues for veterans and civilians. As mentioned, no one knew I was without a roof when I first came there or had been two years at the spa. I know they were pondering how I knew so many details and understood so much about the issue of being homeless.

As part of my duties, I would attend events and meetings for the governor's office and, at one event, there was this one man in the back who was asking all of the right questions, the questions that most people wouldn't ask because they feared what their peers would think. I thought to myself, who is this guy and what does he do? I liked him. After the event was over, there was a lunch in the next building; I chased him across the yard and up the stairs and down a hallway. I tapped him on the shoulder and introduced myself and asked who he was; he responded, Don Burnes. I said that I thought he and I should have lunch or coffee; he handed me his card and we made an appointment to meet. I went back to the gov's office and told everyone about this guy and asked Karla Maraccini, director of community partnerships, if she knew him; Karla knows everyone who is anyone and some of those who aren't. Anyway, she smiled and said he was one of her favorite people.

We were to meet at Panera's, so I arrived early; I had kind of forgotten what he looked like. I was sitting in the corner so that I could see all of the entrances. I looked up and saw this man eating a Danish with a knife and fork and said, "Self, that has to be him." I sent him a text and said, "I am here; I am Michelle, the black one in the corner, just in case you have forgotten what I look like." We talked for what seemed like a couple of hours. I finally asked him, "Why do you do what you do when you don't have to?" When he answered me, I knew I had to work for and with him. From then on, we were joined at the hip. I left the governor's office to go to work for

Dr. Don W. Burnes at the Burnes Institute. I thought this would be the last job of my life, doing work to help service organizations serve people better. Doing evaluations to understand what services are working and producing positive outcomes is invaluable information, and tracking this data is just as important; why keep putting money into what is not working? Working with cofounder Tracey O'Brien and Don taught me so much about doing evaluations and logic models, and having spent two years at the spa turned out to be a blessing because I was able to really say that I had been there, done that, and got the T-shirt. I had experienced the broken systems in place.

I was able to assist Don in teaching a class on homelessness at the University of Denver in the spring of 2014, and it was wonderful. The students all knew I had spent time at the spa and I was very honest with them about my experiences. I believe it was a positive experience for all of us. Business at the Burnes Institute was OK, but not thriving; agencies wanted evaluations, but no one had the money to pay for them. No one wants to face the fact that, when you are really doing your job well, your numbers will go down in services provided because people will become self-sustaining. Just like when parents raise their kids and teach them how to be adults, we hope they move on and can take care of themselves. RIGHT.

In the fall, we came up with the idea of having an open house to let the community know that we were the Burnes Institute and we could help service organizations serve their clients better. Our board of directors, interns, and their significant others, Don and Lynn Burnes, Tracey, Rhiannon, and even my friend Gino, all pulled together and put on a fabulous open house. We even had a proclamation from the governor; no big donations came in, but there was a good turnout, and our name was out there. This was in November of 2014 and, although the open house was a success, there were no big contracts coming our way. I was beginning to panic because I just couldn't lose this job and become homeless again. Old thoughts began to creep into my mind, my sleep began to get worse; I was scared, but I tried to hide it. I always tried to keep my faith. I always felt that God would never let me down and believed what Joyce Meyer taught me in her preaching: that I could do things while I was afraid. Being a member of Lakewood Church in Houston, Texas, I always had Joel Osteen to turn to, to hear his sermons to remind me that God would never forsake me. Of course, I always knew these things, but I needed reminding when things got rough. The day Don called Rhiannon and me into his office to inform us that February would be our last day if a miracle did not happen was awful; I still thought someone would learn to eat paper and shit money to save us. I think this was one of the roughest days of Don's professional career.

And guess what would make the whole situation worse? One of my twin daughters was coming to visit me Valentine's weekend. She was the chosen delegate from my loving family to come to Denver to see how I was really doing. You see my family loves me so very much that they have to see for themselves that I am not suffering. They would do anything for me, even things that I don't want them to do. LOL. They are going to shit when they find out I was homeless for two years and didn't tell them; oh well. Anyway, Don, Lynn, Tracey, Rhiannon, and I made a plan to not let Stacey know anything about the Burnes Institute's downsizing. Stacey arrived Friday morning and I picked her up, took her to meet Don and the interns at the office. The interns were sworn to silence. After a nice twenty-four hours during which no one broke the silence, Stacey and I went to a nice place for dinner. We had so much fun; we laughed so much, and I went into a meat coma because we went to Texas de Brazil. Oh my gosh, I tried everything I could not afford on my own. I couldn't believe it when I saw people getting chicken, something you can eat any time. This is the kind of place that you make a strategic plan about what to eat before you go. Don had told me it would be fabulous and he was right on the money.

When I felt I had eaten Stacey's money's worth, we went home; I could hardly breathe. Remember, in the back of my mind, I am in fear of becoming homeless so I had to eat while I could. When we arrived at my apartment, I didn't get into bed; I fell onto the bed and waited for morning. On the way to the airport, I was thinking, we pulled it off; the family delegate would go home and report to the family counsel that I was a success. I have the most loving family and the great team of friends that I work with here in Denver. I would never want them against me. Now, back to losing my job; the end of February came and it was so difficult. February of 2014 was the month that I moved into an apartment, and February 2015 was the month that I was afraid of losing it. You know, I feel that I do so much stuff for everyone, when am I going to be able to relax and just live without worry? I have been doing public service since I was seventeen years old; I dragged my kids with me to do for others. I received a public service award during the time that I was homeless, and I have learned to even appreciate the bad shit. I don't want much, just a small house that I can own, a small yard for Edgar, a car that is dependable, my health, and a job doing service (that pays). I do know how lucky I am to have a family that loves me so very much, friends that love me, and I survived being homeless and I look at it as a blessing. I do know so many people are doing so much worse; I do live in gratitude every day. I am just venting. It will pass.

With the help of Don and Tracey and the Big Guy upstairs, I have a job at Bayaud being of service to people, and I am still able to do my volunteer work. I am working with a great group of people who care for others, so I am still being blessed.

The most important part of my chapter comes now. I became homeless through no fault of my own, and that should not even matter. I made my move to Colorado with investments, savings, and a plan, all of the things

Suze Orman says you should have. I even had a paralegal degree under my belt, excellent letters of reference, and years of good experience. All of the things that kept me from gaining employment were beyond my control. I have no drug use, no alcohol abuse. I had never missed a day of work due to my PTSD. My mental health issue returned due to becoming homeless, and was exacerbated by the case managers and the system that insisted that they were here to help me but only hindered me, trying and almost succeeding in breaking my spirit. I still never used drugs or alcohol. When I didn't fit the stereotype that case managers thought I should fit, they did not know what to do, and it usually resulted in their being angry and they would check the non-compliance box. I am one of those stubborn people that believes in ethics and what is right is right and what is wrong is wrong and, if it is wrong, I always asked why and wanted to understand. Most people in charge don't like this. I found that, with case managers, the process became more important than the individual. The need to increase numbers was the name of the game; hence, the response, "This is what the program requires." When I asked my case manager to name the disabilities that I had, she didn't know, and she had been working with me almost a year. I realized I was only a number being shoved down the line; next, please.

I found that with the broken systems that were in place, it would have been easier for me to sit on my backside and do nothing, have no goals, no desires but to get some kind of check each month, than to finish my school and get back on my feet and be a success story. Other women in the shelters would tell me how to succeed at doing nothing and how to get a check. All I needed was shelter, that's all, and they put me through hell. Thank goodness I am not a quitter and I had such faith and people like Cameron and Izzy in my life. It was almost like the case managers would be angry if you wanted to be a success and you couldn't be counted in the programs where they wanted you to be. The class system between the staff and clients in shelters is worse than the class system in India. I was not going to Jim Crow it for anyone. In shelters, the fish rots from the head down. Recognize, directors! What I mean by this is, when the staff of an organization are not doing their jobs properly, it sometimes reflects on the attitude, behavior, and accountability to the director.

I say this in the hopes that it will be used as a learning tool. When you are in the business of helping others, no matter what your position is, you must first and often look into your mirror and see and own what you are bringing to the table in your behavior, decisionmaking, and understanding. Check yourself because people's lives depend on it.

I have done a great deal of complaining, but not without having some recommendations in mind. One of my basic beliefs is that communication is the key to almost everything. You could be the smartest person in the world but, if you can't communicate what you know, then what good is your knowledge? Another belief is that, when the leader of an organization is too separated from the people in which they serve, there is a disconnect in the true needs of the services needed, how to administer them, and accountability of staff.

In my many years of therapy and parenting, I have found that emotions that are not recognized and dealt with come back or out in negative ways. In the business of serving people, you absolutely must have self-reflection and understand your emotions, prejudices (both known and unknown), and biases and then deal with them. What staff members—every one—bring to work with them every day will affect peoples' lives, and this must never be forgotten. Transference is a real thing and sometimes people may not be aware that they are doing it. Either way, there must be training and checks and balances to protect clients.

Programs should not be set up as if they are models to run an auto plant where everything is done the same way to produce the same identical product. We are humans of different backgrounds, different makeups, different problems, different wants and desires, and different plans for our futures. Programs should reflect that.

Education should be a focus if the client desires it; not some minimum wage job that can't pay rent, but will count as a number for the case manager to show that a client went to work. Long-term self-sustainable plans should be made, not plans to gain quick numbers and move people along to capture immediate data to turn in high numbers to be rewarded for the most served.

I don't quite know how to dummy this down anymore, but I thought that if a service organization's numbers were to decrease and fewer people were coming through their doors, especially repeat clients, that meant their programs were working the best because people were becoming and staying self-sustainable. Therefore, the lower the numbers, the higher the reward, to increase funds to the programs that are working the best. RIGHT.

I came very close to leaving school because of what was happening to me at the hotel. For me, I recognized the inequity and spoke up, knowing there would be retaliation. Now that the truth is out, I have a responsibility to repair the lies that I have told. Izzy has advised me to tell my family before they find out in the book; that way, I am in control. I have told Toni and Gino; I am still deciding about the family. I am still ashamed but I know they will be hurt because they love me so very much, even though all of this was in the past.

"Homelessness" is something that is still difficult for me to say. It has changed me. It still frightens me; I am still afraid to spend any money or relax. It is funny that I am so hard on myself, but I never feel this way about others that have lost their roof. I wonder if this attitude will ever leave me. For example, when you have been homeless and you get a roof and you go to the grocery store, you buy too much. How much toilet paper can one person use? Rhiannon used to tell me to shake off the homeless mentality. I have made a gratitude board at home and I am even grateful for the bad shit that happens. I feel paranoid about making a mistake because of what others will think because I emit post-homelessness wherever I am. There is always that doubt about my credibility from those who don't really know me. It is a heavy burden—being a black woman with a disability, a service dog, and being post-homeless. I personally believe that, when people make mistakes, it proves they are trying. I wish everyone felt that way. The reason I worry about what others think of me is that it seems that people often don't tend to hear what I say or ask because they are thinking of me and my background.

In summary, I guess I want people to know that the emotional effects of homelessness stay with you, just like those of abuse. Getting housing does not fix it, getting a job does not fix it, and having wonderful friends and loved ones doesn't fix it. All of those things are part of the remedy, but it is like addiction; it is a lifelong work in progress. It is akin to PTSD issues; you try to keep them in their proper place. You try to stop asking yourself why, not just about yourself but about others that you see. I thank God for the strength that I found to keep going; I can never ignore the reality of those less fortunate because this is who I am. I believe I had to experience homelessness to be a better advocate for the homeless and people living in poverty.

Through all of this, I consider myself one of the luckiest persons ever, to have had all of these terrible experiences. I want to get more education but, at this time, what I have going for me is that I can feel what it is really like to be without a roof. To me, that is very important to helping a client keep their dignity and that is what was most important to me. Once your dignity is gone, your hope is soon to follow. Then, all is lost. What it has taken for me to expose myself, my personal information, and my feelings is a chance I am taking in the hopes that maybe just one person will change their attitude about the plight of people who have lost their roof. If just one attitude will change, it is a beginning.

3

The New Demographics of Homelessness

Kerri Tobin and Joseph Murphy

Although "homelessness in one form or another has existed throughout much of human history" (Snow and Anderson, 1993, p. 7), its face has changed dramatically over the past several decades. Once predominantly a problem of single men, homelessness now encompasses a substantial number of women and children. In this chapter, we attempt to understand some basics about the new homeless. How many people are homeless? Into what subgroups are the numbers divided? And what is each of these groups like? We pay special attention to homeless families and children, noting that they now make up nearly 40 percent of our homeless population, and attempt to provide readers with a broad portrait from which to begin to understand the needs of these vulnerable citizens.

Major Trends over the Past Century

Homelessness in the United States is not a new condition (Stronge, 1992); "it has been present in one form or another since at least the second quarter of the 18th century" (Johnson, 1988, p. 8). Or, as Shlay and Rossi (1992) observe, "Social researchers today can look back to a long and rich history" (p. 130) of homelessness in this country. The demographics of those who are homeless have changed throughout the years, however. For example, in earlier periods (1865–1930), veterans comprised about one-fourth of the homeless population (Wallace, 1965). Between 1950 and 1980, there were relatively few veterans among the homeless. Today, the percentage of veterans experiencing homelessness has crept back up to about 12 percent (National Coalition for Homeless Veterans, 2015).

A similar ebb and flow can be seen with women and homelessness. "Prior to the 1870s, women made up a significant fraction of the homeless population of urban America. By the end of the nineteenth century, however, the world of the homeless had become an overwhelmingly masculine realm" (Kusmer, 2002, p. 10). And while that condition held for much of the twentieth century, after 1980 we witnessed a dramatic increase in the number of women without housing, as single adults and as heads of families. And what holds for homelessness in general is also true for youth experiencing it (Wells and Sandhu, 1986). As scholars in this domain remind us, "In the United States, running away from home is not a new phenomenon" (Farrow et al., 1992, p. 718) and "homelessness of children . . . has existed since the beginning of civilization" (Shane, 1996, p. 7).

The visibility of persons without housing has also morphed across the past 150 years. Modern scholars often point to an increased visibility of persons experiencing homelessness in recent decades. But as Kusmer (2002) and others have confirmed, while homelessness during the era from 1950 to 1980 was more confined and thus not as visible to the average citizen, it was never more apparent than in the US industrial age and during the Depression of the 1930s. However, the visibility of homelessness is not evenly distributed across subgroups.

Attitudes Toward Homelessness

Over the past 200 years, society's explanations for the phenomenon of homelessness have changed. And as we explore below, this has meant parallel shifts in society's judgments about and responses to homelessness. For example, at some points, a dominant explanation for homelessness painted it as a life choice freely selected. At others, the image of the homeless as lazy and self-destructive persons unworthy of assistance dominated public discourse. During the Great Depression, however, persons without homes were much more likely to be seen as victims of forces beyond their control, and therefore worthy of a more sympathetic response (Kusmer, 2002; Levinson, 1963; Wallace, 1965). This victim perspective has returned to favor in the modern epoch of homelessness (Karabanow, 2004). Societal responses to homelessness have mirrored changes in how society views its causes. Thus, we see an ebb and flow between more humane and harsher treatments of the overall homeless population, as well as its particular subgroups.

Part of the reason homelessness was considered less of a problem in the mid–twentieth century was that it was, for much of the post-Depression era, associated with the urban centers of the nation and often confined to well-defined skid row areas within those core cities. Today, that portrait is less accurate. To begin with, "skid row [is] no longer a geographically well-demarcated section of the inner city" (Hopper and Hamberg, 1984, p. 38), and the displaced are much more dispersed throughout the city (Bassuk, 1984; Hopper and Hamberg, 1984). Second, homelessness has also become a rural and suburban problem (Kusmer, 2002). In addition, the narrative on homelessness is being rewritten, as those experiencing it in episodic and sporadic ways comprise a much larger percentage of the population than was the case in the past (NAEH, 2003).

Equally important, the causes of displacement are shifting in the modern era. In past times, homelessness was largely attributed to flaws in the character of the men who occupied the low-cost hotels and flophouses in the nation's skid rows. Today, personal conditions in general, and moral failings in particular, remain in the portfolio of causes for homelessness, but much more attention is given to the role of the larger economic environment—to trends in housing and to government policy—in explaining homelessness in the United States (Hopper and Hamberg, 1984; Kusmer, 2002; NCFH, 2014). Family conditions have also been illuminated much more brightly than they were in the past (Hombs, 2001), particularly in this decade (NCFH, 2014).

Counting Homeless Persons: A Note

Although we do not wish to duplicate the work of Martha R. Burt (another contributor to this volume), we think it is important to highlight two important concepts before delving into the numbers ourselves. What follows includes estimates of the proportions of the homeless population, descriptions of its many subpopulations, and other numerically based descriptions. But as Burt shows in Chapter 4, estimates of homeless persons range from just over half a million to 3.5 million.

First, we must not forget that these fluctuations depend in large part on who is doing the counting and the definitions and methods that they use. Shinn and Weitzman (1996) provide an excellent encapsulation of the issue:

> Homelessness is more like a river than a lake. Most people do not stay homeless forever: on any given day, some find housing and others become homeless. Thus, far more people are homeless over an extended period of time than on any given night. To estimate the numbers of people homeless over a period of time, we must examine both the capacity of the river and its speed of flow. (p. 110)

Second, we must not lose sight of the political thread that runs through all of the studies that have attempted to quantify homelessness. Government counts tend to employ the most conservative definitions and least extensive counting procedures, thus consistently producing the lowest estimates (see, e.g., HUD, 2010, 2011, 2012). That these low numbers are used to make budgetary allocations is probably not coincidentally related to the methods used to arrive at those numbers. Advocates, on the other hand, accept higher estimates, as they use broader definitions and more inclusive methods. Again, the relationship between methods and purpose is most likely not accidental.

The larger the problem of homelessness is made to seem, the more public support that calls for funding, at least hopefully. Kozol (1988) warned against forgetting what the numbers mean:

> We would be wise, however, to avoid the numbers game. Any search for the "right number" carries the assumption that we may at last arrive at an acceptable number. *There is no acceptable number.* Whether the number is 1 million or 4 million or the administration's estimate of less than a million, there are too many homeless people in America. (pp. 12–13, emphasis added)

Who Are the New Homeless?

The makeup of the homeless population in the United States now looks different from that of thirty years ago, and even more different from thirty years before that. In this section we examine trends in the modern era, including household composition, race, gender, and marital status, veteran status, and other identifiers that help round out the portrait of today's homeless population.

Household Composition

We start with data from the 1980s, the initial phase of the modern era of homelessness. According to the Urban Institute's study of 1987, which examined homelessness in cities with more than 100,000 residents, 74 percent of people experienced homelessness alone, 18 percent were in families with children, and 8 percent were childless couples (Urban Institute, as quoted in Jencks, 1994, p. 11). During this same time period, Ropers (1988) and Rescorla, Parker, and Stolley (1991) reported that one-third of the homeless population consisted of families (see also Stefl, 1987). A HUD report noted that, while the majority of persons without housing remained single men, 16 percent were now women (HUD, as cited in Shlay and Rossi, 1992). Burt (2001), who led the 1987 Urban Institute study, provided this snapshot of household composition: single men (60.7 percent), single women (14.9 percent), adults with children (14.5 percent), and other men and women (9.9 percent). Looking specifically at men, 89 percent were single, 3 percent were with children, and 8 percent were other. Turning to women, 47 percent were single, 38 percent were with children, and 15 percent were other (p. 60).

Based on a survey sponsored by the federal government, the National Law Center on Homelessness and Poverty (NLCHP) suggested that single men comprised 41 percent of the homeless population, families with children 40 percent, single women 14 percent, and unaccompanied minors 5 percent (NLCHP, 2004a, p. 8). Similar numbers were unveiled in a HUD (2009) report: about 60 percent of people without housing on a specific night in January 2008 were single and 40 percent were homeless as members of a family (p. 8). The National Center on Family Homelessness (2009) recorded single adults at 49 percent of the total homeless population (p. 2) and the National Coalition for the Homeless (2007) estimated that 51 percent of people experiencing homelessness are single men, 30 percent are families with children, 17 percent are single women, and 2 percent are unaccompanied youth (p. 3). The most recent Annual Homeless Assessment Report (AHAR) found 37 percent were people in families (HUD, 2014a).

Gender, Age, Race, and Veteran and Marital Status

Not too long ago, a woman conspicuously living on the streets was a rare phenomenon (Stefl, 1987, p. 56). Researchers who document the gender of homeless individuals affirm that, at least in the recent past, the percentage of women in the homeless population was small, 5 percent or less (Ropers, 1988). During the modern era, however, the number of women has skyrocketed, thus effectively documenting the feminization of homelessness. Indeed, by the mid-1980s, women comprised about 20 percent of the homeless population (Bassuk, 1984; Kusmer, 2002; Roth, Toomey, and First, 1992). Homelessness surged due to the recession of 1981–1982 and, coupled with policy changes made at the federal level during the Ronald Reagan years, by the late 1980s that number was even higher. Roughly 30 percent of the homeless population was female (Toro, 1998). Continued changes to public assistance programs, like the Personal Responsibility and Work Opportunity Reconciliation Act (PRWORA) reforms of the Bill Clinton era, which reduced the levels of funding offered to struggling families, are believed to have contributed to the increasing number of women on the streets. Today, that number is believed to be closer to 40 percent (Substance Abuse and Mental Health Services Administration, 2011).

Age

Analysts also find that people in homeless shelters and on the streets are younger than they were in the past (Shlay and Rossi, 1992; Shane, 1996). Hope and Young (1986) documented a twenty-year age change from the 1950s to the 1980s, from the mid-fifties to the mid-thirties (p. 23; Kusmer, 2002; Roth, Toomey, and First, 1992; Snow and Anderson, 1993), with 65 percent of the population in their late twenties to mid-thirties (Ropers, 1988, p. 38). Culhane and colleagues (2013) examined twenty years of data on people experiencing homelessness in New York City and found that the modal age of homeless family heads remained steady at between age twenty-one and twenty-three for the entire study period.

Race

"Unfortunately, there is an ethnic and racial as well as an economic and emotional aspect to homelessness. . . . In all available data, black families and black youth are overrepresented among the homeless" (Shane, 1996, p. 16).

While there have always been people of color in shelters and on the streets, in the modern era they represent a much more significant segment of the homeless population (Roth, Toomey, and First, 1992; Toro, 1998). "Both Hispanics and African Americans are disproportionately represented in the overall homeless population" (HUD, 2009, p. 38). Black people, in particular, are overrepresented—comprising 40 percent of the homeless population while making up only 13 percent of the general population (Rollinson and Pardeck, 2006, p. 11). And according to Hopper and Milburn (1996), this "disproportionate representation of Blacks seems to be especially prominent among younger" people experiencing homelessness (p. 123) and in families without housing. Racial minorities are also, as HUD (2009) confirmed, "heavy users" (p. 38) of homeless services systems and homeless shelters, as in previous decades (Hope and Young, 1986; Hopper and Milburn, 1996).

Unfortunately, the overrepresentation of people of color in the homelessness population is not unexpected given that, in the United States, poverty is skewed to affect more of those individuals. Systemic racism has historically made it more difficult for people of color to secure well-paying jobs (Decker, Spohn, Ortiz, and Hedberg, 2014), get fair treatment in the housing market (HUD, 2013a), and obtain favorable dispositions in housing disputes (Seabrook, Wilk, and Lamb, 2012). All of these factors add up to more people of color in poverty and experiencing homelessness.

In their comparative studies, Snow and Anderson (1990) noted that in the mid-1980s, minority persons made up 25 percent of the homeless population (12 percent Black, 12 percent Hispanic, and 1 percent other). Bassuk (1984) presented parallel findings, with minorities comprising 23 percent of the homeless population, up from 10 percent in the 1950s and 1960s (Ropers, 1988, p. 38). By the mid-2000s, that number had exploded, more than doubling from the mid-1980s and expanding sixfold from the skid row era of the 1950s and 1960s. The National Survey of Homeless Assistance Providers and Clients found that 59 percent of the homeless population was comprised of people of color in 1996 (Aron and Sharkey, 2002). Burt and colleagues (2001) also estimated that people of color made up 60 percent of the homeless population (p. 58; see also Kusmer, 2002). In a more recent report, the NLCHP (2004b) estimated that, at that time, only 35 percent of the homeless population were white while African Americans comprised 49 percent, Hispanics 13 percent, Native Americans 2 percent, and Asian Americans 1 percent (p. 8; see also Gargiulo, 2006, p. 358). Updated numbers have indicated that there has been little change in these percentages: in 2014, 52 percent of the homeless population was white, 37 percent African American, and the rest other (HUD, 2014a).

Other Identifiers

Studies of those experiencing homelessness sometimes furnish data on demographic characteristics such as veteran or marital status. On the first issue, there is sufficient documentation to conclude that veterans represent an important segment of people without housing, although there is some vari- ability in the estimates. For example, Hombs (2001) reported that "homeless veterans are widely reported to make up about 30 percent of the homeless population" (p. 68). Ropers (1988) suggested that approximately half the men in many cities are veterans of US military service (p. 29). In another study, Roth and colleagues found that one-third of their respondents claimed veteran status (p. 204). And Scolaro and Esbach (2002) pegged the veteran homeless population at 25 percent (p. 2), a figure supported by the work of Toro (1998) who observed that around 25–30 percent of adults without hous- ing had military experience (p. 125). Indeed, among men experiencing home- lessness, up to one-half were estimated to be veterans in the 1980s (Ropers, 1988, p. 39). As is not unusual, the federal government counts put the num- ber much lower, at only 11 percent of the total homeless population in 2014 (HUD, 2014a). In recent years, we have also seen an explosion in the num- ber of female veterans living without housing. In 2014, 10 percent of both sheltered and unsheltered veterans counted by the annual federal government count were women (HUD, 2014a).

Using data from the mid-1980s, Snow and Anderson (1993) showed that only 8 percent of the homeless population were married; the balance were single or divorced. During this same era, Burt and associates (2001) exposed similar pictures. However, we did learn that "homeless women are more likely to be married or to have been married than homeless men" (Stefl, 1987, pp. 55–56).

Employment, education, and income. Although stereotypes of the homeless as bums and hoboes still abound, the available evidence suggests that many people experiencing homelessness are unemployed but actively looking for work. Some are employed full time or part time (Ropers, 1988). It is no sur- prise that the people without housing in these studies were extremely poor (Shlay and Rossi, 1992, p. 136). Coming at the issue from the other side, Medcalf (2008) reminded us that "for many, hard work provides no escape" from homelessness (p. 8). Shlay and Rossi (1992), in their review of sixty studies from the 1980s, computed an employment rate of 19 percent (p. 136; see also Ropers, 1988). Data from the turn of the century show that lawfully employed persons comprised a quarter or more of the homeless population (Scolaro and Esbach, 2002).

More recent reports have suggested that employment among people experiencing homelessness may be around 45 percent (Gargiulo, 2006, p. 358). We should be clear, however, that these numbers do not gainsay the fact that the majority of people without housing are unemployed, many chronically so, and most of the individuals who do have jobs are underem- ployed or work on the bottom rungs of the labor market ladder. It bears noting here that there is no state in this country where a person working forty hours per week at minimum wage can afford a one- or two-bedroom apartment at fair market rent (NLIHC, 2014). Studies that investigated the educational backgrounds of people experiencing homelessness concluded that more than half of the population have a high school degree (Gargiulo, 2006; Roth, Toomey, and First, 1992). Up to a third more have some education beyond high school (Ropers, 1988). As expected, older people are overrepresented among those with limited education; that is, those with less than a high school degree (Ropers, 1988; Roth, Toomey, and First, 1992). So too are women without housing (Roth, Toomey, and First, 1992), especially mothers. "Compared to the national average of 75 percent of all mothers having a high school diploma or graduate equivalency diploma (GED) . . . high school graduation or GED rates for mothers in homeless families range from 35 percent to 61 percent across a number of studies" (Rog, Holupka, and Patton, 2007, p. 2-5).

While up to two-thirds of individuals experiencing homelessness have some source of legitimate income (Roth, Toomey, and First, 1992, p. 206), among almost all of these persons, amounts are extremely low. Shlay and Rossi (1992) documented annual average incomes between $1,236 and $2,088 for families (pp. 136–137). Nearly a decade later, Burt (2001) reported that "half of all homeless adults receive[d] less than $300 per month in income, putting them at about 30 to 40 percent of the federal poverty level" (p. 3) at the time (see also Burt et al., 2001, pp. 75–77). Data about sources of income reveal that public support is limited for homeless persons (NLCHP, 2004b) and that "welfare [is] the most common source of income; earnings are second" (Roth, Roth, Toomey, and First, 1992, p. 206).

Families with children and unaccompanied youth. Children and youth experiencing homelessness are found to either be attached to a family (accompanied homeless children, usually younger) or away from home and on their own (unaccompanied youth, often teenaged). "Homeless families" are defined "as one or more adults with one or more children in their charge" (Shinn and Weitzman, 1996, p. 109). Thus, homeless children are usually those "from birth to age 18 who are accompanied by one or more parents or caregivers" (NCFH, 2009) And as Shane (1996) documents,

> . . . the familial homeless, or homeless families with children, are of all kinds: one adult (mother, father, grandparent, other); two adults (with biological, step-, adopted, or common-law parents, unrelated partner, or other relationship); three generations (grandparent, parent, and child[ren]). They stay in every conceivable place—tents, cars, trucks, abandoned buildings, handmade shacks, shelters, and so on. The children, although predominantly younger, are of all ages—neonates through teenagers. There can be one child or many children in the family. (p. 4)

Actual counts of children who are homeless vary greatly (Cordray and Pion, 2003). A decade and a half ago Burt stated that "during a typical year between 900,000 and 1.4 million children are homeless with their families" (2001, p. 1), and more recently Bassuk (2010) asserted nearly the same: "1.5 million children experience homelessness in America each year" (p. 496). On the more conservative end, the 2010 AHAR stated that 346,620 children resided in homeless shelters at some point during that year (HUD, 2010). The National Center for Homeless Education (NCHE) estimated that 794,600 school-aged children were homeless, according to the broader Department of Education definition (NCHE, 2009). The National Association for the Education of Homeless Children and Youth (2010) reported a 41 percent increase over the 2007–2008 and 2008–2009 school years, with 956,914 children without housing enrolled that year. Additionally, in 2010–2011, the National Center for Homeless Education (2016) reported a 13 percent increase, bringing the total to 1,065,794 children in schools across the country. The US Department of Education found that 1.3 million students experienced homelessness in 2013 (US Department of Education, 2014). Because schools often rely on parent or student self-report to determine housing status, these numbers are unlikely to be entirely accurate. Despite a lack of consensus on exact numbers, however, all reports point to a problem of homelessness among families unprecedented in the United States since the Great Depression and that it is continuing to grow (Bassuk, 2010).

In addition to examining the numbers of families with children experiencing homelessness, it is instructive to look at characteristics they share. Although not all families or experiences of homelessness are alike, the dominant form of family homelessness is a single adult with one or more children (McChesney, 1992; P. M. Miller, 2012; Polakow, 2003). The average family without housing is headed by a woman under age thirty who is a member of a minority group (HUD, 2014a). Her children tend to be young, with 41 percent under the age of six (NCFH, 2009). The most recent AHAR provided the following age breakdown for children in shelters and transitional housing: 51 percent under age six, 34 percent age six to twelve, and 15 percent age thirteen to seventeen (HUD, 2014). Additionally, the experience of homelessness varies. The majority (75 percent) of homeless families experience short-term homelessness (between three weeks and three months) and tend to remain housed afterward; 20 percent have one homeless stay that lasts more than six months; and only 5 percent of families are episodically homeless, having repeated short stays in family shelters (Culhane, Metraux, et al., 2007).

Unaccompanied youth. The phrase *unaccompanied youth* is, as Moore (2007) clarified, an umbrella term for a large variety of young people (Julianelle, 2007; Rotheram-Borus et al., 1996). It is a "generic term to refer to minors who are outside a family or an institutional setting and who are unaccompanied by a parent or legal guardian" (Robertson, 1992, p. 288) and includes youngsters living on the street, in shelters, and in group homes, and those doubled up with friends or relatives. Unfortunately, counts of unaccompanied youth are difficult to estimate; HUD began counting them as a separate category only in 2013. In the most recent AHAR, "194,302 youth and children were homeless on a single night in 2014 [but] given the difficulty of counting youth who are homeless, that estimate is likely an undercount" (HUD, 2014a) and one advocacy group estimates that during a year, "approximately 550,000 unaccompanied, single youth and young adults up to age 24 experience a homelessness episode of longer than one week. Approximately 380,000 of those youth are under the age of 18" (NAEH, 2015).

Runaways. While a variety of typologies, often with common dimensions, are used to capture the phenomenon of youth homelessness, nearly all analysts describe three categories of the unaccompanied homeless: runaway, throwaway, and systems homeless (Barry, Ensign, and Lippek, 2002). McCaskill, Toro, and Wolfe (1998) defined "runaways" as those young people "who [leave] home for at least 24 hours without their parents' permission and whose parents [do] not know their whereabouts" (p. 308). Based on criteria "such as degree of school success, existence of peer influences and/or supports, the degree of criminal behavior involved, and the extent to which the individual is committed to street life" (Rothman, 1991, p. 106), a number of conceptual and empirical efforts have been undertaken to describe homeless runaways. Brennan (1980) built a typology featuring six different portraits of runaways based on behavioral and attitudinal factors: self-confident and unrestrained runaway youth; well-adjusted runaway youth; youth who have failed at home and in school, and who are involved in delinquent behavior; youth who are fleeing excessive parent control; young highly regulated and negatively influenced youth; and young and unrestrained youth.

Throwaways. Throwaway youth, on the other hand, "are young persons who have been told to leave home by a parent or guardian and [who] are away overnight and prevented from returning home" (Hallett, 2007, p. 3). A special category of throwaways is "intervention seekers" (Boeskey, Toro, and Bukowski, 1997, p. 22), those youngsters "whose parents asked them to leave home temporarily with the understanding that the adolescent would return home after a short period of time" (McCaskill, Toro, and Wolfe, 1998, pp. 308–309).

Systems youth. Homeless "adolescents who have been in and out of government systems such as juvenile justice and foster care are referred to as system youth" (Hallett, 2007, p. 3), although, as we noted previously, youngsters in long-term foster care are not considered homeless. Systems youth, according to MacLean, Embry, and Cauce (1999), "are those from family environments that were deemed dangerous enough to necessitate removal from the home and whose subsequent residential placements were unsuccessful" (p. 2). That is, "system kids become homeless when their social service placements are problematic" (Rotheram-Borus, 1991, p. 24). Within these three classifications—runaway, throwaway, and systems youth—special conditions are occasionally highlighted. For example, in the throwaway category, Hammer, Finkelhor, and Sedlak (2002) singled out "permanently abandoned" (p. 5) youth, those youngsters whose families have dissolved around them. Across all three classifications, reviewers have described "street kids," a characterization that refers to youths "who spend all of their time in various public places" (Baron, Kennedy, and Forde, 2001, p. 767). "Most of these youth are under-employed/unemployed, often lack a permanent residence, and spend significant amounts of time without shelter" (Baron and Hartnagel, 1998, p. 166).

The Experience of Homelessness

Although we may be wont to think of homelessness as a monolithic experience, even a cursory look at the literature makes clear that this is not the case. Homelessness varies by time spent homeless, region of the country, and what types of shelter people find. The experience can of course vary in myriad other ways, encompassing emotional and philosophical questions outside the realm of this chapter. In this section, we explore a narrow selection of the ways in which experiences of homelessness can be different.

Time Spent Homeless

Over the years, researchers have demonstrated a keen interest in the duration of homeless experiences, paying particular attention to the number of incidents of homelessness and the length of time for each homeless experience. Data on both expose the "cyclical nature of homelessness for many" (NAEH, 2003, p. 6). Most researchers use a typology that classifies homeless experiences as "transitional, episodic, or chronic," concluding that the majority of people experience only transitional homelessness, which is to say a single incidence of at most a few months' duration (McAllister, Lennon, and Kuang, 2011, p. 596).

Using Point-in-Time data, we learn that on any given night, about half of the population will have been experiencing homelessness for more than a year (Jencks, 1994, p. 13; Bassuk, Rubin, and Lauriat, 1984, p. 1547)—16 percent between thirteen and twenty-four months, 10 percent between twenty-five and sixty months, and 20 percent more than five years (Burt et al., 2001, p. 64). Employing homeless population data across a given year shows that a much smaller percentage of the homeless remain displaced for more than a year, around 12 percent. The average length of homelessness for shelter and street people (the literal homeless) is estimated to be less than six months (Shlay and Rossi, 1992, p. 141) and probably less than three months (Link et al., 1995, p. 352; Roth, Toomey, and First, 1992; Stefl, 1987), although the average is somewhat higher for stays in shelters (US Conference of Mayors, 2007).

Point-in-Time data also reveal that about half of the people experiencing literal homelessness on a given night are experiencing their first episode of homelessness and another one-third have been homeless three or more times (Hombs, 2001, pp. 57–58). Overall then, the homelessness mosaic reveals a pattern, with a hard-core group of chronically homeless individuals, a large number of persons who experience only one episode of homelessness, and a group who cycle in and out of homelessness for short periods of time (Ropers, 1988).

Location

Scholars also track the location of people experiencing homelessness: the prevalence of homelessness in different areas such as cities and rural counties, the concentration of the homeless in specific areas of the country, and the stability (or movement) of homeless persons. On the initial issue, researchers have offered up two insights. First, to a large extent, homelessness remains an urban phenomenon; that is, "the majority of individuals and families experiencing homelessness are located in urban areas" (US Conference of Mayors, 2007, p. 11). An often cited survey conducted in 1996 found that 71 percent of people without housing were in central cities, 21 percent in the suburbs or on the urban fringe, and 9 percent in rural areas (Rollinson and Pardeck, 2006, p. 13) while "for poor people in general in the United States, those figures are 31, 46, and 23 percent, respectively" (Hombs, 2001, p. 57). A more recent survey reported that 75 percent of people in homeless shelters resided in central cities (US Conference of Mayors, 2007, p. 11), largely because of the presence of a greater range of services for the homeless (Stefl, 1987). Another more recent report found that 78 percent of the nation's homeless people live in urban areas (HRI, 2010). We have also learned "that the rate of homelessness is higher in larger cities than in smaller cities. Metropolitan areas with 250,000 or more population had a homelessness ratio of around 13 persons for every 10,000 population; in small metropolitan areas (defined as those with populations of 50,000 to 250,000), the ratio dropped by one-half (to 6.5 persons per 10,000" (Peroff, 1987, p. 42).

Second, while primarily an urban phenomena, rural homelessness is not an insignificant problem (Kusmer, 2002; Roth, Toomey, and First, 1992). People experiencing homelessness "are present outside urban areas" (Stefl, 1987, p. 58), although, as we reported earlier, they are often less visible and therefore more difficult to find. Several types of rural areas generate higher-than-average levels of homelessness. Among these are regions that are primarily agricultural, those with economies that center on declining extractive industries (e.g., mining or timber) and that are located in long-standing pockets of poverty, and those experiencing economic growth. In regions with persistent poverty (e.g., Appalachia), the young and able-bodied often leave to relocate in urban areas in search of employment. If they return home after several years because they have no work, they may find them-selves homeless. Residents in impoverished or primarily agricultural areas may lose their livelihood as a result of changing economic conditions — a lower demand for farm labor because of mechanized and corporate farm-ing, or a shrinking service sector because of declining populations. Finally, many communities alongside major transportation routes receive people lit-erally "off the interstate" — those who are on the road looking for work or simply on the move, who have run out of resources (Aron and Fitchen, 1996, pp. 82–83).

We have also discovered that the homeless experience is somewhat dif-ferent in rural areas (Stefl, 1987). Homeless rural persons are "more likely to be married, and less likely to be residing in their county of birth. Persons interviewed in rural counties reported being homeless for a shorter length of time (median of 36.5 days), compared to homeless persons in mixed and urban counties (medians of 65 and 60 days, respectively)" (Stefl, 1987, p. 58). People experiencing rural homelessness are also "more likely to be female and white than [are persons in] the urban homeless group. The rural homeless group also include[s] more young people" (Roth, Toomey, and First, 1992, p. 204). A 2010 study concluded that a much greater percentage of people experiencing rural homelessness were families with children (HRI, 2010).

While there is not an abundance of research on the issue, available stud-ies indicate that "homeless populations vary geographically" (Whitbeck, Hoyt, and Ackley, 1997, p. 389). For example, while popular belief holds that the homeless live primarily in the Northeast and Midwest, "they are actually more concentrated in the West. Almost one-third of all homeless people are found in the West even though only 19 percent of the country's population lives there" (Peroff, 1987, p. 42).

Those interested in the concentration question also investigate the extent to which homelessness is clustered in defined areas, especially the limited geographical urban area historically known as skid row (Bahr, 1973; R. Miller, 1982). The answer seems to be that people without housing are becoming less clustered and more dispersed (Brickner, 1985; Jahiel, 1992; Ropers, 1988). "Since the late 1960s . . . homeless people have become less confined to specific areas" (Bassuk, Rubin, and Lauriat, 1984, p. 1546). Thus, according to Ropers (1988), "skid row" is best defined "as a condition and not a place" (p. 30): "The 'skid row' way of life no longer appears to be confined to a particular geographical area: it is overflowing, and has become a way of life throughout our cities' streets" (p. 35).

Investigators also spend time exploring the stability (mobility) of persons without housing; that is, the extent to which they stay close to their former homes or gravitate to new locales. The best evidence from the modern era of homelessness (post-1980) suggests that the majority of these people are "stayers," remaining close to their pre-homelessness residence and living in the same area for over a year (Hope and Young, 1986; Stefl, 1987).

> Homeless people typically are perceived as highly mobile, but this study does not support that contention. Overall, 40 percent of our sample had been born in the county in which they were interviewed. Another 24 percent of the sample had lived in the county of interview for more than one year. Only about one-third of those interviewed had moved recently to the county of interview. (Roth, Toomey, and First, 1992, p. 206)

Residency

Finally, a massive amount of attention has been devoted to the residency question: Where do persons without homes reside, or more precisely, where do they sleep at night? The initial cut here is usually made between those experiencing literal homelessness who reside in shelters and on the streets, and those who live doubled up with others or pay to live in cheap hotels and flophouses. Given the studies available to date, three points about the doubled up dimension of the invisible homeless population can be drawn with some accuracy. First, "it is unclear how many people live in doubled-up housing" (J. Wright, Rubin, and Devine, 1998, p. 93). For a variety of reasons, doubled up individuals are especially difficult to count. Second, not surprisingly, estimates of doubled up persons cover a good deal of ground. Shinn and Weitzman (1996) put the number in 1987 at around 3 million, which represented "an increase from 1980 to 1987 of 98% in households with related subfamilies and an increase of 57% in households with unrelated subfamilies" (p. 116). Third, there is a consensus that "there are [at least] as many, if not substantially more, doubled up persons" (J. Wright, Rubin, and Devine, 1998, p. 93) as there are literally homeless individuals. Indeed, some advocates suggest that the number was over 7 million in 2011 (NAEH, 2013a).

Scholars traditionally place those persons who are experiencing literal homelessness into one of two groups: those living in shelters and those living on the streets, acknowledging a good deal of movement between the two groups—and between these two conditions and being doubled up as well. Roth, Toomey, and First (1992) reported that, at the end of 1980, of the total homeless population, 14 percent were people sleeping on the street and 57 percent were shelter residents. At the turn of the century, Hombs (2001), examining the "literal homeless" issue, concluded that 31 percent of this group slept on the streets or in other nonstable venues while 66 percent slept in shelters of one kind or another (p. 57). In a report using Point-in-Time data from January 2008, HUD (2009) estimated that of a total literal homeless population of 664,414, 58.2 percent were staying in shelters (386,361) while 41.8 percent were unsheltered (278,053)—with persons in families being much more likely (72.8 percent) to be in shelters than individuals (49.3 percent) (p. 8). Scholars further divide sheltered persons by type of shelter. For example, HUD (2009) reported that 77.1 percent of all sheltered persons in the one-year period from October 2007 through September 2008 stayed in "emergency" shelters only. Another 17.6 percent stayed in "transitional housing" only and another 5.3 percent stayed in both types of shelters that year (p. D-2). Using Point-in-Time data, the US Conference of Mayors (2008) estimated that 48 percent of the homeless were in emergency shelters and another one-third were in transitional housing (p. 16). Again, as we have shown consistently in this chapter, variability in estimates is a norm in the homeless literature.

Chronic Homelessness, Substance Abuse, Mental Illness, and Incarceration

Unfortunately, no discussion of the demographics of homelessness in the United States would be complete without consideration of those individuals often deemed least deserving of help by our society at large: those struggling with substance abuse, mental illness, or both; those leaving prison; and the chronically homeless. In this subsection, we explore the prevalence of each condition within the overall homeless population.

Chronic homelessness. When most Americans envision homelessness, the chronic is what they see. This vision dates back to earlier times, when the man of the skid row era was considered culpable for his condition and, therefore, "blameworthy for whatever poverty, misery, or suffering accompanied [this] voluntarily chosen lifestyle" (Hombs, 2001, p. 10). Much of the problem was attributed to substance (alcohol) abuse (Kling, Dunn, and Oakley, 1996; Shane, 1996; Stefl, 1987). Though this attitude persists in some places today, federal efforts to alleviate the problem of chronic homelessness have shifted toward a treatment and support model.

Despite common perceptions, most homeless people do not fall into the chronically homeless category. HUD defines a "chronically homeless person" as "either (1) an unaccompanied homeless individual with a disabling condition who has been continuously homeless for a year or more, OR (2) an unaccompanied individual with a disabling condition who has had at least four episodes of homelessness in the past three years" (HUD, 2007, p. 3). Over the past decade, the 2014 AHAR asserted, the number of persons who experience chronic homelessness has decreased by 30 percent, to a number of around 85,000 or 14 percent of the overall homeless population (HUD, 2014a). This population tends to have other conditions that are thought to contribute to their difficulty in finding housing: "The vast majority . . . have a serious mental illness, substance abuse disorder or physical disability, and often a combination of these" (Culhane and Byrne, 2010, p. 5).

Mental illness and substance abuse. As noted above, these populations tend to overlap. A majority of people experiencing chronic homelessness are believed to have mental illness or substance abuse issues, and many have both. Analysts have exposed the extent of emotional and psychological impairments in the single adult population, confirming high rates of severe mental illness, much higher rates than are reported in the general population of adults in the United States (Bahr, 1973; Brickner, 1985; Khanna et al., 1992). Indeed, somewhere in the neighborhood of 10 percent of homeless adults are likely to have a major mental illness such as a schizophrenic disorder (Bahr, 1973, p. 101; Toro, 1998, p. 121)—although, as Ropers (1988) reminds us, this is considerably less than commonly assumed or portrayed. Beyond this, there is considerable variation in reports about the extent of mental illness among individuals without housing, with reports running from around 20 percent to 80 percent and higher (see Bahr, 1973; Bassuk, 1984; Bassuk, Rubin, and Lauriat, 1984; Flynn, 1985; Shlay and Rossi, 1992; Tierney, Gupton, and Hallett, 2008; Toro, 1998). Substance abuse, considered "both a consequence of and a leading factor in the continuance of homelessness among individuals," is even more prevalent than mental illness, with 50 percent of the total homeless population, and 70 percent of veterans experiencing homelessness, believed to have substance abuse disorders (ICH, 2015a). Current statistics put the mental illness rate at around 30 percent, with 50 percent of that population experiencing a co-occurring substance abuse problem (Substance Abuse and Mental Health Services Administration, 2011).

Incarceration. Between 1980 and 2005, the US prison population quadrupled (Pastore and MacGuire, 2005), bringing another variable into the homelessness equation. Additionally, the deinstitutionalization movement of the 1960s and 1970s resulted in many mentally ill persons having no shelter, while the concurrent criminalization of mental illness created a situation that leaves mental illness, incarceration, and homelessness hopelessly entangled (McNeil, Binder, and Robinson, 2005). Persons on the streets, particularly those suffering from mental illness, are at increased risk of being arrested and jailed; conversely, people leaving prison often find themselves with no homes to which they can return (Metraux, Roman, and Cho, 2007).

Researchers believe that as many as one in five people who leave prison become homeless; indeed, a California Department of Corrections study found that in San Francisco and Los Angeles, the percentage of parolees who are homeless is between 30 and 50 percent (NAEH, 2015).

Conclusion

In this chapter, we have presented a picture of homelessness significantly different than most public perceptions of single men sleeping on the sidewalk. Families comprise a significant portion of the homeless population, as do unaccompanied youth. The marked increase in the number of women suggests the feminization of homelessness as well. And the education level of a third of those experiencing homelessness indicates that there is valuable human capital that might be nurtured, rather than ignored.

Although the federal government supports these subpopulations, their continually increasing numbers certainly give an indication that more support is needed. One promising recent trend in family homelessness policy is toward programs like housing first and rapid re-housing, which are similar initiatives focused on finding permanent shelter for families before attending to other issues. These types of programs, initially used for men with addiction and mental health issues, comprised 34 percent of homeless shelters in 2010 (HUD, 2011) and are unlike traditional housing programs because they do not require participant sobriety or participation in supportive services (Kertesz and Weiner, 2009). They follow a somewhat breathtakingly simple logic: people experiencing homelessness are people who need homes; the first step in helping them should be to provide those homes.

Although they are initially expensive, these types of programs have been shown to be more effective than nonhousing interventions at reducing homelessness and its long-term costs (Bassuk, 2010), and no less effective at reducing mental health and substance abuse issues (Tsemberis, 2010). The 2009 American Recovery and Reinvestment Act (ARRA) included a one-time $1.5 billion investment in the Homelessness Prevention and Rapid Re-Housing Program (HPRP). The program unfortunately expired in September 2012 (HUD, 2012). Knowing, as we do after a closer look at the demographics of homelessness, that the population is so diverse that the only real common denominator is lack of housing, the most reasonable policy approach should be to start by providing housing.

4

Three Decades of Homelessness

Martha R. Burt

In this chapter, I provide some important historical context to the homelessness we see today by examining this phenomenon during the three decades that began with the 1981–1982 recession, when homelessness became a significant public issue for the first time since the Great Depression. I discuss potential meanings of "homelessness," factors that influence the levels and types at a given time, methods for enumerating and describing homeless people, the ways those methods affect knowledge, and the growth and changes in US homeless populations during this period. I look at what we know and how we know it; and also discuss what we don't know along with some of the many reasons why we don't, and may never, know. I seek to sharpen our understanding of homelessness that I first articulated in my book, *Over the Edge: The Growth of Homelessness in the 1980s* (Burt, 1992) and expanded in *Helping America's Homeless: Emergency Shelter or Affordable Housing?* (Burt, Aron, and Lee, 2001). Now, as then, I draw on the thinking of the many people who have grappled with the same issues.

What Do We Mean by "Homeless"?
Homelessness has been defined in various ways in different eras, countries, and circumstances. Historically, ideas of homelessness have usually incorporated one or more of the concepts of being without place (not being from here), without family, or without housing. Nomads, peddlers, and tinkerers, people living in caravans, and others whose traditions incorporated moving from place to place would fall into the without place category, as would laborers or whole families forced to leave their traditional place of residence to seek work or avoid famine or war. Men living alone in skid rows or in cheap boarding houses were often considered homeless in the without family

sense of the word because they did not live with family members even though they could and did pay to keep a roof over their heads. As late as 1960, the US Census Bureau classified such people as "homeless."

Finally, people who do not have housing have been considered homeless, including those who lose their housing to flood, fire, earthquake, or war. Whether or not a particular situation is considered homeless also depends on time and place—shelter constructed from plywood, tin, and other scrap under a freeway underpass or viaduct in a US city is not considered housing and the people occupying it are considered homeless. But many millions of people in developing countries consider themselves lucky to have such housing in the slums, shantytowns, and barrios that surround most non-Western cities in the world.

In the United States, federal legislation established a formal definition of "homelessness" in the Stewart B. McKinney Homeless Assistance Act of 1987 (Public Law No. 100-77). The act specified that someone was homeless if "the individual lacks a fixed, regular, and adequate nighttime residence." People sleeping in "a public or private place not designed for, or ordinarily used as, a regular sleeping accommodation for human beings," as well as those staying in shelters for homeless people, are part of the definition. This statutory definition may seem relatively broad and flexible, but as a practical matter, a much narrower working definition has applied—being without housing *last night* or expecting to be without housing *tonight*. Thus, people in precarious circumstances who still manage to sleep in conventional dwellings, however unstable, would not count as being officially homeless from the perspective of receiving assistance supported by public homeless funding. Even so, policymakers and practitioners in many communities may still be sufficiently interested in the at-risk and unstably housed population to design counting methods that have the possibility of including them, since they have a high risk of meeting the official definition of homelessness at some time in the future.

One may argue forever and to no avail about which definition of homelessness is the right one. Ultimately, the choice of definition is a political one, meaning that many influences go into defining a concept like "homelessness," and there is no one right, ultimate, reality. Mostly in the United States, the government's interest has been in establishing as narrow a definition as possible, to limit the number and variety of people that government will have to provide with assistance. Simultaneously, advocates' interests have been in expanding the definition to include increasing numbers and varieties of people, in efforts to increase resources or at least enable more people to share in available resources. Programmatically, a definition sets the boundaries of the population considered appropriate to help or make eligible for assistance. If one is willing to supply only emergency shelter, then the narrow definition of "homeless tonight" serves the purpose of identifying the relevant population.

If one is interested in ending homelessness, then it makes sense to pay attention to people who have met the definition of homelessness for a long time, as resolving their homelessness will greatly reduce the size of the overall population that is homeless on a given night.

But even focusing housing programs on people who are chronically homeless will not stop the flow of people into homelessness for the first time, most of whom are destined to be homeless for only short periods. If one were interested in preventing homelessness among the many poor people who go in and out of homelessness in short intervals—for example, a person who sleeps on the streets two nights a week, in a shelter one night, and with different relatives or friends four nights a week—one would need a definition of homelessness that extends in time beyond one day or night and also takes into account a pattern of unstable housing mixed with sleeping arrangements that meet the definition of literal homelessness. And if the goal were truly to prevent or eliminate homelessness, one would want a definition of "unstable housing" or "worst-case housing needs" so one could apply remedies such as a rent subsidy to the households most vulnerable to homelessness. In the course of pursuing its programmatic responsibilities, HUD has already developed operational definitions for both of these concepts, the former for the purpose of reporting the impacts of homelessness prevention and rapid re-housing programs, and the latter for its routine reports on the status of US housing and worst-case housing needs. In addition, one would pay attention to transition moments such as being discharged from a treatment facility or correctional institution since the risk of homelessness is particularly intense at such times, even though the person being discharged was housed the night before.

Causes of Homelessness

The sine qua non of homelessness, its root cause and the stage on which all else plays out, is extreme poverty. With money, housing; without money, no housing, regardless of whatever other vulnerabilities and disabilities a person or family may have. Even the wealthy may be technically homeless if they are unlucky enough to live in places subject to flood, tsunami, or earthquake but, since they have money, they will be able to stay in a hotel or rental accommodations until they can move back and thus will not meet the official definition of homelessness for more than a day or two. So in general, factors that make a person poor are usually the same ones that can push that person into homelessness.

At its core, homelessness results from an inequality between a household's income and the cost of its housing, as shown at the center of Figure 4.1.[1] Causes of homelessness are factors that influence either the cost of housing or a household's ability to pay for it. If the disparity between the two

Figure 4.1 Factors Affecting Homelessness

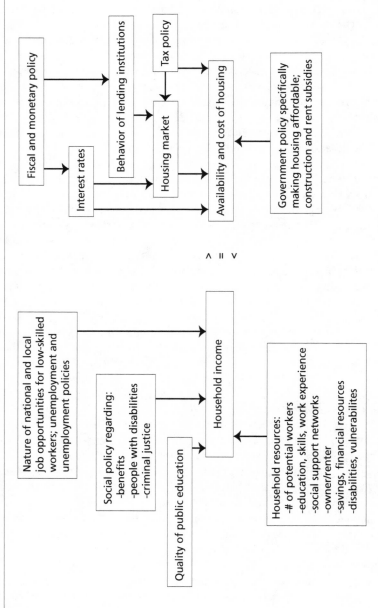

is great enough, the household will not be able to afford housing and its risk of homelessness increases.

Three types of factors are generally acknowledged to cause homelessness, in the sense that they influence the balance at the center of Figure 4.1 and create the conditions, including extreme poverty, that increase the risk of homelessness.

Factors of the first type are structural—these are larger societal trends and changes that affect broad segments of the population. These include changes in housing markets and land use, employment opportunities, wage standards, the quality and relevance of public education, criminal justice policies, institutional supports for poor people and people with disabilities, and discriminatory policies of several varieties.

If, due to any number of factors, housing prices go up, fewer people can afford housing. If unemployment rises or if pay levels of most of the available jobs remain too low relative to the price of housing, fewer people can afford housing. If reckless predatory speculation on Wall Street leads to a foreclosure crisis, more people become homeless. If public education and other institutions do not prepare most people to obtain jobs that pay a living wage, more will be at risk of homelessness. If millions of minority youth are arrested and sent to prison, breaking their ties to community and reducing their prospects for employment on release, their risk of homelessness increases. War and famine are additional structural causes of homelessness. Structural factors determine why levels of homelessness rise or fall in this place, at this time, rather than some other place or some other time.

Factors of the second type are individual—they are the conditions and circumstances that make particular people particularly vulnerable. These include disabilities (e.g., mental illness, developmental disabilities, physical disabilities), illnesses, illiteracy, addictions, and a felony record.[2] They may also include personal circumstances such as domestic violence, too many household members to support on one income, childhood abuse or neglect, or having no family or support network to cushion the effects of economic difficulties (e.g., because one has been in foster care or because of familial abuse). Some factors such as apartment condemnation, fire, flood, hurricane, or having one's landlord fall victim to foreclosure will also affect the risk of homelessness, although they are not strictly either structural or individual.

A third set of factors, public policies, may mitigate structural and individual factors, and thus determine the ultimate level of homelessness in a particular time and place. Emergency relief can often shorten the time spent homeless for victims of natural disasters or war. Guaranteed housing, as enjoyed by citizens of several European countries, can either eliminate the risk of homelessness or shorten the time spent homeless. Alternatively, cuts in publicly supported housing subsidies or policies that exclude the most vulnerable people from receiving them will increase homelessness levels, all other things being equal. Income, housing, and other supports for people with disabilities severe enough to prevent them from working could also prevent their becoming homeless, as could better policies for reintegrating people who have been imprisoned back into the community. Other chapters in this volume explore changes over the past few decades in some of these factors—particularly housing and labor markets and policies affecting them—and discuss the probable impact of these changes on levels and types of homelessness.

Homelessness in the United States in the 1980s

Homelessness has been a presence on the US public policy scene for more than thirty years. It has not gone away, as it was expected to do when it first surfaced as a public issue in the early 1980s. At that time, the 1981–1982 recession pushed people into homelessness at rates that had not been seen in the United States since the Great Depression of the 1930s, when unemployment reached 25 percent and more than 1 percent of the entire population was homeless (Burt, 1992; Crouse 1986). Before the 1981–1982 recession, people who were homeless or precariously housed were generally understood to be mostly single men, living mostly in rundown sections of major cities often known collectively as skid row. Whatever missions, shelters, and soup kitchens existed were located in these parts of town and many saw their mission as saving souls, not as ending homelessness. The 1981–1982 recession changed that reality. During those years, increasing numbers of women and whole families began appearing at skid row facilities, since no other resources or programs offered shelter or food. The situation was so dire that the US Congress took its first step toward involving the federal government in homelessness relief, authorizing the first wave of the Emergency Food and Shelter Program as part of the Job Stimulus Bill of 1983 (Pub. L. No. 98-8).[3]

After about a decade of this new wave of homelessness, Burt (1992) examined changes in several factors for their potential influence on the increasing levels of homelessness being seen around the country. These included housing availability and changes in poverty and household income, income support programs, and supports for people living with mental illness or chemical dependency. All had changed in ways that increased poor people's risk for homelessness. As other chapters of this book address the changes in housing and employment and earning power, I only comment here on changes in public benefits and policies toward people with disabilities. The 1980s saw reductions in the availability of a number of key benefits (Burt, 1992), largely as a result of the expanding influence of smaller government forces and a decreasing public commitment to paying taxes to produce public resources to help those in need (e.g., then President Ronald Reagan's repeated references to "welfare queens" and the effects such messages had on public attitudes). The purchasing power of benefits available through

Aid to Families with Dependent Children had been eroding steadily throughout, not just in the 1980s but the 1970s as well, as states declined to increase benefit levels to keep up with changes in the cost of living. Food stamps, the only program consistently available nationwide and the only one for which single individuals as well as families were eligible, saw reductions in eligibility for about 1 million persons in the 1980s (about 5 percent), and those who retained benefits got less.

A major loss for people with disabilities arose from changes in eligibility determination procedures for Supplemental Security Income (SSI) and Social Security Disability Insurance (SSDI) promulgated administratively by the Reagan administration in 1981 and 1982, which greatly increased the difficulty of establishing eligibility or maintaining it once established through continuing disability reviews. At the same time, many states were pulling back on state-funded welfare, known variously as general assistance, general relief, home relief, and other similar titles. In a number of states, such programs had been the only source of cash income support for people in households without children. Michigan was one of these states where the impact of major cuts to single individuals with disabilities was evaluated; increased homelessness was one of the consequences. All of these benefit cutbacks meant that people who were already poor faced increasing difficulty in being able to afford housing.

For people living with a mental illness or a substance abuse disorder the 1980s and, to an equal and possibly even greater extent, the two previous decades, saw major changes that contributed to the odds that they would become and remain homeless (Burt, 1992). States began emptying their mental hospitals in 1965, when enactment of the Medicaid program made it possible for states to pass responsibility for much of the cost of housing and treating people with mental illness to the federal government as long as patients lived in the community rather than in state institutions. The days were over when mental hospitals supplied at least housing and food for extended periods of time, if not always treatment. The housing that many former hospital residents moved to, single-room-occupancy (SRO) hotels and similar cheap accommodations, also began disappearing or being converted to other uses in the 1970s and 1980s as cities gentrified. Not only did cheap housing disappear, but the availability of the day labor jobs by which many marginal people had been able to earn enough to afford minimal housing also shrank by half or more. So, no housing and no easily accessible source of income made literal homelessness all but inevitable for many who lived on the margins of society. The result was a significant increase in the proportion of people suffering from a mental illness among people experiencing homelessness — from an estimated 20 percent of people who were homeless at a single point in time in 1980 to about 33 percent in 1987. Conversely, the population of people living with a mental illness (1.7 million in 1980; 1.9 million in 1987) experienced significant increases in homelessness during the same period, from about 1.2 percent in 1980 to about 10.4 percent in 1987 (Burt, 1992, p. 120).[4] This was about a ninefold increase.

The same magnitude of increase also occurred for people with an alcohol dependency (Burt, 1992, p. 120). Rates of alcohol abuse were mostly constant among people experiencing homelessness in 1980 and 1987, at about one in three. But because the number of people who were homeless had increased much faster than the overall alcohol-dependent population, the proportion of homeless could be estimated as jumping from 0.38 percent of that population in 1980 to 2.1 percent in 1987 — about a fivefold increase.

No figures for drug dependency are available to make similar calculations, but they are not necessary to make the point because, just as the 1981–1982 recession dragged to a conclusion and the economy began to pick up, the crack cocaine epidemic began. Any reductions in homelessness that one might have expected as people went back to work were countermanded by huge jumps in crack dependency. Emergency room visits involving crack cocaine increased ninefold between 1976 and 1985, and admissions for cocaine abuse to federally supported drug treatment programs jumped fourfold between 1979 and 1984.[5] One consequence for many of those affected was homelessness. Shelters began reporting that their entire population had changed by the mid- and late 1980s, and that crack users predominated in the later period.

People with addictions also suffered a significant setback in the next decade that affected their ability to afford housing; Congress terminated eligibility for SSI and SSDI benefits for people with a primary diagnosis of alcohol or drug dependency. In January 1997, when the new policy went into effect, or shortly thereafter, almost 108,000 people whose eligibility had been based on a substance use disorder lost payment eligibility, comprising 64 percent of all such people (Hunt and Baumohl, 2003).

Homelessness Since the 1980s

After growing at an alarming rate throughout the 1980s due to flat or declining wages for many workers, exploding housing costs, and the continuing failure to provide adequately for people with behavioral health conditions, these same factors have kept homelessness at much the same level since that time. The major exceptions are large increases in family homelessness during the Great Recession of 2008–2009 and reductions in homelessness for specific subpopulations with complex and interacting health conditions that have been the focus of interventions that include subsidies for permanent housing.

Estimates of Homelessness at a Single Point in Time

From a Point-in-Time figure that probably numbered around 100,000 in 1980, the size of the population homeless at a given time jumped to a "most reliable range" estimate of 250,000 to 350,000 in 1983 (HUD, 1984),

500,000–600,000 in 1987 (Burt and Cohen, 1989), and 400,000–800,000 in 1996 (Burt, Aron, and Lee 2001). The latter two figures are derived from probability-based national survey techniques while the first estimate, for 1983, came from provider estimates in their own communities gathered by HUD in an effort to get an initial grasp on the magnitude of the problem at the end of the 1981–1982 recession.

Beginning in 2007, national estimates of population size have been published in a series of Annual Homeless Assessment Reports to Congress. The AHAR data come from Point-in-Time counts conducted in January of most years by Continuums of Care (CoCs) across the country, and from the Homeless Management Information System (HMIS) data reporting on persons using shelters and transitional housing programs (not unsheltered people) at a point in time and over a twelve-month reporting period (Henry et al., 2014).[6] PIT homeless numbers were in the 640,000 to 650,000 range from 2007 to 2010. Overall, PIT numbers have been dropping slowly since then, as time since the recession has increased. The overall PIT population figure stood at about 580,000 in January 2014; within that estimate, the number of people in shelters on the night of the count remained fairly constant at 390,000 to 400,000 from 2007 through 2014.

Approaches to Conducting Point-in-Time Counts and Surveys of People Experiencing Homelessness

We often talk about the homeless population as if such a single stable thing exists. The implication is that counting is a simple matter of enumerating and adding up. But in fact people move in and out of homelessness all the time, making for an ever-changing reality. In addition, there are many ways to count, and each way will produce a different number (or numbers) with a different meaning. Further, each general method will produce different results depending on where you count (both in terms of geographical area and particular locations within an area); when you count (people are more hidden at night, but more mixed in with people who are not homeless during the day); how sparsely populated and spread out the area is you are trying to cover; what rules you set for exploring unsheltered locations; how long you allow the count to go on; whether you want to increase the odds of including certain subpopulations that are notoriously hard to find such as youth; and sometimes also on who is doing the counting. Trying to get a grasp on the homeless population is complicated by the fact that this is a small group relative to the larger population, that its members often have good reason to avoid enumerators, and that it is not the same group from day to day and from week to week.

That being said, how do we gather the data to count and describe, and what effects will the different approaches have on what we think we know?

We consider (1) the nighttime blitz including outdoor locations, (2) service-based enumerations, and (3) data from shelter-based management information systems while also looking at the time frame of the count (including daytimes, extending the count beyond one night), and service-based probability sampling approaches. We look at what it takes to count versus what it takes to describe, what types of information can be gathered by each technique, and the trade-offs between increased knowledge and increased effort and usually cost. We also discuss the issue of duplicate counting and what has been done to avoid an inflated count.

The earliest approach to counting was a one-night blitz, which is still used by most communities today because it is the biggest part of the twenty-four-hour period in the last week of January that HUD specifies as the standard for producing the Point-in-Time count that CoCs must report every year. The idea is to cover in a single night all the territory and locations where you want to count, with the expectation that this will avoid duplicate counting based on the (often not true) assumption that homeless people do not move around much at night. So shelters and other residential programs for homeless people are included as well as a range of outdoor nighttime locations. Counting people staying in shelters on a single night is quite easy; the challenges arise in efforts to cover people who are not in shelters. Such tasks face two horns of a dilemma—how to find and count the people who really are homeless while not also including people who are not homeless. In addition, one does not want to count the same people twice.

The usual approach is to gather a crew of volunteers to do the actual enumeration and maybe also a survey, give them a brief training on procedures, and send them out to walk or drive through predesignated areas and count (and possibly interview) the people they see. This activity most commonly takes place late at night and early in the morning. Preparation for the count includes identifying the locations where the enumerators will search—by far the most challenging part of the job. Do you include indoor locations where people are likely to be awake, such as all-night movies, laundromats, or fast-food restaurants? Do you include public transportation if it runs all night such as buses and subways? What about abandoned buildings, the rear portions of vacant lots, railway yards, the remote sections of parks, shanty-towns and encampments, the hallways of rental buildings? If your territory is mostly rural, without many service locations, how do you cover it? You can miss a great many people by omitting certain locations, or by establishing rules that limit how far your enumerators may go off the beaten path. If your enumerators are covering territory in a car, they will miss everyone who is not obvious.

New York City conducted a study a few years ago to try to estimate how many people its procedures missed (Hopper et al., 2008). One approach was a study that placed volunteers in sites to be included in the search and instructed them to stay awake, observe, and wait to be counted by the enumerators who were supposed to be canvassing their site. A second approach was a next-day survey in feeding programs. Both identified significant portions of people homeless on the night of the count who were not, in fact, counted. The next-day survey was particularly intriguing; most people at feeding programs had not been homeless the night before but, of those who were, 31–41 percent had slept in a place where they would not have been visible to counters and hence not counted. Sleeping locations included the hallway outside an aunt's apartment; a garage in which a person was allowed to sleep after pushing a food cart forty blocks to store it there; a laundry basket sitting on a street corner next to a building, under four blankets; the remote end of a deep vacant lot behind a group of tall metal oil drums; and deep in the recesses of a large park.

Some communities include a survey to be done at night; others conduct surveys the day after the nighttime count and within HUD's twenty-four-hour window. A survey is really the only way to gather data that describe people who are homeless, rather than merely counting them—and it is hard to develop policy without some idea of who the people are for whom you are planning interventions to end their homelessness. For the next-day surveys, CoCs go to feeding programs, warming or drop-in centers, health care for the homeless clinics, outreach programs, and other service locations. They ask where people slept the night before (to determine if they were homeless that night) along with other questions intended to get more descriptive information about the respondents, including how long they had been homeless and information that allows de-duplication in case they were counted the night before. The count organizers also need to include some method for assuring that the people completing surveys in some way reasonably represent all of the homeless people counted. In Los Angeles, for instance, where the survey is conducted some weeks after the count, the count organizers go during the daytime to a representative sample of search areas where the count was actually conducted, and approach and interview everyone found in the area.

Some large cities, feeling they could never cover their entire territory, use a method initially developed by Peter Rossi in his pioneering Chicago studies (Rossi, 1989; Rossi, Fisher, and Willis, 1986). They divide their geography into blocks, and their blocks into those with a high probability of encountering homeless people and those with a low probability. On the night of the count, they go to all the high-probability blocks and to a sample of the low-probability blocks, using statistical techniques to estimate the total number of homeless people in low-probability areas based on what they found in the blocks they sampled. New York City and Los Angeles County, among others, use this technique—although some large cities, such as Houston and Harris County—commit themselves to sending enumerators to every block in their territory. Of course, the accuracy of the results using a sample of blocks heavily depends on the planners' capacity to identify all the high-probability blocks and separate them from the low-probability ones. This in itself is a major challenge because many of the people contributing to sorting blocks into one category or another are familiar with blocks in the daytime when they might be highly populated, but not at night when people make themselves scarce. It takes only a few high-probability blocks misidentified as low probability to throw an estimate of homeless numbers way off because the multiplier used with the low-probability blocks greatly expands the contribution of the misidentified blocks.

The search for homeless people in areas with few services and long distances, such as suburbia or rural areas, or for particular hard-to-find subpopulations, involves additional challenges. One approach is to extend the time period for the count, with appropriate attention given to gathering the information that will allow elimination of people counted more than once. In the 1990s, Kentucky conducted two waves of a survey, each of which covered a two- to three-month period. They involved shelters but also welfare, food, housing, community action, and other agencies where people might turn for help. Two simple questions that determined their likely homeless status were asked of every person seeking assistance at a participating agency. If the answers indicated homelessness, they were asked a few more questions. Only about one in five of the people ultimately deemed to have been homeless on the first day of the survey were counted on that day; the rest trickled in over the course of the survey period. This method allowed the study designers to determine not only the count on the index day, but also the number of people who were homeless when counted but were not homeless on the index day, giving them important information on the flow of people into and out of homelessness throughout a rural state. In 2013, Cleveland allowed a one-week counting period to give itself a better opportunity to include more homeless youth, along with going to some locations especially known to be places where many youth experiencing homelessness congregated.

Estimates of How Many People Experience Homelessness over a One-Year Period

The picture of people who are homeless changes drastically when one considers a time frame considerably longer than one day—the usual alternate period is one year. The picture changes because many people are homeless for only short periods of time—often less than one week—and are replaced by more short-term people as time goes on. But some people are continuously homeless over a long period of time, and they will remain in the population and be counted every time there is a count. The characteristics of people experiencing homelessness for short periods of time differ considerably from the characteristics of those who are homeless for only a short period; thus, it is vitally important to understand those differences so one can design relevant interventions.

Consider the example of a ten-bed shelter and its bed occupancy over a week's time. Five of its beds are occupied by people who have been homeless for a long time, and, therefore, occupy a bed every night of the week in question. Then, assume that the remaining five beds are occupied by persons who stay for only two nights and are replaced by others with a similar bed use pattern. On any given night, we would count ten homeless people, 50 percent of whom would be considered long-term or chronically homeless. But over a week's time, there would have been twenty-five homeless people, five of whom are the same long-term homeless people and twenty of whom are the four people occupying each of the other five beds for two nights each (with the last set of five people coming in on the last day of the week). Now, the long-term homeless people are only 20 percent of the homeless population. This example shows the great importance of knowing about people's patterns of homelessness. Any policies based on population characteristics derived from a single point in time will be systematically flawed.

Two basic approaches to developing an annual prevalence rate are the most commonly utilized in the United States: using information contained in an HMIS and using data from a survey. The former has the advantage of accumulating automatically to an HMIS as homeless assistance programs report the people who have used their services,[7] but the disadvantages include covering only those people who use shelters or other residential programs within the local homeless assistance system and being limited, for most people, to information obtained from only the few, very basic, questions included in the HMIS Universal Elements. The latter approach (a survey) has the disadvantage of having to be gathered through special procedures, but the advantages of capturing information from people who do not use shelters and of being able to ask a relatively broad range of questions.

The first HMIS data used to develop a sense of homelessness prevalence over extended periods of time came from the systems developed by New York and Philadelphia, two cities that covered the costs of providing shelter to all who needed it and, therefore, had to keep track of shelter entries and days of stay to keep track of costs.[8] Culhane et al. (1994) analyzed the data from the late 1980s to reveal patterns of shelter stay. They were able to report the number of people who had a shelter stay over the course of one year as well as the number of homeless on an average day, revealing two things of great importance. First, the number of people using shelters in these two cities over the course of a year was much greater than the average-day count; second, patterns of homeless shelter use appeared to be bimodal. The most common length of stay in a shelter was one day, with many people staying less than a week. On the other hand, about 10 percent of shelter stayers turned out to be long-term homeless. The importance of this 10 percent, from a policy perspective, is that they accounted for about 50 percent of all shelter bed nights over a year's time. This was one fact derived from research that contributed to the policy push to end chronic or long-term homelessness that began in 2000.

Annual prevalence rates now come from data reported by CoCs throughout the country based on their HMIS (i.e., shelter and transitional housing program) data, and reported to Congress annually in HUD's Annual Homeless Assessment Reports. These data show numbers of people using shelter over a year's time to be two to three times greater than the average daily census.

The first estimate of annual prevalence rates developed from survey data was based on the data collected in 1996 for the National Survey of Homeless Assistance Providers and Clients (NSHAPC). NSHAPC used statistically valid probability sampling techniques, covered the entire geographical territory of the lower forty-eight states, used a service-based enumeration technique that included sixteen types of services that homeless people were likely to use, and interviewed over 4,000 people, 65–70 percent of whom were homeless at the time of the interview (many of the rest had been homeless at some point, and all were interviewed at the services where they were selected for the sample). The survey included information on patterns of homelessness, and asked the question of how long the person had been homeless, this time in great detail. Burt (1992), who developed the estimate, (1) took the number of people who said they had been homeless less than a week; (2) assumed that, although the people would be different, the same number of people would have answered the same way any other week of the year; (3) therefore multiplied that number by 51; and (4) added the estimate for the one week the survey was conducted to the result for the remaining fifty-one weeks. After adjusting for multiple periods during the same year, based on answers to a different NSHAPC question, Burt estimated that between 2.3 and 3.5 million people had been homeless over the course of a year, depending on whether one used the lower or the higher NSHAPC Point-in-Time estimate. This annual prevalence estimate translates into about four to five times more people who experienced homelessness at some time during a year's period than would have been counted at a point in time (Burt, Aron, and Lee, 2001, pp. 44–50 and table 2.9). Because of NSHAPC's design, going as it did to feeding programs, health programs, and a range of other nonshelter programs serving homeless people, estimates based on this survey include many people who would have been unsheltered on any given night when a Point-in-Time count would have been done.

CoCs that do surveys as part of their annual or biannual Point-in-Time counts often include questions similar to those used in NSHAPC for the purpose of having the data to calculate a local annual prevalence rate as well as ascertaining how many people are homeless on a given night. Local communities use these rates in their own policy deliberations and goal-setting activities.

Research on annual prevalence rates led to the recognition that only about 10 percent of people homeless over a year's time were chronically homeless, as defined by HUD as (1) having a disability; and (2) having an extensive homeless history—either continuously homeless for a year or more or having experienced four or more episodes of homelessness during the previous three years. Different estimates of how many people this would be ranged from a low of about 150,000 to a high of about 300,000. Numbers in this range were seen as being amenable to solution, so these research-based estimates were one piece of the argument that policymakers should address the problem forcefully, as they did beginning about 2000 and gaining momentum as the decade progressed (Burt, 2003).

Family Homelessness

The Great Recession of 2008–2009 had a major impact on family homelessness. Families struggling economically were hard hit by the foreclosure crisis created by Wall Street investment and banking interests, coupled with the job losses and economic collapse that accompanied the financial crisis, with effects still being felt in 2015. Housing loss happened to homeowners because they could not meet payments on the subprime mortgages they had acquired, and also to renters whose landlords found themselves in the same position. Family homelessness soared in those years. As best as can be estimated, persons homeless in families numbered about 168,000 on a single day in January 2005 (HUD, 2007).[9] In 2007, when the effects of the subprime crisis were beginning to materialize, that number reached about 236,000—a 40 percent increase! Family homelessness numbers stayed in the 236,000 to 242,000 range through 2012, only showing a substantial decrease to 222,000 in 2013 and a further decrease to 216,000 in 2014—still not back down to 2005 levels (Henry et al. 2014).

Reductions in Unsheltered Homelessness

Unlike numbers of sheltered people and persons in families, the number of unsheltered people has dropped quite steadily, from about 260,000 in 2007 to 177,000 in 2014 (a drop of 33 percent; AHAR 2015). There is nothing accidental about this decrease—it stems from deliberate policy decisions, coupled with the funding to implement them, that focused on specific subpopulations within the larger universe of homelessness. These policies have been directed toward people experiencing chronic homelessness and toward veterans, who are sometimes the same people. Major policy initiatives beginning in the early 2000s have spurred investment in permanent supportive housing

(PSH) as the solution to exiting homeless for people with disabilities who experience long or repeated episodes of homelessness. In 1996, there were an estimated 114,000 PSH beds (Burt et al., 1999); by 2006, the number stood at 177,000, and it reached 284,000 in 2014 (AHAR reporting).

The arsenals of homeless assistance systems throughout the country were augmented in this development by expanding federal, state, and local resources devoted to PSH development, ten-year plans to end chronic homelessness promoted by the US Interagency Council on Homelessness (ICH), and significant advocacy work. Federal programs supported housing through HUD's Special Needs Assistance Programs Permanent Supportive Housing grants and Shelter Plus Care (S+C) allocations were supplemented by housing subsidies and supports specifically for veterans, the HUD-Veterans Affairs Supportive Housing (HUD-VASH), and later by the Supportive Services for Veteran Families program, which supplies short-term rental assistance to prevent veteran homelessness or to end it quickly. State and local governments often augmented these federal resources, sometimes dramatically.

Looking at veterans specifically, these policies are responsible for a remarkable drop in homelessness, from about 75,000 at a single point in time in January 2009 to about 50,000 in January 2014 (about one-third). During that same period, the number of unsheltered veterans fell even more dramatically, from about 31,000 in January 2009 to about 18,000 in January 2014 (a drop of 42 percent).

The experience of these three decades points clearly to the solution to homelessness—housing is the answer. What advocates were saying in the early 1980s has come full circle, but now with considerable evidence to back up their claim. When we provide housing to people who have been homeless for a long time, along with the supportive services that help them settle in and stabilize in housing, we end their homelessness.

Conclusion

We have not conquered homelessness. Although we certainly know what it would take to shorten or eliminate most of it and have the evidence of reductions in chronic homelessness in general and among veterans in particular to prove it, comprehensive solutions would take considerable political will to greatly expand programs that make housing affordable (e.g., rent subsidies) and reduce poverty (e.g., better jobs, better education and training) that thus far eludes us. While we have obviously come a long way in the sophistication of our approach to counting and describing homeless populations, we continue to fall far short of ending homelessness.

Early in this chapter, I described factors contributing to the risk of homelessness. On average, these factors increase the risk but, in the end, random events usually furnish the final elements in actually becoming homeless.

Many have likened it to a game of musical chairs—the more people there are circling the few available chairs, and the more stressed any one or two of them may be, the more likely they are to be out of luck when the music stops. A car breaking down and having no money to fix it may be the final straw, as may a serious and expensive illness or medical condition, or a job loss in a recession, or the departure or death of a partner or parent who provided housing. Using data from their study of family homelessness in the 1990s, which provided a huge range of variables to use in predictive equations, Shinn et al. (1998) could account for only a bit more than two-thirds of the variance in identifying which formerly homeless families would reenter shelter. A recent effort to improve on that predictability did a good bit better, but still was not perfect—for families seeking shelter, a screening tool developed by Shinn and Greer (2012) in collaboration with New York City's Homebase prevention program was able to predict with 88 to 89 percent accuracy which families that sought assistance through Homebase would enter shelter unless they received help from the program.

With all the challenges involved in counting and describing people experiencing homelessness, it should be clear that while we have become quite good at describing many homeless people, we will never be perfect. However, the more our techniques and our examination of particular interventions and types of homelessness improve, the more it becomes clear how much depends on what we are looking for, and why. Further, we will have to continue to struggle with the difficulties inherent to predicting who will become homeless right now, and we will never get it completely right because chance plays too big a role.

So why is it important to count and describe? It is obvious that we still have people who are homeless in this country, the argument runs, so why can't we just help them until there are no more people living on the streets or in shelters? And why do we struggle with definitions? Again, many would say, homelessness is obvious, so let's just get on with it.

There are many ways to answer these questions, all of them having to do with politics in the larger sense. To solve a problem, one has to want to solve it, and also be able to solve it. When it comes to poverty and social welfare, Americans have always been conflicted.[10] Our Puritan past (material success indicating being chosen by God and poverty indicating the opposite), overlaid with social Darwinism, says that people have to solve their own problems and that those who cannot are simply unchosen or have lost the battle in the arena of survival of the fittest. There is little room in this ideology, much more dominant in the past thirty or forty years, for collective action by government to help those in need, even the playing field, assure a minimum standard of living to all households, or support other functions of collective social responsibility (although we don't seem to mind paying for prisons or war). We have also had long periods in our history during which this ideology held less sway, when corporations acted on the premise that the well-being of companies and workers went hand in hand. It was during these decades that the most important components of the US safety net were established, including those providing income, housing, health care, and food. The ideological conflicts can easily be seen in the histories of these programs — we want to help, but not too much, and not "the undeserving poor," in George Bernard Shaw's words. So Congress enacts a program and stints on funding, expands eligibility when the level of need becomes a crisis and public outcry increases, and contracts eligibility when the program starts to cost too much, or when undeserving people are perceived to be taking advantage of it.

With respect to homelessness, we need numbers to tell us whether we are making progress. In the early 1980s, before we started counting in any reliable way, the most common responses of communities to homelessness were either to deny that there was any or to maintain that all the homeless people came from somewhere else. Columbus, Ohio, was one of the first communities to develop an information system to track people using its shelters — and one of the first consequences of that tracking, according to local advocates, was the ability to say "here's how many we had last year," and "they are from here!" The result of having that knowledge was that the community stopped arguing and began to search for, and fund, solutions in a systematic way. Columbus was among the first communities to invest seriously in housing first, to develop an approach to prevention and rapid re-housing, and to document the impact of its approaches with changes in numbers.

Are large numbers good, or are small numbers better? That depends on where you stand and what you are trying to do. Advocates tend to think that bigger numbers are better — and therefore more expansive definitions more useful — because only big numbers will have the shock value to move politicians to action. But sometimes big numbers are too big — no one thinks that anything one could reasonably do would make a difference, and so they do nothing. One of the three research results that underlay the decision in 2003 to commit federal resources to ending chronic homelessness was knowledge gained from the NSHAPC that the numbers were small enough to be amenable to actually solving the problem — in the range of 150,000 to 300,000 (the other two pieces of the puzzle were evaluation results showing that PSH works and cost analyses showing that costs of PSH were not much more, and possibly less, than the costs of doing nothing and leaving people homeless). Basically, if we are going to make effective policy decisions, we need accurate numbers and descriptions that accurately reflect the problem we are trying to do something about. And that brings us back to the subject of definitions.

In the policy arena, definitions are *always* programmatic; that is, they always serve one or more purposes related to people, policies, programs, values, and money. Programmatically, definitions tell us which people should get the limited supply of help that is available. Attempts to expand the definition of homelessness beyond the one that HUD uses (e.g., to include doubled up households; to use the Department of Education definition) are attempts by constituencies not currently falling within HUD definitions to access the resources that HUD distributes to end or ameliorate homelessness. To use an example currently surrounded by controversy, HUD's definition pertains to its mission to provide housing, and HUD alone among federal agencies charged with giving assistance to homeless persons has been given the responsibility to reduce homelessness. Its need for numbers and annual counts stems from this responsibility. The Department of Education, on the other hand, has the mission of assuring access to education for all school-age children. The Department of Education calls a child homeless who is living, stably and predictably, with an aunt or grandparent because the child's parent(s) are homeless, since by so labeling the child it can provide transportation to assure continued access to school. The Department of Education counts too — it counts children identified as homeless at time of enrollment by school systems throughout the country. It makes little attempt to identify school-age children who become homeless during the school year some time after enrollment, or children who are not in contact with a school system who are homeless. And it has no defined responsibility for ending or reducing homelessness among school-age children. So the Department of Education's definition serves its purpose, and HUD's definition serves its purpose. Each is valid within its own sphere.

It is essential that we understand the dynamics of homelessness, including risk factors, flows into and out of homelessness, and interventions that can make a difference before and after a person or household becomes homeless in the HUD sense. But it makes no sense, and is in fact a disservice to understanding or developing useful solutions, to create a definition of homelessness so broad that it confuses rather than clarifies.

Of one thing we can be sure — extreme poverty plays a big role in the inability to afford stable housing. It would not be a bad policy decision to provide every household that has a worst-case housing need with a rent subsidy for as long as necessary. We don't need perfect predictability to take that step, just political will, and there can be little doubt that we would reduce homelessness substantially if we took it.

Notes

1. Slightly different versions of this figure were published in Burt (1992) and Burt, Aron, and Lee (2001).

2. For the effects of incarceration policies on homelessness, as well as homelessness on risk of incarceration, see Metraux, Roman, and Cho (2007). For effects of policies for veterans, see Montgomery et al. (2013) and M. Cunningham et al. (2013, chapter 1).

3. After several more waves of emergency funding, the Emergency Food and Shelter Program was authorized as a permanent program with passage of the Stewart B. McKinney Homeless Assistance Act of 1987, and is now on its thirty-third or thirty-fourth wave of annual funding.

4. The increase stems from the increase in the Point-in-Time homeless population by a factor of 500–600 percent coupled with the increase in the proportion of people experiencing homelessness who have a mental illness (from 20 to 33 percent; Burt 1992, p. 120).

5. According to data from the Drug Early Warning Network.

6. The AHARs rely on Point-in-Time counts and data from the HMIS that report data only for people using homeless assistance services, mostly shelter and transitional housing, but sometimes also nonhousing assistance such as supportive services. HMIS data are capable of showing both Point-in-Time homelessness and homelessness over each report's twelve-month reporting period for the people it captures. It took several years for CoCs to achieve a level of competence at collecting and reporting these types of data. The first AHAR went to Congress in 2007; it described the data collection sources and process, and provided limited information on a three-month period in 2005. The first AHAR to report full-year data was submitted in 2009 and was based on 2007 data.

7. Of course, this assumes that a community has an HMIS, and that it covers most of the beds in all or most of the residential programs in the community. Once HUD began pushing CoCs to develop these systems and report data from them every year, it took close to five years before the proportion of CoCs reporting acceptable data with acceptable coverage reached a level that assured reliable annual reporting.

8. The New York and Philadelphia data were limited in the following ways: only these two cities, only people using publicly funded emergency shelters, and only single adults (i.e., no families).

9. That estimate is based on Point-in-Time counts of sheltered and unsheltered persons conducted by CoCs, statistically adjusted for CoCs that did not report qualifying numbers.

10. See Burt, Aron, and Lee (2001) for a more extensive discussion of this premise.

5

A Housing First Approach

Sam Tsemberis and Benjamin F. Henwood

Over the past 30 years, homelessness has become an even more permanent and problematic part of the US landscape. This homelessness crisis that started in the early 1980s was in part a direct result of the federal government's elimination of funding to continue building affordable housing. Homelessness on a large scale continues today, but a community of agencies and a lexicon of program interventions aimed at addressing homelessness have been spawned. In addition to the development of various programs designed to serve individuals who are homeless, the US Interagency Council on Homelessness was created in the late 1980s to "coordinate the Federal response to homelessness and to create partnerships between the federal agencies addressing homelessness and every level of government and every element of the private sector" (ICH, 2008). In the 1990s, the Homeless Management Information System was developed in response to a congressional mandate requiring states to collect information on homelessness to continue receiving federal money from the US Department of Housing and Urban Development to serve a homeless population (HUD, 2001). These systems were developed to provide a better understanding of homeless estimates and trends, which are now provided by the Annual Homeless Assessment Report prepared by HUD.

The 2009 AHAR, which is the fifth and most recent report, concluded that overall homelessness had remained largely unchanged from the previous year, with roughly 643,000 people nationally who were counted as homeless on a single night in January (HUD's "one-night count") and approximately

---

An earlier version of this chapter appeared in V. Vandiver, ed., *Best Practices in Community Mental Health: A Pocket Guide*, pp. 132–150 (New York: Oxford University Press, 2013).

1.56 million people who accessed shelter through homeless services during the course of the year (HUD, 2010). Although overall numbers mask wide variations at state and local levels, and growth in the number of homeless families and those living in rural and suburban areas, the 2009 report noted a more than 10 percent drop in the national number of chronically homeless individuals from the previous year. A working definition of a chronically homeless individual adopted at the federal level is "an unaccompanied homeless individual with a disabling condition who has either been continuously homeless for a year or more, or has had at least four episodes of homelessness in the past three years" (ICH, 2008). In particular, individuals diagnosed with severe mental illnesses disproportionately constitute the chronically homeless population, most of whom have co-occurring addictions (HUD, 2008; National Coalition for the Homeless, 2009; Susser et al., 1997).

It is also true that people with disabling conditions have significantly reduced incomes; they are among the poorest of the homeless, with little chance of a quick economic recovery. If a person depends on a monthly SSI disability check for income, in most places in the United States they would need two or three times that amount to secure housing. People with disabilities are essentially priced out of housing (Cooper et al., 2009). Thus, homelessness can be seen as primarily a problem of poverty; serious mental illness or substance abuse is neither necessary nor sufficient for homelessness to occur; and this combination may hasten the descent into homelessness and certainly impedes the recovery from homelessness. Although serious mental illness typically predates homelessness, substance abuse can occur either pre- or posthomelessness. Either way, homelessness exacerbates both symptoms of mental illness and substance abuse, making the relationship among serious mental illness, substance abuse, and homelessness complex (Drake, Osher, and Wallach, 1991; Mueser, Drake, and Wallach, 1998).

The Promise of Pathways

The Pathways' Housing First program is an evidence-based practice (SAMHSA, 2007) that was developed with this complexity in mind, offering a simple, straightforward solution—provide housing first and then combine that housing with supportive treatment services. The more than 10 percent drop in the number of chronically homeless individuals noted in the 2009 AHAR report can be largely attributed to the rapid growth and dissemination of the Housing First approach that originated from the PHF program. In the past five years, the number of Housing First programs has grown from a few dozen to a few hundred. The National Alliance to End Homelessness reported that more than 400 cities and counties have completed ten-year plans to end homelessness and 67 percent of all plans include a Housing First program (National Alliance to End Homelessness, 2016). In California, an estimated 100 Housing First programs were recently implemented using funds generated by the California Assembly Bill 2034 (the millionaire's tax) that funded the Integrated Services for the Homeless Mentally Ill (Gilmer, Manning, and Ettner, 2009). Housing First programs are also growing in Canada and in Europe. The Mental Health Commission of Canada recently funded a $110 million national initiative to implement Housing First programs in five cities and conduct a cross-site randomized control trial to evaluate its effectiveness (Mental Health Commission of Canada, 2016). In Europe, Portugal, France, Finland, Denmark, Ireland, and the Netherlands are planning the implementation of Housing First programs. In this chapter, we describe the PHF model, its empirical basis, and its consumer-driven service approach that has been the key to its ongoing success.

The PHF Program Model
The design of the PHF program model originated to honor the request of most homeless individuals, which is an apartment of their own in a normal community setting. An invitation to be placed in a home of one's own has proven to be an offer of enormous value that many chronically homeless individuals find irresistible. A key feature of PHF is that the program does not require participation in psychiatric treatment or sobriety as a condition for obtaining housing, thereby removing prerequisites to housing that can be insurmountable barriers for the most vulnerable sector of the homeless population. By adopting a harm reduction approach to substance use, as opposed to an abstinence-based model, PHF has successfully tested the hypothesis that consumers can move directly from homelessness into independent apartment living through the use of flexible team-based support services. In addition to paying 30 percent of their income toward rent, consumers agree to only two other conditions: (1) regular staff visits to their apartment; and (2) the terms and conditions of a standard lease with full tenant rights.

The PHF program model was born out of frustration with, and stands in stark contrast to, traditional approaches to homeless services in which treatment requirements and expectations of consumer stability have interfered with ending an individual's experience of homelessness. The underlying philosophy of traditional approaches is that change must occur at the individual consumer level before that individual can transition into permanent housing. In traditional approaches, consumers must graduate through a series of placements, typically starting with drop-in centers or shelters, through transitional housing, and finally into permanent housing by demonstrating treatment compliance, psychiatric stability, and abstinence from substances (Kertesz et al., 2009; Wong and Stanhope, 2009). If a consumer relapses, becomes unstable, or chooses not to follow rules necessary for congregate living, he or she must leave the program or become institutionalized, which by default entails sacrificing his or her current living situation and the prospect of permanent housing. Success, which is rarely achieved, is attributed to effective treatment and often results in permanent housing in buildings inhabited by other people with psychiatric disabilities (Hopper and Barrow, 2003). The main motivating factor for individual change in this approach is thought to come from a promise of permanent housing. This structurally endorsed incentive presents a high-stakes proposition in which an end to homelessness depends on an individual's ability to first learn to manage conditions that by nature are difficult to overcome and often recurring. The nature of this challenge itself may help to explain why the traditional service approach has had limited success in addressing chronic homelessness (HUD, 2007).

PHF as Empirically Supported

In contrast to the traditional service approach, the PHF program has proven to be remarkably successful and has changed the landscape of what is considered possible for people suffering from chronic homelessness. Research has overwhelmingly demonstrated that Housing First is effective at achieving residential stability for people who have remained homeless for years. Initial evaluations of Housing First in urban areas with primarily street-dwelling people have yielded convincing results; using archival data over a five-year period, researchers found that 88 percent of Housing First consumers remained housed as compared to 47 percent of consumers in traditional residential treatment (Tsemberis and Eisenberg, 2000). In a randomized clinical trial of housing alternatives, individuals assigned to Housing First spent approximately 80 percent of their time stably housed compared to only 30 percent of participants assigned to traditional services after two years (Tsemberis, Gulcur, and Nakae, 2004).

In 2004, the US Interagency Council on Homelessness launched its national Initiative to Help End Chronic Homelessness that was funded by HUD, Department of Health and Human Services (HHS), Substance Abuse and Mental Health Services Administration, and the VA. Seven of the eleven cities funded used the Housing First model and achieved 85 percent housing retention rates after twelve months (Mares, Greenberg, and Rosenheck, 2007). Two years later, HUD published the outcomes of its three-city twelve-month study of Housing First programs and reported an 84 percent housing retention rate for twelve months (Pearson, Locke, Montgomery, and Buron, 2007; Pearson, Montgomery, and Locke, 2009). Similar outcomes were also found for consumers who were long-term shelter dwellers in a suburban county, in which approximately 78 percent of Housing First participants remained stably housed over a four-year period (Stefancic and Tsemberis, 2007). This suggests the model's utility for street-dwelling and shelter-using segments of the homeless population and its effectiveness at utilizing housing stock in urban and suburban environments.

Although the hallmark of Housing First's effectiveness has been assessed through success achieved in residential stability, both quantitative and qualitative research have also documented advantages to Housing First that go beyond residential stability. For instance, consumers rate housing satisfaction significantly higher when living in more independent supported housing settings as compared to congregate or community residences (Siegel et al., 2006). Both single-site and scatter-site housing, as part of Housing First, are significant predictors of consumers' psychological well-being and social integration, respectively (Greenwood et al., 2005; Gulcur et al., 2007). Housing First consumers also described a greater sense of belonging in the world related to having their own home in terms of privacy, normalized daily activities, and a secure base for self-discovery (Padgett, 2007). Important to note is that although some people reported feeling lonely in their apartments, they still preferred independent to congregate housing (Yanos, Barrow, and Tsemberis, 2004).

Additionally, although consumers in traditional programs reported higher rates of substance use treatment, Housing First consumers who had lower rates of treatment utilization yielded no greater rates of alcohol or substance use in a randomized controlled trial (Padgett, Gulcur, and Tsemberis, 2006). Subsequent comparison studies suggested that Housing First consumers may actually use fewer drugs and less alcohol than those in traditional services (Padgett, Stanhope, Henwood, and Stefancic, 2011), yet some individuals maintain Housing First is not appropriate for persons with active addictions (Kertesz et al., 2009). Paradoxically, the traditional service approach with a program requirement of abstinence is no more or perhaps less effective than Housing First programs that use a harm reduction approach, reinforcing the need to target people's internal motivation for recovery rather than program rules (Prochaska, DiClemente, and Norcross, 1992; Rollnick, Miller, and Butler, 2008). Mandating detoxification or rehabilitation stays for substance use also contributes to higher costs in the traditional service approach (Pérez-Peña, 2007).

Indeed, another impetus toward Housing First has come from cost-effectiveness considerations. Put simply, choosing to leave people on the streets has a price. Culhane (2008) noted that homeless advocates have long argued that providing Housing First is significantly less costly than having a person remain homeless, and there is now evidence to support this claim. In a HUD-funded review of cost studies dating back to 1998, Culhane, Parker, et al. (2007) found that, nationally, the average cost for shelter beds was $13,000 or more per year, depending on region and the services available. In New York City, service-enriched shelter beds can range from $23,000 to $33,000 per year and institutional settings such as hospitals or jails can quickly bring those costs to well over $100,000 per year. One study found that the combined average annual cost associated with services such as drop-in centers, shelters, emergency services, police interventions, and incarcerations for individuals who are chronically homeless with severe mental illness is $40,500. When this same group receives Housing First services, the combined rent and service costs range from $17,000 to $24,000, depending on services utilized (Culhane, Parker, et al., 2007). Although funding is needed to support rental costs in Housing First programs, these costs can be offset to some degree through reduction and eventually elimination of outreach, drop-in, shelter, and transitional housing programs, because these step-by-step housing readiness programs are unnecessary when using the Housing First model.

Malcolm Gladwell (2006) put a face on this counterintuitive discussion of cost, homeless, mental illness, and service utilization. His memorable *New Yorker* profile titled "Million Dollar Murray" was written about a man he met in Reno, Nevada; his story is briefly summarized below.

Case Vignette: Million Dollar Murray

Murray was a middle-aged homeless man who lived for ten years in Reno, Nevada. He was a very well-known figure downtown—a veteran who suffered from schizophrenia. Everyone, it seemed, knew Murray: the police, the local merchants, homeless outreach teams, the emergency room staff, the detox center staff, and the ambulance drivers all knew Murray well.

Why does Gladwell give Murray this "million dollar" handle? Because Gladwell, with the assistance of a local police officer, tallied all of the different services Murray received from the City of Reno during the course of the previous ten years. He summed up the cost of the emergency medical service transports, police interventions, jail days, detox days, and hospital days and calculated that in ten years, the City of Reno had spent more than a million dollars on Murray. And yet, Murray remained homeless until the day he passed away.

The service providers in Murray's life repeatedly offered the same services, presumably expecting a different result. Trying to get some people who are homeless into treatment over and over again with housing as an incentive has proven incredibly costly and simply has not and will not work for chronically homeless people like Murray.

More than forty municipalities throughout the United States have conducted cost analysis studies since 2003 to generate strategic planning information as part of their ten-year plans to end chronic homelessness. The findings are striking in their consistency—all demonstrated reduced service use subsequent to housing placement, with cost reductions ranging from $5,266 to $43,045 (Culhane, Parker, et al., 2007). Many researchers have found that the reduced costs of service use fully offset the intervention cost. Despite the consistency of these cost studies, Culhane (2008) pointed out that even when studies of housing solutions clearly indicate that reduced services costs associated with the interventions partially or wholly offset their cost, cost savings do not necessarily transfer between public agencies. Savings accrued from the reduced services utilization of homeless persons are not easily reinvested in housing solutions. Clearly, even when cost savings associated with housing interventions are apparent, there are complicated issues that must be addressed.

Four Essential Program Principles

The Housing First program is a complex community mental health intervention that includes housing and clinical components. The program has numerous operational and administrative dimensions and protocols that are well defined (Pathways to Housing, 2016). The focus here is to present four of the key program principles on which this effective intervention is based.

Consumer-Driven Services

PHF's empirical basis and cost effectiveness, which has resulted in its rapid growth and dissemination, often overshadow the consumer-driven service approach that has been the key to its success. The straightforward effective solution to the problem of chronic homelessness offered by the PHF program requires creative flexible staff members, because honoring consumer choice does not end with providing people with an apartment; ongoing services must also be consumer driven. The program's functional separation of housing from support services is intended to make clear that housing is a basic human right and not something that needs to be earned or used as leverage for treatment compliance, yet ongoing support services must continue to match the stated needs of consumers. This requires the consumer to be either the driver of the treatment or, at minimum, an active collaborator.

The goal of this consumer-driven approach is to shift the initiative for setting goals and pursuing solutions from the provider to the consumer. There is a subtle, but important, transfer in the battle for initiative that must take place when attempting to work in a consumer-driven manner. Consumers with a long history of receiving traditional mental health services have been inducted into a system of care where the initiative and drive of the treatment regimen has been prescribed by providers. They have been told (not asked) what ails them (given a diagnosis that may or may not be consistent with their lived experience or beliefs) and what to do about it. Such clinician-driven approaches direct the treatment and interventions and require the client to be either cooperative or compliant. They are instructed on what medications to take, told how often to meet with their doctors or caseworkers, and provided with specific goals and outcomes for their treatments.

Rarely have their voices been heard. This renders consumers passive in the decision-making process. In such programs, all they are left with is the option to either comply or not comply. If they fail to or choose not to comply, they are usually labeled as "treatment resistant" or "difficult to serve," as if their failure to agree or respond is a personal failing rather than a difference of opinion. This approach has resulted in an overall system of care that many consumers choose to avoid altogether.

In the Housing First model, the client is considered to be the expert on his or her experience. This is the starting point of consumer-driven services and housing, assuming that consumers, and not programs, are the experts of their own needs and wishes. Clients are asked about their priorities and preferences and they actively guide the treatment or services from the beginning. These consumers initiate the service approach because services and housing are designed to respond to their needs and priorities.

The consumer-driven clinician is present, actively listening and prepared to take action, but only when the consumer initiates the plan. (Maintaining this approach is interrupted only in times of crisis when the staff must take an active role, intervening to ensure the health and safety of the consumer.) Consumers, however, are not used to being active, let alone in charge of clinical interactions, so this will take patience and practice for both the consumer and the clinician. For clinicians, there are many instances when it is tempting to point things out to consumers, make suggestions, or simply do things for them. This doing for approach may seem to be expedient or efficient in the short term, but it retains the clinician as the initiator of action and renders the consumers passive. In the long run, it is much more productive to either do with or assist the consumer to do for themselves. In practice, clinicians must be cognizant that although doing things for the consumer may be acceptable during the engagement or initial phase of the program, they want to be moving toward doing things with consumers and finally to teaching and supporting consumers to do things for themselves (and being ready to provide support when asked).

This fundamental approach is given a significant head start in the PHF program because the program starts by working with consumers to help them achieve their immediate self-stated goal — finding a place of their own in which to live. Clients actively work with staff members to select the neighborhood, choose their apartments, and select their furniture and household items. Providing a person who is homeless with a rent-subsidized furnished apartment with few strings attached also serves as an excellent way to achieve trust — creating a therapeutic spike — that then sets the precedent for how all subsequent services are provided. "OK, you're housed; what can we help you with now?" is how the program should unfold. To maintain this approach, clinicians must ascribe to the right values, including a belief in social justice and compassion and being trained in different practices known to be effective for this population (e.g., motivational interviewing, integrated dual diagnoses treatment, and supported employment). This well-trained person must be prepared to meet the consumers where they are, which may mean to simply be there, hovering in readiness but not necessarily doing anything more than that. Ongoing home visits that are part of the program serve to keep lines of communication open between providers and consumers so that when consumers are ready, they have the support they need.

In fact, the home visit represents the heart and soul of the program. It is not simply a social call. It is where and when important communication takes place and where change happens in the person's own environment. In many ways, the home visit starts before the actual visit. It begins when discussing the need to do a home visit with the client and continues while working out a time that is convenient for the client. (Surprise home visits should be done only if there are concerns that a client is in danger or hurt and only after all other ways to contact the client have been exhausted.) Building relationships, after all, takes time, especially when some clients are suspicious of a team's motives and are convinced that the team has the power to take the apartment away (the team does not have that power). During the early phases of the program, clients may deny problems or troubling issues that they are facing. To foster trust, team members must convey acceptance and concern, not judgment. Home visits can create an opportunity to connect and work on developing a deeper and more authentic relationship. To do this, team members must be focused, but not hurried or rushed. Clients will not open up and ask for help unless they first trust the helper; in fact, unless they trust the helper, they may not be home when that helper stops by.

Home visits often include the provision of services such as medication delivery, counseling, and nuts-and-bolts things like helping the client fix a leaky faucet. Much of the routine conversation during a home visit centers on specific clinical services, instrumental or housing needs, scheduling new or follow-up appointments, and family issues and other areas discussed at length during the development of the treatment plan. One of the interesting things about a home visit, however, is how it creates a shift in power dynamics between client and staff member. The home visit, after all, occurs on the client's turf. Coupled with a PHF program philosophy that does not mandate participation in treatment as a condition for keeping housing, this poses an interesting challenge for the team member: clients will welcome or tolerate a visit only as long as they find it useful or engaging. This is why clinicians must fully embrace and respond to a consumer-driven service approach.

Successful home visits provide staff members with an excellent opportunity to assess how someone is doing and examine the condition of the apartment. Team members can learn an enormous amount about clients by carefully observing their living space: What is the meaning of the empty wine bottles on the kitchen counter? Who are the people in that new picture taped to the fridge? The shoes in the doorway are of a different size; who do they belong to? There are still no pictures hanging from these walls . . . does the person feel at home? How comfortable is the client in his or her home? Has he or she settled in, or are there boxes that are still unpacked since the move? Is that a new crack in the wall near the window?

Making a home visit provides an opportunity to make innumerable observations about a client's life. In some ways, it is an intimate experience, in that it allows the clinician access to the very center of the client's life. Clinicians not only can ask about but also can actually observe how their client is managing and maintaining the living space; bedrooms, bathrooms, and kitchens provide great amounts of data to the trained observer. The information obtained during a routine home visit can be stored, noted, asked about, used as a baseline for the client's modus operandi, or serve as a reason to intervene. Answers to these questions will inform how the team approaches the client. This information is also crucial for preventing a possible housing crisis.

There is a lack of formal boundaries when making a home visit, and therefore it is essential that the clinician always maintains his or her clinical and ethical boundaries during such visits. This is a targeted clinical intervention, not a social call. The clinician needs to maintain a professional demeanor at all times and ensure that the visit is consistent with the work that the client has agreed to during the treatment plan.

In fact, honoring consumer choice is especially important in times of difficulty or crisis such as when consumers deplete their financial resources, are under threat of eviction by their landlord, or have relapsed into addiction. Unless there is a danger to the consumer or to others, staff members must support one another in resisting the desire to control or resolve a chaotic situation, and must make every effort to remain in communication with the consumer, exploring options while allowing the consumer to make the decisions. For example, if a consumer is facing eviction by the landlord because she has invited too many of her homeless friends to stay in her apartment, the staff should work with the consumer to determine the best course of action: What options do we have here? Shall we try to negotiate with your landlord? Shall we leave this apartment and start over in another? They need to discuss the lease violations that led the landlord to file for eviction and how these may be prevented from happening again, and explore what steps should be taken next. By making their own decisions under difficult circumstances, consumers can benefit from their experience and learn to make better decisions in the future. Experiential learning, in which consumers are supported in making their own decisions and observing the consequences of those decisions, is one of the cornerstones of recovery. PHF staff members must constantly be offering choices, encouraging self-directed care, and conveying a message of belief that recovery is possible and inevitable.

Separation and Coordination of Housing and Clinical Services

Consumer-driven services are provided by individual clinicians, but are supported by the appropriate organization structures. As noted, PHF functionally separates treatment options from housing supports in a way that mitigates power differentials between providers and consumers. Consumers have the same rights and responsibilities as all other tenants holding a standard lease. They are required to pay 30 percent of their income (which typically consists of SSI benefits) in rent; the program pays the remainder. Consumer choice also drives the provision of housing (location, type, etc.), but housing and neighborhood choices are naturally restricted by the affordability and suitability of available units. Because the apartments that the program rents consist of units available on the open market, there is no need for lengthy project planning and construction. Once the rental stipend is secured or the housing voucher or other subsidy is obtained, the apartment search begins. To ensure the integration of people with psychiatric disabilities into the community, the program limits leases to no more than 20 percent of the units in any one building. Apartments are rented at fair market value and meet HUD's housing quality standards.

The program may offer to become a consumer's representative payee or offer other budgeting services to help ensure that bills are paid. In PHF programs, however, housing loss occurs only for lease violations, not for treatment noncompliance or hospitalization. Some consumers lose their apartment after they relapse, stop paying bills, and are evicted by the landlord. However, because the housing component is separate from the clinical component, the consumers who separate from their apartment are not separated from the team's services; eviction from an apartment does not mean being discharged from the program. Rather than an end to the relationship, a consumer's eviction becomes a learning opportunity on how to avoid future mistakes. Program staff members continue to work with the consumer through a housing loss, preventing a return to homelessness and ensuring continuity of care through crises.

Similarly, if consumers need in-patient treatment, they go into the hospital and, upon discharge, return home to their apartment. By separating the criteria for getting and keeping housing from a consumer's treatment status (yet maintaining a close ongoing relationship between these two components), Housing First programs help prevent the recurrence of homelessness when consumers relapse into substance abuse or experience a psychiatric crisis. When necessary, team members can provide intensive treatment or facilitate admission to a detox center or hospital to address the clinical crisis—there is no need for eviction; after treatment, the person simply returns home.

Support services are provided through whatever type of model matches consumers' needs for which funding can be secured. This is usually provided through a multidisciplinary team approach such as an assertive community treatment (ACT) team or an intensive case management (ICM) team, in which teams are located off-site but available on call twenty-four hours a day, seven days a week, and provide most services in a consumer's natural environment (e.g., apartment, workplace, and neighborhood). Teaming is another vital aspect to maintaining a consumer-driven approach, because colleagues can help keep the corrective instinct of providers in check. In addition, team members help when working with a harm reduction approach that considers alternative paths to sobriety as long as they serve to contain or reduce the many risks associated with behaviors related to addiction such as drug overdose, incarceration, impoverishment, prostitution, malnourishment, unending homelessness, and illness. Harm reduction is consumer driven and seeks to minimize personal harm and adverse societal effects of substance abuse while the consumer strives toward recovery. Consumer choice is the foundation of the harm reduction approach (Inciardi and Harrison, 2000), in which consumers define their needs and goals and the pace and sequence of services.

The choice of ACT or ICM teams is based on current best practices in mental health services and is limited by availability and sustainability of funding. Both of these modalities have excellent outcomes for reducing hospitalization and increasing community tenure while using a recovery-focused approach (Salyers and Tsemberis, 2007). At its core, however, PHF support services need to be flexible and promote consumer choice. This has resulted in the PHF program incorporating such roles as peer providers and primary care as part of available services. Peer services are especially important because they help to reduce inherent power differentials between consumers and providers and provide consumers with a hopeful reminder that recovery is possible. Integrating primary care services through a nurse practitioner or family physician has also become a priority because evidence suggests that chronically homeless individuals represent a stable aging cohort (Hahn et al., 2006) with increasing medical needs and a baseline of early mortality (Hibbs et al., 1994; O'Connell, 2005). In addition, as consumers continue to recover, they may need fewer services. This can be accomplished by using an ACT step-down team or an enhanced case management team. This flexible adjustment process provides a better match between a consumer and higher service needs, increases program capacity, and reduces cost. When the person is fully recovered, there is a complete separation of housing and services because the consumer continues to live in the apartment and continues paying with no need for program services. The services may be simply discontinued, avoiding the need for a potentially disruptive transition.

Recovery Orientation

The PHF consumer-driven approach embodies a recovery orientation that is now the cornerstone of mental health service reform (HHS, 2003; Stanhope and Solomon, 2008). The rise of the recovery movement itself can be understood as addressing long-held misconceptions that serious mental illness is a lifelong, crippling, degenerative condition (Hopper, 2007). Such misconceptions supported the need for long-term residential care that existed in the United States before deinstitutionalization and contributed to a mental health system that did not support, and even discouraged, personal growth. In the past thirty to forty years, many developments have contributed to a changing view that recovery from serious mental illness is possible. Advances in scientific knowledge, particularly in psychopharmacology and some psychosocial interventions, have provided new ways to address symptoms of mental illness (Dickey et al., 2006; Drake et al., 2004). In addition, social movements such as the civil rights and disability movements have advanced recovery by reframing disadvantage and disability from an individual shortcoming to a lack of fit or problem with the environment (Mitra, 2006; Rioux, 2003). Government policies and judicial court decisions have also supported the idea of recovery through a trend toward community integration and societal accommodation (ADA, 1990; HHS, 2003; *Olmstead v. L.C.*, 1999).

Although many of the aforementioned developments laid the groundwork for the recovery movement, the optimistic shift in thinking that recovery is now a real possibility (HHS, 2003) for persons with serious mental illness comes from two distinct sources. The first is longitudinal research that challenges the notion of serious mental illness as a degenerative disease (Harding, 2005). These studies have shown that, over time, many people achieve either full or partial recovery from schizophrenia. The second and perhaps more influential source of the recovery movement comes from first-person accounts of people who have recovered from serious mental illness (Deegan, 1988; Ridgway, 2001). These accounts have framed recovery in terms of consumer empowerment, hope, and promoting wellness through a rediscovery of self. Together, these sources have shown that recovery is not only a possibility, but a reasonably attainable goal for persons with serious mental illness.

Although the Housing First model was not developed explicitly as a recovery-oriented practice, its approach and value base embrace many aspects that are central to the recovery movement. Such recovery principles and their application in practice include: (1) consumer choice and self-direction; (2) person-centered care; (3) empowerment rather than control; (4) strengths-based rather than pathology-based orientation; (5) personal responsibility; and (6) hope for the future (HHS, 2004; Onken et al., 2007). For people with histories of homelessness, substance abuse, and mental illness who face complex challenges resulting from years of cumulative disadvantage, such principles within service approaches are equally important. PHF strives to be recovery oriented by placing consumer choice and a shared decision-making process at the forefront (Deegan and Drake, 2006; Drake and Deegan, 2008; Salyers and Tsemberis, 2007).

Community Integration

Essential to the promise of recovery is that individuals with psychiatric disabilities be integrated into society rather than separated into institutional settings or marginalized by limited opportunities that may result in experiencing homelessness. Before deinstitutionalization, state psychiatric hospitals functioned to both house and treat people with severe mental illness (O'Hara, 2007). Since then, the mental health system has developed several housing models, yet no clear theory of housing and support services has emerged to guide these developments (Newman, 2001). This stands in sharp contrast to housing for people with developmental disabilities, where models have been guided by theories of normalization and social valorization (Wolfensberger, 1983; Wong and Stanhope, 2009). Although the National Institute of Mental Health community support system first articulated the goal of providing the necessary skills and support for mental health consumers to live independently in the community in the 1970s (Stroul, 1989), since then the development of housing approaches has varied from custodial approaches that perpetuate institutional living to more rehabilitative service-intensive models to recent models that separate housing from services in an effort to provide normalized and permanent housing (Wong and Stanhope, 2009).

PHF promotes community integration by using the scatter-site apartment model and working toward the social inclusion of people with psychiatric disorders (Ridgway and Zipple, 1990; Tsemberis et al., 2004; Yanos, Felton, Tsemberis, and Frye, 2007; Yanos et al., 2004). A scatter-site normative model, known as supported housing, has been considered the housing approach most conducive to consumer empowerment and community integration (Blanch, Carling, and Ridgway, 1988; Hogan and Carling, 1992; Rog, 2004; Wong et al., 2007). Program staff members encourage and foster normative relationships with landlords, neighbors, family, and other natural support networks that promote community living, with services tailored to the individual needs of each consumer. This scatter-site housing design is intended to render consumers virtually indistinguishable from other neighborhood residents with similar socioeconomic and ethnic and racial characteristics (Stefancic and Tsemberis, 2007). The model is also consistent with antidiscriminatory legislation such as the Americans with Disabilities Act and the Olmstead Supreme Court decision that mandates that people with disabilities live in the least restrictive settings, both of which are aimed at promoting social inclusion and community integration (ADA, 1990; *Olmstead v. L.C.*, 1999).

Conclusion

The Pathways' Housing First program attempts to build the programmatic equivalent of unconditional love. It seeks out the most vulnerable among the people who have been homeless for years and who have been diagnosed with psychiatric disabilities, addiction disorders, acute and chronic health problems, behavioral problems, or other disabling conditions that may interfere with their social functioning. The program is committed to providing permanent housing and support, and is designed in a manner that provides each client with multiple chances to succeed. The foundation of the program's success is rooted in its client-driven approach. It is extremely effective in engaging clients who others have failed to engage because it offers housing and services on clients' terms and it provides almost immediate access to their own apartment without requiring treatment and sobriety as a prerequisite for housing. Well-trained and recovery-focused clinical support staff members make frequent house calls and support the client to achieve his or her self-stated goals. Whereas some clients move into their first apartment and manage well right from the onset, others may need to relocate to two or even three apartments before they can effectively manage their lives and their housing. The program does not give up; it makes a long-term commitment to do everything possible to help the person escape homelessness and begin his or her journey of recovery.

6

Special Needs Housing

Richard L. Harris

Over the past thirty-six years, Central City Concern has developed an integrated system of health care, employment, and special needs supportive housing for Portland, Oregon's neediest citizens. The health care and employment services are an essential factor in allowing people to live successfully in most of the 1,587 housing units owned and managed by CCC. In turn, CCC's housing options enhance the effectiveness of the supportive services that contribute to the ability of participants to become self-sufficient. What started in 1979 as a small organization with a mission to save old single-room-occupancy housing and provide treatment to public inebriates grew into the present-day continuum of services and housing for homeless people that continues to develop both better programs and needed housing.

In this chapter, I provide a brief outline of the significant events that shaped the programs developed by CCC over the past three decades and some lessons learned from these experiences. The path was decidedly not a straight line to the positive outcomes seen today. Not all activities were completely successful; many failures and problems occurred and, in surmounting them, we gained valuable insight. Of course, none of the growth in services and housing would be possible without active support from the city of Portland, Multnomah county, and the housing and service programs of the state of Oregon and the federal government.

Portland's Homeless of the 1970s and 1980s and the Decriminalization of Public Inebriation

Things began to change for street alcoholics in 1971 when Oregon decriminalized public intoxication. The new approach shifted responsibility from the police, jails, and courts to medical institutions such as hospitals. The initial consequence of decriminalization was an increase in public inebriates on the streets, particularly in the skid row section of Portland's Old Town. As jail was no longer an option to deal with the problem, in 1973 Oregon established a modest tax on beer and wine dedicated to cities, counties, and the state to provide basic treatment services for people with serious alcoholism.

Portland, located in Multnomah county, was the urban center experiencing the largest increase in street alcoholism. It was apparent to civic leaders that public inebriates posed a significant health, economic, and social problem for the community. So, also in 1973, Multnomah county created the Hooper Memorial Detoxification Center, named after the last person to die from alcohol withdrawal in the city jail drunk tank. Hooper Center was composed of two medically supervised programs: a sobering program and a five- to seven-day subacute medical detoxification program. Detox (with about 2,000–2,400 admissions a year) was for those motivated to get into recovery; sobering (with about 18,000–23,000 annual admissions) was for those who were not yet ready to live sober. When CCC took over the programs in 1982, Hooper Center had over 36,000 individual case files and had replaced the revolving door of jail, streets, jail, streets, and hospital emergency departments with a new revolving door: sobering, streets, sobering, streets, detox, streets, and possibly recovery. Decriminalization of public intoxication and the establishment of Hooper Center set the stage for the birth of CCC, initially called the Burnside Consortium. The agency was founded in 1979 with the support of two government grants. The first, a grant from the National Institute on Alcohol Abuse and Alcoholism (NIAAA), focused on late-stage chronic public inebriates and resulted in the creation of the Homeless Alcohol and Drug Intervention Network (HADIN) described below. The goal for this grant was to develop a system of treatment services for the approximately 500 public inebriates who were living on the street or in shelters, missions, jail, hospitals, or SRO housing. At the same time, Portland funded a small program to repair SRO buildings in the city's Old Town neighborhood. The intent of the SRO repair program was to keep the doors open in half a dozen old SROs managed by various nonprofit social agencies for very-low-income people. These goals defined CCC's two-part mission. The situation on the streets, however, caused that mission to expand.

As CCC began the work funded by these grants, it became clear that decriminalization, combined with a non-hospital-based medical program such as Hooper Center, kept people out of jail and provided a more humane system of medical care. However, it did not end the tragedy of public alcoholism and could not, alone, provide a long-term solution to late-stage chronic alcoholism.

Aware of the need for a better approach, over the past thirty years CCC has created an effective response to the challenges of addressing homelessness and addictions. The insights gained by CCC in developing today's

ADFC housing system can be boiled down to the ten lessons set forth in the rest of this chapter.

Ten Lessons Learned by Central City Concern in Developing Its ADFC Housing System

Lesson 1: Individualized coordinated care across the myriad of services is essential to successful interventions. Under the 1979 NIAAA grant to provide services to public inebriates, CCC organized most of the major provider agencies serving the homeless into a formally affiliated group whose goal was to manage and coordinate care for homeless late-stage alcoholics in Portland, mostly in Old Town. Service organizations representing missions, public shelters, public health programs, addictions treatment programs, and case management organizations agreed to share confidential information within the legal framework of a qualified service organization; this approach met the requirements of federal confidentiality laws that regulate the sharing of information about those receiving addiction treatment. The initial group of five contracted agencies and CCC eventually grew to include over a dozen different organizations serving this population. The group, now known as the Homeless Alcohol and Drug Intervention Network, meets every week to present individual cases, with systemwide care plans created for each service recipient. This coordination of services is a huge benefit to each individual and also enhances intervention efforts by identifying the agency responsible for each service. HADIN has turned a loose affiliation of service providers into a network of care. One person at a time, HADIN has developed hundreds of individual treatment and service plans for homeless people with late-stage chronic alcoholism.

Lesson 2: Sober housing is an essential component of the transition from detoxification to sobriety. In 1982, Multnomah county transferred Hooper Memorial Detoxification Center to CCC. The Oregon law that decriminalized public intoxication provided that police could place public inebriates under a civil hold and transport them to a medical facility, home, or (if they had committed a crime) to jail. Hooper Center was the designated medical facility in Multnomah county. Admission under a police hold gave the sobering program the authority to examine and detain individuals who were intoxicated to the point of incapacity until they were able to care for themselves. Those found to have an immediate life-threatening condition could be sent to a local hospital emergency department. Those inebriates who wanted to stop drinking could be admitted, day or night, to the medical detoxification program, while those not yet ready for detox spent time in the sobering program, which provided lifesaving short-term intervention. The civil hold and time in the sobering program prevented inebriates from being left on the streets in their drunken condition, subject to the vagaries of weather, violence, robbery, and unattended health conditions such as infections, wounds, and concussions. There were many repeat admissions to the program; some individuals were admitted hundreds of times. The sobering program's revolving door kept them alive and provided a safety net, but was not an effective recovery strategy.

Hooper Center's medical detoxification program had a similar story. On average, there were in excess of 2,300 admissions per year to detox. Most of the people coming into the program were late-stage alcoholics, and many also used other drugs. The goal for the program was to help individuals through detoxification and to refer them to ongoing postdetox treatment and recovery programs. Nevertheless, in 1982 when CCC took over operation of Hooper Center, the recidivism rate for previous detoxification visits was about 75 percent. The repeat admissions to the detoxification program were related to the lack of postdetox treatment and housing capacity.

Up until the time CCC took over operation of Hooper Center, no one had entertained the idea that homelessness could be ended, either for individuals or for society. For those public inebriates who were motivated to stop drinking, the best choice for recovery was thought to be residential treatment; the problem was there were many more homeless alcoholics than there was treatment capacity. Despite the ability of Hooper Center staff to make referrals to programs across the state, there were few openings in residential treatment programs: about 60 treatment beds compared to the approximately 800 individuals completing detox and in need of follow-up treatment. Assuming an average length of stay of six months, only 120 people per year could participate in residential treatment and, even when one of the few beds became available, getting treatment programs to accept public inebriates was quite difficult.

The result was months-long waiting lists for residential treatment beds. Street alcoholics had no place to stay sober while waiting for an opening in a residential program. If residential treatment was unavailable, the conventional wisdom was that the best that could be done was to provide basic services, keep people in skid row housing, and hope for a miracle. However, living in a shelter or SRO where nearly everybody was drinking was not a successful strategy to stay sober until a bed opened up, even if the resident was attending Alcoholics Anonymous. This situation caused a continuation of the revolving door of sobering—the streets, sobering, then detox, then maybe a treatment bed, or more likely discharge back to the streets. Few observers believed that there was any hope for street alcoholics who were disaffiliated from family, friends, and jobs; the common attitude was to characterize these people as winos, bums, and panhandlers, best to be ignored and forgotten.

Since residential treatment was considered to be the only way for an alcoholic to get clean and sober, the lack of sufficient capacity was a major hurdle for the public inebriate population. CCC had to come up with a new approach to transitioning people from detox to treatment in a sober state. It seemed clear that one element of this solution had to be sober housing.

Lesson 3: Alcohol- and drug-free community housing is the response to the special needs of homeless alcoholics and addicts who are in early stages of recovery. In 1983, the CCC offices were on the third floor of a small SRO across the street from the largest-volume fortified wine retail outlet in Oregon. The second floor had about sixteen units of housing, managed by CCC, in which there were a number of vacancies. Hooper Center staff convinced the housing staff to dedicate the second floor to housing Hooper graduates who were on the wait lists for residential treatment. This was the first attempt at operating alcohol-free housing. Detox staff provided the clients and managed the rooms, the housing department provided the space, and HADIN paid the rent for the sixteen-room space.

Managing the housing with restrictions on alcohol use was a new experience for CCC and was not an immediate success. The postdetox clients were on waiting lists, not yet in treatment. Many clients relapsed, but some stayed long enough to make it to their residential treatment programs. Gradually, as staff and clients learned more about what did and did not work, more clients stayed longer and stayed sober. Fewer relapses occurred and more residents actually made it to residential treatment. After a few months of operation, however, CCC became aware that many residents were more interested in staying in sober housing than in going to residential treatment. The experiment was leading to a new option: staying sober and living as a community in "Alcohol and Drug-free Community" (ADFC) housing.

Once the need for this option became clear, CCC contracted with another agency to provide case management services to the individuals living in the ADFC housing. The case management program started using recovering alcoholic staff as case managers and, gradually, a kind of outpatient treatment process emerged to support the clients who wished to stay. About half of the individuals either stayed in the sober housing or went to residential treatment; the other half relapsed. Despite the absence of a formal data collection process, it was obvious that sober housing was a more successful approach than just discharging people from Hooper Center and waiting for a treatment bed to become available.

Sober housing was showing promise, but a new problem emerged: wait lists. The experiment meant to relieve the wait list problem at residential treatment was successful enough to create its own wait list. Additional rooms were needed.

Some observers considered the alcohol-soaked Old Town neighborhood to be a bad environment in which to get alcoholics sober, so CCC rented three apartments in a residential neighborhood thirty minutes from Old

Town. There was no on-site manager and little case management or recovery support available to the geographically dispersed clients; thus, the first six individuals to occupy this housing all relapsed within weeks, with the next wave of residents quickly meeting with the same fate. CCC closed this effort down after only three months of operation.

This experiment in scattered-site housing resulted in a number of insights useful to understanding what residents needed to be successful. The first problem was the lack of a recovery supportive environment. Living with one roommate or alone did not provide the peer recovery support that results from living with a group of sixteen people in the same situation. The second deficiency was that residents were isolated away from a culturally familiar environment. The third issue was geographic distance from support staff. Understanding these deficiencies reinforced CCC's growing belief that creating an environment where individuals provided mutual support for recovery was the essential ingredient in helping clients stay sober. Armed with this understanding and the desire to dedicate more capacity to sober housing, CCC identified fifty-two rooms on the fourth floor of the Estate Hotel, another of its buildings, as the best option for expanding the model being developed. CCC chose the hotel even though—or perhaps because—it was in Old Town. This model, ADFC housing, became key to CCC's program.

Lesson 4: Treatment and recovery services can vary, but ADFC housing must operate by the basic rules. For CCC, expanding the number of ADFC housing units from sixteen to fifty-two was a big step in program operation and housing management. The agency had grown its portfolio of housing and had gained experience in renovating old SRO buildings to house the homeless. The creation of the fourth-floor ADFC housing forced the housing management staff and the service program staff into a joint enterprise requiring the expertise of both. This joint enterprise was a challenge because the two missions—to house people and to get them sober—did not necessarily coincide. CCC eventually reconciled the two goals, housing and services, and expanded the idea of special needs housing as an effective model for helping many individuals with debilitating problems to become self-sufficient. Accomplishing this reconciliation, however, was a struggle and remains an issue today for many who are in the forefront of homeless policy, as has played out in the Housing First models and the special needs supportive community housing models. CCC, however, has always operated both housing first and special needs housing, as the two models serve different needs.

The Estate Hotel fourth-floor ADFC had numerous program and housing management issues requiring solutions that were outside of the usual landlord/tenant realm. The issues also differed from those typical of an addictions treatment program. Some of the questions that eventually needed answers were: Who pays rent and how is it paid? Who gets access to the housing? How long can or should someone stay? What happens when the housing management and the client service staff differ on who gets to stay and who must leave? What rights and responsibilities do residents or program participants have? Are the people being served tenants or participants? How can alcohol- and drug-free housing exist alongside housing with no restrictions on the use of alcohol? Over the course of the first year of operation, the experience of creating and operating this new type of housing provided practical answers to most of these questions, and the solutions have remained basic to all of the 975 units of ADFC housing CCC operates to this day, enshrined in ADFC housing participant agreements for transitional housing and in lease agreements for permanent ADFC housing. The basic rules are:

- Residents agree to remain free of alcohol and drugs both on and off the premises. This is the basic rule, and there is no tolerance or flexibility allowed. (However, it was and is CCC's practice to follow a policy of intervention before eviction, understanding that relapse is often a part of recovery and may present an opportunity to enhance the individual's recovery.)
- Residents agree to submit to alcohol and drug testing on request.
- If asked to leave the ADFC for violation of the no drug or alcohol use policy, the resident will leave voluntarily.
- Residents must agree to the no use policy both verbally and in writing.
- The resident must agree in writing to maintain his or her ongoing personal program of recovery and to identify an individual who knows of this recovery program.
- All staff working in the housing must also remain free of alcohol and illegal drugs.

The transitional ADFC approach is premised on linking sober housing with support services provided by CCC or another agency: outpatient alcohol and drug treatment, mental health treatment, employment support, and primary health care. All residents are required to participate in services according to their individual needs. For permanent ADFC housing, the requirement is that all residents must participate in an active program of recovery.

Following these basic rules is an important feature of operating ADFC housing, particularly if and when a resident uses alcohol or illegal drugs. Of course, the usual landlord/tenant lease agreements, such as prohibitions against illegal or dangerous activities and timely payment of rent, exist for permanent housing. However, the basic ADFC rules are what differentiate this housing from non-ADFC housing, and these require special ADFC lease forms consistent with federal and Oregon special conditions for ADFC housing (Mandiberg and Harris, 2015).

Lesson 5: Work and employment are essential to recovering self-sufficiency, in both the long and short terms. As more people began to get clean and sober and to benefit from having safe housing, CCC came to understand that clients were not satisfied to just be housed. People wanted independence; they wanted a job; they wanted what most people wanted, a normal life! Understanding that self-sufficiency was a high priority for clients, CCC embraced the goal, realizing that it was integral to achieving its own mission. Work is important to self-esteem and to the feeling of being a contributing member of the community. A big part of resolving the conditions of homelessness and addiction is to move away from dependence on both substances and rent or income subsidies. Having an income removes both the reality and the feeling of dependence, and people who pay their own rent make room for the next person to receive rent subsidies. Steady living-wage employment is key to meeting these goals.

CCC's understanding that work is a central aspect of recovery prompted the agency to establish special employment services that could better meet the needs of recovering addicts. The supported employment model is a fidelity-based best practice to develop employment for people with mental illness. CCC has successfully adapted this model to help people who are homeless and in recovery find employment. The model includes a small caseload, working with the employee and employer for up to two years if needed, and access to education and training.

CCC received a HUD McKinney Homeless Employment Grant in 1989, which included both the sixty-two units of ADFC housing and employment assistance services. CCC provided these services through the CCC Employment Access Center, which also received resources from the city, the state, and the US Department of Labor to serve unemployed, low-income, and homeless people in the central city.

The McKinney grant's funding of rent assistance along with services was a groundbreaking concept in that it combined employment services with housing. At the time, most homeless employment programs were a variation of day labor and sheltered workshop programs. The CCC Employment Access Center, however, focused on helping homeless individuals find employment in the competitive job market. The process of equipping individuals with skills that enabled them to find and keep jobs, and combining this process with case management support and housing, was a different approach. For people in recovery, the program not only combined employment skills and housing, but also provided a supportive ADFC community in which to live.

A unique feature of the ADFC housing supported by the McKinney grant was a rent structure that varied over time once a person was working. Participants paid no rent until after they became employed. At that point, the rent started out at a minimal amount, eventually increasing to 30 percent of income (the HUD standard). CCC divided the rent paid into an individual's move-out account and a rent account, with the move-out account growing over the time the person was employed. Funds in this account were available to cover the costs of moving into permanent housing. This policy accomplished two things: it enhanced the individual's confidence in the ability to work and pay rent, and it made it actually feasible to move into the private rental market. For those people who wanted to be self-sufficient, this program provided a direct and practical way out of addiction and homelessness. Individuals could graduate from the program with a job and a job reference, housing, a rental history and a rental reference, and funds to cover the cost of moving to new unassisted housing. This program demonstrated the power of special needs housing that was supported by services and formed the basis for a community of mutual supportive relationships.

Although the program is different today, the Employment Access Center still helps homeless individuals find work and provides housing. The program is now more oriented toward skill development and preemployment activities; however, getting people connected to jobs remains the primary goal. Over the past decade, the center has placed 250–400 people in jobs each year. Having a job is essential to becoming self-sufficient, not only offering a measure of economic independence but, on a practical level, also providing the means to pay one's own cost of housing and thereby reduce dependence on rent subsidies.

The supported employment model prompted CCC to develop business enterprises that employed clients in recovery. In years past, CCC operated a painting company and a building maintenance and repair company; it currently operates a commercial coffee enterprise and a public street maintenance program. The latter—the Clean and Safe program—functions in partnership with Portland's Business Improvement District. CCC provides the sidewalk cleaning and graffiti removal in downtown Portland. Many hundreds of recovering people have obtained their first job opportunities through CCC business enterprises over the past fifteen years.

Finding that first job often did not work as well for individuals who had been out of the workforce for years, or who had never had successful or legal employment. In addition, although they might be able to find a job, many recovering drug addicts (even though clean, sober, and able to pass a urine analysis) are not good at keeping a job; they lack many workplace skills such as taking supervision, working in teams, going to work on time, and consistently being at work when scheduled.

To address these issues, CCC started the Community Volunteer Corps (CVC). One of the CVC's missions is to provide basic training that will enable people in recovery to succeed in normal workplace situations. A second goal is to provide opportunities to recovering drug addicts to give back to the community as a way to redeem themselves from any problems they may have caused during their addiction. To further both goals, the CVC provides work activities that help to better communities. For example, corps members remove graffiti, clean up schoolyards, remove invasive ivy from parks, and harvest vegetables for the food bank. All successful participants receive a small stipend and are expected to show up on time, learn how to follow instructions and supervision, and work in teams. Participants spend about ninety days working in the CVC until their graduation, when they will have earned a written reference reflecting the jobs they performed. The graduate can then use this reference to gain employment in the conventional workplace. As the name makes clear, all participants enter this program voluntarily. Participants in the program have come to value the CVC reference highly. One indication that this is so is the large number of people who completed the program between 2009 and 2014: 690 total graduates, with over 65,000 volunteer hours given to community service.

Lesson 6: Permanent ADFC housing is a necessary component in a continuum of care. As the Estate Hotel fourth-floor ADFC wait list grew, it became obvious that there was a considerable demand for long-term sober housing. When CCC became aware of a ninety-six-unit SRO hotel among the buildings that the city had closed for code violations, it negotiated to purchase the building using urban renewal funds. On completion of a major rehabilitation, the building (renamed the Sally McCracken) became CCC's first ADFC permanent housing. All ninety-six units in the Sally McCracken were occupied within a couple of weeks by individuals who had been waiting for this housing. The availability of permanent housing units opened up transitional housing units; it thus temporarily reduced the Estate Hotel fourth-floor waiting list and, in turn, the waiting list to get into the detox program at Hooper Center.

Adding permanent ADFC housing and outpatient treatment to the system created a continuum of services and housing focused on homeless late-stage alcoholics and drug-addicted people. Since recovery from addictions is a lifelong process rather than a terminal event, permanent ADFC housing was a necessary component to support recovery. Individuals can get sober, but staying in recovery is more complex than temporarily stopping use. Some people need more time and support to get and stay clean and sober; the damage done by years of addiction and abuse of drugs, alcohol included, requires time to heal. And different people have different needs. Transitional housing by its very nature is time limited. Permanent ADFC housing allows individuals to take the time that they need to stabilize their lives, rather than forcing their recovery into arbitrary time limits. Permanent ADFC housing not only provides a place to live; it creates a recovering community as people stay for the time they need it. Permanent ADFC housing represents a more accurate understanding of the disease of addiction.

Lesson 7: The ADFC model works best when the agency owns and manages the housing and also provides essential services. Combining the housing and program functions into one entity maximizes the ability to ensure that residents (clients) get the best set of services and the customized housing to fit their needs. The challenge is to find a source of funding to sustain this approach.

By 1981, two years after the agency was founded, CCC was managing the 160-room Estate Hotel and the 36-room Rich Hotel. Both buildings were leased, and repairing and managing housing owned by landlords who had little interest in ongoing upkeep was a thankless, fruitless, and unending task. Buildings nearing 100 years old and with years of neglect need a lot more than emergency repairs to make them into manageable, clean, safe housing. While stopgap repairs did keep some SRO buildings in the central city from closing, this approach did not resolve the need for safe, well-maintained, and affordable housing.

An alternative approach would be for the agency to own the housing outright. However, acquiring the resources to buy, renovate, and manage housing for poor and homeless people was an enormous challenge. Clearly, homeless people with no regular income lack the capacity to pay rent. This was a problem since rent revenue to cover operational costs of housing was essential to qualifying for acquisition finance.

A solution to the problem was to convince HUD to allow the project-based Section 8 program to be utilized by nonprofit organizations for support of SRO-type housing. Local and regional HUD offices had expressed doubts as to whether the project-based Section 8 funds could be used for ADFC housing in SROs. In the end, however, the doubts were resolved. HUD, the Housing Authority of Portland, and CCC created a new use for Section 8 rent assistance. Supporting rent for Section 8 individuals in SRO ADFC housing was a significant landmark for HUD, the city of Portland, and CCC, and for the thousands of recovering alcoholics and addicts who have been successful in their recovery as a result of these rent-supported ADFC buildings. Once the agency had a reliable source of rental income, the city and private donors were willing to subsidize, purchase, and renovate the housing. Combining Section 8 rent assistance for SRO housing with private and city funding for purchase and rehabilitation opened a pathway to owning, renovating, and managing housing for very low income and homeless people.

The use of project-based Section 8 rent assistance created a problem, however. Tenants could meet Section 8 income requirements, but there was an issue for some involving HUD restrictions on providing rent assistance to those with criminal records, particularly a record for drug crimes. These restrictions prevented some recovering drug addicts from becoming residents of permanent housing. Working together, the Housing Authority of Portland and CCC eventually found a way to qualify many of these individuals to receive rent assistance; potential residents who were in recovery and who had not been convicted of violent crimes were given an exemption to the HUD prohibition regarding drug crimes. Section 8 rent assistance for ADFC permanent housing became the policy of the Housing Authority of Portland. Section 8 assistance for ADFC housing was a significant step forward because it stabilized the rent assistance sources.

As CCC gained experience in owning as well as managing housing, it became clear that the ownership role was more complex and difficult than imagined. Repairs and improvements to the first buildings involved new fittings, kitchens, paint, and minor improvements to common spaces and rooms. After almost a century of neglect and deferred maintenance, the buildings needed major structural improvements, rehabilitation, and seismic retrofitting to provide safe, sanitary, and permanent housing. Such serious rehabilitation required a considerable investment of resources that CCC did not have. Owning buildings to successfully house very-low-income people required operational subsidies and substantial capital finance for both purchase and rehabilitation.

Portland had a large number of SRO buildings that could be renovated and managed if financial tools were available. Urban renewal funds, known as tax increment financing (TIF), were available in some areas of the city, but such funds were not designed to support nonprofit ownership. Another source of capital was necessary. A new federal program called low-income housing tax credits (LIHTCs) had just been initiated and was to become extremely useful in the development of low-income housing of many types and sizes, enabling the development of thousands of housing units. During the mid-1980s, CCC and the city of Portland adopted the policy that restoring the old SROs was good for economic development and, simultaneously, would help fill the need for low-income housing. CCC identified two buildings that it could purchase and renovate. These two projects were placed into one tax credit deal that combined city TIF funds and investors' LIHTC. As a result, two buildings were completely upgraded to seismic standards, providing almost 200 units of safe housing. This was the first successful LIHTC deal in Oregon.

The agency had now renovated five buildings using the full range of finance and rent-support sources. With the experience of housing management, ownership, and development including full rehabilitation, the housing side of the agency had changed. It was no longer a small, nonprofit, SRO building maintenance program; it was now a robust nonprofit that managed, owned, and developed specialized property providing housing for homeless people.

CCC's mission to help individuals better their lives required it to be a kind of organization for which there was no real model. Our goal was to help people become self-sufficient, not to make profits. The agency had to be both landlord and service provider. The two sides of the organization had separate funders, different cultural values, and different visions of the needs and interests of clients and tenants. At times, the service and housing sides of the organization were both in conflict and in competition for scarce resources.

CCC has addressed this tension by providing diversity in housing types and services, and by providing choice to clients. Employees—both those in recovery and others—can choose to work in sober housing or not. Different types of funding sources can be utilized to their best advantage. Coming to grips with the tension between housing and services made the agency into the organization that it is today. Still, funding for service programs does not usually include money for rent, and rent assistance is critical for homeless people. Similarly, housing funders do not want to pay for services. The search for stable funding for both services and housing is challenging and continues to be a major issue in the debate about how to end homelessness. People who frequently experience homelessness need housing, health and social services, and employment; ignore any one of these components and success will remain elusive.

Lesson 8: Outpatient treatment with special needs housing is more effective than outpatient treatment without sober housing for people experiencing homelessness and addictions. The original Estate Hotel fourth-floor ADFC program revealed that individuals could stay sober living in alcohol- and drug-free housing when the housing is combined with outpatient treatment services. This experience eventually led CCC to establish the Portland Addictions Acupuncture Center (PAAC). The PAAC program provided intensive outpatient treatment largely based on a traditional model of group education and recovery support, combined with acupuncture treatment. Participants also attended twelve-step programs.

By the late 1990s, public and private funders who were concerned about homelessness began asking for outcome data to justify increasing funds being spent in the homeless service arena. In addition, competition for funds was becoming more acute. In this atmosphere, it was especially important to address one of the perennial questions asked of alcohol and drug treatment programs: Do people get sober and remain sober after treatment? This was a perfectly legitimate question, and some officials doubted that treatment is effective. But by that time, about half of CCC's employees were in recovery from addictions, with many being former clients. Personal and work experiences made it apparent to staff that the addictions treatment supported by ADFC housing was working quite well. However, it was important to the agency that this outcome be documented and confirmed by objective analysis. Thus, CCC contracted with Thomas Moore to study the post-treatment success of graduates of PAAC, CCC's outpatient addictions treatment program.

Moore's study was intended to learn whether PAAC participants stayed clean and sober after leaving the program. Most of the clients in the study were late-stage alcoholics, and over half were polydrug users. Most were homeless when entering the program. Some were living in CCC's ADFC housing; the others were living with friends, with family, in non-ADFC housing, or in shelters. The study focused on determining the recovery status twelve months after completion of the PAAC treatment program: How many participants were clean, sober, and successful? The study set a high bar for success, defining it as being abstinent, employed, and housed. Nevertheless, of 287 people who completed the program, 41.9 percent met these criteria, an impressively solid outcome given the serious nature of the subjects' addiction problems. What was even more significant, however, was the breakdown by the type of housing each person had while in treatment. The study found that of those who had lived or were living in CCC's ADFC housing, 87.8 percent met the criteria for success (sober, housed, and employed). Of those in other living situations, only 25 percent were successful (Moore, 2000).

This study resulted in two extremely important findings. First, hard-core drug and alcohol addicts can get clean and sober and stay that way. The PAAC outpatient program was successful. However, a more important finding was that living in ADFC housing more than tripled the probability of success. This finding was stunning. The Moore study confirmed that chances of staying clean and sober are vastly improved when recovering addicts live in alcohol- and drug-free communities. Over the past ten years, CCC follow-up data are consistent with Moore's findings. On average, 65 percent of residents leaving ADFC housing were sober, involved in employment activities, and moving to permanent housing. This outcome cannot be overemphasized; ADFC housing combined with treatment is an effective intervention for homeless people with addiction problems.

Lesson 9: Transitional and permanent housing, where individuals with like issues can receive services and support one another, is an important housing option for many kinds of people with special needs. As CCC continued to grow and develop programs to meet the needs of homeless people, it became increasingly clear that housing was critical to helping people become self-sufficient. Such housing can be crucial for recovering women with children, individuals with mental illness, individuals with addictions, postincarceration felons, and similar people with special needs. As a matter of housing choice, this type of housing is an effective and desirable option. Again, however, funding such housing is a challenge. Three examples illustrate CCC's successful approaches to developing focused housing for people with special needs.

One example was CCC's response to the initial spread of HIV/AIDS in Portland. PAAC was providing acupuncture services to numerous homeless patients living with HIV/AIDS, and stable housing was essential to success in that treatment. HUD's program, Housing Opportunities for Persons with AIDS (HOPWA), provided capital and rent assistance to meet such needs. CCC found a mid-twentieth-century motel and, using HOPWA funds, developed it into a thirty-three-unit housing project to serve homeless people with HIV/AIDS.

A second example is the Letty Owings treatment program for pregnant and parenting mothers and their children. CCC purchased a complex with two- and three-bedroom apartments and turned it into ADFC family housing. After the success of this approach became apparent, CCC took over management of three Housing Authority of Portland apartment buildings that are now operated as ADFC housing for families. More recently a smaller four-plex was purchased and rehabbed as transitional family ADFC housing, and CCC is currently developing another ADFC apartment building in Clackamas county for recovering families.

Special needs housing for persons with mental illness provides the third example, and CCC has pursued three different models. One approach is to rehabilitate existing buildings for that purpose. In one instance, CCC partnered with Mental Health Services West, the local mental health program serving homeless people in the central city, to provide housing for their clients who wanted to live in the community and needed intensive supportive services. Using TIF and LIHTC funding, CCC purchased and rehabbed the Golden West Hotel to serve this need. For individuals who had no income, the program provided rent subsidies through a state and federal homeless mental health program. A second approach is to adapt a basically sound building to serve the needs of people with mental illness as CCC did for the Martha Washington Apartments in downtown Portland in partnership with the Housing Authority of Portland. A third approach is to construct housing specifically intended for homeless people with mental illness. CCC adopted this approach in Clackamas county, which is near Portland, and built a new forty-unit apartment geared to the needs of homeless people with mental illness. CCC owns and manages the housing, which has on-site support services operated by Clackamas county. Regardless of the client need, CCC relies on its experience in operating low-income and ADFC housing as the model for managing special needs housing. These projects operate as communities providing mutual peer support, which offers both the environment and the stability for people to change their lives.

All of this housing has been developed, rehabilitated, or newly constructed combining special needs and conventional low-income housing capital resources such as TIF, LIHTC, and the State Housing Fund. Rent is paid by residents, Section 8, and varying service support programs, mostly relying on public special service funding. The challenge for special needs housing is to develop sustainable funding resources for the simultaneous provision of rent and services.

Lesson 10: Filling the last gap in services: integrated health care—with housing. People being served by CCC had many unmet medical needs that coexisted with their homelessness, poverty, addictions, mental illness, and unemployment. In the early years, most medical services were provided by the Multnomah County Health Department; some were provided by Wallace Medical Concern, a clinic that operated only two evenings a week, and by the Old Town Clinic, which had been serving the homeless population since the early 1980s, mainly with volunteer providers.

In early 2000, Ecumenical Ministries of Oregon approached CCC about taking over the Old Town Clinic. CCC was willing to assume the responsibility for the clinic if a financially sustainable way could be found to operate it. Ultimately, CCC negotiated with Multnomah county to operate the Old Town Clinic as a subrecipient of the county's Federally Qualified Health Center (FQHC) funds. This subrecipient status allowed CCC to operate the clinic as a homeless FQHC and receive its own FQHC designation. The FQHC start-up grant gave CCC the financial basis to operate a health clinic that serves both people with Medicaid and homeless people without health insurance. CCC also made a considerable investment of its own funds; this investment, combined with FQHC funding, allowed it to gradually expand the level and scope of health services. Under the Oregon Health Plan and the Affordable Care Act, a full range of primary care, mental health, and addiction treatment services are now being provided to homeless people in the central city.

Conclusion

Today, as in the past, Central City Concern has operated on the assumption that those experiencing homelessness, addiction, mental illness, unemployment, and physical illness are people with special needs and unique experiences who, when provided with the right tools and a nurturing environment, are capable of transformative change. This change is the responsibility of the individual; creating the tools and the environment for change is the responsibility of the larger community. Drawing heavily on the resources of the community, CCC continues to carry out its mission of providing programs and housing that support people in achieving self-sufficiency.

There are many paths to self-sufficiency. For people who are homeless, housing is an obvious need. Special needs housing and special services work well for some, but not for others. Having a choice is important to people who are experiencing homelessness, as well as to those housed, employed, and reasonably healthy. Thus, CCC has learned to provide a menu of services and different housing options, including housing not linked to programs and services. Further, CCC learned early on that, when individuals experiencing addictions choose to live in ADFC housing and participate in recovery programs, their odds of successful recovery improve dramatically. Put another way, it has been CCC's experience that spontaneous sobriety is truly a rare event and that people with addictions who are homeless benefit most from living in an alcohol- and drug-free environment. ADFC housing is the key special accommodation for people with addictions.

Over its thirty-six years in operation, CCC developed an approach that works for homeless people experiencing addiction and mental health issues. The combination of special needs housing supported by effective services creates an environment of mutually supportive relationships that help individuals make difficult life changes. The housing provides security, safety, and time and support to change and heal. Individuals who have experienced addiction and mental illness are capable of profound change when given the right tools and a supportive environment in which to live. The programs — alcohol and drug treatment, physical and mental health care, and employment services — give individuals the tools they need to become self-sufficient. CCC's story also confirms that the community — local, state, and federal — must be able to provide the resources to facilitate the transformation to self-sufficiency. Adequate affordable housing for the number of low-income persons being served by organizations like CCC will not be available unless we invest capital in buying, rehabilitating, and building new housing projects that serve people experiencing homelessness. In addition, rent assistance must be readily available to cover the cost of operating low-income housing, regardless of whether it is owned by public, private, or nonprofit entities. Funding for housing that fosters mutually supportive relationships among residents with common struggles is an effective long-term change strategy in the work to end homelessness.

7

Systems for Homelessness and Housing Assistance

Jill Khadduri

During the 1980s, requests to city departments for emergency assistance with food and shelter began to rise, and modern homelessness became a national topic (Hopper, 1991; Burt et al., 2002; Buck, Toro, and Ramos, 2004). While assistance was mainly provided by missions and soup kitchens in the skid row areas of cities, a still unresolved debate ensued over whether homelessness was predominately a health issue or a housing issue. Homelessness is a social construct, an abstraction derived from the multifaceted suffering that afflicts the very poor. Academics who began to study homelessness came largely from the health field and treated homelessness as one of the health conditions to which poor people are vulnerable. Over time, however, housing economists began to give it increased attention and to treat it as an extreme form of housing instability or as a housing choice (Buck, Toro, and Ramos, 2004; Ellen and O'Flaherty, 2010).

During the 1980s, shelters began to receive both federal and local government funding, and shelter capacity grew beyond what the faith-based organizations that had traditionally served homeless men provided. An Emergency Food and Shelter Program was authorized at the Federal Emergency Management Agency (FEMA) in 1983. The number of beds in homeless shelters grew from 100,000 in 1984 to 275,000 in 1988 (Burt et al., 2002, p. 3).

HUD was on the defensive while this was going on, and discussions of the federal responsibility for homelessness became politically acrimonious. Officials in the Ronald Reagan administration resented claims that the growth in homelessness during the 1980s was related to cuts in HUD's housing assistance budget. The reality was that housing assistance was growing, not shrinking. The number of assisted households grew, from under 3 million in fiscal 1981 to more than 4 million in fiscal 1988 (Pedone, 1988, p. 39; Weicher, 2012, p.114). The validity behind the charge was that housing assistance was

101

not growing at the same pace as it had during the 1970s, which was a historical peak period, higher than in any earlier or later decade (Schwartz, 2015). To my knowledge, no one has done an empirical analysis that relates the 1980s growth in homelessness to this slowdown. It may not be possible, since there were no attempts to count the numbers of homeless people using consistent methodologies in the 1970s and 1980s.

Reagan administration officials at both HUD and HHS tended to consider homelessness as predominately a health issue fed by mental health deinstitutionalization and by epidemics of substance abuse. In that context, HUD provided housing funds and the National Institute of Mental Health provided other types of support to a demonstration Program on Chronic Mental Illness led by the Robert Wood Johnson Foundation (Shore and Cohen, 1990).

The first HUD study of the national extent of homelessness followed a reasonable methodology, but was attacked by advocates (Kondratas, 1991). The Community for Creative Non-Violence sued HUD for publishing a study that provided a lower national estimate, lower than the 3 million homeless people that advocates had been using and journalists had been quoting. Nonetheless, when enacting the Stewart B. McKinney Homeless Assistance Act in 1987, Congress gave the lead responsibility to HUD: the HUD secretary had convening and administrative responsibility for an Interagency Council on Homelessness. Then, the incoming George H. W. Bush administration promised "full funding for the McKinney Act," and new HUD appointees embraced the department's responsibility for ending homelessness (Khadduri, 2015). Congress had made homelessness a housing issue.

The Ad Hoc Design of Shelter and Housing Programs for Homeless People

The earliest HUD-funded homeless assistance programs were ad hoc and emerged from practice rather than theory or empirical evidence. Emergency shelters had been around for a long time and provided protection from the elements and from hunger, mainly for single men. The Section 8 Moderate Rehabilitation SRO Program, one of the new HUD McKinney programs, was a variant of an older HUD housing assistance program that some communities were using for preventing and ending homelessness.[1]

The origins of transitional housing and its identification as a discrete form of homelessness assistance are more obscure. Authorizations for a transitional housing demonstration program in 1986 and a supportive housing demonstration in 1987 most likely came from observations by providers of emergency shelter that some of the people they were serving needed more than a few days in a shelter to achieve stability (Burt et al., 2002). The earliest use of these demonstrations was to provide housing for people with severe mental illness or chronic substance abuse. The idea that some programs were transitional in nature was introduced by HUD and Congress to distinguish them from permanent supportive housing, but the concept of housing provided in a facility and supported by intensive services was similar.

The legislation that turned these demonstration programs into a permanent Supportive Housing Program (SHP) included a twenty-four-month time limit for the provision of transitional housing, with the possibility of continued services funded by the program for an additional six months. Otherwise, program design was left up to communities (Burt, 2006).

Permanent supportive housing had benefited from a stronger research base. The Robert Wood Johnson demonstration program was largely an effort at systems change to produce better-coordinated community-based systems of care for people with severe mental illness. However, its housing component demonstrated that people with severe mental illness could use scattered-site, tenant-based housing assistance (Goldman et al., 1992; Newman et al., 1994). HUD had originally provided some project-based assisted housing units to the demonstration, but the mental health providers found that what their clients wanted—and were able to successfully use—was tenant-based Section 8 vouchers. That was part of the basis for the Shelter Plus Care Program, enacted in 1990, which uses the same subsidy formula as HUD's housing assistance programs (rent minus 30 percent of income) and permits three types of control of the housing: a tenant-based model that works exactly like a voucher; a project-based model, in which an organization serving homeless people can own the housing; and a sponsor-based model, in which the organization can master lease units and then sublease them to formerly homeless people.

Homeless Assistance Kept
Separate from Housing Assistance

By the end of the 1980s, HUD had decided to keep homeless programs separate from mainstream housing assistance programs—that is, from the programs that form part of the social safety net for people who cannot work or who have jobs that do not pay enough to enable them to afford housing. One of HUD secretary Jack Kemp's first actions in 1989 was to create, within the Office of Community Planning and Development, an Office of Special Needs Programs that brought together HUD management of all the homeless assistance programs, including the formula-based Emergency Shelter Grants Program and the separate discretionary programs that had been authorized by the McKinney Act (Khadduri 2015).

Mainstream housing assistance programs are those for which renters are eligible, not because they are homeless, but because they have very low (often poverty-level) incomes. Those programs—public housing, tenant-based housing vouchers, and privately owned Section 8 projects—were (and still are) managed by assistant secretaries in other parts of HUD. In addition to these three programs that any poor household might be able to use by reaching the top of a waiting list, other offices in HUD continued to manage programs for people who had special needs, but were not homeless: the Section 202 program for seniors and the Section 811 program for people with disabilities.

As part of the decision to administer a separate system for addressing homelessness, HUD kept the eligibility criteria for the homeless assistance programs narrow. That narrow definition came to be HUD's—and most of the federal government's—definition of homelessness. Excluded were people who appeared to be at risk of homelessness because they were temporarily living with other people or because they frequently moved—for example, in anticipation of being evicted. The HUD definition that created eligibility for homeless assistance programs included only people in shelters or on the streets—places not meant for human habitation. For that purpose, transitional housing was treated as a type of emergency shelter, so that people in transitional housing would remain eligible for programs limited to people currently experiencing homelessness such as permanent supportive housing. While the Homeless Emergency Assistance and Rapid Transition to Housing Act (HEARTH Act) of 2009 broadened the federal definition of homelessness, HUD continues to use the narrower definition for determining who is eligible for HUD-funded homeless assistance programs.

Thus, what Congress and HUD did in the late 1980s was to create a separate federally funded homeless services system. A few cities were doing the same thing. New York City created a separate department of homeless services while Philadelphia and Chicago expanded the responsibilities of adult protective services departments to cover emergency shelter. In most cities, the impetus came from HUD through the creation of the Continuum of Care in the mid-1990s. By forcing providers of shelter and services to make a single application for HUD funds, HUD encouraged local communities to create systems with coordinated needs identification and strategic planning.

The unfortunate effect was to leave mainstream housing assistance outside the homeless services system. HUD's vision for the CoC was that the public housing agency (PHA) that administered the public housing and voucher programs would be part of the strategic planning undertaken by the CoC and would make some resources of the mainstream housing assistance programs available to people experiencing homelessness. However, that usually did not happen at all, or the PHA's participation in the CoC was nominal (Spellman et al., 2010; Dunton et al., 2013). Private owners of subsidized rental projects—either HUD-assisted Section 8 projects or housing produced by the Low-Income Housing Tax Credit Program—are even harder to bring into a local system for planning and coordinating resources. The state agencies that make decisions on the use of LIHTC subsidies could be brought into the CoCs of those states' largest cities, but that seldom happens.

Segmenting Homeless Populations and Their Shelter and Housing Needs

Research on the numbers and characteristics of homeless people conducted in the late 1980s and early 1990s established the utility of segmenting the homeless population. The first such segmentation was into individuals and families. By the time Burt and colleagues (2001) analyzed data from the National Survey of Homeless Assistance Providers and Clients in the late 1990s, describing individuals and families as distinct groups among the homeless had become standard. Burt pointed out that people who become homeless alone often have family—partners or children young enough to be part of their households—who are not with them in shelter or on the street during an episode of homelessness. Nonetheless, the patterns of homelessness and the needs of individual homeless people and homeless families are sufficiently different that it became useful—and standard practice among providers of shelter and services—to treat these as separate types of homelessness requiring separate responses.

An important by-product of segmenting the homeless population this way was to establish that most people who become homeless do so alone. An earlier study by Burt and Cohen (1989) that enumerated homeless people using soup kitchens and shelters had already established that 90 percent of homeless households are comprised of individuals. The Annual Homeless Assessment Reports that provide counts and characteristics of people homeless at a point in time or using shelter over the course of a year have consistently shown that about two-thirds of the people who become homeless do so alone (HUD, 2008, 2015 a, b). Furthermore, rates of disability, a marker for people who may need intensive services to avoid becoming homeless again, differ sharply between homeless individuals and adults in homeless families. The AHAR estimates show that 44 percent of people who enter shelters as individuals have a disability, compared to only 20 percent of adults in families (HUD, 2015b).

It has been difficult to make the homeless services system focus most of its resources on people who become homeless as individuals. For example, the Shelter Plus Care Program was proposed by HUD as permanent housing linked to services only for individual homeless people with disabilities. However, when Congress enacted S+C, eligibility was extended to families as well. The share of PSH that serves individuals rather than members of families has been growing but, as of 2013, was still less than two-thirds (HUD, 2015).

A further step in segmenting the homeless population into subpopulations came with the concept of chronic homelessness in the early 2000s. The concept was already there in S+C, which was intended for people whose severe mental illness or substance abuse (or both) was thought to create a risk that they would be homeless over a long period of time. S+C's approach to ensuring that services would be linked to permanent housing was to use a requirement for matching services funding (Fosburg et al., 1997).

By the late 1990s, researchers were finding that most people became homeless only for short episodes. A small subset of the homeless population had long episodes and used most of the homeless services system's resources. The researchers also concluded that people with chronic patterns of homelessness created high costs for other systems—in particular, the health and criminal justice systems—and that those costs might be avoided by providing permanent stable housing (Kuhn and Culhane, 1998; Culhane, Parker, et al., 2007). After consultation among federal agencies, *chronically homeless people* were defined as single individuals with a disabling condition who have been continuously homeless (on the street or in a shelter) for at least one year or have had at least four episodes of homelessness during the past three years (Locke, Khadduri, and O'Hara, 2007). That definition is not perfect, in part because of the difficulty in defining what constitutes a discrete episode. However, it seems to have had some effect on encouraging local homeless services systems to devote more resources to ending the costly patterns of homelessness of particular individuals.

Unaccompanied homeless youth constitute another population group that is useful to distinguish from other groups, both from young people who become homeless with their parents and from people twenty-five years or older who become homeless by themselves. Programs that serve youth differ markedly from programs serving single adults or adults in families. The goal of youth programs is not necessarily to create leaseholders. In many cases, returning to family is a positive outcome, as is living with one or more unrelated people while pursuing education or starting out in the job market. For many years, HHS has administered grant programs that support shelters and transitional programs for youth. Depending on the community, programs for youth may or may not be considered part of the homeless services system, although HUD encourages communities to do so and the AHAR now provides separate counts of unaccompanied children and youth (HUD, 2015b).

Considering veterans a separate subpopulation has a different rationale, as the nature of the services that veterans need and the desired outcomes are largely the same as those for other homeless adults. AHAR data on homeless veterans show that their characteristics are similar to those of all people who become homeless as adult individuals (HUD, 2015). Furthermore, the same interventions work for them when they are challenged by disabilities, notably service-linked permanent supportive housing (Rosenheck et al., 2003). What has led veterans to be treated as a separate subpopulation is the political imperative for not permitting veterans to experience homelessness. Another consideration is the separate VA health system for which veterans are eligible—and which can serve as an entry point and as a source of services.

Categorizing and Studying the Homeless Services Systems Programs

As HUD strove to rationalize the homeless services system during the 1990s, the agency adopted a three-part organization of the housing dimension of the homeless services system: emergency shelter (ES), transitional housing (TH), and PSH. As part of their annual applications for funding, CoCs were required to produce a Housing Inventory Chart that identified projects and units that fell into these categories.

When HUD further decided to require communities to use the Homeless Management Information System to report on the number and characteristics of people using the homeless services system, the HMIS was designed with separate reporting for these three types of programs. When a new program type, rapid re-housing, emerged in the late 1990s and then received substantial funding from HUD under the American Recovery and Reinvestment Act of 2009, HUD added that program to the HMIS as a separate type. The result is that we know a fair amount about the use of programs categorized in this way from the aggregation of local HMIS data reported in the AHARs.

Abt Associates has conducted two recent studies that examine different types of homeless assistance programs. The Cost of Homelessness study examines the patterns of program use and the costs of ES, TH, and PSH programs for both individuals and families in eight communities (Spellman et al., 2010). The Family Options Study is a randomized controlled trial that measures both the impacts and the costs of three interventions to help homeless families achieve housing stability. Two of the interventions, transitional housing and rapid re-housing, are within the homeless services system. The third intervention uses the mainstream Housing Choice Voucher program to provide a permanent rental subsidy.

Both studies measure the costs of the housing or shelter provided to families and also the costs of services when those services are incurred by a program (or a partner) because the person receiving the services is a client of the program. Not included are services for which clients would have been eligible in any case—for example, a mental health program available in the community with no preferential access for the program's clients—even if the program's caseworkers refer clients to those services.

The Family Options Study measures the impacts on housing stability and other outcomes of the three active interventions—transitional housing, rapid re-housing, and a permanent rental subsidy—relative to usual care in which families find their way out of emergency shelter without being given priority access to one of the active interventions. The study followed randomly assigned families and surveyed and collected administrative data about them at eighteen and thirty-six months after random assignment (Gubits et al., 2013, 2015).[2]

Emergency Shelter

Early emergency shelters provided a place to sleep and some meals and often were not open during the day. Over time, especially as shelters for families with children were created, the model for what ES is became less clear. The expectation is that stays in shelters will be brief, and some shelters have time limits. However, federal rules do not impose a time limit, and some communities permit long stays. Analysis reported in the AHAR shows that more than two-thirds of people who use emergency shelters as individuals, and more than 20 percent of people in ES as members of families, stay for less than a week but the distribution of lengths of stay has a long tail, with some people staying at least a year (HUD, 2015). Most emergency shelter is provided in dormitory settings, but family ES often has separate sleeping rooms and sometimes provides a separate apartment for each family. Types and intensity of services also differ widely across shelters (Spellman et al., 2010). The Family Options Study found that services in emergency shelters for families are more intensive than in transitional housing and that the cost per month of having a family stay in emergency shelter is more than $4,800, with services making up 63 percent of the cost (Gubits et al., 2015). Thus, the delineation between emergency shelter and transitional housing is not clear, and the labels can muddle policy choices rather than clarifying them. When the HMIS was being created, researchers and federal staff got together to try to create definitions, but gave up and decided to let communities decide what to call a program when entering data into the system.[3]

Transitional Housing

The design features of TH have also become more diverse and more difficult to pin down, other than the fact that transitional housing must have a time limit no greater than twenty-four months when funded by HUD. Transitional housing provides dormitory-style sleeping arrangements less often than emergency shelters and more often provides private apartments for people homeless alone as well as for families. The type and intensity of services varies a great deal as well. Increasingly, transition-in-place programs have blurred the distinction between TH and PSH, other than the program rule imposed by HUD that only people with disabilities may enter PSH. Otherwise, PSH can have an intensive services period and then a less-intensive period—for example, as people's behavioral health issues stabilize. Thus, the post-transition phase of transition-in-place may look a lot like a less-service-intensive phase of PSH.

Advocates for TH often are more concerned about the need for intensive services for the highest-needs people and would not necessarily object to a program with no time limit.[4] In that sense as well, the definition of TH may blend into the definition of PSH. A stay in transitional housing is also costly, especially TH for families (Spellman et al., 2010). The Family Options Study found that the cost for a family to stay in project-based transitional housing for a month is $2,700, with services making up 42 percent of the cost (Gubits et al., 2015).

Over time, the usefulness of having people go through a transition period has been challenged. In the early 2000s, Culhane showed that family TH was not being used for the most vulnerable families and concluded that the family transitional model might not be cost effective (Culhane, Metraux, et al., 2007). The process of setting up and implementing the Family Options Study confirmed that TH for families often screens out the most vulnerable families and also showed that families deemed eligible for TH often did not want to use it (Gubits et al., 2013; B. W. Fisher et al., 2014). When the Family Options Study measured the impacts of providing a family with a direct referral to an opening in a transitional housing program, improvements to housing stability were slight. Furthermore, despite the intensive services provided by transitional housing, there were no gains in employment or family stability relative to the comparison usual care group, and gains in other measures of well-being were all but nonexistent (Gubits et al., 2015).[5]

For individuals, the challenge to transitional housing has not been primarily driven by cost considerations or by evidence about who uses the programs that follow this model or its lack of impacts. Instead, the challenge has been based on the premise that people with disabilities related to behavioral health have better recovery outcomes when placed in permanent housing immediately rather than going through a transitional period. Proponents of Housing First argue that making permanent housing a reward for compliance with treatment is less effective than using the stability of permanent housing as a platform for recovery (Padgett, Henwood, and Tsemberis, 2015).

On the other hand, TH for individuals is costly. The Abt Associates study of program costs within the homeless services system showed that TH for individuals costs much more than the typical rent of an apartment in the private market because of the costs of the services and because transitional housing programs often use expensive downtown real estate (Spellman et al., 2010).

Permanent Supportive Housing

Within its funding for the homeless services system, HUD started emphasizing PSH in the early 1990s by requesting and receiving more funding for the new S+C program than for the other HUD homeless programs. Maintaining that emphasis became more difficult after funding for S+C and the Supportive Housing Program were combined in the mid-1990s. Applications from

CoCs often emphasized transitional housing—and particularly funding for services—rather than permanent supportive housing. HUD and Congress responded, first with a mandate that a minimum of 30 percent of funds allocated to CoCs (beyond funds used for S+C renewals) be used for PSH and by building incentives for greater use of PSH, in particular for chronically homeless individuals, into the CoC application process (Locke, Khadduri, and O'Hara, 2007).

Sources of permanent supportive housing. Unlike emergency shelter or transitional housing, PSH is considered to be housing. An individual or a family living in housing provided by a PSH program is not considered homeless by HUD for purposes of counting homeless people. However, PSH differs from the large mainstream housing assistance programs—public housing, Housing Choice Vouchers, and privately owned Section 8 projects—in that the intent of the PSH approach is to serve only people who are leaving a current episode of homelessness and who could not sustain themselves in housing without intensive services. Whether all providers of PSH comply with the rigorous targeting implied by this intent is open to question.

PSH is where the boundary between the homeless services system and the mainstream system of housing assistance is most likely to be crossed. Within the homeless services system, most PSH is funded by S+C, which works exactly like a voucher and is often administered by the local PHA. In addition, PSH is the place where the mainstream housing assistance system most often provides resources to augment the homeless services system. The most common contribution of PHAs to the homeless services system is a voucher to be used to help pay the rent in PSH. PHAs typically do this through a partnership arrangement with a provider of services to homeless people, often a particular type of homeless person that is the specialty of the partner organization. The partner organization refers clients to the PHA, which then provides a voucher (or a public housing unit) on a preferred basis. Once the PHA has issued the voucher, the partner organization helps the client find housing (or move into housing the partner owns or controls) and stay permanently housed. For example, partner organizations frequently intervene with landlords if a question involving tenancy obligations arises (Dunton et al., 2013). Another model, less commonly used, is for the PHA to provide graduation housing for people ready to move out of PSH because their need for intensive services has diminished. This increases the capacity of the homeless services system to provide service-supported housing by freeing up PSH units for other tenants with greater current needs.

While many PHAs are providing set-asides of units for PSH, both those PHAs and others could do more (Dunton et al., 2013). PHAs are the primary, but not the only, potential sources of PSH from within the mainstream system of housing subsidies. The state housing finance agencies that administer the Low Income Housing Tax Credit Program often provide incentives within competitions for housing developments that contain some units of supportive housing for people with disabilities, including formerly homeless people. States are often motivated by the 1999 *Olmstead* decision of the US Supreme Court (*Olmstead v. L.C.*), which required states to provide community-based rather than institutional placements for people with disabilities. Again, more states could use LIHTC housing in this way, and the states that already are doing it could do more.

PSH costs less on a monthly basis than either ES or TH. In particular, PSH costs the homeless services system less because services often are provided for and funded by the mental health system or by Medicaid. (The concept behind PSH is that it also will cost less overall by reducing costs to health systems—for example, by reducing emergency room visits and inpatient hospital stays.) PSH also often costs less because it uses ordinary rental housing found in the market rather than downtown real estate with a high value (Spellman et al., 2010).

Over time, however, PSH usually costs more than either ES or TH, because the intention is that the tenure in the housing—and the housing subsidy—will last a long time. This is the reason that both federal funders and local homeless services systems have attempted to target PSH to people who need it the most—people with chronic patterns of homelessness and with severe disabilities. In the Los Angeles region, for example, system planners and their supporters are developing coordinated entry systems to help achieve better targeting of PSH as well as growing overall numbers of PSH units (Brown et al., 2014). This targeting is not easy. It requires an effective link between the coordinated entry system and the entity that has control over the housing, whether an individual housing provider or a housing authority.

Housing First. Housing First is a particular type of PSH for formerly homeless people with disabilities. Housing First emphasizes the central importance of leaseholding in the recovery or stabilization process for people who need behavioral health services to help them control mental illness, substance abuse, or both. Leaseholding means having a place of your own, somewhere that you are in control of whether you can stay there or have to move on. If one satisfies basic tenancy obligations—paying rent, not destroying property, and not unduly disturbing neighbors—one can stay. Housing First posits that mental health services will be more effective while a person is a leaseholder. In Housing First models, intensive services are not mandatory—not a condition of retaining housing—but they are available, often using a research-based approach such as Critical Time Intervention (Locke, Khadduri, and O'Hara, 2007; Padgett, Henwood, and Tsemberis, 2015).

The Housing First movement grew out of a small number of programs that pioneered the model (Pearson et al., 2007). However, a gradual shift toward the Housing First model can been seen within the much-larger Shelter Plus Care Program. In the early years of S+C, the housing was commonly provided in a restricted facility-based setting, especially for people considered to have higher levels of disability. Evaluators took at face value assertions by providers of the housing that this was appropriate (Fosburg et al., 1997). More recently, S+C has typically used the tenant-based model, and discussions of resources for PSH often make no distinction between S+C and Housing Choice Vouchers provided by the PHA, referring to both sources of rental assistance as "vouchers."

The Department of Veterans Affairs has embraced the Housing First concept in its implementation of the HUD Veterans Affairs Supportive Housing (VASH) program, for which funds have been appropriated every year since 2008 (as of this writing). The VA selects homeless veterans to receive permanent supportive housing in the form of a voucher allocated by HUD to a local PHA. The key elements of the model as applied to VASH are that a housing placement must be permanent and rapid and with no preconditions related to sobriety or treatment participation. The veteran is supposed to receive adequate clinical support based on modern recovery philosophy, and the most vulnerable clients are supposed to receive assistance on a priority basis (Kertesz, 2015).

The PSH model has been well tested, including an early evaluation of the VASH program that used a rigorous experimental design and found that VASH vouchers resulted in substantially fewer days of homelessness over a three-year follow-up period (Rosenheck et al., 2003). But additional rigorous evidence on cost avoidance would help make the case for greater resources for PSH. In particular, more evidence is needed on the effectiveness of different service models for people with different needs and at different stages of their recovery process.

Rapid Re-Housing. Rapid re-housing emerged in the late 1990s, growing out of community practice rather than research. Rapid re-housing shares some of the concepts of Housing First, notably the central importance of leaseholding. Advocates for the rapid re-housing approach argue that people are less likely to become homeless again—or at least no more likely—if, as quickly as possible, they are placed in a housing unit over which they have control rather than having a service-intensive stay in either ES or TH (Culhane, Metreaux, and Byrne, 2011).

HUD has funded rapid re-housing through a Rapid Re-Housing Demonstration, through the ARRA-funded Homeless Prevention and Rapid Re-Housing Program, and through an eligible (and encouraged) use of ongoing funding for HUD's homeless assistance programs. Rapid re-housing is a temporary subsidy; HUD program rules permit it to last up to eighteen months, but local programs are often designed to last for a much shorter time. This is

a key difference from Housing First, which is permanent housing with a subsidy of indefinite duration for people with long-term disabilities and, at best,
long recovery periods (Pearson et al., 2007).[6]

Rapid re-housing applies to a broader population—everyone who becomes
homeless—and not just to people with disabilities.[7] Supporters of rapid re-
housing posit that most people do not need the intensive and costly services
provided by many emergency shelters and most transitional housing programs.
What they need is to leave shelter immediately with enough money to pay rent
in a private market housing unit, together with limited case management to
help them find housing and connect to income benefits or employment, as
available and appropriate to the adult's age and any work-limiting disabilities.
This limited intervention avoids prolonging costly stays in programs funded
within the homeless services system.[8] Once they are in their own housing, the
sort of crisis that sends people into homelessness is unlikely to recur.

The Family Options Study found that rapid re-housing led families to
leave emergency shelters more quickly than families who were not given priority access to a rent subsidy. However, rapid re-housing did not lead to
fewer returns to shelter during a period between seven and eighteen months
later (Gubits et al., 2015). This somewhat disappointing finding has led to
some rethinking among advocates of rapid re-housing about how to improve
the program model to make it more effective. One possibility is to lengthen
the expectation for the time a family needs a rent subsidy. The Family
Options Study found that a rent subsidy with no time limit—a Housing
Choice Voucher—led to substantial reductions in returns to shelter, in returns
to either sheltered or unsheltered homelessness, and in other measures of
housing instability such as doubling up in someone else's housing (Gubits et
al., 2015). Rapid re-housing is most often applied to families. The family
portion of the homeless services system is much more expensive on a per
household basis than the portion that serves individuals. Therefore, avoiding
time in emergency shelter or transitional housing seems particularly important for families. According to the perspective behind rapid re-housing, people who become homeless as individuals and who are not among the few
with chronic patterns of homelessness may not even need a short-term rental
subsidy to leave shelter within a few days and not return any time soon.

Whether the rapid re-housing concept—including the temporary character of the housing subsidy—should be applied to chronic or high-needs
homeless people is a matter of active debate as of this writing. Advocates for
applying the concept to anyone who becomes homeless argue that even the
neediest individuals may use a rental subsidy for a short period of time and
not become homeless again. Through progressive engagement—providing a
short-term subsidy and seeing if it works before offering PSH—the limited
supply of PSH can be better targeted to those who will really need it. This
trial-and-error system may be more effective than assessment tools that use

an individual's housing and behavioral health histories and other characteristics to prioritize people for PSH (Culhane, Metraux, and Byrne, 2011).

This point of view reflects the separation between the homeless services systems and mainstream systems, including the mainstream housing assistance system. Advocates and researchers within the homeless services system define their objective as avoiding repeated episodes of homelessness rather than as contributing to the long-term stability and well-being of vulnerable people.

Preventing Homelessness

It would seem logical to try to prevent people from becoming homeless rather than dealing with this extreme form of housing instability after people have entered shelters or started sleeping outdoors. But prevention strategies have faced the problem that homelessness is a rare event and hard to predict. About 1.5 million people in the United States come into homeless shelters in any particular year, which is only about one-half of 1 percent of all Americans and about 3 percent of people below the poverty level (HUD, 2015b). Even if we were to add people who were homeless during a year but never used a shelter, the percentage would still be small.

O'Flaherty (2010, 2011) concludes that homelessness results from a combination of factors; for example, extreme poverty that makes a person vulnerable plus bad luck—what economists call a stochastic event. The best attempts to predict who will become homeless on the basis of collecting a great deal of information about people's characteristics get it wrong about half the time. Researchers in New York City used an assessment tool for families that had applied for prevention assistance to try to predict the 10 percent of those families most likely to become homeless. They found the ages of parents and children and whether the family had been moving frequently to be good predictors. Even then, about half of these highest-risk people who had self-identified by applying for assistance did not become homeless (Shinn et al., 2013).

As its name implies, the ARRA Homelessness Prevention and Rapid Re-Housing Program included a prevention element. Enacted in response to the emerging Great Recession, HPRP was based in part on the fear that job loss and foreclosure would cause large increases in homelessness. HUD implementers were skeptical about the ability to target prevention assistance to those who would otherwise become homeless, but did not apply a ceiling to the amount of HPRP funds that could be used for prevention, in part because of the imperative to spend ARRA funds quickly to create the intended stimulus for the economy.

HPRP relied on caseworkers to make the determination of who would get assistance. Some used screening tools. But HPRP assistance was a time-limited rent subsidy, and therefore HUD regulations provided communities with ambivalent guidance: to receive prevention assistance, a family or individual should be at imminent risk of becoming homeless but also have characteristics such as a history of employment and leaseholding that gave the household a good chance of being able to pay unsubsidized rent after the assistance ended (Cunningham et al., 2015).

Family homelessness grew by only modest amounts during the Great Recession (HUD, 2014a), but whether HPRP had any effect on keeping the numbers down is hard to say. The families targeted by HPRP—those with temporary job loss and histories of leaseholding—may have been the same families that had enough resilience (options for dealing with the bad luck that, according to O'Flaherty (2011), is the proximate cause of homelessness) to avoid literal homelessness. HUD did not attempt to evaluate the impact of the HPRP prevention activities, but instead funded a process evaluation that included a discussion of how prevention programs might be evaluated in the future (Cunningham et al., 2015).

Promising Approaches to Prevention

One prevention program has received a rigorous evaluation based on randomly assigning people to receive the intervention or not. The approach to targeting prevention used by the Homebase Community Prevention program is to focus on those neighborhoods from which most people enter New York City's shelter system. This made sense as a targeting approach since a study from the mid-1990s had concluded that entry into homelessness in New York and Philadelphia was heavily concentrated in the poorest neighborhoods in those cities (Culhane, Lee, and Wachter, 1996).

Prevention is particularly important in New York because it is one of the few cities with a right to shelter. Cities without such policies can control the volume of people entering shelter by limiting shelter capacity; most probably, the result is that most people find alternatives to becoming homeless such as doubling up, while some become unsheltered homeless.

Homebase services include case management, benefits advocacy, conflict mediation, and modest financial subsidies for rent and utility arrears and move-in costs. The evaluation showed that those receiving program services spent substantially fewer nights in shelter than did the control group. Most of the control group did not enter shelter, so targeting to those who would have become homeless was not strong. On the other hand, the cost was fairly low, about $2,200 per household, low enough that the program was able to show savings that covered its costs by reducing nights in shelter (Rolston et al., 2013).

Another promising approach to prevention assistance is to entrust the identification of people at risk of becoming homeless to institutions that, by the nature of their mission, have a great deal of information about highly vulnerable people: the criminal justice, child welfare, and mental health systems. Using these systems has the advantage of avoiding moral hazard, the phenomenon in which people choose to do things because it increases their chance of a reward. People are not likely to become involved with systems such as child welfare, which puts them at risk of losing a child, just to get a small housing subsidy or some case management. On the other hand, criminal justice, child welfare, and mental health are heavily burdened systems. Parole officers, child welfare caseworkers, and mental health professionals might be reluctant to apply either judgment or a formal screening tool to their clients and instead deem all of their clients at imminent risk of homelessness and refer them for prevention assistance.

Broadly-based Prevention Strategies

Targeting prevention assistance would not be such a quandary if the broader social safety net was doing an adequate job of providing people with the resources they need to deal with bad luck or shocks such as job loss, illness, and family breakup. The evidence that an adequately resourced mainstream housing assistance program would go far toward reducing homelessness is strong and is derived from studies at both the household and community levels.

Household-level studies have shown that people assigned to get housing vouchers rarely become homeless, unlike members of a control group. Community-level studies have revealed that more vouchers for poor households are associated with lower community rates of homelessness (Khadduri, 2008, 2010). Growing evidence of the efficacy of housing vouchers for preventing and ending homelessness — for example, from the Family Options Study (Gubits et al., 2015) — may help build the case for returning to the long-standing policy of growing the voucher program through appropriations for incremental vouchers.

Other social safety net programs are important as well. Food stamps (Supplemental Nutritional Assistance Program [SNAP]), Medicaid coverage for the poor and near-poor, and SSI income for people with disabilities give families and individuals a platform for coping with emergencies without falling into homelessness. SNAP is particularly important because it is the closest thing the United States has to a comprehensive source of support for those at the bottom of the income distribution. SNAP should not be made subject to work tests that discourage participation.

Other approaches to preventing homelessness would provide support just at the time of an emergency. Worth testing are renters insurance and a program of repayable emergency loans. Under a renters insurance approach, a tenant would pay a small insurance premium against predetermined events such as job loss, divorce, or major illness. When one of those events caused a tenant to stop paying rent, the landlord would get a payment to cover the rent loss. This insurance might substitute to some extent for screening criteria and security deposits. It might even improve overall housing affordability by reducing rent levels that currently include an implicit insurance premium against the owner's risk that an occupant will stop paying rent several months before moving or being evicted (O'Flaherty, 2011).

Renters insurance would be useful only to leaseholders. Many people who become homeless do so from other people's housing units (HUD, 2015b). Therefore, approaches to prevention targeted to the time of the crisis should include emergency loans that could be used for a broader set of purposes—for example, a security deposit and utility turn-on fees in a different housing unit.

Temporary Assistance for Needy Families (TANF) agencies already can make emergency assistance payments to help families experiencing a crisis that threatens to make them homeless. The Administration for Children and Families at HHS currently has no systematic information on how frequently that is done, what approaches are being used to determine when a crisis is sufficiently serious, or other eligibility factors such as past compliance with TANF work requirements. We do know that caseworker judgment may not be as effective as a formal screening tool. The New York City study targeting homeless prevention showed that, when families applied for prevention assistance, using a formula based on objective data such as age and previous homelessness worked better than caseworker judgment (Shinn et al., 2013).

Making an emergency loan repayable could help make assistance for homeless prevention self-targeting. The knowledge that money will have to be repaid substitutes the family's or individual's own knowledge of the need for assistance, inducing families or individuals to be more careful in requesting a loan at the outset. This screening mechanism is usually better than any determination by a caseworker or other method. Experimentation with emergency loans could test what the terms of a loan would have to be to achieve this self-targeting.

Conclusion

Coming closer to ending the epidemic of homelessness that became apparent in the early 1980s will require breaking down the barriers that have kept the mainstream system of housing assistance separate from the homeless services system. The historic separation of these systems has had several unfortunate effects. Those who control housing assistance do not devote enough of it to targeted programs to end the homelessness of particular people—for example, through set-asides for permanent supportive housing. They are protective of their long-standing waiting lists for assistance and suspicious of queue-jumping by people who use emergency shelters. Those who operate within the homeless services system treat it as a closed system and act as though obtaining housing assistance for their clients is hopeless. Policymakers for homelessness focus on conserving resources within their system and define the appropriate policy outcome simply as reducing the numbers of people served by the homeless services system. They fail to recognize that homelessness is simply a construct, an abstraction built from the various types of suffering that afflict the very poor in the United States.

What is needed is to unite the separate systems, merging the separate system for ending and preventing homelessness into the mainstream social safety net. More housing vouchers for poor people in general would go far toward ending homelessness. At the same time, mainstream housing programs—Housing Choice Vouchers and the Low Income Housing Tax Credit—should be used more extensively for permanent supportive housing for people who experience homelessness and need behavioral health services. We also should experiment with light-touch prevention programs—for example, replicating neighborhood-focused programs like Homebase Community Prevention in other cities, designing and testing rental insurance, and integrating TANF emergency assistance into efforts to prevent homelessness. Sharpening our efforts to fully understand the complexity of what we call homelessness, too often viewed as a unidimensional phenomenon, and making services and housing part of the larger social safety net will go a long way toward addressing this tragedy.

Notes

1. Congress had made exceptions to the usual rules of housing assistance programs for the Section 8 Moderate Rehabilitation Program so that the program could be used in the Pacific Northwest to preserve older hotels that were housing middle-aged and older, otherwise homeless men when those hotels were at risk of being lost to gentrification. The exceptions were put into the law in 1979 by Congressman Les AuCoin who represented Portland. In addition to permitting subsidies to units without complete kitchens and bathrooms, the exceptions made it possible to serve households consisting of single nonelderly people. Until then, the service population for HUD programs consisted only of families with children, households with a member aged sixty-two years or older, and people with disabilities. A confusing aspect of HUD law and regulations is that "family" is now synonymous with "household."

2. Transitional housing in this study is called "project-based" transitional housing to distinguish it from transition-in-place models. Rapid re-housing is called "community-based rapid re-housing" to emphasize the diversity of program models (length of subsidy, rent formula, frequency of case management) chosen by communities. Permanent subsidies usually consist of a housing voucher. This is not permanent supportive housing since the only services provided are directly related to housing placement (Gubits et al., 2013, 2015).

3. The author was part of that process.

4. For a summary of the advocacy argument for transitional housing as it applies to families, see Gubits et al. (2015).

5. In contrast, the Family Options Study found that a permanent housing subsidy had impacts beyond housing stability. Families given direct access to a housing

voucher had fewer child separations and foster care placements. Adults experienced less intimate partner violence and reported alcohol and drug dependence less frequently. Children of study families were absent from school less often and changed schools less often (Gubits et al., 2015).

6. Policy discussions often conflate the Housing First and rapid re-housing concepts, resulting in confusion and misleading claims of demonstrated effectiveness.

7. Or perhaps it applies to everyone who becomes homeless as an adult (or with an adult present). Immediate leaseholding may not be a key objective of programs for youth.

8. For a summary of the advocacy argument for rapid re-housing as it applies to families, see Gubits et al. (2015).

8

Controversies in the Provision of Services

*Jason Adam Wasserman and
Jeffrey Michael Clair*

Social services have obvious importance for any discussion of homelessness. After all, homelessness is a significant social problem, and both public and private sectors need to be engaged to address it. Examining social services generates one of the most substantive pictures of how we conceptualize and collectively feel about homelessness. One of the fundamental problems in providing services is the divergence of ideas about who is homeless and how they might be helped.

In this chapter, we detail various attempts to provide social services, broadly defined, to people experiencing homelessness. Social efforts to remediate homelessness trace as far back as the phenomenon itself. Throughout this long history, we have witnessed significant changes in the structure and character of services, and the past several decades have generated extremely polarizing debates. In particular, the shift from housing ready to housing first programs initially represented a significant shift away from a treatment model whereby homelessness was treated as coextensive with addiction and mental illness. However, mainstream assimilation of housing first strategies has been accompanied by an increasing emphasis on social utility; that is, on promoting the best outcomes for society rather than a focus on the rights and dignity of individuals experiencing homelessness.

In this chapter, we first detail the evolution of homeless services from the preindustrial to the postindustrial eras. We then examine how a diverse set of religious philosophies and cultural norms underpins social services. We conclude by highlighting several key contemporary social conflicts and debates related to homeless service provision.

A History of Homeless Services

As long as there have been individuals experiencing homelessness, there have been various social attempts to deal with them (Snow and Anderson,

1993). Laws governing poor people's use of public space date to the Middle Ages, as the proliferation of almshouses and charity services coincided with the dawn of capitalism and as the erosion of feudal structures in Europe left many of the peasant class dislocated (Arnold, 2004; Axelson and Dail, 1988; Kusmer, 2002). Then, as now, far less effort was directed toward sealing cracks in the social system itself than was directed toward helping those who had fallen through them. In this section, we highlight how often questionable conceptualizations of homelessness underpin homeless services.

The roots of contemporary homelessness in the United States can be linked to shifts in the early industrial economy. In its early years, the vast expanse of undeveloped territory and extensive natural resources in the United States led to migratory industries, specifically coal and lumber, along with the construction of railroads necessary for development (Arnold, 2004; Axelson and Dail, 1988; Kusmer, 2002; Snow and Anderson, 1993). When those industries declined in the late 1800s, formerly transient workers became statically unemployed in US cities. Except for periods of acute economic recession (1890s) or depression (1930s), the size and scope of the homelessness remained relatively small through the end of the 1960s. Nonetheless, stereotypes of homelessness that persist today took root in social conflicts from around the close of the nineteenth century. It was in this time that the disaffiliated man experiencing homelessness came to be perceived as a social nuisance that varied between the clownish drunk (see Figure 8.1) and the dangerous criminal (see Figure 8.2).

Services for those who were poor and homeless during this period took the form of religiously motivated almshouses and soup kitchens. These largely idiosyncratic efforts focused primarily on food and, to a lesser extent, shelter, but they lacked an overall strategy for addressing homelessness as a larger social issue.[1] There were also attempts to criminalize homelessness through vagrancy laws, particularly from 1895 to 1917. One ordinance made it illegal for "any person, who is diseased, maimed, mutilated or deformed in any way, so as to be an unsightly or disgusting object, to expose himself to public view" (City of Paris Illinois ordinance, as quoted in Schweik, 2009, p. 1; see also Phelan et al., 1997).

Social Services
Beginning in the early 1970s, the prevalence of homelessness began to rise in most US cities, owing in part to inflation, vanishing manufacturing jobs, and declining real-dollar wages (Arnold, 2004; Mathieu, 1993; Mossman, 1997). While, historically, economic upturns had gone a long way toward resolving periods of high rates of homelessness, in the 1980s this was undercut by growing inequality such that the poor did not greatly benefit from economic gains. Moreover, cuts in funding for subsidized housing exacerbated the growing crisis of homelessness.

Figure 8.1 *Los Angeles Herald* **Cartoon, December 8, 1907**

Source: Cartoon from the *Los Angeles Herald*, December 8, 1907. Retrieved from the Library of Congress Archives; digitized and archived by the California Digital Newspaper Collection, Center for Bibliographic Studies and Research, University of California, Riverside, http://cdnc.ucr.edu.

Despite the association of social structural factors with rising rates of homelessness in the 1970s and 1980s, social service delivery largely attended to the most immediate needs of feeding and sheltering individual people experiencing homelessness. The image of homelessness continued to center on the "disaffiliated man" (Bahr, 1971), despite climbing rates of homelessness among women and children (Nunez and Fox, 1999). In this period, as before, social service programs portrayed pervasive conceptualizations of homelessness as a form of individual deviance (Lyon-Callo, 2000).

Based on the idea that the emergency shelter model, also known pejoratively as "three hots and a cot," did not address the more complex needs of individuals who are homeless, the 1990s and early 2000s witnessed a shift toward a Continuum of Care model of homeless service (Lyon-Callo, 2000, 2004). The most typical CoC form routes individuals who are homeless to temporary emergency shelters until they can be connected with intensive rehabilitative programs. From there, they move into transitional housing, which often includes continued outpatient rehabilitative support, with a final goal of moving them into independent housing or permanent supported housing. While this model certainly fits the needs of some individuals experiencing homelessness, it also reflects more specific connections of homelessness

Figure 8.2 *Washington Times* Cartoon, October 27, 1907

Source: Cartoon from the *Washington Times,* October 27, 1907. Retrieved from the Library of Congress.

as a form of individual deviance (Lyon-Callo, 2000; Wasserman and Clair, 2011a). In particular, rehabilitative services presume that an individual malady is central to one's homelessness and these programs typically center on substance abuse and mental health treatment; that is, despite strong evidence that homelessness is predicated on social structural factors, this treatment model focuses intensive efforts on addressing the (perceived) deficiencies of individual persons who are homeless.

It has been pointed out by numerous critics that the treatment model effectively medicalizes homelessness (Lyon-Callo, 2000; Mathieu, 1993; Wasserman and Clair, 2011a). Namely, substance abuse and mental health are implicated as the central causes of homelessness, when the reality is far more complex. Moreover, in this model, treating individual "sickness" becomes the central function of social services, excluding the ways that engaging homelessness might require focus on social structural factors. Finally, the CoC model brought with it a more complex bureaucratization and, indeed, an entire homeless service industry (Culhane and Metraux, 2008; Wasserman and Clair, 2010).

Despite criticisms, addressed in detail below, the treatment model began as a well-intentioned and progressive alternative to emergency shelters, which were characterized as callous warehouses for society's poor. Similarly, housing first or rapid re-housing approaches gained popularity in the early 2000s as a critical response to treatment-oriented shelters, which were coming to be perceived as cumbersome, bureaucratic, and inherently judgmental (Pleace, 2011; Rog, 2004). At its core, the idea of this model is simply to address homelessness by providing housing with as few barriers as possible.

Early rapid re-housing initiatives were heavily predicated on social justice notions of housing as a right that ought not require enrollment in a program to treat perceived sickness qua deviance. In 2008, under the Barack Obama administration, the Department of Housing and Urban Development (HUD, 2008) began prioritizing funding for CoCs utilizing a rapid re-housing platform. While many had been reluctant to abandon their treatment models, this had a dramatic effect on proliferating housing first approaches.

However, as various housing first models have been more widely adopted, we have seen a proportional shift from justice to utility. Harm reduction has long been at the center of housing first approaches, including the 1992 Pathways to Housing model often credited as being the first (Tsemberis, 2010). However, the diffusion of housing first into more mainstream CoC structures has emphasized utilitarian concerns that are often defined in terms of cost savings. In fact, as Pleace (2011) shows, there has been a conflation of the housing first proper and other rapid re-housing or "housing led" approaches, which simply place housing earlier in the continuum of care.[2]

Charity Services
Charity services for those who are poor and homeless have a long historical connection with religious organizations. Early soup kitchens and almshouses

organized around various Christian tenets such as "whatever you did not do for one of the least of these, you did not do for [the Lord]" (Matthew 25:45, NIV). However, religious values not only provide impetus for actions to serve those who are homeless, but those values also manifest in the structure and rhetoric of religiously motivated programs.

We have observed that many people experiencing homelessness tend to be relatively religious. One might infer that this is because they tend to come from low socioeconomic status (SES) backgrounds where religiosity is high or because they are frequently exposed to religious charities that involve, and sometimes require, religious participation (both SES and exposure promote religiosity; see Schieman, 2010). Additionally, it is not difficult to understand the appeal of religion among the population experiencing homelessness, particularly when scripture can be interpreted in ways that speak directly to the suffering of the poor. Notions such as the "Blessed are the meek: for they shall inherit the earth" (Matthew 5:5, NIV) and "Do not store up for yourselves treasures. But store up for yourselves treasures in heaven" (Matthew 6:19–20, NIV) can provide solace to individuals experiencing poverty and homelessness. Moreover, these ideas suggest that poverty on Earth is negligible compared to the possibilities of heaven. Similarly, a mantra repeated in the shelters and among those who are homeless is: "God is good, and all the time!" (Wasserman and Clair, 2010, p. 209). This idea of perpetual benevolence reflects and reinforces fatalistic ideas that one's experience of homelessness is natural and just, a sort of cosmic lesson (Kyle, 2005).

In *At Home on the Street: People, Poverty, and a Hidden Culture of Homelessness* (Wasserman and Clair, 2010), we identified three broad archetypes of religious engagement with individuals who are homeless. The ethnographic data at the foundation of that work primarily contained examples of Christian organizations in the southeastern United States; however, it is likely that most major religions spawn groups fitting into any of these archetypes. Religious involvement in homeless services tends to take one of three forms that can be distinguished as: (1) those who work on sinners; (2) those who work with the meek; and (3) those who work for social justice.

Those employing a sinners approach toward those experiencing homelessness fundamentally locate the cause of homelessness in the spiritual character of the person who is homeless. This manifests either as understanding homelessness as the direct result of moral deviance and sin or, perhaps more commonly, as the notion that religious belief is essential to the healing of the person experiencing homelessness. Both have obvious connections to the treatment model, with an underlying assumption that homelessness is the result of sickness (physical, psychological, or spiritual), and that addressing it requires treatment of the afflictions of people experiencing homelessness. In our ethnographic study, we encountered one woman operating as something of a street preacher, who was rumored to run a boarding house and work program. As she preached to a group of men who were homeless, using a bottle of water as a visual metaphor for the Holy Spirit, she said to one: "He says if you repent, and turn from your wicked ways and follow him you can have that life that Jesus has for you." When one man responded, "I repented my sins and asked God," this woman interrupted, "Well, if you received it, why didn't you get up?" The clear implication was that anyone who truly believed in the word of Jesus Christ would inevitably no longer be homeless. The notion that true belief in God brings material reward on earth is shared among a variety of popular prosperity theologians such as Joyce Myer and Joel Osteen (Attanasi and Young, 2012). Even when prosperity is not an explicit component of one's theology, it is widely considered a product of God's grace. Of course, the logical inverse is that poverty constitutes a just condition imposed by God.

The sinners approach to homelessness is not always so direct and explicitly judgmental. In fact, it is more commonly nested in the idea that providing housing, food, work programs, and the like are meaningless without spiritual intervention. We interviewed a religiously oriented homeless shelter director who noted that

> the only programs that work are faith-based programs. You can change all of the outside that you want to. You can put new clothes on 'em, you can feed 'em, you can give 'em a place to live, but if on the inside they haven't developed a new spirit and a new attitude and a new viewpoint on life, they're eventually gonna fall away and have nothing to gain strength from. (homeless shelter director, as quoted in Wasserman and Clair, 2011b)

Almost all of the shelters that we interacted with in the course of our study had a religious foundation, and many of them reflected the centrality of spiritual remediation in this way. Most often, this was seen in language about providing hope. While not inherently religious, the notion of hope for many service agencies was colored by religious notions about belief in God's control of the universe, a belief that everything works as it should.

Many of those religiously oriented service programs that we examined would balk at the notion that homelessness was a punishment for sin. As with the shelter director above, those ideas were more subtle. Similarly, many religiously motivated charities for those who are homeless took a more sympathetic view of homelessness that nonetheless contained implicit judgments. For example, when a number of religious organizations were feeding people experiencing homelessness on Easter Sunday, several volunteers took it upon themselves to sit down at the tables and witness to the individuals experiencing homelessness as they ate. There was a presumption of asymmetry, where some people needed the good news while others had it to share. Empowered less by notions of sin, and more by notions of serving the least of God's children, these volunteers were well meaning. Nonetheless, inherent in the structure of their service, rhetoric, and interactions was a notion of the person who is homeless as pitiable, someone perhaps not immoral but certainly demoralized (see Hoch and Slayton, 1990). The discourse among the volunteers was about providing hope and lifting up, which by implication positions those who are homeless as hopeless and beaten down.

Within shelter programs, particularly those employing a twelve-step model for treating substance abuse, a similar sort of religious fatalism implicitly degrades the self-determination of individuals who are homeless. While many shelters use a language of empowerment, they simultaneously promote a give it all to God ideology, which not only locates one's homelessness in the just hands of a higher power, but credits those same supernatural forces with any accomplishments in the path off the street.

Faith-based perspectives also can underpin social justice approaches to homelessness. Liberation theology emerged from South American Catholics who linked biblical scripture to sociological critiques of exploitation in capitalist societies (C. Smith, 1991). In our research, similar justifications were made clear by the pastor of a church that not only served individuals experiencing homelessness, but also included them in the organization as regular congregants, board members, and so forth. This pastor also helped a group of individuals experiencing homelessness establish a political action group that spoke to the city council and protested police abuses, among other things. In rejecting the individual pathology approach, this pastor noted:

> If Moses would have shown up in Egypt and told [the Hebrew slaves] the problem you all have is that you're sinners, the Hebrew slaves would have laughed Moses out of Egypt. Well, that's what everybody tells the homeless is their problem, that they are sinners. Well, that only bashes them down further, right? In other words religion contributes to the oppression. And so what we do here is we counter that with a message of value. The problem is not that they are sinners. The problem is that they are slaves and injustice has got them here. And not to be hard on themselves but to take care of themselves. And let's work together . . . so we can build a community. (pastor, as quoted in Wasserman and Clair, 2011b)

In taking a scripturally based social justice perspective, this pastor saw engagement with those who are homeless as being concerned not only with caring for individuals, but also with working at a community and societal level in protest of social economic inequality. Religion often provides motivation for groups or individuals to take up homelessness as a cause. However, rather than dictate a particular way of engaging homelessness, various religious perspectives tend to fit among the variety of ways of constructing service programs.

Contemporary Conflicts and Debates About Homeless Services

The developmental trajectory of services not only betrays a changing demographic landscape, but also shifting conceptualizations of homelessness. In this section, we review some contemporary debates about homeless services provision to highlight the ongoing evolution of perspectives on service provision and homelessness more generally.

Services and the Regulation of Public Space

Those who are homeless have long been conceived as a public nuisance, with laws managing the access and appearance of those experiencing poverty and homelessness in public space dating back to the Middle Ages (Axelson and Dail, 1988). Today, the regulation of public space continues, not only in the perpetuation of vagrancy ordinances, but through segregated residential housing and zoning laws that create single purpose spaces (e.g., retail districts) that constitute de facto class segregation (Bickford, 2000; Low, 2006; Wasserman and Clair, 2011c). At a fundamental level, the appearance of those who are poor and homeless in a social space is an existential affront to the order and stability of the social system (Amster, 2003; T. Wright, 1997). Not only does this create an insidious and pervasive social conflict between the citizens experiencing homelessness on one hand and the housed citizens and business owners on the other, particularly within gentrifying urban centers, but also it directly involves homeless services institutions and organizations. As illustrated below, some social services have been utilized to justify the regulation of public space, sometimes even actively participating in municipal initiatives of the sort while others have actively opposed policies and ordinances that target people experiencing homelessness.

Attempts by municipalities to criminalize homelessness are widespread (Amster, 2003, 2008; Mitchell, 1997; Tars et al., 2013). During our four-year period of ethnographic research in Birmingham, Alabama, there were a number of such initiatives, including ordinances that made it illegal to sleep in the doorways of city businesses or to stay on public property and proposals to remove park benches so that people who were homeless could not sit on them. For the purposes of this chapter, however, what is most interesting is how homeless services intersected with these discussions.

Individuals living on the street often establish urban camps under viaducts or along railroad lines (for a full description of several such camps, see Wasserman and Clair, 2010). These camps are cleaned up by city workers with some degree of regularity, often following nuisance complaints by business owners or housed residents or the commission of a crime in their vicinity. Many of those who ran local shelters actually supported the local anticamping ordinance in Birmingham (which did not pass due to fervent opposition from other groups). As they saw it, those on the street were effectively obligated to enroll in the various programs they offered. During one citywide sweep of homeless camps, a homeless shelter volunteered its program clients for the dual role of assisting city workers with disposing of campers' tents and other possessions while at the same time bearing witness about the benefits of its respective service programs.

One shelter director, who technically opposed an urban camping initiative noted:

> I have fought against the anti-camping ordinance. Lead the discussion against it. My concern is that you cannot say people cannot sleep outside when you don't have enough shelter space. But if there comes enough shelter space, uh, that may become a different issue, even from my viewpoint. Because at some point, their rights to be able to stay outside, and the rights of the rest of the citizens in the community may come in conflict. (shelter director, interviewed by the authors, Birmingham, Alabama, June 15, 2006)

While homeless service programs ostensibly advocate for the population of homeless individuals, they often intersect in a more complex way the public distaste for the presence of people who are homeless and the resulting social conflicts. Nearly all service providers sincerely believe they are advocates for those who are homeless. Even while justifying or participating in the dispersal of street communities and supporting legislation that effectively criminalizes homelessness, shelter staff are genuine in their belief that they are acting in the best interest of those living on the streets by trying to persuade or coerce them into a program. At the same time, in doing so they find themselves aligned with groups that clearly have little concern for those who are homeless other than making them disappear, one way or another.

Other service groups, described above, take more decidedly oppositional stances toward the criminalization of homelessness. More recently, there has been a wave of antifeeding ordinances across the country that has targeted groups that provide meals to those who are poor and homeless in public spaces. These types of ordinances are not new, but whether because of an increase in the number of them or because of the arrest of particularly sympathetic figures civilly disobeying them (see, especially, Conlon and Shoichet, 2014), there has been a great deal of media coverage since 2011. Groups from churches and collectives such as Food Not Bombs continue to protest these ordinances (Ng, 2011).

For us, there was an illustrative juxtaposition of these homeless services organizations against the more mainstream providers when the local Food Not Bombs group in Birmingham received a cease-and-desist letter from the metropolitan CoC. The more official mainstream homeless services providers noted that Birmingham Food Not Bombs was upsetting local businesses and the city government and requested that its efforts be channeled through the existing services. What becomes clear in this anecdote is homeless services providers (of all varieties) become integrated into social conflicts. Rather than finding themselves allied in their concern about the issue of homelessness, service providers often find themselves divided by local social and political debates.

Unintentional Shelters: The Roles of Hospitals and Prisons

Despite the divergent philosophies of service and homelessness itself, almost all agree that, in most cities, there are not enough shelter beds to accommodate the population of individuals who are homeless. While a small minority chooses to live on the street (and even then, we have to understand how these choices are influenced by social forces), and a larger contingent chooses the street over the types of service programs that are available to them, most areas remain in dire need of more beds (though certainly in more dire need of affordable and supported housing stock). When the extremely limited availability of shelter space (temporary and permanent) is combined with the criminalization of homelessness and the physical and mental health vulnerabilities that individuals face while they are homeless, hospitals and jails (or prisons) become de facto shelters.

Hospital usage by those who are homeless, particularly those living on the street, represents a complex and expensive problem. For one, individuals experiencing homelessness, especially those living on the street, are exposed to weather, physically demanding and dangerous working conditions, and violent crime (Huey, 2012; Wasserman and Clair, 2010). Housing status, victimization, mental illness, and substance abuse all predispose those who are homeless to greater hospital use (Kushel et al., 2005). Individuals experiencing homelessness sometimes utilize emergency departments as service agencies; that is, places to access food, shelter, and even clothing. Accessing basic services at hospitals is often a matter of necessity rather than preference, particularly when other services are scarce or difficult to access. Moreover, the discharge of patients who are homeless that technically no longer qualify for hospital-level care, but who have no place to recuperate safely and effectively, causes high rates of recidivism.

There are enormous costs associated with overuse of emergency departments.[3] Data from 1992 suggest that, even adjusted for substance use, individuals who were homeless stayed in the hospital 36 percent longer per admission than other patients (Salit et al., 1998). "The costs of the additional days per discharge averaged $4,094 for psychiatric patients, $3,370 for patients with AIDS, and $2,414 for all types of patients" (Salit et al., 1998, p. 1734). Data from 2006 suggest that each emergency department visit costs $688 while the cost of overnight admittance is $3,320 (reported in Kertesz and Weiner, 2009 based on data from the 2006 Medical Expenditure Panel Survey). A Canadian study found that "homeless patient admissions on the psychiatric service cost $1,058 more than housed patient admissions (95% CI, $480, $1,635) even after adjustment for length of stay" (Hwang et al., 2011, p. 350).

Discharged patients who are homeless also experience high rates of recidivism due to institutional practices among hospitals by which the hospitals often fail to provide needed additional supports in their care and discharge plans (Kertesz and Weiner, 2009). Patients experiencing homelessness are often discharged with paper prescriptions and no way to fill them, sent back onto the street with no way to change bandages, no access to bathroom facilities, or without transportation to area shelters where they might need to recuperate. At the same time, shelters are often uninformed and ill equipped to handle a client's medical needs. As a result, we have seen the development of specialty shelters called "respite shelters" that allow discharged patients who are homeless to recuperate from illness or injury (Zerger, Doblin, and Thompson, 2009). One study in Boston, Massachusetts, found that "discharge to a homeless respite program was associated with an approximately 50% reduction in the odds of readmission at 90 days post-discharge, compared to discharge to streets and shelters" (Kertesz et al., 2009, p. 135). A study in Chicago yielded similar results (Buchanan et al., 2006).

Hospitals have become de facto shelters for some individuals experiencing homelessness. This is not to say that most patients who are homeless are intentionally scamming these services. Rather, emergency department overuse by those who are homeless results from complex factors, including the inaccessibility of more appropriate services, lack of access to health care resulting in the use of the emergency department for primary care, and institutional practices that lead to treating and streeting patients who are homeless, resulting in inevitably high recidivism.

Jails and prisons also have a disproportionately large number of individuals experiencing homelessness in their populations. Homelessness increases the probability that one will commit a crime, either by promoting criminal behavior or through the criminalization of behaviors endemic to experiencing homelessness (e.g., loitering). Moreover, the social and economic instability introduced by incarceration and ex-convict status make the formerly incarcerated vulnerable to homelessness (Kushel et al., 2005; Pager, 2003).

A disproportionate number of incarcerated persons have a history of homelessness. Using a national sample, Greenberg and Rosenheck (2008) found the rate of homelessness among adult inmates was four to six times higher than in the general population. Another study of incarcerated veterans showed 30 percent of a large national sample from the United States had a history of homelessness, a figure five times higher than homelessness in the general population of adult men (Tsai et al., 2014).

The relationship between homelessness and incarceration is complex and difficult to establish. Clearly, both operate in ways that are mutually reinforcing. It is easier to see how homelessness can lead to short stints in local jail systems, simply by virtue of the fact that individuals who are homeless are forced to do things in public that those who are housed are more able to conceal (Waldron, 2000). However, individuals experiencing homelessness also may be more likely to resort to crime for survival. Quantitative evidence is largely lacking, but Tsai and colleagues (2014) did find that incarcerated veterans with a history of homelessness "were also significantly more likely to

be currently incarcerated for a property offense or probation/parole violation" (p. 364). Greenberg and Rosenheck (2008, p. 98) found that adults
experiencing homelessness were more likely to be incarcerated for property
crimes, but also to have previous "criminal justice system involvement" for
violent crimes. A great deal more work has examined the risk of becoming
homeless among the formerly incarcerated. A study of prisoners released to
New York City found that 11.4 percent entered a homeless shelter within two
years (Metraux and Culhane, 2004). Lack of case management exacerbates
the issue. While parolees receive supervision that can serve to some extent as
a form of case management, those who are released after serving their full
sentences are typically on their own. In the Metraux and Culhane (2004,
p. 145) study described above, rates of postrelease shelter stay were markedly
lower for those who were unsupervised (7.5 percent). We suspect that rates of
homelessness for this group are actually markedly higher, but that they simply are not accessing the shelter services at a rate equivalent to parolees and
therefore were not captured in the study.

Patterns of incarceration in the United States clearly intersect with patterns of homelessness. The two phenomena come with common disadvantages in terms of economic barriers and social stigma that make accessing
and retaining housing difficult. Once homeless, the odds of committing a
crime and getting arrested appear to increase dramatically while the odds of
experiencing homelessness are radically higher for those exiting incarceration. Where homelessness and incarceration cyclically feed each other, jails
and prisons, like hospitals, become unintentional shelters.

The Homeless Management Information System

As noted above, throughout the 1980s there was growing concern over the
limitations of the emergency shelter model. Part of the problem was that there
was little coordination of efforts between various service providers, leading to
duplication of services in some areas and gaps in others. As these idiosyncratic homeless services came under the umbrella of Continuum of Care
organizations, coordination and collaboration became an important challenge.
At a very basic level, promoting coordination between agencies required a
system of data sharing on clients who were moving in, around, and through
the CoC. At the same time, there was a general need for better, more comprehensive, and standardized data so that homelessness could be analyzed across
regions and at a national level. The HMIS has become an integral part of case
management and service provision in response to these challenges. However,
despite a preponderance of support, critical concerns remain.

The HMIS refers to a set of technical standards rather than to a particular program. Individual CoCs are tasked with developing and implementing
their own systems, with support from HUD. While this affords CoCs the
ability to customize their data collection (within the HUD requirements) to

fit local concerns, it also adds a layer of responsibility and cost to already strained CoCs (though adjustments to funding in 2001 eased some of that burden). "Since 1999, HUD has provided standards and technical assistance to phase in local HMIS systems" (Barrow et al., 2007, pp. 3-13), and by 2007 the majority of CoCs had at least begun to implement such systems (Leginski, 2007). In 2009, the passage of the HEARTH Act required all CoCs seeking or receiving CoC Program and Emergency Solutions Grant funding (the major source of funding for many homeless service agencies) to utilize an HMIS system that met HUD standards.

The vast majority of literature on the HMIS focuses on its utility for understanding characteristics of the population of individuals who are homeless and implementing evidence-based solutions. Poulin, Metraux, and Culhane (2008) note that, before the widespread adoption of these data systems, the majority of agency-collected data on clients who are homeless was cross-sectional. Since HMIS data frameworks are shared across agencies, information can now be tracked longitudinally because it is connected to clients themselves rather than client visits at each agency. This allows more sophisticated analysis and a better ability to make inferences about causes of homelessness. The size of data sets also provides more power to analyses while the standardization of data collection allows for comparisons across regions (Poulin, Metraux, and Culhane, 2008).

Concerns were voiced throughout the development of HMIS data and technical standards, though they appear to have centered largely on issues of data privacy and burdens to clients and providers (Guiterrez and Friedman, 2005; HUD and Culhane, 2004). With respect to the latter, Hoffman and Coffey (2008) argue that "an emphasis on numbers and statistics . . . affects both those experiencing homelessness and the providers, who may be experiencing their own loss of dignity and respect with difficult working conditions and bureaucratic pressure to produce HMIS statistics" (p. 208). Guitierrez and Friedman (2005) note that the HMIS imposes technical requirements on CoCs that "seldom match available expertise" (p. 514). In its Final Notice in 2004, HUD responded to these concerns by stating that "the burden of data collection must be balanced against the benefits of HMIS" ("Homeless Management Information Systems; Data and Technical Standards Final Notice," cited in HUD and Culhane, 2004, p. 45890). Other concerns centered on the limitations of the data for accurately enumerating and surveying the population of individuals who are homeless. In particular, individuals experiencing homelessness who do not use services are not likely captured in an HMIS, a selective bias that obscures a particularly important subgroup. Leginski (2007) posits that HUD acknowledges such limitations, but reiterates the advantages of the HMIS.

While the discourse about the HMIS reported in the commentary and response section of the HUD and Culhane (2004) Final Notice revealed relatively minor and resolvable concerns about data integrity and interpretation, there have been more critical concerns discussed in the literature. Notably, there is concern about an increasing focus on standardization and measurement that denigrates a more holistic perspective of local providers and clients who are homeless themselves (Hoffman and Coffey, 2008). That is, more robust qualitative understandings of individuals who are homeless can be lost in the quantification of homeless cases. This is particularly true where enrollment criteria for programs become rigidly anchored around the best evidence derived from aggregate-level data. The more evidence-based conditions are actively targeted by programs, the more individuals with complex problems will fail to qualify for them. Perhaps the most glaring instance of this involves dual-diagnosed individuals, particularly with mental health and substance abuse issues, who therefore often fail to qualify for either type of program because the mental health programs will take only sober persons and substance use programs avoid those with significant mental illness. Willse (2008) notes that the HMIS replaced a "case notes" system "in which a social worker produced narrative accounts of clients," a more qualitative account that may also be lost in the drive toward quantification (p. 231).

Another critical concern that has been raised suggests that the HMIS functions as a mode of surveillance. Some have questioned whether there was any real boundary between managing information about those who are homeless and managing individuals experiencing homelessness themselves (Willse, 2008). Perhaps this seems paranoid but, given the political policies described above, it is not difficult to imagine HMIS data being used to bolster vagrancy laws and other antihomeless ordinances.

There are utilitarian benefits to the HMIS, and HUD has clearly acknowledged some of its limitations. At the same time there seems a real risk that, as funding flows into evidence-based programs supporting clients who fit into particular operationalized categories of need, those limitations will be forgotten or at least pushed aside. Criteria attached to funding can cause programs to cluster around particular approaches. For example, when services are funded on the basis of enrollment in treatment programs, assistance for homeless individuals who do not need or want treatment becomes scarce. While rapid re-housing approaches have gone a long way to correct many of the shortcomings of the treatment model itself, it is worth carefully observing if the standardization and quantification introduced by the HMIS effectively guide programmatic models in particular directions, but that also may leave new gaps in service.

Wise Boundaries or Harmful Barriers

Despite the current trend toward rapid re-housing approaches, the debate between housing first and housing ready continues in important, though perhaps more subtle, ways. In particular, as various communities have undertaken rapid re-housing initiatives, sometimes reluctantly since HUD funding now largely depends on it, there has been a palpable shift in the underlying justifications for housing first. Additionally, a similar iteration of the housing first versus housing ready debate continues over the provision of low-barrier and no-barrier shelter.

In some ways, debates over the best way to provide services are understandable. After all, the stakes are high and those involved are typically well-meaning and passionate advocates. However, conflict over the right way to provide homeless services also reflects their institutionalization and the vested interests of service providers, whether conscious or not, in particular ways of doing business. As J. Wright, Rubin, and Devine (1998) notes, "We hear of turf battles between groups trying to protect their fiefdoms, sometimes even at the expense of the people who are homeless they are presumably trying to serve" (p. 213).

Housing ready approaches tend to center on the notion that successful re-housing requires sobriety, mental health management, and the like (Kertesz et al., 2009). In this way, the treatment model positions rehabilitation as the gateway to housing. Housing first perspectives see that gateway as a barrier and, at least superficially, focus on homelessness as a housing issue rather than one of substance abuse or mental health. Thus, providing housing is prioritized over other kinds of services and treatment. Treatment model advocates often suggest that the provision of housing (or even temporary shelter, as discussed below) to those who are not actively sober constitutes enabling addicted or ill individuals to continue the destructive lifestyle at the root of their homelessness (see accounts in Wasserman and Clair, 2010). Of course, this presumes that drug use and mental health issues are primary causes of homelessness, as opposed to the effects of being homeless (Wasserman and Clair, 2011a). Moreover, it presumes that withholding housing is a legitimate and effective way to coerce treatment. Additionally, treatment approaches not only expand the time it takes from becoming homeless to being re-housed but, as Culhane and Metraux (2008) note, in the process of enveloping people who are homeless into long-term rehabilitative programs, many CoC systems have lost focus on re-housing. Finally, the treatment model presumes, at its core, that the way to address homelessness is to "fix" the individuals experiencing it, which not only assumes that homelessness is tied to individual deficiency but draws the focus from the role of social structural factors. Housing first emerged in opposition to several of those assumptions.

As housing first models have proliferated, they appear to have become underpinned less by social justice concerns and to a greater extent on the notion that it is easier and more efficient to deliver services, including treatment programs, to persons with stable housing. This represents something of a conflation of housing first logic with that of the housing ready treatment model, for which the goal of housing represents a carrot (an effective entice-ment for sobriety) while the punishment of returning to the streets represents a stick (see descriptions of several specific programs in Kertesz et al., 2009). Of course, there remain key differences. Housing first presumably eliminates the role of housing as a punishment or reward. Instead, housing is provided regardless of sobriety status. At the same time, when CoCs taking up rapid re-housing approaches center their justifications on the utility of stable hous-ing for the delivery of treatment services, they retain potentially problematic notions at the heart of the treatment model, where clients who are homeless are inevitably in need of fixing.

Arguably, housing first models emerged as a rejection of treatment-ori-ented homeless services. As criticisms of the dominant paradigms become over time more mainstream, their conceptual boundaries must become broader and more inclusive to capture wider support. However, this also means that the ideological contours of housing first also become more nebu-lous (see Abbott, 2001; something noted by Pleace, 2011). Housing first models now appear to simply mean providing housing with relative speed (as compared to the older continuum of care model), but do not necessarily entail many of the ideological notions around which they originated.

The provision of low- or no-barrier shelters—where sobriety is not required or, in some cases, substance use is allowed in the shelter itself—contains similar dynamics, particularly where (1) justifications of those efforts can center on the inherent right to shelter or around utilitarian notions of harm reduction; and (2) where criticism of them has centered on enabling problematic behavior. Justifications of the Pathways to Housing program, one of the earliest Housing First models, discussed harm reduction as:

> a pragmatic approach that aims to reduce the adverse consequences of drug abuse and psychiatric symptoms. . . . Consumers are allowed to make choices—to use alcohol or not, to take medication or not—and regardless of their choices they are not treated adversely, their housing status is not threat-ened, and help continues to be available to them. (Tsemberis, Gulcur, and Nakae, 2004, p. 652)

Homeless shelters employing harm reduction strategies also have emerged where barriers inherent to the treatment model have been relaxed. Often, these are based on utilitarian considerations that it is safer for individuals experiencing homelessness as well as the wider community to allow intoxi-cation or even active substance use within shelters rather than relegating them to the street. However, there also are social justice considerations at the heart of harm reduction models, particularly where eliminating judgments about substance use remains central. According to Pauly (2008), "Harm reduction shifts the culture from one where resources may be rationed on the

basis of deservedness to one in which everyone is seen as deserving of care"
(p. 6).

Additionally, low-barrier shelters expand rather than contract notions of
citizenship, serving as needed inclusive spaces for those who are especially
marginalized and deemed hard to house (Evans, 2011). This type of inclusiv-
ity also has both utilitarian and humanitarian elements. With regard to the
former, providing space and opportunity to participate in the community,
regardless of sobriety status, may simultaneously provide a foundation on
which sobriety might be achieved. With regard to the latter, harm reduction
shelters might represent the only spaces in which those who are homeless
and use substances are not deemed unworthy and excluded from social life.

Criticisms of low- or no-barrier shelters have tended to reprise the logic
of treatment shelters. Concern centers on enabling those who are addicted to
substances to continue their behavior, sometimes being assisted in it with the
provision of clean needles and even the direct provision of alcohol in the
case of managed alcohol programs (Podymow et al., 2006; Hwang, 2006).
However, several studies have indicated that the managed distribution of
alcohol resulted in greater retention and even less alcohol consumption
(Collins et al., 2012; Podymow et al., 2006).

The expansion of harm reduction shelters may likely see a shift in discourse, if it has not already, away from principled considerations—for example, providing safe space based on the inherent dignity of individuals experiencing homelessness—and toward more utilitarian notions. While the notion
of harm reduction may have prima facie consequentialist appeal, it is not the
only possible justification for such an approach (Evans, 2011; Pauly, 2008).

Conclusion

The evolution of homeless services, particularly across the past four decades,
is terrain rife with ideology and conflict. How one understands homelessness—for example, as fundamentally a function of individual or structural
dynamics—and how broadly one conceptualizes the rights implied by citizenship both strongly influence how one views the fundamental role of services. The core of this debate is whether one perceives service as remediation
of problematic behavior, or an opportunity to address systemic problems. The
rationales employed by service providers tend to be heavily pragmatic (both
in terms of costs and client outcomes) even when employing a housing first
approach, but there are more principled ways of thinking about these issues
(Wasserman and Clair, 2013).

Perhaps a more fundamental dilemma can be abstracted from the homeless service milieu: there are difficulties inherent in establishing programs
for individuals. The former, almost by definition, are developed around
evidenced-based typologies while in many cases nonfitting individuals

distinguish themselves from types in ways that are important to working with them. This is a dilemma that appears to attend most, if not all, models of service. Even where Housing First centers on limiting the programmatic structures surrounding assistance, rapid re-housing models have become more programmatic in practice where they have been diffused across CoCs.

An advocate for those who are homeless in our ethnographic study once remarked:

> It strikes me that part of the dilemma is societies demand rules to function and if you don't fit the rules, then you are classified as homeless or deviant or criminal or something. Society made up of people as complex and diverse and in a society that is complex, you are going to have folks that don't fit the rules. (Homeless advocate and founder of health care program for the homeless, as quoted in Wasserman and Clair, 2011b)

Perhaps a more fundamental problem at the heart of service model debates concerns the implication that there is a right or a best way to deliver services (Wasserman and Clair, 2013; see also Kertesz and Weiner, 2009). Discourse surrounding homeless services provision often appears to proceed without a questioning of certain fundamental assumptions. One group starts first by critiquing an older way of doing things and proposes what is supposed to be a new and better way. The proponents of the older way reject the new ideas as reckless or impossible to implement in some way and point to their own successes. Yet few step back and recognize that with a population as complex and diverse as those who are homeless, perhaps there is no right or best way at all. There is nothing to suggest that different service models cannot coexist to meet the needs of a diverse population. Instead, simply abandoning that assumption "could legitimize the simultaneous existence of alternative services underpinned by alternative logics that are able to fill in the gaps" (Wasserman and Clair, 2013, p. 180).

To create these diverse landscapes of service requires reexamination of fundamental assumptions at various levels. Among providers themselves, there must be recognition of the ways that programmatic approaches at some point inevitably limit the ability to meet the complex needs of individuals. Loosening programmatic criteria where possible within particular agencies helps attenuate this, as do conscious attempts across CoCs to create diverse sets of programs. Collaboration within CoCs specifically ought to promote diverse services and CoCs should be mindful of ways that commitments to overarching philosophies of service exclude valuable ideas and create gaps. Instead, CoCs should avoid endorsing particular value-laden programmatic concepts, working instead as facilitators of diverse service landscapes and fostering strong collaborations between agencies even where they have differing philosophies.

At a higher level, the attachment of funding for homeless services providers to particular philosophies of service should be minimized in favor of funding a diverse array of services. Agencies applying for funding could just as easily be asked to attest to the role they will play in addressing gaps in service and how they will collaborate with other agencies since they can attest to how well they fit prefabricated programmatic models.

At all levels, however, there must be a fundamental change in how we think about the issue of homelessness. The ideological pendulum of homeless services provision will simply keep swinging between various positions until there is an epistemic shift underneath the discourse that undercuts an oppositional mentality itself and allows for that diverse service landscape to develop and coexist.

Notes

1. Although in that respect, Franklin Roosevelt's New Deal with its focus on relief and job creation might be considered a de facto homeless service program. Also, many would point out that homeless services in most cities are still undercoordinated at best.

2. From here on, we use the uncapitalized "housing first" to denote the full range of such programs.

3. We caution that we use "overuse" in a factual way, not to indicate malicious intent on the part of a patient who is homeless.

9

How We've Learned
to Embrace Homelessness

David L. DiLeo

The way we think about our history weighs heavily on our perceptions of homelessness and our traditional approaches to dealing with it. Like other dehumanizing institutions in our past, homelessness is imbedded in our national life and generally understood as an unintended consequence of our basic values, perhaps even a natural consequence of civil and economic liberty. In this chapter, I explore how the virtues of our social, economic, and political systems unwittingly rationalize and even encourage the neglect of our most vulnerable citizens.

The Obstacle of Belief:
Denying Humanity and Blaming the Victim

It was in 1997 when, at a conference in Atlanta, I first heard these words in this sequence: "Holocaust denial." That there could be such a thing stunned me a bit. Isn't the Holocaust in every textbook? I was having a little trouble imagining this level of antihistory. But the speaker confidently asserted that the question of whether the Holocaust ever even occurred would, within a generation, be passionately debated (Lipstadt, 1997). She was certain that, when the last survivors of that era passed, ideologues would cultivate doubt among an unlettered public and provide interest groups with ample opportunity to create a counternarrative. The myth of the Holocaust, as political agenda, was not far off.

Deborah Lipstadt's presentation was not about historical evidence. Or justice. Or compassion. It was about belief, and as I show below, popular conventions seriously impede the ability of homeless advocates to broaden coalitions, compete for resources, and generate support for neighborhood facilities. Getting people to believe something is apparently not that hard.

Reinforcing traditions galvanized by prejudice across centuries is even easier. But how is it that we are so often willing to suspend rational thought, accept myths, tolerate stereotypes, and utilize straw men in political discourse? How can we plumb the depths of the cognitive dissonance required to blame plagues on a religion, burn witches, enslave Africans, or pray away the gay? Indeed, how are we prepared to tolerate—and even embrace—another generation of the dystopian antipathy that is homelessness?

One answer lies imbedded in the beliefs and bigotries toward people in poverty that we have unconsciously internalized. At some cellular level, too many of us still believe that people experiencing homelessness are living in a way that corresponds to their value as human beings. They live on skid rows, mainstream opinion implies, for the same reasons that—in other cultural contexts—slaves lived on plantations, or Native Americans on reservations, or Jews were sent to death camps: enough of us still believe they deserve to be there. We have shrouded homelessness in myths, evaded responsibility, and have ourselves become deniers. Of course, as I have been energetically reminded "state-sponsored neglect is not the same as state-sponsored murder" (D. Lipstadt, personal communication, February 5, 2015), and I am not here arguing the moral equivalence of the Holocaust and our tolerance for homelessness. But I am suggesting that two societies got to those different places on the same road: subjective and specious judgment about another person's humanity. Because we prefer emotionally fulfilling illusions to real engagement with our history, because we blithely accept the human consequences of free-market competition, and because we uncritically accept the ancient dogma of free will, we are complicit in the dynamics that foster poverty and homelessness.

Like other derided minorities, persons experiencing homelessness in the United States today are iconic others. Despite what economists, social scientists, or clinicians may tell us about the complex and differentiated causes of homelessness, what the general public believes about people experiencing it—uninformed and unencumbered by analysis or association—determines our tepid policy responses. Our lack of comprehension relegates more than half a million of our fellow citizens to our streets each night. It is reinforced by our very human tendency toward unexamined belief, and a prejudice against poverty that was hardwired into our culture before even our founding as a nation.

Two important historical examples of generally accepted policies that affected millions of people are: the policies that brutalized European Jews and the positive good theory that consigned 4 million Americans of African descent to plantations. Similarly, people experiencing homelessness in the United States today are profoundly disadvantaged by the cultural and political norms we have inherited, and which we have unthinkingly internalized. Without much discernment, far too many of us regard our poor and homeless neighbors as drunk, lazy, and crazy, and we blame—more often than we support—people with needs. Conquering homelessness is presently beyond our reach because too few of us are willing to meaningfully engage the issue, or confront our own roles in its perpetuation. With what we sincerely believe is good reason, we seem to prefer judgment to discernment and tough love to meaningful institutional change.

Americans support what is, effectively, culturally endorsed neglect of our most vulnerable citizens. Powerful dogmas like free will, free enterprise, and rugged individualism encourage it. Popular culture supports it. But when the mythic bark is stripped from US history, it turns out that our own freedoms and prosperity were not forged with individual initiative, or free will, or free enterprise. Slaves were not set free. Freedom was taken in countless acts of cooperative civil disobedience; legal, moral, and political agitation; and military conflict. Thousands of industrial workers died winning the right to bargain collectively and protect themselves from the caprice of the market. Women organized, marched, and demanded the right to vote. It required decades in court, sit-ins, and bus rides to achieve the semblance of equality in educational opportunity. And Congresses legislated pathways to middle-class prosperity and economic security with a long list of empowering benefits ranging from publicly subsidized education and infrastructure, to the virtual creation of industries, and on to the facilitation of our modern consumer economy. Even as rights and attainments were secured by the raw exercise of economic, legal, and political power, belief in the self-made man persists and it reinforces our class assumptions. If there is a mythic ladder of success, then there must be a bottom rung. Homeless people occupy that space.

Cognitive Failings

This cultural template of people experiencing homelessness is easily imbibed because believing comes naturally. It is mostly unconscious, and it is effortless. While our brains are impressive cognitive machines capable of abstract reasoning, artistic creation, intuition, they are also what historian of science Michael Shermer (2011, p. 171) calls "belief engines"—and specifically evolved to sort, judge, and explain. There are significant evolutionary advantages in creating compasses for navigating the chaos of life and, particularly, to the group cohesion created and enforced by belief systems. Socialized humans are naturally believing beings.

But our cognitive equipment is also dangerous. Our ability to get complicated things right—the laws of gravity or the principles of thermodynamics—does not preclude our getting other things wrong. We all operate multiple software programs whose functions sometimes overlap (Bloom, 2005). Using some, we can comprehend human emotion and read body language; with others, we may invent geometry, build temples, explore outer space, or invent a new app. Problems arise when our software crosses boundaries, prompting us to construct explanations for phenomena beyond our scientific competence. Our forbearers were notorious for drawing explanations of the physical world from a reservoir of myths, simply because we are all hardwired to explain things even when we actually don't understand them.

A typical pre-Enlightenment error, illuminating in this discussion of homelessness, was to attribute natural phenomena to human agency. Before geosciences, for example, earthquakes were linked to forces that humans could explain: God or, the gods, must be pissed. In the absence of a scientific explanation, a mythic one—predictably involving the default of human agency—was serviceable. In this world, "to peasants," an old Roman proverb wisely tells us, "all beliefs were true; to philosophers, all beliefs were false; but to the emperor, all beliefs were useful." Institutions of power were built on myths, and elites harvested the innocence of the masses in developing instruments of exploitation and coercion. While some may still claim that deities cause earthquakes, most of us now understand that shifting tectonic plates make the ground shake. But before science (think ignorance) or without science (think innocence), we are biologically built "to infer intention where none exists" (Bloom, 2005, p. 110).

One cognitive error made with respect to people experiencing homelessness is that we infer intention, which is merely a refined way of saying that we blame poverty on poor people. This is useful. It is both convenient and natural to believe that people experiencing homelessness have chosen their lot in the same way we have chosen ours. We all have free will—a concept subjected below to more scrutiny—and persons who are homeless have exercised theirs poorly. We judge them and, by making a self-referential claim, elevate ourselves. We are easily seduced by what anthropologist Pascal Boyer calls "hypertrophy of social cognition" (Boyer, as quoted in Bloom, 2005, p. 110); that is, we see design, intention, and agency in places that it may not exist.

Homelessness advocates presently suffer from a cultural lag that frustrated scientists in the past as they were confirming explanations for phenomena that ran afoul of traditional beliefs. Complexities of indigence are now well understood, and there will someday be a tipping point in the politics of poverty. When human capital deficits, disaffiliation theory, neuroethics, clinical and social pathology, and impersonal economic forces are more generally understood, the debate about why some folks find it challenging to support themselves will turn from one based on free will to one that appreciates the utter randomness of evolutionary fitness and the vagaries of market capitalism. Rights will someday accrue to citizens as a function of their humanity, and not merely their means, their physical or social fitness, or their mental health.

Labels and Prejudices

But for now—and for enough of us to keep the problem unconquered—an ideology that supports homelessness powerfully influences the cultural landscape. For the short term, people experiencing it will continue to exist more vividly in our thought world than in our physical world. They will continue to occupy the ideological space we have created for them, and remain inscrutable foreigners in our midst: unknown, unpredictable, and dangerous. The homeless man on the street doesn't get the same break as our Aunt Sally suffering from Alzheimer's whom we love, and visit, and touch. He is abstracted, then categorized, as slothful, indigent, and alcoholic. No address? No respect. A person with means goes to Betty Ford for rehab; the homeless go to the alley behind the 7-Eleven to sleep it off.

So our cognitive dilemma—the obstacle of belief—is that we import a prescientific critique of people experiencing homelessness, along with a bunch of raw stereotypes, into our scientific world. The conventions to which we remain passively shackled were born in an age that knew not of systemic unemployment, outsourcing, wage poverty, bipolar disorder, schizophrenia, PTSD, or underdeveloped prefrontal cortexes. Despite what science tells us, we have been hardwired to believe that poverty, mental illness, and homelessness are mystical problems of character, and even countenances with evil. And in our politics, when it comes down to competition for resources, ideology trumps analysis.

It seems a good bet that anyone picking up this book has puzzled over what to do for the homeless person at the proverbial stop sign. Of course there is empathy—we are biologically built to feel it—but, as it turns out, very often a paralyzing empathy deficit. We feel that something should be done but, within seconds, our intellects provide an escape and we end up being driven not by what we feel, but by what we believe: "this inebriated or schizophrenic man is beyond my help" or "this lazy man is not deserving of my help." This strong ideological response is not created in an emotionally enriched space shared with a person, but has been peremptorily constructed in our minds.

We are insulated within the social spaces we occupy, essentially segregating ourselves from people with needs and effectively rendering them invisible and unknowable. People experiencing homelessness occupy physical spaces that make denial possible—shelters, underpasses, and alleys—and they occupy compartments in our minds that make denial easy.

Our modern attitudes remain mostly obsolete echoes of an unexamined past. The values that shape our responses to homelessness washed ashore in the early seventeenth century as we inherited our attitudes about poor people from Elizabethan England. After the enclosure movement (as commonly shared land became privately owned), homelessness, as a political issue, was born. Land scarcity produced conflict. Antivagrancy laws, poorhouses, debtors' prisons, fences, sheriffs, and courts protected propertied people from the wandering poor. Elites, and particularly Protestant clergy, wrote the story of poor people.

The Protestant Work Ethic

An emerging commercial class encouraged poor people to know their place (Bremer, 1976, p. 9). As wages began to be paid to hired hands, piety, industry, sobriety, punctuality, and personal discipline became its hallmarks. As the Atlantic seaboard became *New* England, a vigorous Puritan work ethic dominated its emerging ethos. In the harsh and labor-scarce American wilderness, little sympathy was shown to low achievers.[1] Work became a form of worship, and poverty was consciously taught to be a type of moral depravity. Landowners enjoyed the imprimatur, saints. Landless poor were sinners. In a community that embraced predestination (salvation determined before birth and unknown until death), spiritual anxiety propelled achievement and wealth became a reassuring sign of election. Property was seen as a manifestation of visible sainthood,[2] poverty and vagrancy as signs of sin and indolence. A template for dealing with homelessness in America was thus born. In this dynamic variant of Christianity, providing for the poor was considered an unwarranted interruption in the redemptive process they must endure, and destitution was a taste of a hell they deserved.

Across New England, the birthplace of American democracy, poor people were comprehensively disenfranchised. If one were not a sanctified church member, one did not own land, hold office, or vote. What one historian of Puritanism calls "the agony of uncertainty" (Morgan, 1958, p. 8) encouraged believers to achieve, but also to rebuke the destitute as validation of their own psychological and economic security.

The Obstacle of Prosperity: Capitalism and Wealth

Along with a militant version of Christianity, capitalism also came on the first ships. Pilgrims (of the Plymouth Company), Puritans (of the Massachusetts Bay Company), and merchant adventurers settling the Chesapeake (of the Virginia Company), all sailed in vessels bought and paid for by joint stock entities and were obligated by their charters to return value to shareholders. At the moment of its conception, and in the spirit of the classical colonialist model, America was designed and built to produce wealth in the most efficient way possible for business owners. Within the first few decades of English settlement, all manner of expedient measures were rationalized under that grand commission. Proprietary charters, the exploitation of Native American peoples and lands, contract and child labor, indentured servitude, the domestication of women and girls, slavery, and what we would today call wage theft, were all hallmarks of early American capitalism.

Reverberations of these founding institutions bode ill for people experiencing homelessness. The otherwise disparate impulses of capital accumulation and the ethics preached by Jesus of Nazareth were married by a peculiar catechism of work as worship. Inability or unwillingness to toil was "symptomatic of the lack of grace" (Weber, 1958, p. 159). A culture, informed by a radical theism, also embraced a radical secularism that was expressed in the marketplace. Property and money became American sacraments. Puritan stalwarts supposed a "providential God," as historian Gordon Bigelow (2005, p. 35) told us was "one who built a logical and orderly universe." Hence, New England's commercial economy was widely believed to be the fulfillment of a divine plan and "the free market was a perfectly designed instrument to reward good Christian behavior and to *punish and humiliate* the unrepentant" (p. 35, emphasis added).

While they are decidedly not economic actors, we have been conditioned to think of people experiencing homelessness in economic terms (and this endnote is guaranteed to amuse).[3] In our world, nearly everything is commoditized. Water is bottled and sold, space is owned and rented, and even our consciousness is harvested by incessant commercial messaging. But people experiencing homelessness are superfluous. They don't add value to an enterprise, they make few demand purchases that stimulate the economy, they don't normally invent or innovate, and they don't create much wealth with their labor power. So, with respect to those who are perceived to retard an economic agenda or, by their mere presence, cause our property to depreciate, the United States could not have been founded at a more inopportune time and could not presently be a more inconvenient place. In this country, being poor seems vaguely subversive.

The Irony of Wealth

But what, really, is wealth? As it turns out, it is not some nominal amount of money, but rather a differentiation of money. Wealth is not about having some, or even a lot, but demonstrably more than other actors in the market. Wealth and poverty are strange bedfellows and, in a sense, mutually reinforcing phenomena. Seen in this light, wage depression and poverty become innate prerequisites to wealth creation. And wealth is most certainly not the result of individual initiative. When government grants a patent, builds a road, creates an offshore tax haven, bails out a bank, or sends cavalry to kill Native Americans so railroads can be built, it is subsidizing business by means of corporate socialism. Similarly, middle-class socialism—Pell Grants, Medicare, social security, or the big daddy of all federal housing subsidies, the mortgage interest deduction—significantly augments the economic security of a powerful political class. Corporate and middle-class benefits dwarf indigent services because they are ideologically associated with growth, material abundance, and essential Americanism. While what we naively refer to as the free market may in fact produce the greatest good for the greatest number, it is emphatically not designed to alleviate either poverty or homelessness. It is, ironically, designed and built to encourage them. Solutions to homelessness will therefore, inevitably, be derived from nonmarket forces.

The past couple of years have seen a torrent of studies about the wealth gap, and new terms like the 99 percent and the 1 percent. This is peculiar insofar as the wealth gap is not only presently a feature of US capitalism; it has been its defining dynamic. Except for just 3 of our 228-year history as a country, worsening income inequality has been a pretty normal phenomenon.[4] Intentionally created wealth differentials—while providing incentives to strive and innovate—inexorably price some people out of access to things like rent, food, transportation, and health care. So why are some reading here for the first time that wealth is a function of poverty, and that our system is designed to produce poor people? Part of the answer lies in our embrace of a narrative—entrenched in traditional K-12 curricula and reinforced by a profit-driven media—that encourages our denial, and a long tradition of our economic elites rationalizing self-interest with inspiring rhetoric. At our founding, the concept of a global capitalist market became America's gift to the world; since our founding, we have been its most aggressive proponent. When the United States projects power, a commercial objective (a canal, a resource, land, markets, bases for more power projection) has propelled the initiative. "America's empire," Canadian member of parliament Michael Ignatieff (2003) insightfully notes, "is not like empires of the past. It is an empire *without consciousness of itself as such,* shocked that its good intentions arouse resentment" (p. 2, emphasis added).

How Low Can We Go?

One rung up from the homeless on the mythic ladder of success are the working poor, and our treatment of human capital in our low-wage labor market ensures the perpetuation of chronic homelessness. When even our largest and most profitable corporations pay minimum wage and deny workers benefits and promotion, market theory grants them the cover of freedom and celebrates their competitiveness. Market share expands. Stock shares soar. As profitability is derived from depressing labor costs, shareholders are treated to benefits, and workers to a steady decline in purchasing power. Poverty flows, ironically, from what we are told are the virtues of our system. Even the founder of modern capitalism, Adam Smith, saw this coming, and decried the materialism embedded in our passionate attachment to the market: "Virtue," he once reproved, "is more to be feared than vice because its excesses are not subject to the regulation of conscience." If we argue so vociferously about the minimum wage, it's not too hard to comprehend why we respond so harshly to people who can't work or can't find work.

Social and Economic Justice

So, how do global capitalism and foreign policy impact what has tradition-ally been regarded as a domestic issue? Without, here, critiquing the benefits of US hegemony, suffice it to say that the military industrial complex domi-nates the political landscape. It wraps defending freedom abroad in the flag and minimizes our attention to reparative justice at home. We rightfully mourn our fallen service men and women, but tolerate the culture of death visited on our own citizens abandoned on our own streets. It exhausts the political energy of our democracy and conflates military adventurism with essential Americanism. In so doing, it ensures that competitive open door global capitalism dwarfs its ideological rivals, and we end up proportionately disinclined to support progressive social issues at home.

Wealth in the United States is almost never spoken about in terms that include shared assets (roads, clean air or water projects, public parks and libraries, community centers or Little League), but only by the narrow index of assets privately owned. But while only a tiny few of us are shareholders, we are all stakeholders. Even if we don't own a piece of property or a share of stock, we most certainly have an interest in how the property might be used and how a business might treat its employees. In what is sometimes called the "tragedy of the commons," we have ceded to private interests extraordinary power over our lives.

Myths about the American dream—and how attainment is achieved through individual effort—hinder our reading of the empirical evidence. Peo-ple with means seem quite willing to ignore a great deal of history and to pay protection money in the form of welfare, if only to avoid addressing more fundamental issues. People experiencing homelessness, losers in the capital-ist race for maximizing self-interest, are tolerated for the simple fact—and perhaps only for that fact—that not everyone can be a winner. Economically secure people don't fear homelessness! They may even welcome the oppor-tunity to donate to worthy causes. What they fear is any conversation about economic justice, which implies that they might be asked to make ethical rather than economic calculations (Freeland, 2012, p. ix). If you are a person experiencing homelessness in the United States, the dominant political and economic ethos make for rough sledding. When people with means give food to the poor, they may be thought of as saints. But when they inquire as to why they are poor, they are inevitably marginalized as some form or degree of leftist,[5] at which point their voices are evicted from legitimate political discourse. We are charitable without making structural changes, and then end up living in a world that is designed, built, and regularly fine-tuned to create more as opposed to fewer homeless persons. In that world, fresh thinking, not driven by economic rationalization but by a reappraisal of our common humanity, may be required.

The Obstacle of Justice: Two-tiered Citizenship

I won't soon forget Christmas morning 2012. Sent to forage for orange juice, I found an open liquor store at 6 A.M. near my home in San Clemente, California (in a middle-class neighborhood near a homeless enclave). After exchanging pleasantries with the clerk, he asked, not wanting to make change, if I had ten cents. Noticing I had only a twenty, a homeless man next to me at the counter, whom I had not brought into my peripheral vision, sheepishly slid a dime in my direction. A homeless man, about sixty years old, rummaging through his tattered pockets trying to retrieve enough change to buy a stale muffin—his Christmas breakfast—wanted *me* to have *his* dime. This was a bit unnerving. Because he deals directly with that level and kind of transaction each day, he was more alert to my need, and willing to engage, than I was to his. I felt weirdly ashamed. He was more tuned in to my need (a fu*#ing dime) than I was to his (a wholesome meal, medical attention, perhaps some meaningful companionship, and a couple of nights of solid sleep).

As a person of means, I benefited from his deference and kindness more than he benefited from mine. Retail clerks, business and professional people of all sorts, and, particularly, politicians pander to people like me. Because I work, pay my bills, and own a home, I get services and rents from government and from the market. Lots of them. I can borrow money on the equity in my house, trade on its value, stuff my wallet with all kinds of magic plastic, donate money to a political party or cause, and I don't have to pee in a cup to declare a mortgage deduction on my tax return—the way a San Diegan does to get a hundred bucks in food assistance (Taibbi, 2014, pp. 316–320). Because I have a job and an address, a better class of citizenship accrues to me than to an American person without those things. I am affirmed by the state and by the market because of my means, not because of my humanity. There is no meaningful equality in this and there is certainly no compensatory or reparative justice in this.

We have created a two-tiered system of citizenship in the United States. On one tier are the worthy. If you inhabit this place, you have a good chance of living a good life, increasing your longevity by being regularly tested for treatable diseases, avoiding arrest, and, if arrested, a good chance of avoiding jail. You can vote, get a library card, a table at a restaurant, memberships at clubs that spawn more access to more advantages, and, in the twilight of your days, you aren't means tested for your social security check. If you have a drug addiction, chances are it is a safer kind, single-malt Scotch, prescription narcotics, or cocaine, the powdered variety. All kinds of things accrue to you because of your station. The benefits you receive from society are synergistic and, throughout life, increase your access and privilege. A salaried position becomes a pension; owning a home, a higher credit rating; accumulated sick leave, paid vacation; and missed time on the job is covered by workers' compensation.

If you are on the other tier, working poor or homeless, you are looked on with suspicion, denied services, and blocked out of options. Your life is hard and your longevity measured. Your preferred vice is probably cheap wine, and the drugs in your world are dangerous and powerfully addictive (like teeth-rotting meth). Often public places, including voting booths, are closed to you (Holland, 2013). You are more likely to get arrested, get robbed, and get mugged. We have essentially criminalized poverty and homelessness in the United States, and living on the street is cruel and unusual punishment. The depravations of life without reliable shelter—the cold, the heat, the denial of basic dignity—are like the coercive measures to which detainees are subjected behind the walls of places like Abu Ghraib or Guantanamo, and, in that context, understood as torture. And as if living on the edge is not hard enough, your character and humanity are constantly being judged by people around you.

That's our social contract: people with means are given progressively more by the state and the market through the exercise of political and economic power. People without means forage. What colonial Puritans called saints and sinners are now, effectively, propertied and unpropertied Americans. This caste system is objectionable on a few levels. One is that it brutally disenfranchises people who either can't work or can't find work, and another is that its injustices are multiplied over time. But most problematic is the conceit of the worthy because that is what perpetuates poverty and homelessness. This conceit, for most of us unconscious, includes the powerful dynamics of condescension and judgment. Those who have made it consider themselves superior—more virtuous—than those who haven't. But like Adam Smith, we'd be wise to contemplate this claim.

Is it warranted by the facts? Did we who have attained—as the code is written—sacrifice, play fair, and work hard to get ahead? Or did we just stay in line and receive our benefits from the social contract? Did we create the circumstances of our success as the expression of some dynamic character trait, piety, temperance, and virtue, or were we merely born with certain genetic advantages, with access to determinative class privileges and to an advantageous portion of human capital? It seems as though we've made middle-class attainment about as challenging as a high school diploma, and then celebrate it in the privacy of our own thoughts—particularly during the political seasons—as some cosmic achievement.

The Theory of Just Deserts

The conceit of people with means complicates life for homelessness advocates. By itself, it is unbecoming. But as University of Nevada, Las Vegas, professor of social work Leroy H. Pelton (2006) insightfully argues, it does something much worse: it encourages "active derogation" of poor people. Our willful ignorance of how we have benefited from the system through the exercise of political and economic power induces us to rationalize our own attainment and deride the less successful. "The truth is," Pelton told us with a whiff of understatement, "most of us have been getting something for nothing." Indeed, that is "the very object of community." But in our illusions about our history, and our own lives, we have created a social contract infected with a capricious virus of desert (p. 15).

We believe that we deserve our lot (often based on unexamined assumptions) and we believe that people experiencing homelessness deserve theirs (also based on unexamined assumptions). This is ironic, if not perverse, because we all receive from society inestimably more than we contribute. Desert theory is a manufactured fiction. It turns out that getting what we deserve is really about asserting political and economic power, and protecting our benefits with an army of rationalizations. We establish what is deserved and undeserved along what Pelton (2006) argues are "highly contestable lines" (p. 14). If it protects our assets, we are proficient at rationalizing almost anything (think fracking or tobacco subsidies). Claims about what we deserve "arouse intense passions" (p. 15) and bring out whole arsenals of persuasion sometimes called "politics."

The Obstacle of Politics: Divisions of Status and Class

So, if there are far more poor people than rich ones, why is that not reflected in policy—and why is the reverse actually the case? It turns out that in an egalitarian democracy, with all citizens being theoretically equal under the law, people still want to distinguish themselves and scratch the itch for prominence. So, along with a desert theory of justice, embedded in our political culture are anxieties about status. Particularly in a society without titles of nobility, or birthright, people are people and like to be differentiated. This makes majority rule—expressed as a class interest—improbable. There was, for example, no collaboration between poor whites and slaves (insofar as they were separated by color) to challenge the supremacy of the planter class. There was no poor man's bond between Italian and Irish immigrants (insofar as they were separated by ethnicity) to fight the white Anglo-Saxon Protestant establishment in nineteenth-century Boston. Recently, the largely urban Occupy Movement fizzled when it tried to appeal to the suburbs. Even though there are far more poor people than rich ones, we don't have a poor people's political agenda. Things like race, ethnicity, ideology, religion, and region ensure that they won't work together.

Consider this stunning aspect of our politics: today's Tea Party rank and file share objective class interests with the working poor (health care and nutrition challenges, job insecurity, college for their kids), but espouse an ultraconservative ideology identical to that of the energy tycoons, the Koch brothers. This is our democracy's Achilles' heel, and it goes a long way toward explaining why we can't end homelessness. Most Americans share concerns with the poor, but they don't identify with them because they are engrossed in an ideology—useful to economic elites—that encourages nativism, judgment, and a heavy dose of anti-intellectualism. Americans don't trust the clinical sciences, the social sciences, or, most especially, academic history, which is largely regarded as a conspiracy against their freedoms insofar as it is based on skepticism—as opposed to mythic glorification—and because it exposes too many inconvenient truths.[6]

As it turns out, we want to govern ourselves and much of the world while knowing as little about ourselves or other nations as possible. "It isn't that Americans view the past as irrelevant," essayist Lewis Lapham (2012) poignantly reminds us, "it's that they regard it as the stuff that dreams are made of, straw spun into gold, camera-ready for the preferred and more profitable markets in prime-time myth" (p. 28). So homelessness is a paradoxical expression of our marketplace of ideas in which the mythic competes favorably with the empirical. Homelessness flourishes because our history is tortured beyond comprehension by willful efforts to politicize it. Too often, the enthusiasm with which we embrace an idea—self-reliance, the free market, limited government, low taxes—may be measured in inverse proportion to actual knowledge about how a cultivated commons has, in fact, created more opportunity for more people.[7]

The Role of Government

Government is the only entity that can provide a safe shelter for every person experiencing homelessness in the same manner that it provides every ten-year-old with a fifth-grade teacher, or every senior a Medicare card. But when it comes to poor people, we have a negative response to state power being exercised on their behalf. This reflex derives from a unique version of Christian theology weighted more heavily by sin than by grace, and an originalist view of ourselves, born in the eighteenth century and recently exhumed by business interests.[8] The hypocrisy in this is positively startling: we neither want to create a dependency society, except for the middle class, corporations, and banks, nor a too powerful government, except in ways that it can police a world in which our multinationals can flourish.

We are paranoid about each other and about authority. Conservative ideologues, Al Gore (1992) reminds us in his fight with them about climate politics, have ensured that people remain "deeply suspicious of any effort to focus their moral attention on a crisis in the material world that might require a new exercise of something resembling the moral authority of the state" (p. 247). Even though a preponderant number of us support a new regime of gun safety laws, we can't legislate it—can't even bring it to a vote. Climate politics? Dead on arrival. Comprehensive immigration reform, no way. Our political system is hamstrung by atavistic impulses and professional messaging that render it dysfunctional. To add insult to injury, during our election seasons, professionally field-tested messages employ the rhetoric of freedom and equality to defeat the purposes of freedom and equality. So we have a democratic process, but not a democracy. So long as homelessness is consigned geographically to restricted spaces, so long as it remains compartmentalized in our minds, and so long as it remains imbedded in mythic images of our history, change will be challenging.

Beyond Belief: Changing Perceptions

Every US historians' favorite Winston Churchill quotation speaks to our ingenuity for avoiding hard truths: "The Americans," he once rebuked, "may be counted on to do the right thing, after all the other alternatives have been exhausted." Given our resources and the moral and political imagination we have often displayed in the past, we are capable of making dignity an inalienable right, and providing a decent existence for all our people. While homelessness is now emotionally tolerated and intellectually rationalized, it won't lie forever untouched. Like one of Taylor's Relics,[9] it will someday be consigned, as other forms of barbarism have been, to the dustbin of history.

So what's the right thing to do? Programmatically, as the authors demonstrate in this volume, that's not a hard question. Many advocates confidently know what to do and how to do it, but universally grieve the lack of resources and will. So, to move the needle, homelessness coalitions need to be significantly enlarged, the intersection between middle-class and poor people's issues more fully comprehended and ideological conservatives invited to tasks normally initiated by liberals. All of that will require a change in public perception—a cultural change—on which the additional will and resources are dependent.

Here's a first step: acknowledge that homelessness is not a failure of character, but the failure of an otherwise dynamic system to provide enough gainful employment for people who can work and sufficient services for those who cannot. This will require more general confidence in our clinical and social sciences, and the abandonment of archaic beliefs. To this end, we would benefit from a conceptual reengagement with a new vocabulary and new perspectives. Some of each are offered here.

Homelessness can be conquered, but it must be made a conservative concern. Reform moves quickly when injustices are injected into our consciousness with new language and are seen in new light. Abraham Lincoln's party changed history by effectively making emancipation a conservative issue, and by demonstrating that slavery grievously injured all Americans, both white and black.[10] Details came later. Thurgood Marshall argued *Brown* in 1954 without illusion about ending racism, but asserted only the narrow point that segregation in public schools was unconstitutional. Legislation was not far off. In their argument against California's Proposition 8 in 2012, David Bois and Theodore Olsen did not challenge homophobia, but maintained only that it was unlawful to deny Fourteenth Amendment protections because of an intrinsic human condition. In an instant, marriage equality became an American, and not a gay, issue.

Continuing to permit our fellow citizens to live without shelter, security, and nutrition is the functional equivalent of leaving them enslaved, segregated, and discriminated. Homelessness is not a poor people's issue. It is an American issue, and needs to be rebranded as a concern in which we all have an interest, the solutions to which imply generalized benefits. If opportunity can trickle down, it can also spring up. The political argument needs to be made, not about how poor people benefit from antipoverty programs, but how all Americans do. Here is a string of such inducements to consider.

Services and Training

More professional services will give civilians options other than numbing ourselves to the plight of the poor, or directly assisting them when we are not confident in doing so. When homelessness is more regularly addressed by more trained field practitioners, police departments and other service providers will benefit from the efficiencies implied in fewer nuisance calls. It is now well known that governments at all levels—as the people of Salt Lake City are discovering—save money by housing and serving, rather than policing and incarcerating (Carrier, 2015, p. 33).[11] Absent a spurious moral judgment, it makes no sense to give thirteen years of primary education to all our children, and then abandon a small percentage of able-bodied adults who need additional skills and services to become more fully self-sustaining. Jobs get created when we invest in the poor—just like they do when we build jet fighters or warships. Property values appreciate. What's good for people is good for business. While it is presently not politically popular, that's the proven Keynesian message (Hughes, 1983, p. 523).[12] Given our present political climate, we might consider neologisms like *democratic capitalism* or *conscious capitalism* to challenge the historic power of that forbidden idiom socialism—so effectively employed by critics of antipoverty initiatives. Conservatives must be called on to demonstrate enough confidence in the market to embrace antipoverty initiatives as good investments, and positive proof of the entrepreneurial ethic.

The Myth of Free Will: Blaming the Victim

But there is also a harder case to make: at some point, we will need to revisit our veneration for the myth of free will. So long as we blame poverty on poor people, changing the culture will be daunting. Much like the fiction of an independent force that we have for millennia called evil, free will is an artifact of an age when men were dependent on myths, and before they aspired to govern themselves. This dogma predates the Enlightenment, natural selection, evolutionary psychology, and neuroscience—all of which compellingly posit a causal universe—but it trumps all of them. If our political ideology continues to rest on the pillars of free will or just deserts, our tendency to sort and judge will be encouraged. It may be time to acknowledge that the doctrine is but a comforting illusion that we have for too long allowed to dominate the politics of poverty. Clinical and social sciences are shattering old wisdom. Complex neurological and biological factors beyond our control—and even our awareness—create the space we call our lives, and that our conscious thoughts haphazardly identify as our reality. It may be time to acknowledge that arbitrary genetic gifts and the advantages to which we had access during our development are what we have for centuries been calling "the designs of Providence" or "expressions of free will."

The Challenges Ahead

Eminent scientists, like sociobiologist Edward O. Wilson (2014), are now confidently telling us that the human brain is among the most complex systems in the universe. That our mechanisms can be congenitally or environmentally diminished and lead to indigence may be—like gender, or skin color, or sexual orientation—an intrinsic human condition. What we have long regarded as questions of character or moral development may in fact be hereditary or environmental predispositions. This should cause us to ponder—and perhaps enlarge—the meaning of equality.

On the legal front, homelessness is rapidly becoming the next civil rights frontier. At this writing, poor people in Detroit, unable to pay their utility bills, are suing the city for turning off their water (Thompson, 2014). Their appeal to the United Nations Charter and their demand for access to water as a universal human right are pregnant with implications: if water wins, one can imagine a template for cases about shelter, nutrition, and health care.

In Richmond, California, officials addressing the perverse irony of homelessness in the midst of empty houses are inverting the normal uses of eminent domain to keep people in their homes by restructuring loans to correspond with present market values. If the housing market is based on pride of ownership, a logical inference may be made that this is also true for poor people. The American Civil Liberties Union (ACLU) is waging a Dignity for All campaign, asserting rights of people experiencing homelessness. While just two states presently have a statute, it has become a fertile field for activists. An Illinois law (SB 1210, 98th Illinois General Assembly) adopted in 2013 and evocatively entitled Rights for the Homeless Act, states that "a person experiencing homelessness has the right not to face discrimination due to [a] lack of permanent mailing address, [the] address being that of a shelter or service provider." Shelters are, incrementally, becoming legitimized domains of law.

Renewed engagement with homelessness will, in its wake, bring other challenges into sharper relief. As we more thoughtfully engage our history and consider new definitions of wealth that include accountings of the commons and of the future, we will surely become a more compassionate culture. One might wonder how an ideology emanating from an eighteenth-century agrarian community might dominate our lives the way it does. But here we are. Perhaps, as at Gettysburg, a new birth of freedom is called for, and new definitions of liberty and prosperity and wealth may be required.

They may include emancipation from a foreign policy that is dependent on weaponry, and a conception of freedom not based solely on material expectations. I can imagine a generation of Americans that doesn't subordinate sustainability to profitability, or confuse capitalism with consumerism. And this is not an antibusiness sentiment. These principles are part of a new corporate ethos expressed by prominent chief executive officer Ray Anderson and others who came to realize they had been practicing an "intergenerational tyranny"—a sort of taxation without representation—by putting people at risk who will inhabit the planet after we are gone, and by not more fully democratizing prosperity (cited in Hawken, 1993, p. 23).

We've come a long way from the eighteenth century and Jonathan Swift's "modest proposal"[13] for dealing with homelessness. But we have a long way to go. A vaulting demographic curve, accelerating environmental degradation, ideologically charged terrorism, and rampant militarism all conspire to demand a new approach to living on this shared space that we call "our planet." The incremental tasks associated with ending homelessness—affirming the vagaries and varieties of social experience—will no doubt go a long way toward reintroducing us to our humanity and, ultimately, to saving our species. And that's a conservative argument.

Notes

1. John Winthrop's iconic 1629 sermon, "A Model of Charity," includes the admonition: "In all times, some must be rich, some poor; some high and eminent in power and dignity. Others mean and in subjection."

2. Puritan elites gladly paid window taxes (windows then being expensive adornments) to display their wealth and piety. Standard volumes on the Puritan work ethic include Edmund S. Morgan, *Visible Saints: The History of a Puritan Idea* (1963) and Richard Bushman, *From Puritan to Yankee: Character and the Social Order into Connecticut, 1690–1965* (1965).

3. A man I once helped at an off-ramp insisted on exchanging a joke—too raunchy to repeat here—for money. I've always assumed that the sign he was carrying—"Not Drunk"—was designed to help passersby get beyond condescension and judgment and, in the spirit of capitalist exchange, the joke was told to complete a principled fee-for-service transaction.

4. War production and government stimulation from 1942 to 1944 caused the US gross national product (GNP) to more than double. The number of Americans earning enough to pay income taxes increased sevenfold. The Keynesian model produced "the greatest—indeed, the only—redistribution of income downward in the nation's history" (Goodwin, 1994, pp. 624–625).

5. "When I give food to the poor, they call me a saint. When I ask why they have no food, they call me a communist" (quotation attributed to Archbishop Dom Helder Camara of Brazil, *Essential Writings*).

6. In ultraconservative quarters, academic history is thought to be a conspiracy against American heritage because its "standards of evidence and methods of analysis are based on skepticism" (Lepore, 2010, p. 16). Apparently, Americans don't like to question their assumptions too much.

7. One observer of our political culture has referred to conservative orthodoxy as a "derangement" in explaining how ideology occludes rational analysis of our history (T. Frank, 2004, p. 2).

8. "Originalist" views of the Constitution and of the "founding" are actually manufactured legal and commercial critiques of US history designed to "take back our political system from Communists, New Leftists, and other revolutionaries" (Yeomans, 2012, p. 14).

9. "Taylor's Relics of Barbarism" included polygamy, infanticide, sanguinary games, torture, caste, and slavery (Taylor, as quoted in Palmer and Colton, 1984, p. 551).

10. Abraham Lincoln's winning coalition in 1860 was comprised primarily of free-soilers. It was decidedly not the progressive, racial equality–minded abolitionists that provided the margin of victory, but conservative Northern whites not wanting to compete with slave labor in the new territories. White and conservative interests, ultimately, tipped slavery over.

11. Salt Lake City fathers discovered that supportive care costs, on average, $16,282 less per client than the emergency room, shelter, and policing options.

12. "Thus the war [World War II] was the Keynesian message illustrated. Government expenditures could and did wipe away the depression" (Hughes, 1983, p. 523).

13. Jonathan Swift (1729) proposed that rich people devour—as a protein source—the children of poor people. While he was (one would hope) being tongue-in-cheek, it speaks to what was permissible discourse in his lifetime.

10

Homelessness Is About Housing

Sheila Crowley

Homelessness is not an inevitable or permanent condition of life in the United States. It is a problem to be solved. If we choose to, we can end it. Rather, homelessness in this country today is the manifestation of the failure of multiple systems and institutions to provide a secure social safety net below which no member of our society is allowed to fall. Those who are becoming homeless are beset with the most complex set of vulnerabilities and the weakest support systems. The only certain common denominator about persons experiencing homelessness is that they have a housing problem. The primary cause of homelessness is an acute shortage of affordable and available housing for our poorest citizens. Among other challenges, ending homelessness will require a housing solution.

Insufficiently supported in the past few decades, the housing sector has failed to provide an adequate supply of decent and affordable units. This was not always the case. As recently as 1970, the market showed a small surplus of rental housing that people in poverty could afford (Daskal, 1998). Today, there is a staggering nationwide shortage of 7.1 million rental homes that are affordable and available for extremely low income (ELI) households[1] (NLIHC, 2015). To understand the pervasiveness of modern homelessness, one needs only to comprehend these two data points.

Explaining the Affordable Housing Shortage

To talk of a national housing shortage of 7.1 million affordable rental housing units illustrates the magnitude of the problem, but also can make it seem like the problem is overwhelming. A national number also allows people to assume that the problem is somewhere other than their state, county, or city. In truth, there is no place in our country where someone working full time at

159

the prevailing minimum wage can afford to rent a modest one-bedroom home (Bolton et al., 2015). Nationally, there are just 33 affordable and available rental units for every 100 ELI renter households. The shortage ranges from 15 units per 100 ELI renter households in Nevada to 56 units in South Dakota (NLIHC, 2015). The Housing Wage is what a full-time worker (40 hours a week, 52 weeks a year) must earn to afford the rent on a modest two-bedroom home. Nationally, the Housing Wage is $19.85 an hour ($41,288 a year), but the Housing Wage varies across the country with a high of $39.65 an hour ($82,472 a year) in the San Francisco metropolitan area.

These data confirm that no region of the country is immune from the low-cost housing shortage. Homelessness is a problem in the biggest cities and the smallest towns. The magnitude of homelessness varies considerably from place to place, but no community is providing enough affordable housing for all its residents.

Housing policy uses cost burden as a measure of affordability. A household is housing cost burdened if it spends more than 30 percent of its income for its housing; it is severely cost burdened if total housing costs exceed half of household income. The lower one's income, the more serious cost burden becomes. Nationwide, 75 percent of ELI renters have a severe housing cost burden (NLIHC, 2015).

Faced with untenably high housing costs, people cope in a variety of ways. They seek out more income with second or third jobs, or resort to extralegal means of satisfying the landlord. They scrimp on other necessities, forgoing heat or food or medicine. They are at the whim of unreliable, but no- or low-cost, forms of childcare or transportation. Any disruption in pay—illness, car trouble, attending a parent-teacher conference—can upend even the most carefully planned budget. Non- or late payment of rent looms large every month, and is a source of unrelenting stress.

Poor families have high rates of involuntary residential mobility (forced moves) due to eviction. Facing eviction for falling behind in rent, many struggling tenants, (especially women) move out ahead of the process server (Desmond, Gershenson, and Kiviat, 2015). The next housing situation is sure to be worse than the last. People careen from living with friends and relatives to stays in cheap motels to sleeping in their cars, and finally to emergency shelters or the street.

Tracing the decline in the supply of low-cost rental housing and the concomitant rise in homelessness starts in the 1970s with stagnating wages and growing income inequality. Urban revitalization and gentrification brought the permanent loss of hundreds of thousands of low-cost city dwellings, often the housing of last resort for the poorest of the poor. An estimated 1 million single-room-occupancy units were lost in the United States between 1970 and 1980 (K. A. Frank, 1998, p. 539). The traditional housing economic model relied on *filtering* in the housing market. New housing in better neighborhoods is built to attract an upwardly mobile population who vacate older housing in less desirable neighborhoods. Rents in the older housing go down, making them affordable for lower-income people. This way, the supply is constantly replenished. But filtering can bring rents down only so far. Once the rent that the prospective tenants can afford goes below the minimum cost to maintain and operate the housing, the owner will stop investing in the property or look for other ways to use the property that will provide a return (Apgar, 1993). With falling incomes and the resulting mismatch between what it costs to operate even the lowest-cost housing and what low-income people could pay, the supply of low-cost housing dwindles and eventually disappears.

A major overhaul of federal housing programs occurred in the 1970s. The Housing and Community Development Act of 1974 established the Section 8 program to replace public housing to produce and subsidize new affordable rental housing. The Gerald Ford and Jimmy Carter administrations had ambitious budgets to add tens of thousands of new units and housing vouchers for several years. However, the federal investment took a precipitous decline in the early days of the Ronald Reagan administration (Dolbeare and Crowley, 2002). Additions to federally subsidized housing dropped by 66 percent from the 1970s to the 1980s (Burt, 1992).

Support for low-income housing programs took another big drop in the mid-1990s in the wake of the Gingrich Revolution (Dolbeare and Crowley, 2002). The FY1997 appropriations bill for the US Department of Housing Development zeroed out new housing assistance for the first time (DeParle, 1986). While some HUD budgets in the ensuing years have added a modest number of vouchers, there have been more losses than gains. The FY1997 budget marked the onset of a two-decade defensive posture to protect HUD low-income rental housing programs.

Both the Bill Clinton and George W. Bush housing policies extolled the virtues of homeownership and sought to push the national homeownership rate ever higher. Major foundations and civil rights groups saw homeownership as asset building and a way out of poverty. Deregulation of the mortgage industry led to easy and risky credit for many people who aspired to homeownership, but for whom it was not a prudent choice (Baker, 2004).

The idealization of homeownership had the effect of devaluing rental housing. Local officials wanted more homeowners and fewer renters, and directed public funds to expanding homeownership. Communities fought the siting of new multifamily housing, especially for low-income households, anywhere near them. The loss of low-cost rental housing must also be examined through the lens of persistent race discrimination. Resistance to investing in and siting of new low-income rental housing is often a thinly disguised objection to people of color moving into a neighborhood. Not surprisingly, the supply of rental housing continues to decline.

In 2008 the housing market crashed, and foreclosures swept the nation as taxpayers bailed out major financial institutions. Former homeowners flooded the rental market and low-income renters were pushed down even further. More new households are choosing to rent in an unstable economy, putting greater pressure on an already inadequate rental housing supply. Renters were directly affected by foreclosure when their landlords lost their properties to foreclosure. Forty percent of the households that lost their homes to foreclosure were renters (Pelletiere, 2009, p. 3).

Today, the macroforces that fuel the rental housing shortage continue unabated. Low-wage workers (10th percentile) earn 5 percent less than they did in 1979 and middle-wage workers (50th percentile) earn only 6 percent more than they did in 1979 (Mishel, Gould, and Bivens, 2015). The rental housing vacancy rate fell to 7 percent in the last quarter of 2014 (US Census Bureau, 2015), and most of the supply is concentrated at the high end of the market. Rents are 15.2 percent higher than they were at the end of 2009 (Whelan, 2014).

Current Federal Housing Programs

Primarily through HUD, the federal government directly funds a variety of low-income housing programs. Housing is also subsidized through the federal tax code. While only 25 percent of eligible low-income renters receive federal housing assistance due to lack of funding (Center on Budget and Policy Priorities, 2015), all eligible homeowners can take advantage of federal tax subsidies for homeownership. Federal housing policy is out of balance, favoring owner-occupied housing over rental housing and higher-income homeowners over low-income renters.

It is useful to distinguish between older programs enacted prior to the 1980s and newer programs; the older programs are gradually shrinking and are wholly inadequate to the task of addressing the low-cost rental housing shortage.

Older Programs

The older programs begin with the 1937 US Housing Act passed during the Great Depression. They include public housing, housing vouchers, and project-based Section 8 as well as several smaller programs. Together, these approaches provide 4.6 million homes for 10 million people (HUD, 2013b). These serve predominantly ELI households (over 70 percent) and rents are based on 30 percent of household income.

While part of the social safety net, these programs differ from most other safety net entitlements (e.g., food stamps and SSI) and are funded on the mandatory side of the federal budget. HUD programs are not entitlements and are funded through annual appropriations on the discretionary side of the federal budget. As a result, they are susceptible to the vicissitudes of an appropriations process that is fraught with partisanship and the pet projects and peeves of individual members of Congress.

The most recent and egregious evidence of the vulnerability of these programs is the Budget Control Act (BCA) of 2011, which set in motion the catastrophe known as *sequestration*, deep across-the-board cuts to all discretionary programs that took effect in 2012. The results were so devastating that Congress passed temporary legislation in 2013 to ameliorate some of its worst effects. Sequestration came back with a vengeance as Congress took up the FY2016 appropriations bills. Congress was forced to provide additional sequester relief in order to fund the federal government for FY2016. Most HUD programs still lost ground and will continue to do so in the foreseeable future.

Public housing. The 1937 act created public housing that, at its peak, consisted of 1.4 million rental housing units. Public housing is owned and operated by some 3,400 Public Housing Agencies, most of which operate 200 or fewer units. PHAs are governed by local boards, whose members are appointed by local city, town, or county councils, but are funded and regulated by the federal government.

The history of public housing cannot be separated from our racial history. In many cities, especially in the South, public housing was built to maintain racial segregation (Silver and Moeser, 1995). Large, urban public housing projects where black and Hispanic families live in concentrated poverty is how public housing is generally perceived. Public rejection of public housing as a viable government program can be traced to the demolition of the infamous thirty-three-tower, fifty-two-acre Pruitt-Igoe development in Saint Louis in 1972 (*The Economist,* 2011). Today, 71 percent of the 2.3 million residents of public housing are people of color (HUD, 2013).

In the early days, public housing was occupied by families whose wage earners were able to pay the modest rents that PHAs charged. Rents started to go up when more revenue was needed to cover public housing operations in the 1960s, rendering public housing unaffordable for many residents. The solution was the enactment of the Brooke Amendment in 1969. Named for its sponsor, Senator Edward W. Brooke (R-MA), the rule provided that rents in public housing were not to exceed 25 percent of the income of individual tenants; the federal government would pay the difference between the amount of rent collected from tenants and the cost to operate the housing. The Brooke rule was raised to 30 percent of tenant income in 1981, where it remains today (Pelletiere, 2008) and applies to all of the older programs.

Declining investments in the capital needs of an aging housing stock and growing concern about crime and drugs prompted Congress to establish the National Commission on Severely Distressed Public Housing in 1989. In its

1992 report, the Commission estimated that 6 percent (84,000) of public housing units were severely distressed (National Commission on Severely Distressed Public Housing, 1992).

In response, Congress enacted the HOPE VI program in 1992, which authorized the demolition and redevelopment of public housing and relocation of residents. In 1996, Congress repealed the long-standing one-for-one replacement rule, allowing PHAs to demolish more units than they replaced. By the late 2000s, more than 70,000 public housing residents had been displaced and more than 88,000 units were demolished (Crowley, 2009). Few of the displaced residents have returned to redeveloped neighborhoods and many fewer units have been rebuilt than were demolished.

Under the Barack Obama administration, HOPE VI has been replaced by the Choice Neighborhood Initiative (CNI). Rather than focusing on a particular public housing development, CNI seeks to revitalize specific neighborhoods where a project is located. CNI has many more tenant protections that did HOPE VI, but is funded at a fraction of what HOPE VI received. Its impact remains to be seen.

Another public housing experiment is the misnamed Moving to Work (MTW) demonstration program that began in 1996. MTW continues today with thirty-nine MTW PHAs that operate 12 percent of the nation's public housing and housing vouchers (Couch, 2015). Under MTW most of the federal regulations that govern public housing and vouchers are waived and PHAs are allowed to experiment with new models of operation and programming, some of which may have promise but others, such as time limits on housing assistance or doing away with the Brooke rule, can be harmful for residents. Unfortunately, HUD failed to implement any MTW evaluation protocols, so the effects of the various experiments are unknown.

Today, PHAs are calling for significant expansion of MTW, primarily as a way to cope with declining federal funds. Advocates have objected to any further MTW expansion in the absence of a robust (and funded) evaluation plan and tenant protections. The FY2016 HUD appropriations bill allows HUD to add 100 more MTW agencies over the next seven years with significant evaluation requirements. It should be noted that some MTW PHAs are using their MTW flexibility to direct more resources toward housing for people who are homeless.[2] What is not known is if these initiatives are reducing rental housing for other ELI families to help families who are homeless.

Public housing is the most vulnerable HUD program. Today, there are only 1.1 million public housing units, 300,000 fewer than at its peak. Congress repeatedly cuts public housing funding. Bringing public housing units up to current physical standards would cost $26 billion, an unattainable sum in the current budget environment. President Obama requested a total of $6.820 billion for public housing operations and capital needs for FY2016.

Housing vouchers. Vouchers are a market-based approach to providing rent assistance to low-income households. Rather than subsidize a physical unit that is rented to an eligible household, an eligible household receives a voucher and looks for a home to rent in the private market. Vouchers are the most common form of tenant-based rent assistance (TBRA). Today, 2.4 million households are assisted with housing vouchers (HUD, 2013).

Experiments with TBRA, as an alternative to public housing, started in the 1960s. The idea went national with the Section 8 program of the Housing and Community Development Act of 1974. Section 8 refers to Section 8 of the 1937 US Housing Act, as amended, and includes both the voucher and Section 8 project-based programs. Section 8 privatized low-income housing; while the federal government still pays for housing, the housing itself is owned and operated by private landlords and developers. For the most part, vouchers are administered by PHAs, which collect fees from HUD to do so. State agencies also receive vouchers to distribute to cities and counties that do not have PHAs, where local Departments of Social Services or other local public or nonprofit agencies administer the program.

Vouchers can be used to rent units that meet federal housing quality standards and for which the cost does not exceed Fair Market Rents (FMR) set by HUD for geographic areas. In most of the country, the FMR is set at the 40th percentile of area rents; in some high-cost areas, FMRs are set at the 50th percentile. The costs of vouchers rise with the cost of all rents in an area, requiring an increase in the appropriation each year just to maintain all vouchers in use.

An important attribute of the voucher program is that it offers holders greater choice in where recipients can live, including the possibility of moving to neighborhoods with better schools and job opportunities. Civil rights and fair housing advocates see vouchers as a means of reducing racial segregation in housing. However, rents in better neighborhoods often exceed what a voucher will cover, limiting the mobility of holders.

The voucher program has grown considerably in recent years, but not because Congress is expanding housing assistance. Rather, tenants who are displaced from public housing that is being demolished or revitalized are given vouchers to help pay the rent in their new homes. Tenants in project-based housing also receive vouchers when the owners of the properties in which they live opt out of their Section 8 contracts to turn the development into market rate housing or dispose of the property altogether. Most of the growth in the program in the past twenty years is the result of the loss of hard units in the public or project-based housing stock. The administration's budget request for TBRA for FY2016 was $21.123 billion.

One final variation in the voucher program is known as *project-basing*. These vouchers are attached to specific hard units to make the units affordable to income eligible tenants. A PHA can project-base up to 20 percent of its vouchers, and about 100,000 vouchers have been project-based (Sard, 2015). Project-based vouchers encourage the production or preservation of affordable rental housing because owners can be reasonably assured of ongoing subsidies to maintain the financial stability of their properties.

Project-based rent assistance. Project-based rent assistance (PBRA) encompasses the Section 8 project-based program and several smaller programs. For the purposes of this analysis, PBRA also includes the Section 202 elderly housing program and the Section 811 housing for people with disabilities program. Together, these programs comprise 1.05 million units, in properties that are privately owned and publicly subsidized. HUD provided the capital needed to build the properties and provides the operating assistance to cover the difference between 30 percent of tenant income and the contract rent negotiated with HUD.

Unlike public housing that remains affordable because of public ownership, PBRA contracts will expire at some point in the future and can be lost to the affordable housing supply. Many PBRA properties are owned by nonprofit mission-driven organizations that exist for the purpose of providing affordable rental housing. An important way to preserve this housing stock is to facilitate its transfer to nonprofit owners. Although not as old as public housing, the Section 8 portfolio is aging and in need of recapitalization to preserve it for future tenants. Funding for the PBRA programs has not been as grim as it has been for public housing. The president requested $11.392 billion for the PBRA, Section 202, and Section 811 programs for FY2016.

Rental Assistance Demonstration. The Rental Assistance Demonstration (RAD), authorized in 2012, allows PHAs and owners of private HUD-assisted properties to use their existing federal housing assistance as leverage to borrow funds for capital improvements. PHAs and owners compete to participate in RAD. Up to 185,000 units of public housing and 22,000 privately owned units are authorized (Gramlich, 2015). HUD has requested that the cap be lifted entirely in its FY2016 budget, but reservations about RAD among key legislators make that unlikely.

RAD offers PHAs the opportunity to convert their annual public housing operating and capital funding to either project-based vouchers or project-based Section 8. PHAs can then leverage the Section 8 contracts to raise funds for capital repairs or redevelopment. PHAs with approved RAD conversions can apply for LIHTCs, as well as mortgage their properties.

Today, RAD is the only avenue available for PHAs to access the capital needed to preserve public housing units. However, RAD also exposes these units to risk should the PHA default on any loan. For this reason, residents of public housing are wary of RAD, despite numerous protections built into the legislation.

Summary. Public housing, vouchers, and project-based rent assistance represent a huge investment by the taxpayers in decent and affordable housing. They are the legacy of a time when Americans believed it was possible to ensure a decent home for all our people and they remain the most affordable option for millions of low-income families. Waiting lists are years long, and yet people flock to apply when a PHA announces it will open its waiting list for new applicants. The demand far exceeds supply while those on wait lists remain on the streets.

Some conservative legislators think the solution to the demand for housing assistance is to make it time limited. Under this proposal, current tenants would be required to move out after five years to make room for people on the waiting list. There are at least three problems with this proposal. First, more than half of the leaseholders of these programs are elderly or people with disabilities, for whom public or assisted housing is permanent housing (NLIHC, 2012). Second, the average time for a household to receive housing assistance is seven years. When elderly and disabled residents are excluded, the average time a household receives assistance is less than five years (HUD, 2013). Residents who are not elderly or disabled and who receive housing assistance for more than five years tend to be the poorest people with the most complex set of problems. Ending their housing assistance after five years, thus forcing them into the private housing market, would invariably consign them to homelessness.

Newer Programs

The low-income housing programs enacted since the mid-1980s are smaller in scope and serve many fewer ELI households than the older programs. Most are not subject to the Brooke rule, so tenants can be housing cost burdened.

The Low-Income Housing Tax Credit. The last major overhaul of the US tax code occurred in 1986; numerous tax breaks were eliminated, including some that benefited owners of rental property. They were replaced with the LIHTC and, since that time, the LIHTC has supported the financing of 2.4 million rental housing units.

The LITHC is not a HUD program; it is based at the Department of the Treasury. Each year, Treasury allocates the tax credits to state Housing Finance Agencies (HFAs) on a per capita basis. The HFA produces a Qualified Allocation Plan (QAP) that outlines priorities for projects for the coming year. Developers submit applications and compete for the tax credits. HFAs receive requests that far exceed the number of tax credits available to allocate.

When an award of tax credits is made, the developer sells the credits to investors who provide the funding for the project and use the LIHTCs to reduce their federal tax liability over a ten-year period. Most investors are banks and other large corporations. The LIHTC is a federal tax expenditure that the Office of Management and Budget (OMB) projects will cost $8 billion in 2015 (OMB, 2015).

When using the LIHTCs, a developer has two low-income unit set-aside options, and must remain with the chosen option during the required low-income occupancy period of at least fifteen years. The options are: (1) at least 20 percent of the units are occupied by households with income below 50 percent of AMI; and (2) at least 40 percent of the units are occupied by households with income below 60 percent of AMI. Rents in LIHTC units are not based on income; instead, they are based on 30 percent of whichever AMI is applicable to the unit (30 percent of 50 percent AMI or 30 percent of 60 percent AMI). In either case, the LIHTC rents are rarely affordable for ELI households.

Until recently, there was no national reporting requirement of who lived in LIHTC properties. To better understand how ELI households benefit from the LIHTC program, Bolton, Bravve, and Crowley (2014) examined the data on a random sample of LIHTC developments in five states. The sample was composed of 104 properties with a total of 8,578 units. Of these units, 36 percent were occupied by ELI households. However, 69 percent of the ELI households were also receiving some form of rental assistance that made their homes affordable. Federal housing vouchers made up 90 percent of all rent assistance provided. Of the ELI households who did not have vouchers or other forms of rent assistance, 87 percent were housing cost burdened, with 57 percent paying more than 50 percent of their income for their housing (Bolton, Bravve, and Crowley, 2014).

Today, the LIHTC is the major source of funding for low-income rental housing, but its usefulness as a tool to address the shortage of rental housing that ELI households can afford is limited. ELI tenants need other forms of assistance. Given the dearth of new federal housing vouchers for the foreseeable future, relying on them to serve many more ELI households in LIHTC properties is unrealistic.

A voucher is a rich subsidy. The NLIHC's analysis suggests that voucher holders tend to live in the 60 percent LIHTC units, with the voucher paying for the difference between 30 percent of household income and the higher LIHTC rents. The allowable rent with a voucher can be higher than the LIHTC rent, providing the developer with extra revenue (Bolton, Bravve, and Crowley, 2014). The question is: What do developers do with the extra revenue? Does it go to increase profits or is it used to reduce rents for unassisted ELI tenants? More research is needed to unpack these questions.

HOME. The HOME Investment Partnerships Program was authorized as part of the National Affordable Housing Act of 1990. Administered by HUD, it is a block grant to participating jurisdictions, which are all states and several hundred local jurisdictions. Its purpose is to expand the supply of affordable housing for low-income people. HOME can support a wide array of housing activities for both rental and owner-occupied housing.

Like the LIHTC, HOME is not targeted at ELI households. For home-ownership activities, beneficiaries can be households with incomes up to 80 percent of AMI. For rental housing, 90 percent of funds must be used for households with incomes up to 60 percent of AMI, with the remainder going up to 80 percent of AMI. If a rental housing development has more than five HOME-funded units, 20 percent of them have to be reserved for households with incomes at or below 50 percent of AMI.

HOME can also be used for TBRA with an initial contract of two years that can be extended. Since its inception, HOME has been used to support 287,000 TBRA contracts. However, most HOME funds are used for hard units. Almost 1.2 million homes have been delivered using some HOME funds; 61 percent have been for homeownership activities (Bolton, 2014). Like other HUD programs, HOME is funded through annual appropriations. At its peak, HOME was funded at $2.03 billion in FY2004. Funding has declined to $900 million in FY2015, an all-time low. As a block grant, HOME is susceptible to cuts in tight budget years, and the sequester has taken a big chunk out of it.

The Affordable Housing Program of Federal Home Loan Banks. The Affordable Housing Program (AHP) is not federally funded, but it is federally mandated. Since 1990, the Federal Home Loan Banks, which are federally chartered lending institutions, have been required to put 10 percent of their annual profits into AHP. Since that year, $3.7 billion has been distributed to assist 600,000 households. Nearly three-quarters (72 percent) have had incomes of 50 percent of AMI or less, and over three-quarters (76 percent) of the housing supported by AHP is for renters (Federal Housing Finance Agency, 2014). AHP is a small program, but has a dedicated funding source, making it less susceptible to congressional whims. There is no requirement that rents be set at 30 percent of tenant income.

Housing Opportunities for Persons with AIDS. Established in 1990, HOPWA is primarily a block grant program run by HUD, funded through appropriations and distributed to 139 jurisdictions. It pays for a range of housing-related services for people living with HIV or AIDS. The Obama administration has requested $332 million for FY2016.

McKinney-Vento homeless assistance programs. The last major new programs that support low-income housing are the HUD programs that were established in 1987 and reorganized by Congress in 2009. Over the history of McKinney-Vento, the emphasis has shifted from emergency and transitional shelter to permanent housing for people who are homeless or at risk of becoming so.

The permanent housing programs funded through McKinney-Vento are largely devoted to assisting long-term homeless people with mental illnesses and other disabling conditions. Rents are based on 30 percent of tenant income. Almost 350,000 people who were homeless now have permanent homes (Berg, 2015). The McKinney-Vento programs are funded through appropriations. The president requested $2.48 billion in his FY2016 budget.

In recent years, the relationship between rent and income has changed with the advent of Rapid Re-Housing. The concept is to move people from homelessness into housing as quickly as possible or to prevent them from losing their homes in the first place. Assistance is the form of a shallow subsidy to tide the family over until they can get back on their feet financially, usually with a time limit. The best programs provide intensive home-finding and case management services (NAEH, 2014b). Success is measured by how many families stay out of the homeless services system once their assistance ends. However, there are no data on whether families become stably housed and, given the housing shortage, these families remain at risk (Davis and Lane, 2012; Dvorak, 2014).

The total value of the low-income housing programs reviewed above will be at best $50 billion in FY2016, but they will not make a dent in the 7.1 million unit shortage of rental housing affordable for ELI households. On the other end of the economic spectrum, higher-income homeowners enjoy substantial housing subsidies paid for by the US taxpayers.

Tax Subsidies for Homeowners

Tax expenditures are tax breaks for corporations and individuals that have been enacted into law over the years to subsidize some activity that an interest group or politician has determined is worthy of government support. The 169 tax expenditures reported by OMB for 2016 amount to $1.31 trillion in uncollected federal revenue (OMB, 2015).

The mortgage interest deduction (MID) is a federal tax expenditure that allows some homeowners to reduce their annual federal income tax. The Sixteenth Amendment to the US Constitution establishing the federal income tax was enacted in 1913. When the income tax was implemented, certain business expenses were allowed to be deducted, including interest on all loans. At the time, most personal and business finances were intermingled and few people had home mortgages. When federally insured and thirty-year mortgages multiplied after World War II, the MID became more widely used. The earliest estimate of the cost of the MID, done in 1977, was $4.7 billion (Dolbeare and Crowley, 2002).

The federal government produces two different estimates of the annual cost of the MID. The estimate from OMB in the president's FY2016 budget proposal projects MID to cost $75.26 billion in 2016, growing to $102 billion by 2019. In August 2014, the Joint Committee on Taxation (JCT) of Congress estimated the cost of the MID to be $81.6 billion in 2016 (JCT, 2014). Both OMB and JCT show the MID to be lower than in recent years, primarily because of the sluggish housing market.

The tax code includes other subsidies for homeowners; also allowed are the deduction of state and local property taxes ($35.5 billion in 2016 using OMB numbers) and the exclusion of capital gains on home sales ($39.5 billion in 2016 per OMB). OMB also includes a tax expenditure called an exclusion of "net imputed rental income." Imputed rent accrues to homeowners because they do not pay taxes on the income they derive from not paying rent, even though they take tax breaks (MID and property tax deduction) for the costs of owning a home. OMB projects the cost of the imputed rent exclusion to be $82.4 billion in 2016. JCT does not provide an estimate of the cost of the imputed rent exclusion.

OMB projects the total cost of tax expenditures that subsidize homeowners in 2016 to be $233 billion, 18 percent of the cost of all tax expenditures. The federal tax code provides no housing-related tax breaks for taxpayers who are renters, unlike several states that have renter tax credits.

When filing their annual federal income tax returns, taxpayers can deduct the interest paid on home mortgages of up to $1 million, a deduction based on the size of the mortgage, not on the value of the house. The interest can be on mortgages on first and second homes. In addition, the interest on up to $100,000 in home equity loans can be deducted for a cap of $1,100,000 on the value of mortgages eligible for tax breaks.

The degree to which the MID reduces a taxpayers' taxable income depends on their tax bracket. Taxpayers in the 33 percent tax bracket can reduce their taxes by 33 percent of the amount of interest paid, but someone in the 15 percent tax bracket can reduce their taxes by just 15 percent of the interest paid. To benefit from the MID, a taxpayer must file an itemized tax return. JCT reports that 166 million tax returns were filed in 2014, but only 29 percent were itemized. Only 21 percent of all tax returns claimed the MID. The top 61 percent of taxpayers (incomes of $100,000 or more) who claimed the MID received 82 percent of the total benefit. The top 18 percent of taxpayers (incomes of $200,000 or more) received 42 percent of the benefit (JCT, 2014).

The MID is a regressive, expensive, and inefficient housing subsidy. Contrary to popular belief, it is not an incentive for middle-class renters to become homeowners. Rather, it encourages people to buy bigger, more expensive houses and take on more debt. The MID has no effect on the decision to move from renting to owning for low- and moderate-income households. It may be an incentive for upper-income homebuyers in loose housing markets, but at a high cost to the taxpayers. In tight housing markets, the MID inflates the cost of homeownership for everyone and puts it out of reach for most households (Hilbur and Turner, 2014).

The Future

Across the country, people are engaged in smart targeted initiatives to help individuals and categories of people dealing with homelessness, such as veterans, obtain and maintain stable solutions. Nonetheless, there were 25,000 homeless children in New York City in 2015 (Coalition for the Homeless, 2015). They need more and deserve better. In the current political climate, the future of federal housing policy and programs can seem bleak. However, there is cause for hope.

The National Housing Trust Fund

After an eight-year campaign, the National Housing Trust Fund (NHTF) was established as a provision of the Housing and Economic Recovery Act of 2008. The primary purpose of the NHTF is to close the gap between the number of ELI renter households and the number of homes renting at prices they can afford. At least 90 percent of the funds must be used to build, preserve, rehabilitate, or operate rental housing, and at least 75 percent of the funds must be used for rental housing that benefits ELI households. One hundred percent of all NHTF dollars must be used for households with incomes of 50 percent of AMI or less.

The statute specifies an initial dedicated source of revenue to come from an assessment of 4.2 basis points on the new business of Fannie Mae and Freddie Mac, the two secondary mortgage market giants. The NHTF is to receive 65 percent of the assessment. Not an appropriated program, funding for the NHTF is on the mandatory side of the federal budget.

Unfortunately, during the financial crisis in September 2008, Fannie Mae and Freddie Mac were placed into a conservatorship overseen by the Federal Housing Finance Agency (FHFA), which placed a temporary suspension on any assessments for the NHTF. Six years later, on December 11, 2014, the FHFA director lifted the temporary suspension and directed Fannie Mae and Freddie Mac to begin setting aside the required 4.2 basis points on January 1, 2015. Sixty days after the close of calendar year 2015, the amounts set aside are to be transferred to HUD for the NHTF.

HUD published proposed regulations to implement the NHTF in 2010 and issued the interim rule on January 30, 2015. After states have gained experience in implementing the NHTF, HUD will open the interim rule for public comment and possible amendments.

The NHTF is a block grant to states. The funds are to be distributed by formula to states based on factors that measure the housing needs of ELI and very-low-income households as well as the costs of housing construction in the state. A state agency will administer that state's NHTF program and make grants to capable entities to create new affordable housing opportunities.

The first funding from the assessment on Fannie Mae and Freddie Mac for the NHTF will be between $250 and $300 million, a small down payment on what has the potential to become a fund of several billion dollars a year. The NHTF statute permits Congress to designate other funds to NHTF as it so chooses.

Fannie Mae and Freddie Mac remain in conservatorship. The Obama administration, many members of Congress, and numerous analysts and pundits want to end the conservatorships, wind down Fannie Mae and Freddie Mac, and establish a new model for the secondary mortgage market. In 2014, three bills to do so were considered by Congress that would have also provided funding for the NHTF by applying a 10 basis point fee on transactions through the new system. This fee was estimated to eventually generate $5 billion a year and all three bills would have allocated 75 percent to the NHTF.

Unfortunately, none of the bills were passed before the end of the Congress in December 2014. However, reform of the housing finance system is inevitable. NHTF advocates will remain vigilant to ensure that whatever new system emerges will provide robust funding for the NHTF.

Mortgage Interest Deduction Reform

Low-income housing advocates also have designs on major funding from federal tax reform. It has been nearly thirty years since the last reform of the federal tax code, and there is widespread agreement that it is time for another overhaul. Tax-writing committees in the Senate and the House have held hearings, requested proposals, and formed working groups. Like housing finance reform, tax reform is inevitable. While all see the need for reform, to what end is not so clear. Should the goal of tax reform be to reduce the deficit, lower tax rates, or generate new revenue for new spending?

When tax reform happens, close attention will be paid to closing tax loopholes or tax expenditures. Because the MID is one of the largest and most regressive of all tax expenditures, it is under particular scrutiny. Numerous tax reform and deficit reduction panels and commissions have called for changes to the MID (National Commission on Fiscal Responsibility and Reform, 2010; President's Advisory Panel on Federal Tax Reform, 2005). Economists and tax policy experts across the political spectrum criticize the MID as being inefficient and poorly targeted (Hanson, Brannon, and Hawley, 2014; Toder, 2014). The Bipartisan Housing Commission called for using savings from reform of the MID to fund housing assistance for all ELI households (Bipartisan Policy Center, 2013).

In 2013, the NLIHC launched the United for Homes (UFH) campaign.[3] UFH proposes smart simple changes to the MID that will reduce taxes for millions of low- and moderate-income homeowners who do not currently benefit from the MID, and raise billions of dollars in new revenue that can be invested in rental housing for people who are homeless and for cost-burdened ELI households.

First, UFH proposes to reduce the cap on the size of a mortgage for which the interest can be deducted to $500,000. The $500,000 cap is on the size of the mortgage, not the price or value of a home. Someone with a mortgage over $500,000 would still get a tax break, but only on interest paid on the first $500,000. Only 4.6 percent of all mortgages in the United States between 2011 and 2013 were over $500,000. Further, mortgages of $500,000 or more are geographically concentrated. In only 3 percent of all counties in the United States did the percentage of mortgages over $500,000 exceed 5 percent.[4] Most people who borrow money to buy a house would not be affected by the proposed new cap.

UFH also proposes converting the tax deduction to a nonrefundable tax credit of 15 percent. A tax deduction reduces one's taxable income; a tax credit is a direct reduction of one's total tax bill. Taxpayers do not have to itemize their tax returns to benefit from a tax credit, making tax credits more accessible to lower-income households. Generally speaking, tax credits are flatter and fairer.

Under the UFH proposal, the number of homeowners who will get a tax break will grow from 39 million to 55 million, with most of the increase being households with incomes of less than $100,000 a year. Higher-income households with mortgages, primarily those with incomes of $200,000 or more, will pay higher taxes.

These two changes to the MID, phased in over five years, would generate $230 billion in new revenue over ten years (Eng, 2014). UFH proposes that this revenue be used to capitalize the National Housing Trust Fund. According to a 2013 national poll, 60 percent of voters favor the UFH proposal to reform the MID and 76 percent favor building more affordable housing in their states to help end homelessness.[5]

Representative Keith Ellison (D-MN) has introduced the Common Sense Housing Investment Act, which would change the MID as proposed by UFH and direct 60 percent of the revenue raised to the NHTF and 40 percent to other low-income rental housing programs. Under Ellison's bill, it is possible to end homelessness and the housing shortage for ELI households without costing the federal government another dollar. The proposal is budget neutral; it simply uses existing federal housing subsidies more fairly and more efficiently. Changes to the MID are coming. The challenge for the housing community, especially the defenders of the MID in its current form, is to come together to assure that new revenue generated by MID reform is used for housing.

Conclusion

Over the past forty-five years, we have failed to maintain an adequate investment in the housing safety net for our poorest citizens. In 1970, there was a surplus of low-income housing units that the very poorest could afford and before the major explosion in the number of people experiencing homelessness. Since 1970, a shortage of 7.1 million units has developed for ELI persons, and this doesn't even include almost 600,000 persons experiencing homelessness. Simultaneously, federal tax policies provide a projected $233 billion for homeowners in tax relief, and much of this subsidy goes to those wealthy owners who can take advantage of itemized tax deductions when filing their returns. There is something horribly wrong with this picture.

To reiterate the beginning of this chapter, homelessness is not an inevitable or permanent condition of life in this country. It is a problem to be solved. If we choose to, we can end it. That will require preferring equity and fairness over greed and residential separation. It will require changing the will of the public to advocate for a more balanced distribution of housing resources. It will require electing officials who will challenge the status quo, and inspire all of us to care and give more. Only then will we be able to provide housing for the very poorest among us.

Notes

1. Extremely low income is 30 percent or less of the area median income (AMI). In most of the country, ELI for a family of four is less than the federal poverty threshold. Housing is considered affordable if it costs no more than 30 percent of household income.

2. For example, see the San Diego Housing Commission at www.sdhc.org/.

3. See the United for Homes website at www.google.com/?gws_rd=ssl#q=united +for+homes+campaign.

4. Based on calculation of Home Mortgage Data Act data by the National Low Income Housing Coalition. See http://nlihc.org/sites/default/files/UFH_Mortgage _National.pdf.

5. Poll commissioned by the NLIHC. See http://nlihc.org/sites/default/files/2013 _Belden_Russonello_MID_Survey_Data.pdf.

11

Work, Wages, Wealth, and the Roots of Homelessness

Bristow Hardin

*There is nothing more dangerous than to build a society with a large seg-
ment of people in that society who feel that they have no stake in it; who
feel that they have nothing to lose.*

—Martin Luther King

Economic developments over the past forty years have significantly
eroded the security of the great majority of Americans, especially those at the
bottom of the wealth and income pyramids. These changes are inexorably en-
twined with the growth in income and wealth inequalities to levels not reached
since the 1920s. That's hardly news, of course. But it is worth repeating since
these structural conditions and dynamics and the lack of affordable housing
discussed by Sheila Crowley in Chapter 10 of this volume are the fundamental causes of homelessness. Moreover, these are not inevitable or natural economic processes, but rather predictable results of economic policies implemented since the late 1970s.

The growth in US income inequality that the Organisation for Economic
Co-operation and Development (OECD, 2014a, p. 1) has characterized as
"spectacular," has been mirrored by increases in wealth inequality. While
Pope Francis deems "inequality . . . the root of social evil" (Pope Francis, as
quoted in Wade, 2014, p. 6), many economists deem it the necessary price of
economic prosperity and maintain that policies to mitigate it, such as
increased taxes on higher-income groups and increased support for low-
income people, are economically counterproductive. And former British
prime minister Margaret Thatcher proclaimed that "it is our job to glory in

inequality and to see that talents and abilities are given vent and expression for the benefit of us all" (Thatcher, as quoted in Wade, 2014, p. 1).

Many homeless people work; many others want to work, but cannot find jobs; those that can find work typically earn meager wages; and others cannot obtain work to support themselves and their families because of limited skills, physical or mental disabilities, or childcare responsibilities (NAEH, 2014a; ICH, 2015c). But the economic plight of those experiencing homelessness is only the tip of a huge and daunting iceberg.

In this chapter, I first profile the factors that highlight the precarious economic security and limited opportunities of most US workers and families — trends in workers' employment, unemployment, and wages, and household incomes and wealth holdings. Then, I review the official poverty measure and trends in poverty rates. After that, I discuss the neoliberal policies that have undermined the economic and social well-being of the great majority of US workers and families since the late 1970s, inequality and social protections in other countries, and the economic and social costs of inequality. I conclude with a discussion of policies that many analysts argue would significantly improve the labor market opportunities, wages, incomes, and economic security of the great majority of US families. Absent the implementation of these or similar policies, the well-being of most Americans, especially the poorest among us, will improve little and far more likely worsen.

In the chapter, I concentrate on developments since the late 1970s because 1979 was the last business cycle peak before the implementation of the neoliberal policy regime: tax reductions for corporations and upper-income groups, cuts in the income supports and protections for moderate- and low-income households, regulatory changes that increase corporations' power over workers, and trade and investment frameworks that have shaped the transformations of the global economy. I highlight data for the peak years of economic cycles — 1979, 1989, 2000, and 2007 — as well as for 2010, the first year of the recovery from the Great Recession, and 2014 (or the most recent year for which data are available). Data for peak years of the business cycle are appropriate benchmarks because they minimize variances due to cyclical conditions (thus providing a consistent comparative standard) and represent when the material well-being is greatest for most of the population and the average worker or family.

I encourage readers to pay special attention to those figures that include the bottom quintile, since persons who are employed and are homeless or at risk of homelessness almost invariably fall into this bottom group, and those who are not working are in even worse financial shape.

Labor Market Transformations Since the 1970s
The economic Golden Age from the end of World War II until the late 1960s to early 1970s brought prosperity to US workers and corporations alike.

Economic growth rates were robust, workers' real (inflation-adjusted) wages and incomes grew in tandem with steadily improving productivity, corporations enjoyed healthy profit rates, and inequality declined. The neoliberal policy regime emerged from the political conflicts that ensued with the end of the postwar boom.[1]

Unemployment and Underemployment

Official unemployment rates have varied since the late 1970s. (In the official data, workers are employed if they work as little as one hour a month and they are unemployed only if they are actively seeking work.) The unemployment rate fell from 5.8 percent in 1979 to 5.3 percent in 1989 and then to 4.0 percent in 2000. After that, it increased to 4.6 percent in 2007, after six years of economic growth, and then reached 9.6 percent in 2010, the first year of the post–Great Recession upswing, and fell to 6.2 percent in 2014. Note the numbers of workers who futilely sought work in those years: 7.1 million in 2007, 14.8 million in 2010, and 9.6 million in 2014 (Bureau of Labor Statistics; labor force statistics from the Current Population Survey, annual average data, http://www.bls.gov/cps/tables.htm).

Data regarding "underemployed" workers—those who are officially unemployed as well as involuntary part-timers (who want a full-time job, but cannot find one) and "discouraged workers" (who want to work, but gave up looking because they could not find it)—provide a more complete picture of workers' limited job opportunities. As Table 11.1 shows, the rates and numbers of the underemployed are significantly higher than those who are officially unemployed; for example, the underemployment rate grew from 8.3 percent in 2007, to 16.7 percent in 2010, and then fell to 12.0 percent in 2014. Note that 16.2 million workers were underemployed in 2007, 29.8 million in 2010, and 23.2 million in 2014, when the official unemployment rate was only 6.2 percent.

Two other important measures of workers' job prospects are the job seeker/job opening ratio (the number of unemployed workers to available jobs) and data regarding the "long-term unemployed" (persons unemployed for at least six months), both of which provide another perspective on the labor market. The job seeker/job opening ratio reached 5.8 in 2009 and then fell to only 3.4 three years later (Hathaway, 2013; Bureau of Labor Statistics, Labor Force Statistics from the Current Population Survey, various years). The long-term unemployment rate at business cycle peaks more than doubled during the 1979–2007 period, jumping from 8.7 percent in 1979 to 17.6 percent in 2007. It then reached 43.4 percent in 2010 before falling to 33.5 percent in 2014 (Bureau of Labor Statistics, Labor Force Statistics from the Current Population Survey, various years).

Unemployment rates have long been one of the most striking measures of enduring racial and ethnic inequality in the United States: in good times and bad, white unemployment rates are typically half the rates for blacks,

Table 11.1 Unemployment and Underemployment, 1979–2014

	Rates (%) and Number of Persons (in 000s)					
	1979	1989	2000	2007	2010	2014
Unemployment						
Rate (%)	5.8	5.3	4.0	4.6	9.6	6.2
Number (in 000s)	6,137	6,528	5,692	7,078	14,825	9,617
Underemployed						
Rate (%)			7.0	8.3	16.7	12.0
Number (in 000s)			13,332	16,182	29,758	23,153

Note: Author's calculations from Bureau of Labor Statistics (BLS), Labor Force Statistics from the Current Population Survey (CPS).

and the unemployment rates for Hispanics fall roughly midway between those of whites and blacks. For example, in 1979, the unemployment rate for whites was 5.1 percent compared to blacks' and Hispanics' rates of 12.3 percent and 8.3 percent. In 2000, whites' unemployment rates were only 3.5 percent versus 7.6 percent for blacks and 5.7 percent for Hispanics. The rates for all groups spiked because of the Great Recession—peaking at 8.7 percent for whites, 16.0 percent for blacks, and 11.7 percent for Hispanics in 2010. By 2014 the rates for whites, blacks, and Hispanics had fallen to 5.3 percent, 11.3 percent, and 7.4 percent, respectively (Bureau of Labor Statistics, Labor Force Statistics from the Current Population Survey, various years).

Wages and Income
Wage and income trends starkly highlight the diminishing economic well-being of US workers over the 1979–2014 period; while the wages and incomes of most workers stagnated or fell, those at the top end, especially the top 1 percent, captured the lion's share of the overall increases in incomes and real wages.

Wages. Figures 11.1 and 11.2 show the changes in the median real weekly wages for wage and salary workers for all workers and by sex and race/ethnicity, respectively, from 1979 to 2014. As Figure 11.1 shows, the median weekly earnings for all workers were relatively flat. Note that these stayed flat only because the 21 percent increase in women's earnings (from $547 to $662) offset the 8.6 percent decline in men's earnings (from $877 to $802). Even then, men's weekly earnings remained 21 percent above women's.

Figure 11.2 highlights changes in white, black, and Hispanic workers' real weekly earnings over these years. As the figure shows, white workers' weekly earnings were relatively flat over the 1979–2014 period (in 2014 they

Figure 11.1 Changes in Wage/Salary Workers' Median Weekly Earnings by Sex, 1979–2014

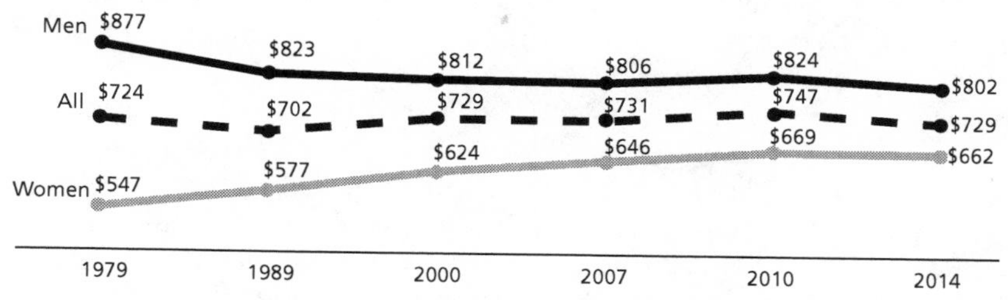

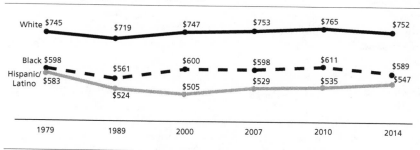

Source: Author's calculations based on Bureau of Labor Statistics; labor force statistics from the Current Population Survey.

Figure 11.2 Changes in Wage/Salary Workers' Median Weekly Earnings by Race, 1979–2014

Source: Author's calculations based on Bureau of Labor Statistics; weekly and hourly earnings data from the Current Population Survey, various years.

were 0.9 percent higher than they had been thirty-five years earlier) while black and Hispanic workers' earnings fell 1.5 percent and 6.2 percent, respectively.

The 1979–2013 period was also marked by significant changes in the shares of workers in different categories who were working for poverty-level wages (or less). (A full-time year-round worker in 2013 needed to earn $11.49 an hour to support a four-person family at the poverty level.) The percent of the total workforce earning poverty-level wages increased slightly, from 27.1 percent in 1979 to 27.5 percent in 2013 (EPI, 2014). This would have been much greater except for the sharp decrease in the share of women workers earning poverty-level wages, which fell from 42.1 percent to 31.5 percent. Note that even with this decline, nearly one in three women workers earned no more than poverty-level wages in 2013. Over this same period, the share of men who were poverty-level wage earners increased from fewer than one in six (15.7 percent) to nearly one in four (23.7 percent). The trends by race and ethnicity are all too familiar. The percent of white workers earning poverty-level wages declined slightly from 1979 to 2013 (from 25.1 percent to 22.5 percent). The share of black workers earning poverty-level wages declined slightly, from 37.5 percent to 35.7 percent, while the share of Hispanic workers with poverty-level wages increased, from 37.9 percent to 42.2 percent. Thus, in 2013, over one in three black workers and two of five Hispanic workers earned only poverty level wages.

Figure 11.3 shows the changes in workers' real wages at different wage percentiles from 1979 to 2013. As it reveals, while the wages of workers at the lowest percentile fell by 5.3 percent, the wages of workers at all other percentiles increased. Moreover, the higher the wage percentile, the greater the wage increase: the increases ranged from 0.9 percent for workers at the 30th percentile to 31.5 percent and 40.6 percent at the 90th and 95th percentile, respectively.

However, even as low-wage workers' wages fell significantly over the 1979 to 2013 period, their educational attainment levels increased. The percent of low-wage workers (those in the bottom fifth of wage earners) with a high school degree increased from 55 percent to 78 percent and the percent of those with a college education increased from 24 percent to 44 percent (Bivens et al., 2014, p. 42).

Income. Figure 11.4 shows the growth in the real after-tax income from 1979 to 2007 for different income quintiles. As can be seen, the top 1 percent of households saw their incomes leap by 278 percent, dwarfing the growth in the incomes of other groups: the incomes of the top 20 percent of households other than the top 1 percent grew by 65 percent, while the incomes of the fourth, middle, second, and lowest quintiles grew by only 43 percent, 35 percent, 28 percent, and 18 percent, respectively.

Figure 11.3 Changes in Real Wages of Workers at Selected Percentiles, 1979–2013

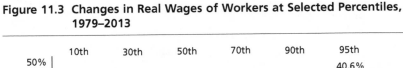
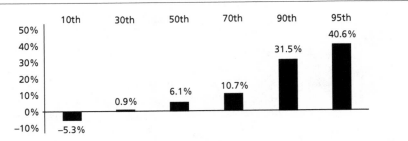

Source: Economic Policy Institute, 2014.

Figure 11.4 Growth in Real After-tax Income from 1979 to 2007 by Income Group

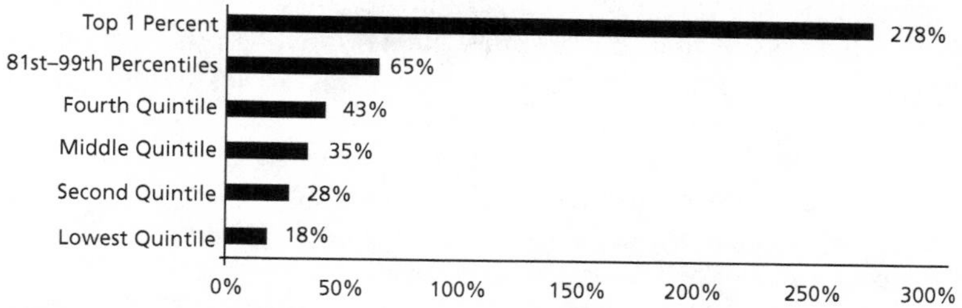

Top 1 Percent — 278%
81st–99th Percentiles — 65%
Fourth Quintile — 43%
Middle Quintile — 35%
Second Quintile — 28%
Lowest Quintile — 18%

0%   50%   100%   150%   200%   250%   300%

Source: Congressional Budget Office, 2011, Summary figure 1.

Figure 11.5 highlights another perspective on these trends; it shows the shares of total US income captured by different income quintiles and the top 1 percent in 1979 and 2007. The share captured by the top 1 percent more than doubled, from 10.5 percent to 21.3 percent. Put differently, the top 1 percent had more than one-fifth of all US income in 2007. At the same time, the shares of all other groups declined. The already meager share accruing to the lowest fifth fell from 2.9 percent to 2.5 percent.

The biggest losers were the middle three quintiles: the second quintile's share fell from 10.1 percent to 7.3 percent, the middle fifth's from 15.3 percent to 12.2 percent, and the fourth quintile's from 22.4 percent to 19.0 percent. The share of the top quintile minus the top 1 percent dipped from 39.1 percent to 38.6 percent.

Wealth

Wealth—what people own minus debts—can be a more important dimension of economic and social security and well-being than income. For most people,

Figure 11.5 Changes in Percentage Shares of Income by Quintile, 1979–2007

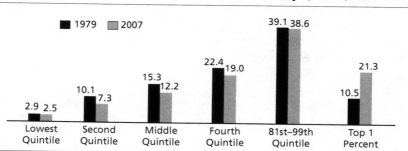

■ 1979   ▨ 2007

Lowest Quintile: 2.9 2.5
Second Quintile: 10.1 7.3
Middle Quintile: 15.3 12.2
Fourth Quintile: 22.4 19.0
81st–99th Quintile: 39.1 38.6
Top 1 Percent: 10.5 21.3

Source: Congressional Budget Office, 2011, Summary figure 2.

income is what they earn from working. The better off also receive income from their wealth holdings: dividends, interest, and any rents or royalties on properties they own. Wealth enables people to avoid economic disasters—including the loss of their homes and homelessness—in the face of crises precipitated by unemployment, catastrophic medical costs, disabling injuries, family breakup, or other calamities. It also enables families to pay for college without incurring huge debt, avoid penury in retirement, and enjoy comforts that might be unaffordable on their incomes alone.

There are two major categories of wealth: total net worth, which includes all marketable assets, such as the value of one's home, minus debts, including mortgages, credit cards, and so forth; and financial wealth, which is net worth minus net equity in owner-occupied housing. As will be clear from the figures and tables that follow, the value of their home comprises the overwhelming share of most Americans' wealth. Financial wealth is a much better indicator of families' economic security than net worth since few households can readily sell their homes to cushion financial losses without incurring further hardships and, of course, some may not be able to sell their home without incurring significant losses. Moreover, since it includes the value of stocks, bonds, and bank holdings, financial wealth provides an indicator of the control over investment capital, corporate entities, and so forth.

Wealth is even more inequitably distributed than income and, like income, has grown more unequal over the past three decades.[2] The share of net wealth (i.e., including the value of their homes) of the bottom 80 percent of households fell from 19 percent in 1983 to 15 percent in 2007, and then to 11 percent in 2010, in large part because of plummeting housing prices during the Great Recession. The share of the top 1 percent remained relatively stable: it was 34 percent in 1983 and 35 percent in 2010. The 81 percent to 99 percent wealth group captured the losses of the bottom 80 percent, as its share increased from 46 percent in 1984 to 54 percent in 2010.

Figure 11.6 highlights the growing concentration of financial wealth at the top, and the limited and declining financial wealth held by the bottom 80 percent. The share of the bottom 80 percent fell from 9 percent in 1983 to 5 percent in 2010; the share held by the top 1 percent remained roughly stable; and the share of the 81 percent to 99 percent group increased from 48 percent to 54 percent. Put differently, of every 100 people, the richest person owned 42 percent of all financial wealth in 2010; the next richest 19 people owned 54 percent; and the remaining 80 people held a meager 5 percent.

The mean net worth (including an owner-occupied home) and financial wealth of different percentiles highlight the massive inequities of different wealth classes. In 2010, the average net worth of the bottom 40 percent of households—some 23.3 million households with 61.6 million members—was negative $10,600 and their average financial wealth was negative $14,800.[3] The middle 40 percent of households, some 46.5 million with

Figure 11.6 Distribution of Total US Financial Wealth Among Wealthy Classes, 1983–2010

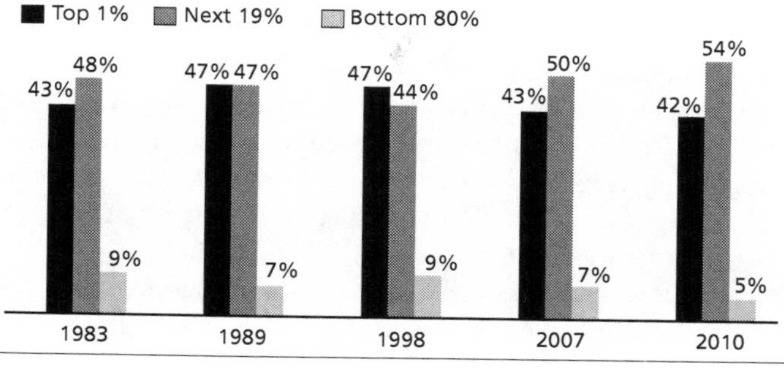

Legend: ■ Top 1% ■ Next 19% ▨ Bottom 80%

Bars by year:
- 1983: 43%, 48%, 9%
- 1989: 47%, 47%, 7%
- 1998: 47%, 44%, 9%
- 2007: 43%, 50%, 7%
- 2010: 42%, 54%, 5%

Source: Domhoff, 2015.

123.2 million members, had an average net worth of $61,000 and average financial wealth of $12,000, providing them little cushion in the event of an unexpected crisis. The fourth quintile and top 20 percent of households had an average net worth of $216,900 and $2,061,600 and financial wealth of $100,700 and $1,719,800, respectively. The top 1 percent—some 1.2 million households—had average net worth of $16,439,400 and financial wealth of $15,171,600.

White households' wealth holdings dwarf those of black and Latino households. While the median wealth holdings of all households fell from 2007 to 2010, the median wealth of black and Latino households was devastated. White households' median net worth fell by over a third (35.8 percent) from $151,000 to $97,000 while black households' net worth was nearly halved (−49.5 percent) from $9,700 to $4,900 and that of Latino households plummeted 86.5 percent, from $9,600 to $1,300. While white households saw their financial wealth fall by 39.7 percent, from $45,900 to $27,700, the median financial wealth of black households was nearly eliminated (falling from $6,000 to $1,000) and that of Latino households was wiped out (dropping from $4,000 to $0).

The Pew Charitable Trusts (2015) reports that, "the majority (55 percent) of American households . . . can replace less than one month of their income through liquid savings" while the typical low-income household "has the equivalent of less than two weeks' worth" of readily available liquid resources." Even by pooling all resources, including costly-to-access retirement accounts and investments, "the typical middle-income household can only replace about four months of lost income" (p. 1).

As these data highlight, because of their limited wealth, millions of households may face disaster, including losing their homes, in the event of unexpected events such as unemployment, disability, or catastrophic medical costs. Those who become homeless have likely lost all of their wealth and, once homeless, will have little opportunity to accumulate assets of any sort.

Poverty Estimates and Their Mismeasurement

The official measure of poverty has been criticized since its establishment in the early 1960s. The main line of criticism has concentrated on a range of methodological shortcomings.[4] However, far less attention has been focused on what is a more fundamental failing: the official poverty level and the Supplemental Poverty Measure developed to address the official measure's methodological shortcomings are capped at levels below which households are materially deprived, and both significantly understate the extent to which US families suffer economic insecurity and deprivation. Some of the many indicators that highlight these realities include the following. First, respondents to Gallup Poll surveys since the 1940s have consistently said that "the minimum amount of yearly income a family of four" needs "to get along" in their communities is significantly higher than the official poverty line. In the most recent survey, this amount was 2.5 times the poverty threshold (J. M. Jones, 2007). Second, the Economic Policy Institute recently calculated the income needed to afford a family "an adequate standard of living" for six different family types in 615 communities around the country. The median income to sustain this living standard was 2.7 times the official poverty level (E. Gould et al., 2013). Third, as Fremstad (2010) observes, research shows that most low-income Americans who "experience food insecurity . . . [and] . . . various other forms of economic hardship . . . have incomes that put them above the current official poverty line" (pp. 27–28, emphasis in original). Finally, many low- and moderate-income families often spend more than their incomes, which can be much higher than the poverty level, to meet their basic needs. For example, CNN Money (2015) recently reported that low-income Americans—those in the bottom 30 percent of the income scale—spend "182%, of their annual income mostly on basic needs like housing, food and transportation." To meet their needs, these families must "dip into savings, lean on family or go into debt." And an analysis by the Pew Charitable Trusts (2015) found that "just under half of families" report "household spending greater than or equal to their income" (p. 1).

Only with these realities in mind should readers consider the data in Table 11.2, which shows poverty trends based on the official poverty measure between 1979 and 2013. The official poverty rate was above 11.3 percent in all of the peak years of the economic cycles in this period and the financial crisis drove it to 15.1 percent before it declined somewhat thereafter. However, the number of persons in poverty increased steadily throughout these years, from 26.1 million in 1979 to 46.3 million at its highest in 2010 and then dropping slightly to 45.3 million in 2013. The table also shows that

Table 11.2 US Poverty Rate by Race and Ethnicity, 1979–2013

	1979	1989	2000	2007	2010	2013
All Races						
Rate (%)	11.7	12.8	11.3	12.5	15.1	14.5
Persons (in 000s)	26,072	31,528	31,581	37,276	46,343	45,318
White						
Rate (%)	8.1	8.3	7.7	8.2	9.9	9.6
Persons (in 000s)	14,419	15,599	14,735	16,032	19,251	18,796
Black						
Rate (%)	31	30.7	23.6	24.5	27.4	27.2
Persons (in 000s)	8,050	9,302	8,441	9,237	10,746	11,041
Hispanic (any race)						
Rate (%)	21.8	26.2	22.7	21.5	26.5	23.5
Persons (in 000s)	2,921	5,430	7,876	9,890	13,522	12,744

Note: U.S. Bureau of the Census, Current Population Survey, Annual Social and Economic Supplements.

blacks and Hispanics must endure far higher poverty rates than do whites. Black poverty rates were typically three times (or more) greater than whites, and Hispanic rates were nearly that much greater. That the differences in the poverty rates of blacks and Hispanics narrowed relative to whites in this period was due less to reductions in their rates (indeed, Hispanics' poverty rates were higher in 2013 than in 1979) than to the increases in the poverty rates for whites.

The Causes of Inequality and the Declining Economic Security of US Workers

At the broadest level, changes like the economic transformations and upheavals since the 1970s are endemic features of capitalism. However, these changes were neither inevitable nor natural. Instead, they were the results of the neoliberal policy regime that emerged from the economic and political conflicts over the past four decades. Key aspects of these policies include regulatory changes, globalization, changes in labor market institutions, and specific tax and spending policies.

Regulatory Changes

Regulatory changes implemented over the past four decades are typically termed "deregulation." But as Wade (2014) notes, this is "misleading" because "there is no such thing as a free or unregulated market. The crucial question . . . is regulation to benefit whom?" (p. 14). The regulatory changes since the 1970s—whether legal or de facto—have established new rules that have significantly benefited corporations and those at the top of the wealth and income scales.

Globalization

Globalization—the integration of international trade and labor and financial markets—accelerated since the 1970s. The trade agreements that regulate and organize these changes provide significant protections for investors and intellectual property and copyright protection, but include de minimis labor and environmental standards. It is widely recognized that the globalization of production processes has eliminated jobs and exerted downward pressure on the wages of workers in the United States and other higher-wage countries (Bivens, 2013; Bivens et al., 2014; ILO, 2015; IMF, 2014; Mishel et al., 2012; Mishel, Schmitt, and Shierholz, 2014; Scott, 2012, 2015; Stiglitz, 2012). Among recent examples of these impacts in the United States, Scott (2015) estimated that trade with China eliminated some 3.2 million US jobs in the twelve years after China joined the World Trade Organization (in 2001). Bivens (2013) estimated that "growing trade with less-developed countries lowered wages in 2011 by 5.5 percent—or by roughly $1,800—for a full-time, full-year worker earning the average wage for workers without a four-year college degree" (p. 218).

That some 100 million workers—about 70 percent of the workforce— lack a four-year degree starkly highlights the significance of these developments. Researchers also report that offshoring puts downward pressure on the wages of mid-level workers as well as higher-wage white-collar workers and may account for the slowdown in the wage growth of college-educated workers since the mid-1990s (Blinder and Krueger, 2009; Autor, Dorn, and Hanson, 2013; Mishel, Schmitt, and Shierholz, 2014). Researchers from the University of Edinburgh and the Federal Reserve Bank reported that offshoring is a "leading potential explanation" for the decline in the US labor share of US national income over the past twenty-five years (Elsby, Hobijn, and Sahin, 2013, p. 1).

Labor Market Institutions

Labor market institutions such as the value of the minimum wage, unionization rates and worker protections, and income supports significantly affect the well-being of all but the highest-paid workers, but they are especially important for lower-paid workers. Changes over the past four decades significantly diminished the protections that these institutions provided workers.

The real value of the minimum wage was $9.58 in 1968, nearly a third higher in real terms than the current level of $7.25. Since the minimum wage serves as a wage floor, this eroding value fueled wage reductions for lower-paid workers who are disproportionately women and people of color. This erosion hits those experiencing homelessness particularly hard. The National Employment Law Project and Economic Policy Institute (2015) estimated that increasing the minimum wage to $12 an hour (a 10 percent increase in real terms over its 1968 value) by 2020 would directly benefit more than one-fourth of all workers, half of the workers with annual family incomes less than $40,000, nearly one-third (32 percent) of women wage earners, 37 percent of black workers, and 40 percent of Hispanic workers. Were they fortunate enough to find employment, such an increase would substantially benefit those experiencing homelessness.

Deunionization

Deunionization has reduced the ability of workers to improve or defend their earning ability. "Union density"—the percent of the workforce in unions or otherwise covered by collective bargaining agreements—is a critically important measure of workers' bargaining power. The portion of the US workforce in unions has declined steadily since the mid-1950s, when about one-third of workers were union members. By 2013, only 11.2 percent of all workers (and 6.6 percent of private sector workers) were union members (Bureau of Labor Statistics, 2015).

Mishel, Schmitt, and Shierholz (2014) cited a range of research regarding the extent to which deunionization has fueled inequality in recent years, such as the overall growth of wage inequality between men and women as well as widening wage gaps between white- and blue-collar men and between high school- and college-educated men. Figure 11.7 provides another perspective on trends in deunionization and income inequality. At the same time that the union share of the workforce fell from 25.4 percent in 1979 to 11.2 percent in 2013, the share of income captured by the top 10 percent increased from 32.3 percent to 47.0 percent.

Figure 11.7 Changes in Union Membership and Top 10% Share of Income, 1979–2013

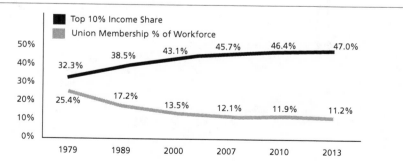

Tax and Spending Policies

Since the late 1970s, key income supports for workers and families have eroded while top income groups have enjoyed increased benefits from trends in tax and some spending policies. Figure 11.8 highlights one critical change; that is, the share of their incomes that the top 1 percent of households paid in federal taxes fell from 37.3 percent in 1979 to 29.5 percent in 2007.

Figure 11.9 highlights another perspective on the effects of policy changes since the late 1970s; it indicates the percentage shares of federal transfers going to different income quintiles in 1979 and 2007.[5] As those data show, the percentage share of federal transfers going to the bottom 20 percent of households fell dramatically over this period, from 54.2 percent to 36.1 percent, while percentage shares going to all other quintiles increased.

The 1996 Clinton-Gingrich welfare law is another measure that undercut the economic security of low-income families, eliminating the federal

Figure 11.8 Top 1% of Households' Percentage Share of Federal Taxes, 1979–2007

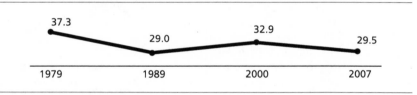

Source: Congressional Budget Office, 2011, figure 18.

Figure 11.9 Percentage Share of Federal Transfers by Income Group, 1979–2007

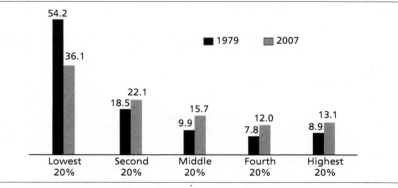

Source: Congressional Budget Office, 2011, figure 18.

entitlement to poor families provided through the Aid to Families with Dependent Children (AFDC) program established by the Social Security Act of 1935 and replacing it with the Temporary Assistance for Needy Families program. From 1996 to 2011, the maximum benefit for a family of three fell from 51.4 percent to 28.4 percent of the federal poverty line (author's calculations from HHS, 2013).[6] Further, Pavetti (2014) reported that in 1979 some 82 percent of poor families with children received AFDC benefits, but in 1996 only 68 percent of such families received TANF support and in 2013 only 26 percent did. In addition, from 1996 to 2011, the average monthly caseload of families receiving TANF benefits fell from 4.7 million in 1996 to 1.7 million in 2011.

Discussions about government subsidies and benefits provided to households seldom focus on "tax expenditures," which are "any reductions in income tax liabilities that result from special tax provisions or regulations that provide tax benefits to particular taxpayers" (Joint Committee on Taxation, 2014, p. 2). The Congressional Budget Office (CBO, 2013) notes that these "exclusions, deductions, preferential rates, and credits"[7] reduce tax revenues and also "resemble federal spending by providing financial assistance to specific activities, entities, or groups of people . . . [and] . . . like traditional forms of federal spending, contribute to the federal budget deficit; influence how people work, save, and invest; and affect the distribution of income" (p. 1).

Of course, most people use less technical terms to describe these provisions; they call them "tax breaks" or "tax loopholes." And as most laypeople suspect, the share of these benefits received by the richest taxpayers is far greater than the share of all other taxpayers. The top 1 percent of households received 17 percent of the value of the ten largest tax expenditures in 2013, leaving 83 percent to the bottom 99 percent. The top 10 percent garnered fully 39 percent of all tax expenditure benefits in 2013, leaving 61 percent for the bottom 90 percent of households. The distribution share going to the top classes would be significantly greater except for the earned income tax credit, for which eligibility was capped at about $48,000 for a family of four in 2013.

What do these tax breaks cost? As former Senate minority leader Everett Dirksen (R-IL) is reported to have observed in an oft-quoted comment, "a billion here, a billion there, soon you're talking real money." The CBO tagged the total costs of these tax breaks at $848 billion in 2013, of which $144.2 billion went to the top 1 percent and $330.7 billion to the top 10 percent. In describing the costs of direct spending programs, analysts often cite their costs over a ten-year period. Based on CBO data, over the 2014–2023 period, the tax expenditure benefits for the top 1 percent and top 10 percent will total $1.98 trillion and $4.54 trillion, respectively (author's calculations based on CBO, 2013, tables 1 and 2).[8]

Inequality in the United States and Other Rich Countries

The neoliberal policy regime has been implemented, to a greater or lesser degree, by all rich countries since the late 1970s or early 1980s. Although the extent of inequality and the severity of its consequences have varied, as Henwood (2014) observes the United States became "the affluent world's undisputed inequality champ" (p. 1). This reality is reflected in data for other rich countries (e.g., Canada, Western Europe, Japan, Korea, Australia). For example, only the United States fails to provide universal health insurance coverage (OECD, 2014c); the United States has significantly higher rates of overall poverty and child poverty (OECD, 2014a); and the United States has far greater income inequality on various measures such as the share held by the top 1 percent and the ratio of income received by those at the 90th percentile to the incomes of those at the 50th and 10th percentiles (OECD, 2014b).

While some may believe the types and magnitude of inequality profiled above are morally and ethically unacceptable; others may have a more hard-headed realistic perspective, accepting the premise articulated by many mainstream economists: inequality, though regrettable, is necessary to promote economic growth, innovation, work effort, and economic and social well-being. Developments since the late 1970s have demonstrated that these assumptions are wrong. This conclusion is supported by a broad body of research, including that by preeminent mainstream organizations such as the International Monetary Fund (IMF) and the OECD. For example, a staff report of the IMF notes that "there is growing evidence that high income inequality can be detrimental to achieving macroeconomic stability and growth" (IMF, 2014, p. 4). Another IMF staff analysis concludes that "lower net inequality is robustly correlated with faster and more durable growth, for a given level of redistribution," and that "the combined direct and indirect effects of redistribution—including the growth effects of the resulting lower inequality—are on average pro-growth" (Ostry, Berg, and Tsangarides, 2014, p. 4).

A recent OECD analysis found that "income inequality has a negative and statistically significant impact on subsequent growth" (Cingano, 2014, p. 16). The analysis calculated the impact that the increases in inequality from 1985 to 2005 had on countries' economic growth rates from 1990 to 2010. It concludes that the US "growth rate would have been more than one-fifth higher had income disparities not widened" (Cingano, 2014, p. 18).

Research has also clearly demonstrated that inequality is associated with significantly elevated rates of a wide range of health and social ills (Stiglitz, 2012; Wilkinson and Pickett, 2009; Cingano, 2014). Wilkinson and Pickett's (2009) analysis and summary of a wide range of research show that inequality is strongly and directly correlated with a large range of indicators of health and social well-being (or the lack thereof). They marshaled data from the latest research on key indicators in rich countries and in the fifty states and the District of Columbia. Their findings were striking. Wilkinson and Pickett conclude that levels of "social problems have little or no relation to the average incomes in a society" (p. 11); rather, they directly correlate with levels of income inequality within a country or state. Both among rich countries and among states in the United States, as rates of income inequality increase, so too do the levels of a range of social problems, including: life expectancy, infant mortality, mental illness, obesity, teenage births, homicide, incarceration, use of illegal drugs, lower literacy achievement, lower math scores among young people, and high school dropout rates. Countries' scores on the UN Children's Fund (UNICEF) index of child well-being (which is comprised of forty different indicators) are directly correlated with inequality: the greater the inequality, the lower the index score, and vice versa. Wilkinson and Pickett (2009) also found that "women's status is significantly worse in more unequal states [in the United States], although this is not a particularly strong relationship" (p. 59). Internationally, women's status was also linked with levels of inequality.

Social mobility—or the lack thereof—is likewise directly correlated with inequality: countries with less inequality have greater social mobility. Historical trends in the United States provide an additional perspective on this. After World War II, rates of social mobility—measured as the percentage of sons' incomes explained by their fathers' income—consistently increased until 1980. After that, however, social mobility markedly declined. Over the next two decades, the percentage of sons' income explained by their fathers' income more than tripled, increasing from about 10 percent in 1970 to 33 percent in 2000.

As the inequality leader among rich countries, it is unfortunate but unsurprising that the United States had the lowest scores on nearly every measure of health and social well-being analyzed by Wilkinson and Pickett (2009). It is also not surprising that the negative consequences of inequality cited above are endemic among the poorest of the very poor, those experiencing homelessness.

Policies to Improve the Economic Security of Workers

Policies that would meaningfully improve the economic security and well-being of the great majority of US families are hardly mysterious. Indeed, key measures are the opposite of the neoliberal policy regime that has held sway since the late 1970s. These policies include increasing the minimum wage, enforcing and strengthening laws to protect workers' collective bargaining rights, increasing the income and social supports for lower-income and unemployed workers and their families, and enforcing laws prohibiting race and gender discrimination. Complementary policies would include raising taxes on the wealthiest households, not engaging in trade pacts that foster offshoring to areas without comparable worker and environmental standards, and not bailing out too-big-to-fail institutions. Public investment to improve the nation's crumbling infrastructure—roads, bridges, water systems—as well as in research and development, efficient public transportation, renewable energy, education, and broadband would yield significant long-term economic benefits while creating millions of jobs. Other measures are long overdue such as policies that are taken for granted by families in most other rich countries: access to quality, affordable health care, more paid sick leave, paid family leave, and childcare.

Merely highlighting the need for and benefits of the types of policies profiled in the previous paragraph is currently beyond the pale of acceptable realistic political discourse. In the present political environment, these policies are unacceptable because they would primarily benefit the "wrong" people—the great majority of US workers and families. Multiple factors, especially the campaign finance system, make these policies unacceptable. For example, in the 2014 electoral cycle, the top 1 percent of donors accounted for 29 percent of disclosed contributions to federal campaigns, some $1.8 billion (Olsen-Phillips et al., 2015). Unsurprisingly, recent research has demonstrated that legislators' real constituents are not most voters (Gilens, 2005, 2012; Barber, 2014; Gilens and Page, 2014). As Gilens (2005, p. 778) reports, "actual policy outcomes strongly reflect the preferences of the most affluent, but bear virtually no relationship to the preferences of poor or middle income Americans."

One can and should criticize the ethical and moral impact that current policy has on most US families, especially those who are homeless. At the present time, in political and economic conflicts, ethics and morality can seem almost irrelevant.[9] To end homelessness and increase US households' economic well-being, more just and effective public policies must become imperatives, not choices. This requires us to struggle to alter the political terrain and discourse so that legislators will understand the need for these changes and enact them.

Notes

1. The literature on these developments is vast. Useful introductions are found in Harvey (2005), Glyn (2006), and Gindin and Panitch (2013).

2. Cogent and informative discussions of wealth are provided in Domhoff (2015) and Wolff (2010). Unless noted otherwise, the data in the following three paragraphs are from Domhoff (2015).

3. The population estimates in this paragraph are the author's calculations based on data in US Census Bureau (2014), table S1101, "Households and Families."

4. Among other shortcomings, the official measure does not reflect (1) households' actual expenses on the goods in their consumption baskets; (2) households' available resources (e.g., in-kind benefits from programs such as Medicare and Medicaid; Supplemental Nutrition Assistance Program, formerly known as the food stamp

program; housing assistance) and their expenses (e.g., out-of-pocket medical expenses, childcare, taxes), and regional variations in housing costs (G. M. Fisher, 1992; Citro and Michaels, 1995; Blank and Greenberg, 2008; Fremstad, 2010; E. Gould et al., 2013; Short, 2014).

5. Transfers include cash transfer payments—such as social security, unemployment insurance, and welfare benefits—along with estimates of the value of in-kind benefits—from programs such as Medicare, Medicaid, the Children's Health Insurance Program (CHIP), and the Supplemental Nutrition Assistance Program.

6. These are the median maximum benefits provided by the fifty states and the District of Columbia.

7. Income exclusions include employer-sponsored health care, pension contributions (e.g., 401(k) accounts), capital gains transferred at death, and a portion of social security benefits. Major deductions are for home mortgage interest, property taxes, and charitable contributions. Tax credits are the child tax credit and the earned income tax credit. The preferential treatment of capital gains consists of a maximum 20 percent tax rate on capital gains income. (The marginal tax rate for married couples filing jointly with an annual wage of $17,850 was 15 percent in 2013.)

8. Estimates assume that top 1 percent and top 10 percent shares of tax expenditures over the 2014–2023 period will be the same as in 2013.

9. Some, of course, believe alternative policies are themselves immoral. For example, in a letter to the editor of the Wall Street Journal, billionaire investor Tom Perkins likened public criticism of the "one percent" to Nazi attacks on the Jews (Perkins, quoted in Krugman, 2014).

12

Rights, Responsibilities, and Homelessness

Collin Jaquet Whelley and Kate Whelley McCabe

Over the past three decades, the rights of persons experiencing homelessness, and society's responsibility to care for them, have changed according to several metrics. During this time, the responsibility of implementing homeless policy has devolved from the federal government to states, municipal governments, local communities, and individuals. Today, a patchwork of nonprofits, religious groups, and municipal agencies, partially funded by unstable charity, form the ground floor of homeless policy. At the same time, the legal rights of persons experiencing homelessness have eroded. While often adverse to these municipal policies, federal and state law has, with few exceptions, remained stagnant. Through it all, however, the moral case for taking responsibility for persons experiencing homelessness has remained consistently dynamic. In this chapter, we examine the devolution of responsibility for homelessness, contrast it with the evolution of the rights and responsibilities of persons experiencing homelessness, and explore the conceptual underpinnings that inform those fluctuations.

Rights and Responsibilities Under the Law

The legal rights of persons experiencing homelessness have eroded at the municipal level through the enactment of laws criminalizing the behaviors associated with life without shelter. Although they are in tension with the new laws, federal and state law has not evolved to the same degree. Thus, the net effect has been that the homeless are experiencing a loss of rights. While it is possible that advocacy in our courthouses and statehouses can reverse this trend, given the barriers to doing so, it should not be assumed that any progress will take place.

There are two relatively simple starting points for outlining the legal rights of the homeless and concomitant responsibilities of the housed: federal constitutional law and state homeless bills of rights. Federal constitutional provisions and civil rights statutes are primary legal tools used by, and on behalf of, the homeless to combat the antihomeless laws that have become so prominent in the past few decades (NLCHP, 2014). So-called homeless bills of rights—few in number, but also currently on the rise—may become an independent source of rights for people experiencing homelessness (Rankin, 2015). There are significant barriers to vindicating the constitutional rights of the homeless. Nevertheless, persons experiencing homelessness enjoy the following rights under the US Constitution.[1]

The First Amendment

The First Amendment may exempt persons experiencing homelessness from antiloitering, antibegging, and anti–food sharing laws. Begging is constitutionally protected speech, and laws that prohibit begging, or loitering for the purpose of begging, may violate the First Amendment's Free Speech Clause if they target the content of the speech itself or fail to leave open adequate alternative channels for the speech (NLCHP, 2014). The free speech guarantee may also benefit the homeless by entitling philanthropists to express their religious beliefs by sharing food with them in public places (NLCHP, 2014).

The Fourth Amendment

The Fourth Amendment right to be free from unreasonable searches and seizures may entitle people experiencing homelessness to be free from the confiscation and destruction of personal property stored in public spaces. A city must follow constitutionally adequate procedures when confiscating and disposing of the personal property of persons experiencing homelessness. Failure to do so—for example, by not providing adequate notice to the homeless community before commencing a sweep—may constitute an unconstitutional seizure under the Fourth Amendment (*Lehr v. Sacramento,* 2009; *Pottinger v. City of Miami,* 1992; *Kincaid v. Fresno,* 2006; *Justin v. City of Los Angeles,* 2000).

The Eighth Amendment

The Eighth Amendment's prohibition of cruel and unusual punishment may entitle persons experiencing homelessness to be free from antisleeping, antisitting, or anticamping laws. "Because many municipalities do not have adequate shelter space, homeless persons are often left with no alternative but to sleep and live in public spaces" (NLCHP, 2011, p. 19). When cities impose criminal penalties for sustaining life in public where there is a lack of shelter, cities may run afoul of the Cruel and Unusual Punishment Clause of the Eighth Amendment (NLCHP, 2014).

The Fourteenth Amendment

The Fourteenth Amendment's Due Process Clause may entitle individuals experiencing homelessness to be free from laws prohibiting them from living in cars and those that prohibit loitering. At least one court has ruled that a city's ordinance prohibiting persons from living in cars was unconstitutionally vague under the Due Process Clause (*Desertrain v. City of Los Angeles,* 2014). Moreover, the US Supreme Court has held more than once that antiloitering ordinances that did not give clear notice of what conduct was prohibited or allowed for arbitrary enforcement were unconstitutionally vague (*Chicago v. Morales,* 1999; *Papachristou v. City of Jacksonville,* 1972). According to the National Law Center on Homelessness and Poverty, "Many loitering ordinances use similarly broad and vague language and could [therefore] be challenged as violating the Due Process Clause of the Fourteenth Amendment" (NLCHP, 2011, p. 20).

The Fourteenth Amendment right to travel may entitle those experiencing homelessness to be free of anticamping and antisleeping laws. Laws that deny access to a necessity of life in a certain locality violate the right to travel by unconstitutionally discouraging ingress into that place (*Memorial Hosp. v. Maricopa County,* 1972). According to the NLCHP, "Advocates have contended that arresting people for sleeping outside violates the fundamental right to travel by denying access to a necessity of life, i.e., a place to sleep" (2011, p. 20). At least one court has agreed that laws criminalizing sleeping in public unconstitutionally restrain the movement of persons who are homeless within and to a locale (*Pottinger v. City of Miami,* 1996).

In addition to federal constitutional law, the rights of people experiencing homelessness and the responsibilities of the housed are articulated in the Homeless Bills of Rights enacted in Puerto Rico, Rhode Island, Illinois, and Connecticut (Rankin, 2015). Unlike federal constitutional rights, state statutory rights are effective only within the state or territory. Nevertheless, especially to the extent the recent enactment of these laws may be emulated by other jurisdictions, they are worth examining.

Puerto Rico's Homeless Bill of Rights

In addition to establishing an administrative body and processes to achieve the stated purpose of "eradicating homelessness" (Act to Create the Multi-Sector Homeless Population Support Counsel, 2007), Puerto Rico's act declares that individuals who are homeless have certain positive rights. In particular, the act declares that homeless persons have a right to shelter, nourishment, medical care, access to public services, assistance in entering the workforce, protection by law enforcement, free legal advice, a free postal address, access to support groups and counseling, and access to public spaces such as "town squares, parks and . . . other public facilities" (Act to Create the Multi-Sector Homeless Population Support Counsel, 2007, p. 5). Further, the act appropriates $250,000 annually for the completion of its stated purposes (Act to Create the Multi-Sector Homeless Population Support Counsel, 2007, p. 10). However, for reasons only understood by those who enacted it, Puerto Rico's act was not drafted so as to be enforceable in a court of law; for this and other reasons, the act is vulnerable to criticism on the grounds that it is more visionary than helpful (Rankin, 2015).

Homeless Bills of Rights in Rhode Island, Illinois, and Connecticut

Rhode Island and Illinois have recently enacted laws for the stated purpose of "ameliorat[ing] the adverse effects visited upon individuals and communities when the state's residents lack a home" (Homeless Bill of Rights, 2012, p. 2; Bill of Rights for the Homeless Act, 2013, p. 5). The laws, which are nearly identical, prohibit the government from denying a person their rights, their privileges, or access to public services solely because that person is homeless (Homeless Bill of Rights, 2012; Bill of Rights for the Homeless Act, 2013). In particular, the acts guarantee persons who are homeless an equal right to use and move freely in public spaces, the right to be treated equally by all state and municipal agencies, the right not to face discrimination while seeking or maintaining employment, the right to emergency medical care free from discrimination, the right to vote, the right to register to vote, the right to receive documentation necessary for voting free from discrimination, an equal right to privacy in records, and an equal right to privacy in personal property. Notably, both acts provide for enforcement in court, and enable judges to award prevailing plaintiffs with costs and reasonable attorneys' fees.

Connecticut's law contains a similar articulation of purpose and recitation of negative rights, but omits any reference to enforcement or attorneys' fees (An Act Concerning a Homeless Person's Bill of Rights, 2013). While Connecticut's law is certainly vulnerable to attack based on its lack of meaningful enforceability, all three can be critiqued on the grounds that they merely articulate rights that homeless persons held in common with housed persons prior to enactment (Rankin, 2015) and thus, like the Puerto Rico Act, are only symbolic.

What do these federal constitutional and state statutory rights mean to the lives of persons experiencing homelessness? Legal rights may or may not be enforceable in a court of law (Rankin, 2015). While many federal constitutional rights, including those explored above, are enforceable through federal civil rights statutes. as discussed above at least some of the homeless bills of rights that already exist are not. It is tautological, moreover, that not even enforceable rights are self-executing (Cross, 2001). This means that to guarantee that any right makes a difference in the life of any individual person, even an enforceable right must be formally invoked through a lawsuit;

in other words, even enforceable rights must be enforced. Unfortunately, enforcement by litigation is expensive, difficult, and often futile, especially for homeless persons and their advocates (Rankin, 2015). Yet without enforcement, the rights outlined above cannot make a meaningful, concrete, and timely impact on peoples' lives.

At least some legal scholars believe, however, that there is more to rights than their enforcement value. In the context of homeless bills of rights, for example, Rankin (2015) concludes that the laws "are more likely to have an incremental social and normative impact than an immediate legal impact," and that "even so, these new laws are an important step toward a long-overdue rights revolution for [the homeless]" (p. 4). This is because, Rankin (2015) argues, "judicial enforcement is not the only relevant venue for realizing rights; other government agencies and social settings negotiate rights and contribute to their definition" (p. 44). Rankin (2015) claims that

> this perspective liberates rights from the confines of the judiciary, recogniz-
> ing that rights are "claimed and negotiated in a wide variety of settings, in-
> cluding courts but also legislatures, agencies, the workplace, the media, pub-
> lic squares and private interactions, and how these various forms of activism
> influence one another in complex ways." (Rankin, 2015, p. 44; quoting
> Southworth, 2000, pg. 14)

Even if Rankin is correct, liberating rights to extrajudicial settings does not mean that, to be enjoyed, even through the indirect means of incremental social and normative change, they do not still need to be claimed in these forums. Legislatures and agencies must be lobbied; conversations must be started and pursued in workplaces as well as in the media and in other public and private spaces. In other words, realization of rights in Rankin's sense still requires advocacy. Are we exercising that agency? Are we starting these conversations, authoring these media pieces, and lobbying our elected officials on issues important to homeless persons? Are we engaging in this advocacy? Absent a positive answer to these questions, all we have are unenforced rights and responsibilities, invisible to their holders.

Political Priorities According to Antihomeless Laws

Over the past thirty years, an increasing number of cities and towns have responded to their growing responsibility to address the rise of homelessness by passing ordinances that criminalize the behavior of individuals living in public spaces, otherwise known as "antihomeless laws" (NLCHP, 2011; Mitchell, 1997). While antihomeless laws are not the only municipal response to homelessness, they reveal how the public understands it and prioritizes and distributes rights and responsibilities. Through antihomeless laws, the public puts boundaries around its responsibility for the homeless and prioritizes assuaging its fear of poverty and desire for cultural regulation above individuals' needs to engage in activities necessary for survival.[2]

Cities that pass antihomeless ordinances commonly implement a slate of similar and, at times, overlapping laws (Beckett and Herbert, 2008).[3] While antihomeless laws technically only criminalize unwanted behavior or restrict the space within which unwanted behavior may take place, in practice the laws criminalize homelessness. T. Wright (1997), Mitchell (1997), Gowan (2010), and others agree that the message to those experiencing homelessness is clear: "Get out, you are not welcome, and you have no right to be here." Most importantly, scholars argue that this is how those experiencing homelessness understand this message (Gowan, 2010; Robinson, 2013; T. Wright, 1997). Municipalities employ antihomeless laws as a response to attitudes held by the public, including that: (1) homelessness is a threat; (2) it is bad for business; and (3) the community must hold its own amidst shifts in race and class.

The Homeless Threat

Some believe that homelessness threatens society. In their broken windows theory, J. Q. Wilson and Kelling (1982) insist that there is a causal relationship between the visibility of disorder, a lack of attention to small-scale disorderly behaviors, the deterioration of community intervention and outlook, and rising crime (Hinkle, 2014). According to this theory, the existence of small-scale disorder creates an environment in which disorder becomes more widespread, possibly leading to violence and culminating in the destruction of the community. The theory equates visible homelessness with the disorder that provokes serious crime. Indeed, J. Q. Wilson and Kelling (1982) argue that the "unchecked panhandler is, in effect, the first broken window" (p. 4).

This fear of the homeless threat—in which visible homelessness is a harbinger of a city descending into chaos—emerges in discourse that supports antihomeless laws. It has been championed by city mayors, like New York's Rudolf Giuliani, and political scholars, like Fred Siegel. Moreover, citizens of cities such as Denver and San Francisco have openly expressed a physical fear of those experiencing homelessness (Corman and Mocan, 2005; Gowan, 2010; Whelley, 2013). In short, homelessness has been equated with criminality, degeneracy, and danger (T. Wright, 1997; Amster, 2003; Siegel, 1997; Gowan, 2010).

The connection between homelessness and danger is significantly perceptual. Results of studies evaluating the implementation of broken windows theory are mixed (Corman and Mocan, 2005; Hinkle, 2014). Fear of the homeless and the perception of a homeless threat are unfounded; violent and sexual victimization of those experiencing homelessness is much more prevalent than that of the general public (Huey, 2012; Bender et al., 2014).

While incarceration rates are higher among those living on the streets, the crimes that persons experiencing homelessness commit are most often nonviolent, drug related, or associated with survival behaviors (Link, Schwartz, et al., 1995; Donley and Wright, 2008).

When cities pass antihomeless laws out of a fear of the threat of homelessness, the right of the public to address an unfounded feeling is placed above the right of an individual to exist in public without housing in the face of shelter and affordable housing shortages. For example, if a city criminalizes the ability of those experiencing homelessness to cover themselves with anything besides clothing while not providing shelter for all who live on the street (as is the case in Denver), the right of the public not to see people using blankets, cardboard, tents, or tarps in public is placed above the right for someone without housing to protect themselves from the elements (Whelley, 2013).

Bad for Business

Fear of the homeless and of crime is not enough to explain the recent resurgence of antihomeless laws. Donley and Wright (2008), Link, Schwartz, et al. (1995), and others have indicated that large portions of the public do not feel threatened by the homeless, but rather empathize with their struggles for survival. Passage of antihomeless laws can also be explained by a neoliberal economic viewpoint, which sees people experiencing homelessness as being bad for business and uses that as justification to restrict their movements in public space.

The global embrace of the neoliberal economic model,[4] popularized by Milton Friedman and others in the 1980s, is the primary suspect for the growing prevalence of antihomeless laws. Neoliberal economic political goals include opening markets to global competition, removing regulations and other market interventions, privatizing public assets, reducing taxes, and dismantling, limiting, and devolving welfare and redistributive systems (Harvey, 2005; Friedman, 1980; Mitchell, 2003).[5] As cities focus on economic growth strategies that attract capital and depart from the Keynesian policies of the past, they must develop marketing strategies that support this goal (Beckett and Herbert, 2008; Mitchell, 1997, 2011).

Similarly, Križnik (2011) observes that contemporary cities are primarily focused on the global competition for capital and, as a result, must resort to marketing strategies that are primarily focused on attracting wealth. The recreation of spaces, used as marketing tools, involves restructuring the meaning and purpose of space. These marketing strategies have been expanded to the legal regulation of space, including the growth in antihomeless laws. Beckett and Herbert (2008) observe that, "from a political-economic perspective, the intensifications of urban social control measures [antihomeless] stems from the ascendance of neoliberal global capitalism and the related transformation of urban economies" (p. 16).

Scholars like N. Smith (1996, pp. 207–222) and Mitchell (2003, pp. 190–191) interpret the rise of antihomeless laws as an explicit example of revanchist policy. *Revanchism* refers to policies that simultaneously support neoliberal growth and consolidate control over the economy and its profits with the wealthy elite (N. Smith, 1996, pp. 42–45, 207, 214). To Mitchell (2003) and Smith (1996), revanchism is less about fear of disorder and crime and more about perceived economic threats. N. Smith (1996) defines "revanchist policies" as vengeful policies implemented and supported by the wealthy to regain economic control of space taken from them by the cultural and political shifts of the 1960s and 1970s, and to make large profits from controlling the reshaping of urban space. Taking back city space from the unrest and policies of the mid–twentieth century therefore is not only a cultural strategy, but can be a profitable strategy as rent gaps are found and exploited through the upward development of once-degraded spaces, previously inhabited by low-income and homeless residents.

Revanchism remains a contentious theory, but the reality that cities are neoliberalizing is widely accepted.[6] The neoliberal economic perspective adds to the homeless threat perspective by combining fear of safety and fear of economic catastrophe. Link, Schwartz, et al. (1995) found that "most people believe" that the presence of persons experiencing homelessness "makes neighborhoods worse, spoils parks for families and children, and threatens the quality of urban life" (p. 553). This evidence supports the idea that the focus of a city's response is the effect of those experiencing homelessness on the public rather than the oppression and discrimination of those experiencing homelessness. Therefore, the private pursuit of wealth is placed above the right of those living in public spaces to engage in survival behaviors.[7]

Culture Shift and Moral Panic

The rise in antihomeless laws may also be attributable to the moral panic brought about by cultural changes in the community. This theory is unique because it does not expressly link attitudes about homelessness with the passage of antihomeless laws, and because it seldom explicitly appears in public discourse about such laws. Essentially, the theory posits that affluent persons experience moral panic when races and classes mix and thus champion policies that avoid race and class diversity or, in other words, engage in cultural revanchism. This policy prioritization confirms what we already know: caring for the homeless is one of the least profitable industries. Unfortunately, our attempts to delegate responsibility to the business community for addressing homelessness do not change this fact.

Racism compounds antihomeless sentiments. T. Wright (1997) argues that the presence of nonwhite populations created the perception of disorder in a community. Donley and Wright (2008), applying a similar theory to homeless populations, argue that perceptions of fear are more prevalent when a higher proportion of those experiencing homelessness are minorities. Lee, Tyler, and Wright (2010) cite two studies indicating that "whites, males, and political conservatives are more likely to believe in individual causes [of homelessness], hold negative opinions, and endorse restrictive measures to address the problem" (p. 13).

The fear of diversity affects public spending as well. Hopkins (2011) found a connection between race and criminal justice spending. While no association exists between diversity and social welfare spending, according to Hopkins substantial evidence indicates that as a city becomes more diverse, it spends proportionally more money on criminal justice. Ferrell (2001) and Sennett (1970) bring the concepts of class and creative space to the discussion. They documented how new residents of renovated spaces, who move to gentrified locations to find authentic and cultural urban experiences, immediately seek to cleanse the building and its surroundings of the preexisting culture—namely, the street culture. New residents inevitably support development projects that rehabilitate the blighted areas surrounding them and fill the abandoned public spaces with new private cultural spaces. The new spaces, once home to the homeless and runaway youth, are cleansed of street culture. These observations compliment Sennett's (1970) hypothesis that urban culture is turning away from a respect for the cultural creativity born in disorderly urban public spaces and toward the pursuit of unattainable purity and structure fueled by a puerile fear of disorder, change, and otherness—in other words, fear of the city itself.[8]

Wyly and Hammel (2005) and Mitchell (1997) conclude that this gentrification was a key aspect in explaining antihomeless laws. Wyly and Hammel (2005) found that "gentrification is generally correlated with one strand, explicit anti-homeless laws, but most of the variation among cities [of severity and type of law] comes from the broader urban context in which reinvestment and revanchism have emerged" (pp. 11–12). Some of the variables playing out in a broader urban context are racial and class segregation, or integration, and inequality (Wyly and Hammel, 2005). While the homeless threat and neoliberal explanations hold a degree of truth, some quantitative evidence points toward the cultural shift hypothesis. When comparing the number of antihomeless laws across US cities, cities with growing Democratic Party political strength are becoming more diverse and are integrating racially tend to have more antihomeless laws (Whelley, 2014). Rather than saying all change causes moral panic, however, it seems that cultural changes actively instigate antihomeless laws and thus moral panic (Whelley, 2014; Ferrell, 2001; Sennett, 1970; Pruijt, 2013; Johnsen and Fitzpatrick, 2010; Van Eijk, 2010). Moreover, these same quantitative results support T. Wright's (1997) assertion that the perception of disorder grows in the presence of diversity and poverty. Cities with the most integrated communities and highest nonwhite populations (i.e., the highest experiences of diversity) tend, predictably, to have more antihomeless laws (Whelley, 2014).

A society's reaction to the moral panic caused by cultural shifts is sometimes called "cultural revanchism," a politics of revenge on the lower classes by the upper classes. The lower classes include the homeless, but also include other populations that don't fit into a traditional picture of a revanchist's vision of a healthy city. This strategy includes the effective regulation of class and race by law to avoid or assuage moral panic (Prujt, 2012; Johnsen and Fitzpatrick, 2010; Van Eijk, 2010). If cultural regulation is the driving force behind antihomeless laws, then the public right to address moral panic and regulate cultural environments becomes the right that the public seeks to uphold and, in doing so, pushes the rights of the individual to engage in survival behaviors to the periphery.

While there are other possible reasons why cities are passing antihomeless laws, these three explanations dominate the literature and public debate. Together, they provide a sinister commentary on the origin of laws affecting those experiencing homelessness: the reason why cities criminalize homelessness is not to help the homeless, but to hide them. Whatever the reason(s), antihomeless laws elevate the public's desire not to encounter those experiencing homelessness above the needs of those who are homeless to engage in survival behaviors.

Rights, Responsibilities, and Deservedness

Conceptual frameworks of homelessness inform public priorities by defining who is to be deserving of help. How we think and talk about segments of our population influences the rights we extend and responsibilities we collectively embrace.[9] According to Mitchell (2011),

> a traditional division between "deserving poor" (women, children, and those who behaved themselves in ways dominant society deemed sufficiently grateful to charity) and "undeserving poor" (men of working age, those who lived on the streets or in encampments and refused to enter shelters or rehabilitation programs). (p. 934)

has been reestablished in the United States.[10]

The deservedness concept is embedded in the United States welfare systems, which are means tested, meaning that they limit the recipients of assistance by requiring a demonstration of need (Adolino and Blake, 2010). The division between eligible and noneligible is in itself a separation of deserving from undeserving.

The individualized nature of current federal homeless policy reinforces the institutionalization of means testing social services. Cronley (2010) observes that federal policy "interpreted homelessness according to the individual perspective and thus provided short-term emergency relief and social programs that address individual level problems" (p. 323). Unfortunately, by targeting pockets of need for relatively short periods of time, funding streams are divided into subcategories of deservedness. Government and local funding arrive in the form of program and agency silos that work with specific subpopulations rather than a broadly defined homeless population. Therefore, agencies must prioritize and focus on subpopulations rather than addressing need comprehensively in a community.

One's conception of the degree to which an individual experiencing homelessness deserves assistance is also influenced by one's perspective as to the causes of homelessness. Conceptual divisions with regard to the causes of homelessness involve a conversation concerning individual choice or the lack thereof. Gowan (2010) derived three conceptions of choice from individuals living on the streets of San Francisco: "sin-talk," "sick-talk," and "system-talk." These apt terms clarify the three dominant frameworks for understanding the causes of homelessness: the independent agency perspective, the individualized medical (medicalized) perspective, and the structural perspective.

Sin-talk is shorthand for the individualized agency perspective, which holds that those experiencing homelessness are homeless because they are deficient, deviant, and make bad choices. The sin is the behavior deserving of blame such as drug use, attitude, or laziness (Gowan, 2010). This perspective supports the idea that people are homeless by choice, that their choice is illegitimate and criminal, and therefore those experiencing homelessness are undeserving of help (Lyon-Callo, 2000; T. Wright, 1997; Amster, 2003; Mitchell, 2011; Gowan, 2010). Once the individuals are deemed undeserving, an evaporation of public responsibility occurs, the right for those experiencing homelessness to occupy public space disappears, and the responsibility to address homelessness is placed entirely on the shoulders of those experiencing it.

Sick-talk refers to an individualized and medicalized perspective that complicates the assumption as to the degree to which people have complete control over their fall into homelessness. While not necessarily blaming the character of the individual, the focus of blame remains on the deficient nature of that individual. In other words, medicalized perspectives blame homelessness on an individual's pathology or pathologies (Gowan, 2010).

Support for the individualized and medicalized perspective abounds. Mental illness, substance abuse, and trauma are vital to the construction of an accurate understanding of persons experiencing homelessness. People are afflicted with illnesses and traumatic experiences without regard to choice. Adverse childhood events or traumatic experiences continue to be a predictor of adult functioning (Larken and Park, 2012). Counts of adverse childhood events continue to be connected with homelessness, physical health, mental illness, learning disabilities, and possibly substance abuse (Cutuli et al., 2015). The co-occurrence of substance abuse with other forms of disability is well documented, yet even without co-occurrence, research indicates that addiction diminishes one's capacity to make independent choices (Parsell and Parsell, 2012). Under the individualized and medical perspective, the population of deserving poor expands—from none to some—and by doing so, increases the public's responsibility to act.[11]

System-talk is shorthand for the concept that homelessness is structural. According to Neale (1997), "A structural explanation of homelessness locates the reasons for homelessness beyond the individual, in wider social and economic factors" (p. 49). A structural approach holds that the structure of society is responsible for the production of homelessness through such mechanisms as a poorly functioning economy, inadequate affordable housing stock, and soaring medical expenses that drive people into bankruptcy. Structural producers of homelessness include economic inequality and the rise of rents and housing costs, have been well-researched, and cannot be discarded (O'Flaherty, 1996; Ellen and O'Flaherty, 2010; Quigley, Raphael, and Smolensky, 2001). Wasserman and Clair (2010) posit that "a significant number of people are disenfranchised by macro level forces. They therefore are not completely responsible for their condition or at least it seems that society significantly shares in that responsibility" (p. 165).

Under this structural perspective, because society is responsible for creating the environment causing people to be homeless, it therefore is society's obligation to change the environment in such a way as to allow people who are homeless to improve their living conditions and become self-sustaining. This perspective effectively makes all citizens in poverty deserving of help. And because the homeless are largely not to blame for their situation, the behaviors that they must partake in on a day-to-day basis are unavoidable behaviors of survival. Any attempt to criminalize their survival behaviors is effectively criminalizing a person who has no other choice but to be homeless (Mitchell, 1998).

Structure Plus

In reality, individual free will, myriad pathologies, and systemic factors intersect and combine to explain the causes of homelessness. Parsell and Parsell (2012), Nicholls (2009), and Fitzpatrick (2005) agree in that they frame the choices people make within the context of their structural and pathological realities. In short, according to this fourth and final perspective, choices exist but are limited by our abilities and the environments in which we make choices. The inclusion of agency, medicalization, and structural perspectives creates a conception of homelessness that is completely deserving. There is no means test capable of identifying deservedness by examining and incorporating the structural, pathological, and choice components that contribute to each homeless individual's experience. Nor will one solution to homelessness emerge from such a combined perspective; structural elements must be addressed, but services should be molded to fit individual needs rather than being prescribed by service professionals, private agencies, public funding, or government agencies.

Parsell and Parsell (2012), Nicholls (2009), and Fitzpatrick (2005) include choice in their comprehensive framework. While understanding that choice is influenced, choice is a vital piece of recovery that must not be overlooked. Individual choice must be respected, encouraged, and supported. Emerging client-centered, evidence-based practices, such as motivational interviewing, empower choice while respecting the context in which behaviors play out. Some individuals thrive in sober living settings and some excel in less restrictive settings. Some families only need a place to live while others would benefit from financial management support, job training, childcare, and other services. The reality is, if we want to help, the help must be in a form defined by the client rather than the agency, municipality, state, or federal government. Yet positive choices require real opportunities in terms of structure (housing and employment) and medical care. Thus, society is responsible not only for addressing the structural production of homelessness, but also for supporting those who experience illness, addictions, trauma, incarceration, and homelessness. And if these programs are to be informed by evidence-based practices like housing first, motivational interviewing, harm reduction, trauma-informed care, and other person-centered models, the requirements to access care must be less informed by arbitrary means tests and more by the needs of the person. Only after opportunity is provided in the way that respects an individual's needs, history, culture, and humanity can we honestly discuss whether some people just want to be homeless or are homeless by choice.

Rights and Responsibilities According to Public Policy

The responsibility to implement homeless policy has been devolving from the federal government to states and municipalities for the past thirty years.[12] The Richard Nixon, Gerald Ford, and Ronald Reagan administrations consolidated welfare spending in block grants administered to states, effectively transferring responsibility for the implementation of welfare policy to those states. Prior to this shift, large federal structures of the New Deal era and comparatively higher tax rates constituted the core of social welfare policy. During his tenure, President Reagan also pushed for the reduction of welfare spending and the reduction of taxes (Starling, 2008; Gowan, 2010). States and municipalities were left to search for independent funding sources to cover existing programs during the very time that the country experienced drastic increases in homelessness and poverty (Mitchell, 2011; Gowan, 2010). Many cities looked to their business communities to help cover this gap.

Under President Bill Clinton, the Personal Responsibility and Work Opportunity Reconciliation Act of 1996 accelerated the devolution of responsibilities both symbolically and functionally. Symbolically, PRWORA established as the government's perspective that the poor needed to be more self-reliant, were not being held accountable for their individual responsibilities, and would defraud the government if not watched carefully. Significantly, two of PRWORA's goals were that: "(1) individuals should take more responsibility for themselves and (2) work, not welfare, is the goal of public assistance. [Functionally] The burden of administering this new program [PRWORA] was shifted entirely to the states" (Starling, 2008, p. 116). This burden was accompanied by the concomitant cost of implementing and building new homeless care infrastructures (Starling, 2008).

Today's homeless policy consists of a patchwork of private nonprofit organizations; state, county, and local government programs; and faith-based service agencies. Under direction from the Clinton administration, states divided control of homeless policy implementation into separate Continuums of Care (Gowan, 2010) that are most often controlled at the city, county, or regional levels, but may also be controlled in part by states and territories. Because these state and municipal governments have accepted their new responsibilities in different ways, the quality of care for persons experiencing homelessness is geographically inconsistent.

Changes in welfare policy, however, are not the sole contributors to welfare devolution. The neoliberal economic policy shifts of the past thirty years—replacing investment in social services by investment in private growth—are, the evidence suggests, the primary culprit (Mitchell, 2011; Harvey, 2005). Neoliberal economic political principles not only seek to shrink government but also dismantle, limit, and devolve welfare and redistributive systems (Harvey, 2005; Friedman, 1980; Mitchell, 2003). Moreover, there is little debate that neoliberalism has had an immense effect on our cities.

Cities have become important growth engines for many economies around the globe, especially in the United States (Palmisano, 2014; Logan and Molotch, 2007; M. Davis, 2004). This trend, which is called "urban neoliberalism," involves the opening up of new market forces in urban space and urban housing markets, the privatization of public assets such as public housing, and a political and economic commitment to attracting private capital investment above all else (Mitchell, 2003, pp. 167, 163–181). US cities are seeking to attract wealth through public subsidies of corporate projects as well as through marketing strategies to brand cities as clean, safe, and exciting places to play (Wyly and Hammel, 2005). The neoliberal goal is to build a clean, pure, safe environment for tourists, shoppers, and conventioneers, as well as spaces for those with expendable incomes to spend in new retail, sports, entertainment, and luxury housing venues (Mitchell, 2003; Amster, 2003, Sennett, 1970; Ferrell, 2001). As part of the neoliberal turn, US cities are also trying to attract direct foreign investment in developments and postindustrial industries such as high-tech, biotech, and financial services (Florida, 2012; Križnik, 2011).

City development and redevelopment projects are taking place at great speed across the globe, and many US metropolitan areas are following the same trajectory of population growth and development. Development projects create new spaces that are designed not only to react to growth, but also to attract it. Urban growth can help create jobs and wealth and attract new industries. However, one aspect of these new urban growth dynamics is the fact that newly developed urban spaces are not always produced in a way to meet the needs of entire populations. More often, the needs of the multinational corporations and power brokers who control investment dominate the creation of new urban spaces and, as a result, their needs are met before the needs of broader society.

Harvey (2012) argues that "the actually existing right to the city, as is now constituted, is far too narrowly confined, in most cases in the hands of a small political and economic elite who are in a position to shape the city more and more after their own particular needs and hearts' desire" (p. 24). Turner (2002) and others echo this assertion, insisting that the transfer of public property to private entities, accompanied by public funded subsidies for large private investors, transfers power over the direction of city growth to private corporations. This transfer constricts the democratic use of and control over public space, and prioritizes the transfer of public funding that could have been used for social programs and low-income housing to private corporations.

Lobao, Adua, and Hooks (2014) found evidence confirming that neoliberal policies have grown across the country, that devolution of responsibility is increasingly reaching localities, and that the privatization of social services tends to happen in those localities that have the most business friendly policies. They also confirmed that neoliberal policies instigate the privatization of public social services. Governments, federal to local, are outsourcing the responsibility of implementing, taxing, and funding homeless policy. By outsourcing responsibility, the national, state, and local governments have effectively decreased their capacity to adapt to and meet changing needs. Today's privatized services have emerged as the tool to which our nation, states, and localities turn when fulfilling the responsibility to address social need. The path toward privatizing social services shrinks government to the point that it no longer has the capacity to care for its citizens (Klein, 2007). Nevertheless, homeless policy implementation is being handed from the federal government to states, from states to county and municipal governments, and from government to private nonprofits, businesses, and faith-based organizations.

Conclusion

The rights of persons experiencing homelessness and society's responsibility to care for them are in flux. Local communities are being given progressively more responsibility to address poverty. Yet if the legal status of those persons experiencing homelessness in our communities and the prevalence of homelessness are any measures, this devolution of responsibility is unfair and ineffective. This is perhaps because the privatization of social services puts the responsibility to care for vulnerable citizens into the hands of those who are not directly accountable to the people. Under the neoliberal paradigm, we see it as being against our economic interest to make financial demands of businesses. In fact, attracting business usually involves the citizenry giving away money in the form of tax breaks and tax increment financing. Neoliberal economic policies have concentrated great power in the business community. While, morally speaking, great power comes with great responsibility, the law will not enforce the effective discharge of that responsibility unless and until the electorate demands it.

Businesses have no special legal responsibility to help the people who live on their doorsteps but, in many locations, they do have the right to evict them through antihomeless laws. While there may be moral responsibilities held by shareholders, ultimately this moral responsibility is no different than any other segment of the population. In fact, because businesses must prioritize shareholder earnings above other responsibilities, charitable giving from businesses is not the most effective or sustainable method of filling the gaps in homeless funding. If society wants to place people above property, then we need laws that are built and enforced with that goal in mind.

The responsibility to address homelessness is not spread evenly across society, as it should be, at the federal level. The days of the New Deal are long gone. However, a societal responsibility is one in which all should share equally in the burden. We must not rely on charity from the business community alone. Rather, serious homelessness policy involves levying taxes, building affordable housing, reviving large-scale public works jobs, and rapidly disseminating and implementing evidence-based practices across all continuums of care.

Right now, we don't live in a world in which these things seem possible. Our federally elected officials do not stand up to special interests to defend the poor, and the electorate is not demanding that this change. Society is still blaming those experiencing homeless for their situation without any factual evidence to back up those assertions. Yet despite differing views as to the causes of homelessness, it remains a pervasive national tragedy for which we all bear a collective responsibility. Unless and until we start behaving accordingly, however, those experiencing homelessness will be literally left out in the cold.

Notes

1. The law is a contextual animal with few absolutes. For example, whether rights have been abridged often depends heavily on surrounding facts (*Clark v. Community for Creative Non-Violence,* 1984). Moreover, rights are constantly evolving (Bopp, La Rue, and Kosel, 2011). Finally, not all rights are enforceable in a court of law (Rankin, 2015) and, moreover, even enforceable rights must be enforced, a task that requires significant resources (Cross, 2001). As a result, the most precise way to understand rights is to speak in terms of which arguments apply to what factual scenarios and have some likelihood of being successful if pressed competently by an adequately resourced advocate in a court of law.

2. Antihomeless ordinances may criminalize, for example, sleeping or camping in public, sleeping in cars, loitering, panhandling, going to the bathroom or bathing outside, or distributing food in public places (NLCHP, 2011; ICH, 2012). Some ordinances prohibit behaviors in specific locations while others are citywide prohibitions.

3. Mitchell (1997) among others argues that these packages of antihomeless laws are "simply erasing the spaces in which [people experiencing homelessness] must live" (p. 305).

4. This model includes harsh revanchist aspects such as large-scale evictions resulting from municipally sponsored land grabs.

5. Beckett and Herbert (2008) argue that for "cities that depend upon capital investment, tourism, retail, and suburban shoppers for their economic well-being, the environment on commercial streets has become the subject of much official attention" (p. 17).

6. Lobao, Adua, and Hooks (2014) found significant quantitative evidence supporting "path dependency in economic development policy across U.S. localities" (pp. 659–670), meaning that implementations of neoliberal policies are self-reinforcing, as others have predicted. If there is a connection between the neoliberalization of localities and the implementation of antihomeless laws, and if cities around the globe continue to adopt neoliberalism, we should expect antihomeless laws to continue to grow in number.

7. The prioritization of the protection of private property over the rights of individuals has been an element of US policy since our very beginnings. The Bill of Rights was adopted years after ratification while intellectual property and the ownership and value of slaves were protected in our founding document. Moreover, in Federalist Paper 10 & 51, James Madison defended our Constitution by arguing that ambitions of the masses should be set against each other in such a way that the rights and property of the elite class would be maintained. These foundational priorities have ascended to greater heights because of the abandonment of Keynesian policy and large public programs of the New Deal and the embrace of neoliberal policy. The protection of private property and the implementation of antihomeless laws clearly require those experiencing homelessness to respect public and private property near businesses. In most cases, "respect" is synonymous with "stay away." While it might sound nice to have businesses help and employ those they find on their doorstep, there is no law requiring them to do so. Moreover, if there were such a law, not all businesses would be burdened equally.

8. According to Sennett (1970), "by defining the 'outsider' and the 'otherness' the 'we' becomes solidified with other 'we's' to separate themselves from the reality of pain and the toughness of life" (p. 39). By separating ourselves from the other, our fear of the others—in this case, people experiencing homelessness—is reinforced (Bannister, Fyfe, and Kearns, 2006).

9. Gans (1995), Mitchell (2011), Gowan (2010), and others describe a concept of deservedness, specifically targeted at the poor and homeless, that has been entrenched in discourse and policy since before the first settlers came to the shores of the new world. The followers of Martin Luther and other Protestant and puritanical religions incorporated religious moral judgment into law (Gowan, 2010). Moreover, the pervasive individualism that the new settlers embraced by necessity is a cultural aspect that many Americans cling to. Public debate and welfare institutions continue to promote these concepts and, beneath this reality, public constructs of homelessness compete for control of the debate concerning rights and responsibilities.

10. This compartmentalization of deservedness based on age, gender, or behavior is largely cultural in that, in the United States, men of working age are thought to be more responsible for taking care of themselves and thus less deserving of help (Gowen, 2010; Wasserman and Clair, 2010). Conversely, in other cultures like South Korea, it is the man of working age that is deemed deserving of service (Song, 2011).

11. The adoption of an individualized and medicalized framework has led to mixed results. Under the framework, responsibilities are driven by the study of individuals. Evidence-based best practices continue to emerge from these studies. If the medicalized understanding of homelessness is truly adopted, bringing best practices to scale becomes a moral and political obligation. However, imbedded in the current medicalized approach, Lyon-Callo (2000) argues that injecting "'disease' within the discourses of 'helping' actually obliterates discussion of alternative [structural] explanations" of homelessness and makes structural discussions peripheral (p. 30). Moreover, city officials have misused medicalized perspectives to argue in support of anti-homeless laws out of compassion because they operate under the understanding that people need to be pushed and corralled into the arms of care (Whelley, 2013; Gowan, 2010).

12. *Devolution* refers to the transfer of federal policy control to local policy control.

13

In Pursuit of Quality Data and Programs

Tracey O'Brien

Few deny the importance of providing quality programs and services that support individuals and families experiencing homelessness. But how do we know if these programs and services are working? The providers on the front line certainly think they are making a difference, but how much of a difference, for whom, and for how long, and what are the long-term outcomes for those experiencing homelessness? Are resources being well spent? Are lives improved as a result of programs and interventions? To ascertain whether or not interventions are effective, programs require user-friendly management information systems, evaluations that measure outcomes and not just outputs, innovative data sharing initiatives, and organizational cultures that do not simply tolerate inquiry but are invested and interested in results. Finally, quality data are critical to answering these questions.

> We need research and data to identify trends in homelessness and changes in demographics, for example the shift from individuals to families. I don't think that has ever been reflected in the programs that are being funded. If we had some professional expertise in terms of evaluation and good data, we could identify those programs that are making a difference and are serving their clients well.
>
> — Stakeholder meeting participant

In this chapter, I offer a case study of a Colorado organization's response to its community's clamor for program evaluation and effective use of data. I give a brief overview of the accepted principles of program evaluation and present some of the barriers that are common to conducting such evaluations. I discuss the value of data and give examples of data collection efforts, including data warehousing. I then present some of the accomplishments and challenges of two of the primary data sources on homelessness, and conclude

215

with a call for funders and decision-makers to support the need for quality data, research, and evaluation, in light of their frequent requests for program accountability.

Community Call for Research and Evaluation Support

In 2011, the seven-county Metro Denver Continuum of Care held a strategic planning session with community stakeholders during which practitioners, researchers, and policymakers proposed the creation of a research institute to address homelessness and related issues in Colorado. The group suggested that the work of the institute would encompass research, program evaluation, and interpretation of primary and secondary data to inform local, regional, and state decisionmakers, service providers, funders, and the public about the complex issues surrounding homelessness. The primary intent was to provide key stakeholders with accurate information, specific to Colorado, to help create effective policy and to improve outcomes for homeless individuals and families. The strongest argument for an institute centered around the idea that data, research, and program evaluation are essential for developing plans to end homelessness, for developing programs to serve homeless populations, for assessing cost-effectiveness, for informing public policy, and for determining the most efficient use of resources. The group recognized that communities, cities, and regions across the country are using data to understand and coordinate client services, potentially transforming outcomes for homeless individuals and families.

Instead of basing the development of such an undertaking on the philosophy "that if we build it, they will come," several local researchers held community meetings, conducted key informant interviews, reviewed local and national homelessness research and data organizations, and attended a conference offered by the National Human Services Data Consortium. These community meetings and interviews were held with service providers, researchers, funders, state and local government leaders, and leaders of several prominent local nonprofit organizations. The purpose of the meetings and interviews was to further explore the need for state or regional program evaluation and research on issues of homelessness. Stakeholders passionately articulated that the effective use of comprehensive data on homelessness and quality program evaluation were the greatest needs, and that those needs should be addressed by a research organization comprised of professionals with a keen and sustained focus on issues of homelessness.

Meeting participants identified specific projects in which such an institute would play a significant and important role. For example, the state's CoCs would need substantive technical assistance on an ongoing basis to meet the HEARTH Act evaluation requirements. All stakeholders expressed their desire to raise public awareness and sensitivity and to provide information on best practices to improve interventions and services for individuals and families experiencing homelessness. The stakeholders provided a long list of potential projects, needs, and topics where research and evaluation would make a tangible difference in Colorado's ability to address homelessness. In response, the Burnes Institute on Poverty and Homelessness was created and was granted its nonprofit status in December 2013.

Irrespective of the data needs identified by the community, there were, and still are, many barriers to overcome. Colorado is without a central entity or clearinghouse for relevant data and stakeholders resist data-sharing practices. As a first step, Colorado's CoCs needed to facilitate a statewide system that would bring Homeless Management Information System data together for a comprehensive picture of homeless populations and services across Colorado. Further, without a goal to include data from other systems—such as health and mental health, corrections, and human services—Colorado will not reap the benefits of having a holistic picture of homelessness and issues related to poverty in Colorado. Such a picture would provide a comprehensive data set to inform state, regional, and local plans to streamline systems, inform policy, and improve resource allocation.

The goals for the institute remain, and are best represented by, a single word: impact. All institute activities are focused on creating a positive impact on the lives of those experiencing extreme poverty and homelessness—through technical assistance to create capacity, streamline systems, inform policy, and guide evidence-based funding allocations. To date, the institute has provided research and evaluation support to a diverse group of organizations. It continues to work with local organizations, although it faces the commonly reported challenges of conducting effective program evaluation, foremost among them, project-specific funding that is less than ideal.

Program Evaluation: What Is It and Why Do It?

Evaluation plays a central role in organizations that view program evaluation as a strategy and not merely an external requirement. These organizations use evaluation as a valuable tool that can strengthen the quality of their programs and improve services to their clients. Most questions that organizations probe through evaluation lie in three categories: (1) What did we do? (2) How did we do it? (3) What difference did it make? The most common reasons for program evaluation are to discover what is working, to promote these successes to the community and to funders, and to improve practice—in this context, improve the practice of those that provide direct services to homeless individuals and families. Evaluation increases a program's internal capacity for self-assessment and strategic planning and adds to the knowledge in the field. It has the potential to lead to policy development, coalition building, and may help raise the public's awareness.

In this chapter, I do not describe the technical aspects of evaluation. There are countless resources available on the web and in workshops, classes, and workbooks. However, it may be useful to understand that program evaluation is a systematic method for collecting and analyzing information about programs, and then answering questions about process and impact.

There are many different types of program evaluation, although typically they are categorized in terms of two broad types:

1. *Process/implementation evaluation:* Are the program's services or activities being implemented as planned? Is the program reaching the intended target population; that is, the intended number of participants or clients? How do the participants perceive these services and activities?
2. *Outcome evaluation:* Are the recipients of the program's services experiencing the desired changes in knowledge, attitudes, or behaviors? Is the program having an impact on the people it serves?

Traditionally, programs track outputs; for example, the number of services provided, the number of people being served, and the number of resources distributed. However, in recent years, there has been a heightened focus on outcomes and outcome measurement. For some time, organizations have been increasingly pressured to provide evidence that their services are having a positive impact on clients. This is a significant change in evaluative expectations placed on organizations—expectations that require leadership and sufficient resources that support data collection strategies, a management information system, computer capability, and adequate staffing.

Figure 13.1 illustrates that outcomes have become the priority in the discussion of outputs versus outcomes. Among the many tools that Google provides, Ngram Viewer has scanned millions of books and indexed the terms referenced in them (Google Books Ngram Viewer). The Ngram Viewer graphs how many times one or more of these terms appears over a given period of time.

The discussion of outputs and outcomes begins to climb starting in 1950 to the mid-1960s. However, since about 1965, references to the concept of outcomes dramatically exceed the focus on outputs. The graph reflects the current thinking in the field, which may be summarized in one word—results. Increasingly, programs are required to provide evidence of impact in measurable quantifiable terms, rather than simply describing an organization's services.

Challenges of Effective Evaluation

For some, evaluation is simply not feasible—organizations may not have the elements that signal readiness for evaluation. To engage in an effective

Figure 13.1 Outputs Versus Outcomes: Frequency of References

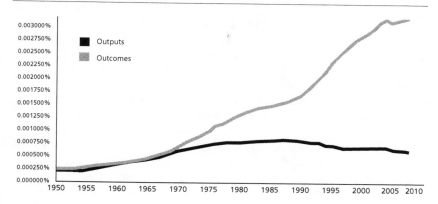

evaluation, a formal program design or model must be in place and have adequate staffing, equipment, and technology. Evaluation requires data and, with that, data collection procedures and a management information system to house the data and to produce meaningful reports.

Agencies and organizations face funding and internal capacity challenges. Program evaluation is seldom built into programs from the start, and is rarely funded. Foundations that support direct services require information about results, but historically do not allow program budgets that include a line item for evaluation. Many organizations are interested in learning whether their programs are effective, but too often are unable to carve out the time or the budget to support evaluation. The Center for Effective Philanthropy surveyed 177 nonprofit leaders, finding that 81 percent of those surveyed believe that their organizations should demonstrate the effectiveness of their services, but 71 percent reported they received no funding support for any evaluation efforts (Brock, Buteau, and Herring, 2012).

And funding is not the only barrier. Numerous methodological issues exist in tracking and gathering data on homeless individuals and families. Management information systems can be expensive and require internal capacity for data tracking. Overworked and underpaid service providers often feel that evaluation will add to their workload, and rightly so; some resist evaluation due to the perception that it reduces human experience to simple measurable constructs.

While these barriers are real, there are other, less obvious ones as described by an expert in the field of program evaluation (Fulop, 2011). Fulop states in his blog that the "no money" claim actually conceals the real barriers to effective evaluation. First, he argues that organizational leaders do not invest in expanding skills within the organization that would support evaluation. Given leaders' lack of confidence in this area, they are unable to build a culture that supports evaluation and effective use of data. Second, agencies see no positive incentives for program evaluation—many cannot identify even one example of a public presentation of program results, a celebration of program effectiveness, a consequence suffered for not producing an evaluation, or had even one funder provide resources specifically for program evaluation. Third, Fulop refers to the old adage, "the Emperor wears no clothes," whereby organizations fear negative evaluation findings. Although these barriers do exist, we should not hold them up as insurmountable—quality programs depend on it. "We need to understand," Fulop continues, "that program accountability and evaluation is the source of power and empowerment. Without evaluation how can we improve or measure progress? Program evaluation is the stuff that makes program giants, changes things, and disrupts unmet needs" (Fulop, 2011).

Data Drives Impactful Programs

Data collection is challenging. It requires time, resources, determination, and a clear plan. The Burnes Institute works with a number of local agencies that use multiple data systems, which makes data analysis and interpretation particularly difficult. For example, over the years, agencies may experience a data system that has become obsolete, or a specific system may be required by a major funder, or the agency creates an additional data collection system to produce the reports it needs.

Using Data to Inform Programs

Agencies that use data to improve programs and inform decisionmaking have tangible evidence of their progress and success. A recent report examined a number of nonprofits whose data-driven decisionmaking practices were responsible for their outcomes and overall progress (Bernard and Pope, 2014). The study reported that the framework for successfully using data to improve programs generally involves six steps: (1) defining a goal for the data; (2) identifying what data to gather to help reach a goal; (3) storing data in a way that is accessible; (4) establishing a means of collecting data; (5) reporting and analyzing what the data means; and (6) acting on what is learned from the data (Bernard and Pope, 2014). Here, we offer several excellent examples of organizations that are using data to inform and support communities, improve practices, and implement outcome management tools.

eLogic Model Manager

A shining example of a data management and evaluation tool, eLogic is a web-based software application that allows for data collection and analysis, effectively supporting the program evaluation needs of an agency. It is a comprehensive intake, assessment, and outcomes-based client management system that is both logic model based and affordable to grassroots nonprofits. The development of eLogic was based on the belief that agencies needed data management systems that inform programs, not just funders, and support both internal and external evaluation. Fred Richmond, software developer and chief executive officer of the Center for Applied Management Practices, offers his own description of this valuable tool:

> eLogic is a state-of-the-art web based software application with a database that allows for data collection and analysis and transforms text to data. It serves not only to describe a program of human service delivery (as a regular logic model does), it uniquely drives the database for supporting client/case management and the program evaluation needs of the agency. eLogic compiles reports on client demographics, needs presented, services/interventions administered and outcomes attained, also referred to as achieving a satisfactory level of well-being. It is a tool that helps provide the "evidence" in evidence based practice and supports longitudinal analysis.

A Local Collaborative: Colorado eLogic Evaluation Network

Five nonprofit agencies in the Metro Denver area formed a collaboration called the Colorado eLogic Evaluation Network (CEEN). The members are agencies serving homeless individuals and families and other at-risk populations. Each agency is committed to measuring impacts to guide program improvement, to engage in evaluation to support planning and program management, and to provide staff with ongoing feedback.

CEEN's guiding principles include:

- A commitment to using data to improve the social impact of organizations.
- The belief that evaluation is an integral component of an agency's program and daily operations.
- A focus on creating an internal agency culture that will strengthen and solidify an outcome measurement system.
- The goal that the collaboration will have a greater impact than that of the individual organizations in conducting evaluation activities and disseminating results to decisionmakers and to the public.
- The requirement that the collaboration will share evaluation strategies and methodologies, effective practices, and implementation techniques and trainings among CEEN members.
- A commitment to continuous improvement of client services and quality of work-life of agency staff.

CEEN is in its infancy but, if it reaches its goals, it can serve as a model for other collaborations that are committed to outcomes management.[1]

Beyond Colorado:
Examples of Data Sources and Warehousing

Communities across the country are addressing the challenges and solutions of data collection, data analysis, and data warehousing that span public sectors, including human services, criminal justice, and housing and homelessness. Individuals and organizations are using integrated data for performance measurement, program planning, and systems change.

Data warehousing (i.e., the integration of human services agency data) can answer critical questions about at-risk populations based on a cross-system analysis of services. Some states are creating data warehouses that include HMIS data through partnerships with their local CoCs, regional or local planning entities that coordinate housing and services for homeless families and individuals. In Colorado, for example, there are three CoCs: (1) the Metropolitan Denver Homeless Initiative (MDHI), the Metro Denver area Continuum comprised of seven urban counties; (2) the Pikes Peak CoC (El Paso County); and (3) the Balance of State Continuum comprised of Colorado's remaining fifty-six counties.

Agencies that provide services to homeless individuals and families in Colorado do not have a working plan for data sharing across these agencies and, therefore, are far from internalizing a philosophy that would advocate for sharing their CoC's HMIS data with the state. However, the opportunity likely exists, given the Data Integration Initiative of the Colorado Department of Human Services, the intent of which is to develop an integrated behavioral health services data collection system that addresses client or patient behavioral and physical health service needs. As stated earlier, an integrated data system, or a data warehouse, would provide a holistic picture of the characteristics of, and the system of services provided to, our most vulnerable citizens. Below are examples of other states that are fully engaged in this effort.

Michigan's Data Warehouse

Michigan's data warehouse (MDW) is a valuable statewide resource and is one of the most broadly used state government enterprise data warehouses in the nation. It has transformed outcomes (health and human services) and saved hundreds of millions of dollars by providing useful data and information. The warehouse contains information from state and federal agencies. Each agency maintains its own data in the warehouse, but data are shared when authorized by the agencies in formal agreements. Some examples of questions that can be answered are:

- What is the cost of supporting the homeless population?
- What patterns of service usage relate to patterns of homelessness?
- How many foster care children end up homeless and how do they differ from those who do not?

- How do changes in state programs and allocations impact the homeless population and private sector providers?
- How effective are our efforts to help the homeless?
- What are the trends and patterns of homelessness that can direct policymakers with strategic directions?

The Ohio Human Services Data Warehouse

Ohio is currently involved in a statewide data consolidation effort. The state expects that, through the analysis of data across systems of services, it will gain a more thorough understanding of trends and mobility patterns and be able to assess the impact of investments in housing and human services at a level that would inform funding and policy decisions at the state and local levels. Currently participating are two state agencies, the Ohio Housing Finance Agency and the Ohio Development Services Agency. They are joined by eight CoCs across the state. The Ohio CoCs collaborated to "leverage learning across the multiple communities, and to facilitate the creation of a statewide system that brings HMIS data together for a composite picture of the homeless population and services across Ohio" (Holtzen, n.d.). The group's goal is to include data from state systems — such as from corrections, health and mental health, and human services — so as to develop a comprehensive picture of homelessness and issues of poverty.

Some states, such as in the Ohio example, recognize that data sharing and data integration are crucial to answering critical questions about individuals experiencing homelessness and have turned this recognition into action. Data initiatives can simultaneously maintain the privacy and security of client data while providing detailed information about issues of poverty and homelessness.

Availability of Data on Homelessness

Apart from the research and data collection efforts for specific projects across the country, the primary sources of data on homelessness are through the Point-in-Time homeless counts and the HMIS. Based on our local experience in the Metro Denver area, both data sources have challenges. The PIT effort has been historically underfunded and is laden with data collection processes that are extremely labor intensive, and the HMIS is a source of frustration for many of its users.

Agencies serving homeless individuals and families in the Denver area have been using the HMIS for years and many still report they have no ability to easily access the data. It does seem that public and private organizations are forever in the midst of technology upgrades and promises of user-friendly systems. The Denver area CoC has been through more than one HMIS software provider at great expense and time given to data migration, and yet a number of service providers report the need for a data management system apart from the HMIS. However, HMIS is here to stay, and in the next section I offer examples of CoCs successfully using the HMIS.

The Homeless Management Information System

The HMIS is a software application designed to record and store client-level data, including the characteristics and service needs of the homeless community. All agencies receiving federal funds from the HUD McKinney-Vento housing assistance program are required to participate in the HMIS, as are Emergency Solutions Grant and Supportive Services for Veteran Families providers. The experiences of agencies using the HMIS vary wildly, ranging from difficulty accessing any data via reports to the need for greater technical support. Further, linking the HMIS with state agency data would allow for a comprehensive understanding of service use, mobility, resource use, gaps assessment, and outcomes.

The National Human Services Data Consortium (NHSDC) is an excellent resource for CoCs and others interested in effectively utilizing the HMIS. It is focused on the best use of information technology to manage human services. The NHSDC provides "information, assistance, peer to peer education and lifelong learning to its membership and other interested parties in the articulation, planning, implementation and continuous operation of technology initiatives to collect, aggregate, analyze and present information regarding the provision of human services" (NHSDC).

Twice every year, NHSDC holds a conference that offers information and sessions that address policy and planning, data sharing and collaboration, and technical applications particularly around the HMIS. It advocates for CoCs to integrate continuous improvement into their planning processes and to use data for performance management and evaluation. Consultants with the Burnes Institute attended the NHSDC conference in 2011 and 2013. In these sessions, CoCs and service providers described their use of HMIS data to inform their program planning, including plans to end homelessness, to inform resource allocation, and for continuous improvement, performance measurement, and research and evaluation. Historically, HMIS users in Colorado have had difficulty utilizing the HMIS system to its full advantage. A number of users complain that they are unable to extract useful data, either in raw form or in reports. Beyond the challenges of individual users, the HMIS would be best utilized if there were a community-wide agreement for sharing data. The following are examples of some of the accomplishments and successes using the HMIS that were presented at the conferences. The goal here is to demonstrate that the HMIS can be used as an effective tool when leaders are committed to learning more about homelessness through research and evaluation.

The Iowa Institute for Community Alliances

The Iowa Institute for Community Alliances (IICA) has nearly ten years of HMIS data and has merged it with criminal justice data. IICA reports that many of its non-HMIS partners would like to merge their data with the IICA data set. In 2011, IICA using criminal justice data was able to look at where the two populations overlap (e.g., felony arrests are significantly more likely to lead to a shelter stay, but not necessarily to long-term homelessness). Additionally, IICA looked at economic causes of homelessness and conducted analyses based on persons actually experiencing homelessness versus individuals at risk of homelessness. It analyzed national indicators that are available on a monthly basis and conducted regression analysis to explore the relationship of change in national indicators and the changes in the homeless population; when any of the economic indicators changed (e.g., food services, personal savings, homeowner vacancy rates, state and local spending), the rate of homelessness changed. These national indicators are freely available. IICA has been able to learn more about how prevention clients differed from homeless clients (e.g., transportation was a big factor); most homeless clients had significant medical data, active chronic health crises, and a significantly higher disability rate.

The Michigan Statewide HMIS Implementation

The Michigan Statewide HMIS (MSHMIS) is one of the most diverse information system implementations in the nation. In the MDW, MSHMIS combines the HMIS records with mainstream services provided by the state. Its participating partners are from the Departments of Human Services (youth and housing) and Community Health. The partners are evolving to a single point of entry across the state and are using MSHMIS to drive systems change. Given that the data system is statewide, it is possible to see where clients are accessing services across the state. For example:

- People often leave a shelter because of rules and regulations and not because they choose to leave.
- Regarding the number of times clients are served: over three years, statewide, about 70 percent touched the system once and did not come back into the system.
- The presence of a disability is an important factor in accessing emergency shelter.
- Operationalizing homeless episodes is critical to all analysis and is difficult to define and apply consistently; length of time of crisis requires automating exits.

The Alliance to End Homelessness in Cook County

The Cook County CoC uses analysis of HMIS data primarily for internal strategic planning. For example, when looking at the length of stay for transitional housing and emergency shelter, it found that little was known about where people go when they leave a shelter, and discovered that the shelters were not consistent about how they determined an exit. The CoC encouraged its emergency shelters to start talking with each other to develop a common exit policy. Additionally, the CoC uses HMIS data to inform the following:

- Most appropriate housing for the hardest to serve clients (persons with disabilities, chronically homeless).
- Discharge planning.
- Homeless prevention—how many people are turned away from services and why.

The Bay Area Counties Homeless Information Collaborative

The Bay Area Counties Homeless Information Collaborative (BACHIC) is a group of representatives from eleven CoCs that formed a collaborative in an effort to combine expertise and to develop the HMIS for the entire region. The intent of the Collaborative is to provide a more complete picture of homeless population characteristics and services across the eleven counties. (California Ten Year Chronic Homelessness Action Plan, 2010).

The Columbus, Ohio, Continuum of Care

All of the service providers in the Columbus CoC participate in the HMIS.

> Columbus has HMIS coverage of 98 percent of shelters, 91 percent of transitional housing, and 95 percent of permanent supportive housing providers. The HMIS operates as an open system, which makes more of the client information available to all providers in the system including emergency shelter history and receipt of financial assistance. HIPAA-protected (Health Insurance Portability and Accountability Act) health information and domestic violence related information cannot be viewed. (NAEH, 2010)

The providers track client- and program-level outcomes and progress on more than thirty measures, which is tracked quarterly. They review program performance standards on a yearly basis and incorporate the results into an annual agreement with each agency, which includes an annual Program Outcome Plan. The Plan becomes the basis for performance-based contracts and evaluation. If a program consistently fails to meet its performance targets, the agency has to participate in a quality improvement program (NAEH, 2010). The National Alliance to End Homelessness offers a wealth of tools and resources, including more specific information about the Columbus model.

Point-in-Time

A Point-in-Time count is a snapshot of homelessness taken by counting those who are homeless at a particular time. HUD, the primary source of federal funding for housing support for homeless populations, requires that all CoCs conduct a PIT survey every two years during the last ten days of January.

PIT data have limitations. For a number of reasons identified below, the data generated from the PIT are unreliable. It is difficult to count people who are experiencing homelessness. The one consistent finding in the research on homelessness is that surveys undercount homeless populations. Persons experiencing homelessness are easily missed; they might not be receiving services on the night of the PIT, or they might not be at a participating agency during the count.

> Certain subpopulations of people experiencing homelessness are particularly difficult to count. By definition, unsheltered persons are not in places where they can easily be counted. Often they simply cannot be found when they are staying in automobiles and other kinds of invisible living situations. Other groups who are difficult to include in the PIT count are youth, adults and children experiencing domestic violence and undocumented persons. Unaccompanied youth tend to avoid systems of care. Often they do not access adult-oriented services due to concerns about detection and safety, and tend to be more mobile throughout the day than are homeless adults. Victims of domestic violence are undercounted largely due to confidentiality and safety concerns and hesitate to complete surveys. (Metropolitan Denver Homeless Initiative, 2014)

Understandably, undocumented people are afraid of being identified.

Some CoCs treat the homeless count as a census (vs. a sampling methodology), which then causes the sheltered count to be entirely dependent on the level of participation of service providers and volunteers. Further, variation in numbers of surveys collected may be based on external factors such as weather. For example, fewer surveys were collected in the seven-county Metro Denver area in 2014 than were collected in 2013. Although there were likely reasons other than weather for fewer surveys in Metro Denver, we do know that in 2014 the weather was extremely severe. Many volunteers who normally would be out collecting surveys were unable to get to their assigned location, and staff were occupied with providing direct services to people seeking shelter from the elements rather than spending time administering and collecting surveys.

Because HUD requires CoCs to collect data on the total number and characteristics of all homeless people, both sheltered and unsheltered, CoCs must determine the most effective methodology by considering its volunteer and agency commitment, capacity, resources, and other competing interests of its key stakeholders. A CoC may treat the count as a census, or utilize a sampling method, or both. Given the difficulty of counting people who are experiencing homelessness, utilizing a random or nonrandom sample, possibly in combination with a census approach, seems to make the most sense for most CoCs, especially when reporting subpopulation characteristics. To further our understanding of the effectiveness and efficiency of the PIT count, a graduate intern with the Burnes Institute, Monika Schneider, compared the PIT processes in three different cities: New York City, Houston, and Metro Denver (Schneider, 2015). New York City's PIT survey is well resourced and has built an extensive pool of volunteer support. New York City (NYC) uses a stratified random sample to conduct the count. The city is divided into approximately 7,000 areas based on the census block groups and these areas are then identified as being either high or low density, depending on the probability of finding a person experiencing homelessness. These probabilities are based on observation and past experience. Approximately 3,000 enumerators volunteer from midnight to 4 A.M. on the night of the PIT—quite an impressive volunteer effort. NYC contracts with an academic institution to conduct a quality assurance check of the count's methodological compliance. An interesting detail of NYC's count is its plant-capture method, which entails placing decoys into areas where volunteers are administering surveys. The decoys track the number and area where enumerators survey the decoys and "the results from the decoy count are then used to adjust the final count estimate" (Schneider, 2015, p. 9).

Houston has built a strong network of agencies to conduct its PIT count. The collaboration includes the Coalition for the Homeless, the University of Texas School of Public Health, and the City of Houston Department of Health and Human Services. In recent years, Houston implemented an Incident Command System that facilitates a systematic planning process and clear chains of command and supervision, which are reflected in the PIT enumeration structure. Houston utilizes a census approach. Approximately 600 volunteers are divided into roughly 80 teams called "surface teams"; each team includes a driver, a service provider, one person who is currently homeless or has experienced homelessness in the past, and a community volunteer. Prior to the count, staging area captains, co-captains, and the surface and outreach specialist teams are trained and become familiar with the geographic area where they will conduct the count. Houston utilizes the HMIS to count persons in emergency shelters, and shelter providers are given the opportunity to confirm the numbers counted on the night of the PIT. Shelters not using the HMIS complete a form to enumerate their clients who are homeless. Houston emphasizes its marketing strategy as key to its extensive community buy-in, including evident support from elected officials and law enforcement (Schneider, 2015).

The Metropolitan Denver Homeless Initiative is the CoC comprised of seven urban counties in the Metro Denver area. Historically, MDHI has approached the PIT as a census count. For the 2015 count, it implemented several changes in an attempt to improve its accuracy. First, instead of counting homeless persons and those at risk, it limited the count to the HUD definition of homelessness, substantially reducing the effort of surveying, data cleaning, and reporting. In the most recent count, MDHI focused on locations where, in prior years, high numbers of individuals were found to be homeless. The CoC shortened its lengthy PIT survey, used its HMIS to gather transitional housing data, counted those who refused to participate in the PIT count but who were clearly homeless, and assigned four AmeriCorps volunteers to the PIT effort. Next year, MDHI expects to utilize the HMIS to count emergency shelter clients as well as persons in transitional housing.

These and other PIT efforts illustrate that the counts standing the greatest chance of achieving the most comprehensive data are: those with adequate funding; those that engage in long-term planning and form relationships with a broad spectrum of partners; and those that have an extensive public and private buy-in, a network of dedicated volunteers, and an effective marketing strategy.

Although certain populations of people are difficult to find and to count, and various external factors introduce instability, the PIT count is important because it is the only measure that captures the scope of people experiencing homelessness. Reporting information on homelessness can increase public awareness of the issue. HUD uses the information from the local counts in a congressionally mandated report, which is meant to inform Congress about the number of homeless individuals and families and the effectiveness of federal programs and policies to end homelessness. Locally, PIT counts are intended to help communities effectively plan their homeless services system. Even so, do we know if the quality of data collected through the PIT count is worth the cost of the count? More importantly, how are the PIT findings actually utilized to inform policy, and do they make a significant contribution to ending homelessness?

Conclusion

Quality programs need quality research and evaluation. Both require resources and data. Data collection practices, data management systems, and software programs used by communities as I have described in this chapter can be valuable resources in addressing homelessness. Organizations face sizable barriers to their ability to track outcomes and show the effectiveness of their programs. Given that the primary purpose of program evaluation is to improve the lives of those we serve, and considering the barriers to quality data and evaluation, are funders, decisionmakers, leaders, and service providers prepared to act?

Given the call for programs that truly work, Johns Hopkins University initiated the Listening Post Project, which asked questions of a nationwide sample of nonprofit organizations about program innovation and performance measurement (Salamon, Geller, and Mengel, 2010). Nonprofit leaders were asked what obstacles stand in the way of innovation and performance measurement. The leaders reported that the major barriers of performance measurement are resource constraints, such as little staff time and internal evaluative expertise, and the related barrier of the cost of good evaluation. The demand is there; organizations are asked to provide evidence of their effectiveness, but do not have the resources necessary to demonstrate impact (Salamon, Geller, and Mengel, 2010). It is time to address the reality of high expectations, coupled with little funding to meet those expectations. Even for federally mandated data collection activities, such as the HMIS and the PIT count, HUD should reexamine the utility of the data and provide the resources necessary to accomplish a substantially improved effort.

Best practice is a term that has been overused and, as a result, has lost its meaning. Perhaps a better term is *good practice;* quality data and evaluation highlight good practice and will improve services that can profoundly affect the lives of our most vulnerable citizens. Agencies and organizations must play their part as well. Without an organizational culture that values transparency and supports the vibrancy that comes from real exploration of accountability and outcomes, evaluation and data have little relevance.

In the current environment, policymakers, funders, and practitioners all respond to numbers and to measurable evidence of impact. However, few provide the necessary funding to improve data collection systems such as the HMIS and the PIT, much less support of the other data management needs of service agencies and organizations. If we are to influence policies and develop and support programs that mitigate poverty and homelessness, it is critical to provide the comprehensive data so necessary for evaluating the effectiveness of programs and services. Decisions at all levels that are made without data are likely to be irrelevant at best, and misguided at worst. Unless we are prepared to undertake such efforts, we are destined to continue blindly consuming resources and perpetuating programs without any evidence that the current policies and practices truly improve the lives of individuals and families experiencing homelessness.

Notes

1. For more information about CEEN, please contact Donald W. Burnes of the Burnes Center on Poverty and Homelessness at donwburnes@gmail.com.

2. The Burnes Center acknowledges and thanks Monika Schneider, a social work graduate intern who developed the PIT comparison material in the text. Her final paper includes case studies of New York City, Houston, Denver, and Atlanta, with a table comparing the PIT study in each city on a number of elements, including methods and perceived strengths and weaknesses. For more information and to receive a copy of the final paper, contact the Burnes Institute on Poverty and Homelessness.

14

Public Opinion, Politics, and the Media

Paul A. Toro and Corissa Carlson

It was 1980. Ronald Reagan had just been elected to his first term. As the early years of his administration rolled out, a dramatic tide of concern developed in the media about what seemed to be a rapidly growing new problem: people on the nation's streets (Baum and Burnes, 1993; Buck, Toro, and Ramos, 2004; M. M. Jones, 2015; Link et al., 1994, 1995; Toro and McDonell, 1992; Toro and Warren, 1991). Some blamed a stagnant economy. Some blamed Reagan and his conservative policies. Others were confident that the deinstitutionalization of the mentally ill that had occurred during the prior two decades had exacerbated this new social problem (M. M. Jones, 2015). Advocacy groups became organized and professionals of many stripes (including social scientists and the medical community) became engaged with what was coming to be seen as a major challenge.

In this chapter, we review the forty years since 1974 and analyze the interaction between media and professional interest in homelessness during this period, public opinion, politics and social policy, and the actual prevalence of homelessness. Considering the linkages among these various forces can help us develop a more thorough understanding of homelessness. This, in turn, can contribute to our developing solutions for ending it. A careful analysis of these links can also provide insight into how such forces might positively contribute to action on other social issues.

The Prevalence of Homelessness

Toro and Warren (1991) note that the definition of homelessness and the methods for estimating its true prevalence became controversial during the 1980s as the nation first attempted to tackle the issue. They observed that the lowest estimates tended to come from government agencies such as the

231

US Department of Housing and Urban Development and were based on point prevalence (i.e., how many people are homeless on a given night). In more recent years, the Point-in-Time counts provided by local HUD-funded agencies throughout the nation have become widely cited (e.g., NAEH, 2015). The US Census has used similar methods, starting in 1990, to estimate the point prevalence of homelessness nationwide (Culhane et al., 2013). Higher numbers have come from methods that estimate prevalence over time. Culhane et al. (1994), for example, used administrative records on service utilization to estimate the three-year prevalence of homelessness in two large cities (New York and Philadelphia). The highest estimates have come from telephone surveys that obtain large national random samples. These surveys assess lifetime prevalence and find rates of 6–7 percent in the United States (Link et al., 1994; Tompsett et al., 2006). Toro and Warren (1991) note that these high rates are still underestimates because (1) they do not include those who are currently homeless (because few of them have telephones); and (2) they do not project the risk for homelessness across the respondent's full life span. Correcting for these two sources of underestimation, Toro and Warren (1991, p. 125) conclude that over 10 percent of the US population could be expected to experience homelessness at some point in their lives. Such a high lifetime prevalence rate ranks homelessness among a wide range of other serious social and health problems, including alcohol use disorder (13 percent), major depressive disorder (8 percent), breast cancer in women (12 percent), and prostate cancer in men (15 percent).

Toro et al. (2007, 2008) used the same survey methodology to interview large random samples by telephone across nine different developed nations, including the United States, Canada, the United Kingdom (UK), France, Germany, Italy, Belgium, Poland, and Portugal. Homelessness has, in recent decades, become identified as a major social issue in all of these nations. The issue was identified in the UK media during the conservative Margaret Thatcher era, around the same time as it was identified in the US media during the conservative Reagan era. Homelessness became a prominent issue in the other nations later (especially in Poland, where it did not gain significant media attention until after the communist system collapsed in 1989; see Toro et al., 2014). A wide variation in the overall lifetime prevalence of literal homelessness among citizens across these nations has been observed. The highest rates of homelessness have come from the United States, the UK, and Canada (6.1–8.6 percent) and the lowest from France and Germany (2.2–2.4 percent), with intermediate rates from Italy, Belgium, Poland, and Portugal (3.3–4.3 percent).

Many explanations for this variation in rates have been proposed, including (1) differences in income inequality and poverty; (2) the availability of low-income housing, especially in urban areas; (3) the robustness of the social safety net, including income and housing supports and health and social services; (4) different patterns of substance use and abuse; (5) the strength of family and community ties; and (6) the intensity of immigration (see Hobden et al., 2007; Shinn, 2007; Tompsett et al., 2003, 2006; Toro et al., 2007, 2008; Toro and Rojansky, 1990). While the variation in the prevalence of homelessness among nations is clearly of interest, the fact that in recent decades homelessness has appeared within virtually all developed nations of the world is also of interest. This ubiquity suggests that broad global structural forces are at work which, in fact, include some of the same ones listed above to explain the variation in rates across nations. In particular, a set of forces associated with the postindustrial economy (Adams, 1986) seem likely culprits. These forces may be the ultimate result of unfettered capitalism in a global context and include the growing income disparity between the rich and the poor (see Phillips, 2008; Reich, 2010). The United States has seen steady growth in its income disparity since before the 1980s (US Census Bureau, 1998), coinciding with the entry of homelessness into the national limelight. The so-called gentrification of urban areas previously providing a substantial stock of low-income housing as well as the weakening of the social safety net are other postindustrial forces that may be associated with the growing income disparity.

While there is no definitive way to know exactly how the prevalence of homelessness has changed over the past forty years in the United States, it does seem likely that there have been some fluctuations, perhaps due to the changing status of the overall economy. For example, based on their telephone surveys with large nationally representative samples of adults conducted in 1993–1994 and again in 2001, Tompsett et al. (2006, p. 50) found that the lifetime rate of homelessness had dropped from 8.1 percent to 6.2 percent over that eight-year period. This drop could be due to the fact that, in this eight-year span, the United States saw its strongest economic performance in many decades (Reich, 2010). A similar drop in the estimated prevalence of homelessness during the 1990s economic boom has been observed in the US Census data and administrative shelter data from New York City (Culhane et al., 2013). These data sources have also shown a rise in the prevalence during the recessionary 2000s.

We are really in the dark about the prevalence of US homelessness in the 1970s and early 1980s before the first estimates were produced. That being the case, we can only speculate about the possible influence that the actual prevalence had on the media expansion of the early 1980s. For sure, reading many of the media accounts of that critical early period, one gets the impression that reporters were genuinely surprised and appalled by what seemed to be a new emergency situation (see M. M. Jones, 2015), and seemed to be grasping for explanations for this situation. So, as many reporters might agree, perhaps the prevalence was growing in the 1970s and into the 1980s, prompting the media to report on the growing national crisis that homelessness was becoming. Did the slow rise in the prevalence of homelessness during the 1970s reach some sort of tipping point in the early 1980s? We will never know, with certainty, the answer to this question.

Media and Professional Coverage

Before 1980, homelessness was infrequently covered in the news media and, when it was mentioned, it often reflected an image of the stereotypical skid row derelict (i.e., an older white single alcoholic male; the "old homeless," according to Rossi, 1990, p. 955). Starting in the early 1980s, the news media began to cover homelessness in detail and as a recognizable social problem. Around this time, there was also a noticeable shift in labeling: the keywords "vagrant" and "vagrancy" began to be replaced by the somewhat more neutral terms "homeless" and "homelessness" (Buck, Toro, and Ramos, 2004; p. 164), a change that was virtually complete by the late 1980s (M. M. Jones, 2015). This change reflected a move from the stereotype of homeless people being tramps and hoboes having various internal flaws of character to the current perception of those experiencing homelessness as being, at least in part, victims of external circumstances (Baum and Burnes, 1993; M. M. Jones, 2015), and was explicitly favored by a number of advocates for people experiencing homelessness (Baum and Burnes, 1993; Baxter and Hopper, 1981; M. M. Jones, 2015). The media readily picked up the new terminology.

A number of causes for this change of perception and associated rise in media coverage in the 1980s have been proposed (Buck and Toro, 2004; M. M. Jones, 2015). First, the Reagan administration's cutting of social programs during the recession of the early 1980s departed sharply from previous government policy and was often criticized as being hard-hearted. The subsequent mobilization of Reagan's political opponents and activists for people who are homeless played a significant role in helping to bring homelessness into the media's consciousness. Second, the development and gentrification of many inner cities resulted in the disappearance of cheap hotels and flophouses in the poor districts where large numbers of marginal people had lived (Adams, 1986; M. M. Jones, 2015). Though we have no way to know with certainty, given the lack of studies on the prevalence of homelessness before the 1980s, it appears that the decimation of so much low-income housing caused many to become homeless. For sure, many activists at the time attributed this apparent rise in homelessness to the loss of low-income housing, and the media quickly picked up on this idea (Baxter and Hopper, 1981; M. M. Jones, 2015).

Third, widespread media coverage of the winter deaths of a number of people who were homeless vividly demonstrated the seriousness and urgency of this problem (M. M. Jones, 2015). Mitch Snyder, perhaps the most prominent of the homeless advocates who thrust themselves onto the national stage during the 1980s, in fact openly carried the ashes of a homeless man who had frozen to death (see Baum and Burnes, 1993). Fourth, there was growing concern that the deinstitutionalization of mental patients during the 1960s and 1970s had led to many former patients being dumped into the communities and, ultimately, finding their way onto the streets (e.g., M. M. Jones, 2015; Koenig, 1978; Goleman, 1986). Fifth, we were seeing increasing numbers of the "new homeless" (Rossi, 1990, p. 956) among the overall homeless population. Such persons included younger adults and youth, minorities, women, and homeless families (mostly young women with young children). The growth of such groups made it more difficult to blame people who are homeless themselves for their plight. Furthermore, greater heterogeneity of the population made it easier for the public to imagine themselves becoming homeless. Finally, in 1986 the Hands Across America charity event, which involved over 5 million people joining together to raise money to combat homelessness, was extensively covered in the news media.

Buck, Toro, and Ramos (2004) used systematic methods to examine both media and professional coverage on homelessness over the thirty-year period from 1974 to 2003. After minimal coverage in the 1960s and 1970s, the amount of media attention on homelessness exploded in the mid-1980s (see Figure 14.1). For example, the *New York Times* published 357 articles on homelessness in 1987, an average of almost 1 per day. The ever increasing media coverage, and perhaps growing professional and public concern,

Figure 14.1   Trends in the Volume of Newspaper and Professional Coverage on Homelessness, 1974–2013, and McKinney Act Federal Funding, 1987–2013

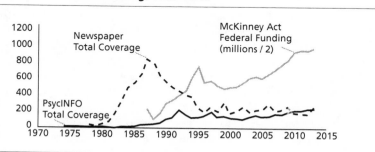

Source: Data presented are, in part, from Buck et al., 2004; Calson, Toro, and Buck, 2015; and Toro and Warren, 1991.

Note: Newspaper coverage reflects the summed total of homelessness articles from four major newspapers with national circulation. Professional coverage reflects the summed total of homelessness records indexed in the PsycINFO database, mostly consisting of journal articles but also including book, chapters, authored books, dissertations, and other reports. McKinney Act funding is presented for fiscal years and is in millions of dollars divided by two (to better fit alongside the other trend lines presented).

helped to prompt passage of the Stewart B. McKinney Homeless Assistance Act (Public L. No. 100-77), the first major federal response to the problem of homelessness in the United States. Though President Reagan was not known as a supporter of people who were homeless and poor, a substantial and veto-proof bipartisan majority in Congress voted for passage of the McKinney Act and Reagan signed the act into law in 1987 (the peak year of media coverage). Although it is impossible to know the actual causal connections between media coverage and congressional action, it seems quite likely that the relentless media coverage of the early to mid-1980s pushed politicians to recognize this new social problem (Baum and Burnes, 1993). Something had to be done about the perceived emergency of homelessness in the nation, and throwing money at the problem seemed the least that Congress could do.

Buck, Toro, and Ramos (2004) found that media coverage declined in the late 1980s and early 1990s, possibly because the topic had been covered in depth for many years and the media felt the need to move on to more current topics (one of those topics became the Gulf War that began to heat up with the 1990 invasion of Kuwait by Iraqi forces; see Figure 14.1). Starting in 1995, media coverage plateaued, with around 200–300 articles per year across four major nationally distributed newspapers (i.e., the *New York Times*, the *Washington Post*, the *Los Angeles Times*, and the *Chicago Tribune*). In a recent update of the Buck, Toro, and Ramos (2004) study, using the same methods and considering coverage in the same four newspapers through the subsequent ten years (2004–2013), it was observed that the media coverage essentially maintained the plateau that began in the late 1990s, with minor variations from year to year (Carlson, Toro, and Buck, 2015).

Buck, Toro, and Ramos (2004) also analyzed the professional literature indexed in the PsycINFO database (which not only includes the field of psychology, but many sources from other social sciences and the health and mental health professions). They found almost no coverage devoted to homelessness during the 1970s and into the mid-1980s. Professional coverage (largely consisting of journal articles) eventually experienced a rise beginning in the late 1980s, and reached a peak in 1992. Thus, the initial rise and peak in professional coverage followed similar changes seen in media coverage by about five years. Professionals, like politicians, seem to have responded to many years of intense media coverage on homelessness. Compounded by the typical year or two publication lag in most professional outlets, it took until the early 1990s for the professional literature to show a major response to the growing intensity of media coverage that had begun a decade earlier.

Certainly, many professionals may have been truly outraged by the apparent growth of homelessness, leading them to become engaged with and write about it. However, it is also quite possible that many of them were acting to some extent as mercenaries who saw large amounts of federal and other funding being thrown at the problem, both to conduct targeted research and to develop various interventions to assist people experiencing homelessness. Many jumped on the bandwagon to obtain some of these generous funds for themselves, their agencies, and their clients. Since that time, we have observed the development of a full-blown *homelessness industry,* which includes a wide range of often well-coordinated services offered to people experiencing homelessness, growth of advocacy organizations, and growing numbers of researchers studying the problem. We do not wish to criticize this industry, but we do wish to note its existence as well as its growing power and influence.

The professional coverage seemed to drop somewhat after 1992, then plateau during the mid- to late 1990s, with about 150–200 articles appearing annually in PsycINFO throughout this period. Over the subsequent decade (2004–2013), however, the professional coverage increased gradually (see Carlson, Toro, and Buck, 2015, and Figure 14.1). The level of professional coverage in the most recent years now slightly exceeds the early peak level of 216 publications observed in 1992 (218 in 2011, 229 in 2012, and 233 in 2013). It seems that the topic of homelessness has become almost mainstream in the past decade: an array of different disciplines now produces a wide range of research studies and provides many different services specifically targeted to homeless populations. It now seems difficult to predict if or when the professional coverage will truly plateau or drop. It has not dropped so far, even though the media coverage has been flat for two full decades now.

A content analysis performed by Buck, Toro, and Ramos (2004) coded 574 randomly selected newspaper articles published over thirty years (1974–2003) and Carlson et al. (2015) coded an additional 250 randomly selected newspaper articles published over the subsequent ten years (2004–2013). Consistent with prior research (e.g., Lind and Danowski, 1999), there were consistent changes in the amount of newspaper coverage by season, with less coverage in the spring (March through May) and summer (June through August) and more coverage in the fall (September through November) and winter (December through February). It has long been noted that the cold weather and holidays prompt many human interest media reports on homelessness, and many service agencies obtain the bulk of their donations during and around the holidays.

The analysis by Buck, Toro, and Ramos (2004) revealed a relative emphasis on a factor labeled "skid-row alcoholic" during the earliest period (1974–1981), a sympathetic focus on mental illness and various structural causes of homelessness during the period of increasing coverage in the mid-1980s, and an emphasis on the need for long-term services for homeless people during later years (i.e., 1988–2003). The past decade (2004–2013) has seen the lowest level of coverage on the skid row alcoholic and the highest levels of coverage on homeless youth, economic resources, the role of public policies, and the need for long-term services (Carlson, Toro, and Buck, 2015). One interesting feature of the most recent media coverage (2004–2013) has been extensive attention given to veterans experiencing homelessness. During this past decade, a full 14 percent of the newspaper articles focused at least somewhat on veterans, with most of these (11 percent of the total) presenting veterans at a high intensity or as the major theme. While Buck, Toro, and Ramos (2004) failed to even code for the presence of veterans in their analysis (due to a low base rate), it seems likely that the 14 percent observed most recently represents a real upsurge in the coverage on veterans. This upsurge could be due to the large numbers of veterans returning from combat in the Middle East, many of whom have had difficulties reintegrating into the civilian economy and have often been diagnosed as having post-traumatic stress disorder.

Professional and Academic Interest

A similar content analysis of 324 professional journal articles over thirty years (1974–2003; see Buck, Toro, and Ramos, 2004) plus 161 more over the subsequent ten years (see Carlson, Toro, and Buck, 2015) showed that, over the entire forty-year time period, the deficits and deviant characteristics of people experiencing homelessness (e.g., substance abuse and criminal behavior) were discussed to a significantly greater extent than the structural causes of homelessness. This difference in the focus of coverage was especially noticeable in the professional publications (vs. the media). In response to such overemphasis among professionals on what is wrong with homeless people, Shinn (1992) called for researchers to move beyond person-centered research and service approaches that emphasize mental and substance abuse disorders toward approaches that examine social, political, and other structural factors that affect homelessness. Unfortunately, it appears that, to date, researchers as a whole have not taken Shinn's advice to heart. As in the media coverage presented above, coverage concerning veterans was also often observed among the professional journal articles coded from the past decade (2004–2013; 8 percent of the total 161 coded).

The interest in homelessness has varied across disciplines over the past 40 years. While medical publications accounted for a majority of the earliest publications (56 percent of the relatively small number published during the 1974–1986 period; many of these were opinion or editorial pieces), they accounted for a small minority in the past decade (only 11 percent of those published during the 2004–2013 period). Psychology and other outlets, on the other hand, showed a gradually increasing interest, with only 5 percent and 40 percent (respectively) of all publications in the 1974–1986 period, but 18 percent and 48 percent of all publications in 1998–2003 and 14 percent and 62 percent in 2004–2013. The other category of publications included many multidisciplinary journals (e.g., *AIDS and Behavior, Addictive Behaviors,* and *Sex Roles*).

The methodological rigor of the studies reported in the professional literature has steadily improved over the years. For example, in the earliest time period (1974–1986), only 6 percent of the empirical articles reported reliability or validity data on measures used, whereas 44 percent reported such data in the 1998–2003 period and 50 percent did so in 2004–2013 (Buck, Toro, and Ramos, 2004; Carlson, Toro, and Buck, 2015). Similarly, only 15 percent of the empirical articles in the earliest 1974–1986 time period involved longitudinal data, as compared with 32 percent in the 1998–2003 period and 85 percent in the 2004–2013 period. M. M. Jones (2015) explains this growing methodological rigor as resulting from rapid dissemination of findings from the first generation of federally funded research projects in the early 1980s and from subsequent generations in the late 1980s and early 1990s. The growing methodological rigor observed could also be partly due to the entry of more psychologists and other research-oriented professionals into the homelessness arena.

The Media, Politics, and Social Policy

Following the passage of the McKinney Act in 1987, we saw a series of other policy and funding initiatives. These included special requests for proposals from the National Institutes of Health and other federal agencies (e.g., the Department of Labor and the Administration for Children and Families). In addition, interest in better serving homeless populations and developing research understanding has increased among many foundations. We have seen the development of a coordinated system of funding for services for homeless people through HUD. In most major cities in the United States, there now is a Continuum of Care (CoC) agency that applies to HUD for funds that are then dispersed to service agencies throughout the city. The CoCs are required to conduct biennial prevalence counts of the local homeless population and to evaluate the service system in their area.

While it is difficult to get a firm grip on the total amount of funding targeted toward homelessness over the past forty years, it seems likely that it has steadily risen since 1987. Funding budgeted for McKinney Act programs, for example, has risen more or less gradually from about $500 million in 1987, to about double that ($1 billion annually) in the mid- to late 1990s, to nearly $2 billion in the most recent years, 2000–2013 (Buck, Toro, and Ramos, 2004; Carlson, Toro, and Buck, 2015; Toro and Warren, 1999). Whether this steady rise will continue, given the current budgetary gridlock in Washington, DC, is anyone's guess. But given the growing influence of the homelessness industry described above, it seems that there will be plenty of political pressure to maintain or continue to increase funding targeted to homelessness.

We have already suggested that the intense and growing coverage by the media in the mid- to late 1980s prompted both politicians and professionals to act. Some in the media might challenge this view, preferring to see the media as responsive to public opinion, the situation on the ground (e.g., the actual prevalence of homelessness), and politics. According to this view, the media simply reflects the reality that exists, but does not create an alternate reality. There is, nonetheless, some evidence that the media can help shape public opinion and prompt political action concerning a range of social issues, including homelessness (see Baum and Burnes, 1993). Although factors affecting policy decisionmaking are undoubtedly complex, social problems that receive a large amount of favorable attention in the media tend to be addressed with policy initiatives (Sabatier and Mazmanian, 1981). Politicians and policymakers often rely on the media to gauge public attitudes and the opinions of their constituents (Hutson and Liddiard, 1994).

Media, Politicians, Professionals, and Advocates

The timing of the various rises of interest in homelessness (i.e., media vs. politicians vs. professionals) bears careful examination. In particular, it is clear that the media were the first of these three actors to show an active interest (see Figure 14.1). With the amazing increase in coverage shortly after Reagan's election in 1980, the media would seem the most likely candidate as the opinion leader. Political and professional interest followed, after a few years, in the mid- to late 1980s. Whether the slowly rising professional interest, along with the continued rapid rise of media interest, prompted the politicians to respond by passing the McKinney Act, or if the passing of the McKinney Act produced a sea change that lifted both professionals' and politicians' boats to new levels, is unclear. Most likely, all three forces operated in a reciprocal fashion (Tompsett et al., 2003) and fueled greater interest among all three. Such reciprocity makes good sense, especially as time moved forward and the media, politicians, and professionals studying and serving homeless people all repeatedly interacted with each other. Coverage of homelessness in the professional literature, for example, can have an impact on media and policy decisions. Advocates for people experiencing homelessness often use research reported in professional outlets to support the need for services and policy change, and professionals have respected positions in their communities that give them opportunities to influence local as well as national policies (Toro and Warren, 1999). Furthermore, organized bodies representing various scientific and service disciplines (e.g., the American Psychological Association [APA]) regularly attempt to engage in interactions with the media and inform public policy decisions based on sound science. One recent example of such an attempt came from the APA's Presidential Task Force on Psychology's Contribution to End Homelessness (see Bray et al., 2010).

Examining the three trends in Figure 14.1 over the past decade (2004–2013), it is noticeable that both the professional interest and the federal funding levels have increased gradually during this time period while the media interest has, essentially, remained flat since 1995. While we cannot be certain about the cause of the now long-lasting lack of media interest, it could be the end result of the intensity of coverage in the 1980s and early 1990s. Such intensity could not be maintained; homelessness no longer seemed to be news and, as noted earlier, there have been many other competing topics to occupy the media's attention (perhaps, most notably, the September 11 attacks and the subsequent wars in Iraq and Afghanistan).

Perhaps the parallel trends for funding and professional interest reflect the regular collaboration between homeless advocates such as the National Alliance to End Homelessness (NAEH) and professional researchers and service providers. Consider, for example, NAEH's Research Council, which was formally launched in 2006 and includes many of the nation's top researchers on homelessness, and NAEH's regular national conferences, which draw hundreds of attendees (mostly service providers and policymakers). This collaboration has perhaps led to continuing pressure on politicians to boost federal funding. The media no longer seems as influential as they were in the 1980s. It is possible that the professionals and the advocates have taken up the torch in recent years while the media have remained on the sidelines. Based on extensive interviews with many activists, researchers, and government officials active during the 1980s, M. M. Jones (2015) recently suggested that some of the early advocates, such as Mitch Snyder and his Community for Creative Non-Violence, were effective at engaging the interest of the media through regular press briefings and bold events such as the "Reaganville" tent city erected across from the White House on Thanksgiving 1981. Advocates represent yet another kind of player that may have operated in a reciprocal fashion with the media, professionals, and politicians (Baum and Burnes, 1993).

We noted above that both the media and professional coverage on veterans experiencing homelessness seem to have shown a dramatic rise in the past decade, an increase that coincided with the explicit federal policy vowing to end homelessness among veterans by the end of 2015. The roots of this policy began during the George W. Bush administration, as many veterans of the Iraq War were becoming homeless on their return home. The formal policy has developed unabated throughout the Barack Obama administration. Tremendous resources have been invested in this policy, including funds for the Supportive Services for Veteran Families (VASH) program that provides short-term assistance to prevent homelessness for at-risk veterans and to rapidly re-house veterans already homeless, and the HUD-VASH program that provides a permanent rental subsidy and long-term case management for veterans with disabilities. By most accounts, it seems that this infusion of resources has paid off. For example, a recent report of the US Interagency Council on Homelessness (ICH, 2013) documented a 17 percent decline in the total national number of homeless veterans over the four-year period from 2009 through 2012 (based on the Point-in-Time (PIT) counts provided by the CoCs nationally). An even more recent NAEH report (2015) notes that the overall national prevalence of homelessness (also based on PIT counts) dropped by 9 percent from 2009 to 2014 as the nation slowly recovered from the Great Recession, while the national prevalence among veterans dropped by over four times that amount (39 percent) during this same six-year period.

Public Opinion

Starting in the late 1980s, a series of public opinion surveys on homelessness have been conducted in the United States and other developed nations (e.g., Link et al., 1994; Link, Schwartz, et al., 1995; Tompsett et al., 2006; Toro et al., 2007). By the 1990s, some in the US media suggested that the public had experienced compassion fatigue with regard to homelessness (Baum and Burnes, 1993; Link, Schwartz, et al., 1995; Toro and Warren, 1991). An increasing number of newspaper, magazine, and television news stories proposed that Americans had grown impatient with and even hostile toward the plight of homeless people (e.g., *ABC News Nightline*, 1990; Blasi, 1994; Janofsky, 1994; Ratnesar, 1999; Wilkerson, 1991). However, research evidence from the various surveys has not supported this interpretation at all. For example, surveys continue to find that a majority of the public supports increased federal spending on homelessness and would pay more taxes to help people who are homeless (Link, Schwartz, et al., 1995). Such data led Buck, Toro, and Ramos (2004) to conclude that "if anything, it seems more accurate to say that it is the mass media that have experienced the fatigue" (p. 167). Not only is the public generally concerned about homelessness, but citizens are also reasonably well informed about the characteristics of people who are homeless. Toro and McDonell (1992) found that the public did not, for example, overestimate the rate of mental illness among those who are homeless if the commonly cited actual rate of around 33 percent was used (often based on having ever been in a psychiatric hospital). It was only when more stringent definitions of mental illness were used (e.g., specific serious diagnoses based on a structured interview) that the public overestimated, as one might expect if they were responding to stereotypes. Similarly, the public overestimated the number of homeless people with criminal histories when a narrow definition of such a history was used (i.e., a felony conviction), but underestimated when a broader definition was used (i.e., having ever been arrested; see Toro and McDonell, 1992).

While it is impossible to rule out the possibility that changing public opinion helped prompt the media to greatly expand coverage in the 1980s because the first opinion surveys were not conducted until late in that decade, it seems likely that the growing media coverage on homelessness not only prompted interest among politicians and professionals but also among citizens in the general public. Public interest and concern was maintained at least through the end of 2001, when the most recent national survey was completed (Tompsett et al., 2006). Similar levels of compassion have also been found in more recent local surveys (e.g., Agans et al., 2011, in Los Angeles; Metz and Weigel, 2015, in Denver) as well as surveys taken in other developed countries, including Canada and many European nations (Hobden et al., 2007; Tompsett et al., 2003; Toro et al., 2007, 2008).

Conclusion

Whatever the prevalence of homelessness, whatever changes in its composition have been manifest over time, the extent of homelessness over the past four decades has been surprisingly robust and has shown little hope of a dramatic reduction anytime soon. Even when tremendous resources are devoted to eliminating it, we have been unable to do so. The case of services for veterans experiencing homelessness is a fine example in this regard; while over the past several years we seem to have made tremendous progress in reducing the number of veterans experiencing homelessness, we are far from reaching the goal of totally eliminating this subgroup from among the larger homeless population (ICH, 2013). Similar attention has been directed toward the chronically homeless (i.e., those homeless for long periods of time and having serious disabling conditions) over the past decade or so, with similarly modest gains observed (NAEH, 2015).

Even under the best possible economic conditions, such as those seen during the 1990s, homelessness has remained at epidemic levels. This is the bad news. The good news is that we have begun to demonstrate that it is possible to make a positive impact, if we are willing to devote the necessary resources. The cases of homeless veterans and the chronically homeless are fine examples of this, as is the growing number of solid demonstrations that we can intervene to prevent homelessness and help those already experiencing it to become stably housed and experience other positive outcomes (e.g., Milburn et al., 2012; Nelson, Aubry, and Lafrance, 2007; Szarzynska and Toro, 2015; Toro et al., 1997; Tsemberis, 1999).

For the reasons we have documented, it seems likely that the media will continue their consistent, but low-level, coverage on homelessness. It also seems likely that, at least for the time being, public attitudes toward people who are homeless will remain relatively sympathetic. Perhaps the low level of media coverage will be enough to maintain that sympathy. On the other hand, professionals show no sign of letting up on the intensity and sophistication of their investigations of homelessness, and advocates show no signs of relenting in their push for funding and new approaches to caring for people experiencing it. The coordinated efforts of the professionals and advocates might be the biggest ray of hope that we may ultimately reduce, and possibly eliminate, homelessness.

15

Community Planning and the End of Homelessness

Samantha Batko

In 2000, the National Alliance to End Homelessness (the Alliance) published *A Plan, Not a Dream: How to End Homelessness in Ten Years* (Ten Year Plan) (NAEH, 2000a). It boldly asserted that homelessness, which at that time was generally considered an intractable social problem, could be conquered. It laid out a path forward that employed data, prioritized prevention of homelessness and permanent housing solutions, and encouraged the engagement of mainstream systems. In the wake of the plan's release, the federal government and hundreds of local jurisdictions across the country developed their own ten-year plans, many of which echoed the strategies outlined by the Alliance.

These ten-year plans were instrumental in building momentum and setting priorities locally but, over time, ten-year planning efforts have been eclipsed by other decisionmaking processes, emerging best practices, and federal requirements. Regardless, the federal government and local jurisdictions still use the framework outlined in the Alliance's Ten Year Plan as well as community plans from across the country to prevent and more quickly end homelessness for families and individuals.

Emergence of Ten-Year Planning

When the Alliance published its Ten Year Plan in 2000, widespread homelessness had existed in the United States for about twenty years. This phenomenon began in the 1980s with growth in homelessness that had not been seen in the United States since the Great Depression. This burgeoning of homelessness first emerged during the recession of 1981 and 1982. As the recovery from that recession progressed in the mid-1980s, the unemployment rate fell and the nation's overall economy improved, but homelessness continued to grow.

This increase is generally attributed to harmful trends in housing affordability. Using American Housing Survey data, Daskal (1998, p. 11) found that a drastic change had occurred in the availability of housing that was affordable for low-income renters between 1970 and 1985. In 1970, there was a surplus of 300,000 low-cost rental units in comparison to the number of low-income renters. In contrast, by 1985, there were 8.9 million low-income renters, but only 5.6 million low-cost rental units—a deficit of 3.3 million low-cost units. Deinstitutionalization, the explosion of crack cocaine, and reductions in social welfare and general assistance are also widely credited as contributors to homelessness, since they may have further impacted the marginalization of already vulnerable populations.

Regardless of the causes, by 1984, the US Department of Housing and Urban Development estimated 250,000 to 300,000 people were homeless on a given night (HUD, 2007, p. 3). In 1987, the Urban Institute estimated that, in cities with a population of over 100,000, nearly 230,000 people were homeless on a given day (Burt and Cohen, 1989, p. 36). Based on the National Survey of Homeless Assistance Providers and Clients, Burt (2001) estimated that at least 800,000 people were homeless in the United States, including about 200,000 children on a given night in 1996.

Up to this point, the primary national response to homelessness was to provide shelter to keep people safe and food to provide basic necessities. Burt (1999, pp. 14–17) found that food pantries represented the largest portion of homeless assistance programs with an estimated 9,000 such programs, and emergency shelters the second-largest response with about 5,700 programs. Few resources were spent on helping people transition from the streets to independent housing in the community.

The Alliance's Ten Year Plan (NAEH, 2000b) acknowledged that food and emergency shelter programs had limited abilities to independently prevent people from becoming homeless, change the underlying income and housing affordability issues that contribute to homelessness, or respond to the continually growing homeless and at-risk populations while still meeting the crisis needs of people experiencing homelessness. Instead, the Alliance's plan focused on a reorientation from individual programs managing individuals and families to community-wide planning to prevent people from becoming homeless and helping them find housing as quickly as possible.

The plan, informed by emerging research on homelessness, the experiences of advocates and service providers, and the efforts of leaders working to address homelessness in communities across the country consisted of four appropriately designed main elements: plan for outcomes, close the front door, open the back door, and build the infrastructure.

Plan for Outcomes

The first element of the Alliance's Ten Year Plan was a call for outcome-driven planning by local jurisdictions. At the time, there were a limited number of communities undertaking strategic planning to address homelessness. Outcome-driven community planning required two activities: the collection and strategic use of local data, and long-term planning of a systemic response that engaged stakeholders beyond targeted homeless assistance programs.

What do people who experience homelessness in your community look like? Why did they become homeless? What homeless and mainstream assistance are they receiving or do they need to access? What assistance is available in your community? How are people using that assistance? The purpose of these data was to assess the effectiveness of existing homeless assistance and to identify gaps that needed to be filled.

Paired with the collection of data to inform community-level planning, the Alliance's Ten Year Plan advised communities to develop long-term plans that went beyond the scope of a jurisdiction's homeless assistance providers to include diverse stakeholders, with the goal of prevention when possible and immediately re-housing anyone who became homeless. The Alliance outlined stakeholders that could be involved in those planning efforts, including (but not limited to) state and local mental health departments, state and local corrections departments, veterans affairs officials, substance abuse providers, governors' and mayors' offices, and housing developers and operators. The collection and use of data and the buy-in of diverse stakeholders as advised by the Alliance permeated the ten-year plans developed by the federal government and communities across the country.

Close the Front Door

Closing the front door to homelessness, the second element of the Alliance's Ten Year Plan, encouraged communities to adopt strategies to stem the flow of people becoming homeless. At the time that the Alliance proposed closing the front door, most homelessness prevention efforts focused on stopping evictions by paying past due rent and utility payments. The Alliance suggested a more comprehensive view of homelessness prevention that placed the onus of keeping people housed on mainstream systems tasked with taking care of vulnerable populations. This would require the engagement of entities such as the criminal justice, child welfare, and health and mental health systems to prevent people being served or exiting those systems from becoming homeless. In the end, both system and emergency prevention were among the most common strategies included in community plans to end homelessness. Despite this, localities continue to struggle with how to target prevention resources and how to successfully prevent discharges from institutions onto the streets.

Open the Back Door

The third element of the Alliance's Ten Year Plan called for quickly re-housing everyone who became homeless. The plan advocated a Housing First approach to help people access permanent housing and connect with appropriate services, with a focus on minimizing time spent in shelter. Housing First was an emerging and promising strategy based on solid research that analyzed the needs and behaviors of people experiencing homelessness. Its adoption, however, would require a philosophical reorientation of the homeless assistance field, from fixing people and then helping them access housing, to helping people access housing as a platform from which to address other issues.

Prior to the advent of Housing First, homeless assistance attempted to keep people in programs for long periods of time to fix the problems that were assumed to have made them homeless. The theory was that, when those problems were addressed, people would be able to find and afford housing and exit homelessness. In contrast, Kuhn and Culhane (1998) found that the majority of individuals who became homeless remained so for short periods of time and often did not become homeless again. For these people who are not homeless for long, the Alliance recommended helping them return to housing quickly and connecting them to mainstream services.

For the small subset of individuals who became homeless and remained so for long periods of time, permanent supportive housing, long-term housing, and service assistance were emerging as aspects of the model. Kuhn and Culhane (1998) found that this group was likely to have mental, physical, or substance abuse disabilities that interfered with their ability to maintain housing. Permanent supportive housing was found to be effective in ending homelessness for this group, and less expensive than emergency shelter or the jails, hospitals, and other public services that these individuals regularly used.

With the increase in homeless families and limited resources, jurisdictions were also experimenting with short-term assistance to help families quickly exit homelessness. These efforts, sometimes referred to and later more commonly known as rapid re-housing, were having success in areas in which they were being piloted. Later, Culhane, Metraux, et al. (2007) found that homeless families followed the same patterns as homeless individuals with regard to short one-time incidences of homelessness, indicating that the application of a rapid re-housing model for families might be the most effective way to quickly end their homelessness. The eventual adoption of permanent supportive housing and rapid re-housing, both by the federal government and in local ten-year plans, reflected a significant change in homeless assistance nationally that has continued to the present.

Build the Infrastructure

Lastly, the Alliance's Ten Year Plan called for communities and federal policymakers to address the systemic problems that lead to homelessness crises: the shortage of affordable housing, insufficient incomes, and lack of appropriate services. The assistance system can prevent people from spending lengthy periods of time homeless, but cannot avert housing emergencies without improving the broader housing, income, and service deficits. The supply of affordable available housing for low-income populations needs to be increased, and public benefits and services that help people pay for and meet basic needs must be supported. However, while creating affordable housing became one of the most popular strategies in local ten-year plans, the country's affordable housing situation has continued to worsen.

Following the release of the Alliance's Ten Year Plan, the concept of ten-year planning proliferated nationally. In 2002, in the President's Fiscal Year 2003 Budget Proposal, the George W. Bush administration set a goal of ending chronic homelessness in ten years. In addition, three cities (Indianapolis, Chicago, and Memphis) completed their own ten-year plans. In 2003, the US Conference of Mayors adopted a resolution in response to a call from then executive director of the US Interagency Council on Homelessness, Philip Mangano, who challenged 100 cities to initiate plans. By 2004, about 100 communities had initiated planning efforts and, by 2006, ninety ten-year plans to end homelessness were complete.

Strategies in Local Ten-Year Plans to End Homelessness

Limited analysis has been completed on what strategies were included in local ten-year plans, or what success was achieved by implementing them. In 2003, the Alliance followed up on its Ten Year Plan with a toolkit detailing ten steps that communities should take to end homelessness that were based on the four elements outlined in the Alliance's Ten Year Plan. In addition to giving communities a template for local ten-year plans, these "ten essentials" provide a framework from which to assess what strategies were included in those plans. Table 15.1 details the strategies outlined in the ten essentials, how they correspond with the broader elements of the Ten Year Plan framework, and the percentage of community plans that included those strategies.

At the time the Alliance introduced the ten essentials, some communities were already undertaking those activities. And not surprisingly, many communities incorporated the strategies outlined by the Alliance in their local ten-year plans. M. Cunningham et al. (2006) found that 90 percent of plans identified public stakeholders participating in the ten-year planning process; most frequently, public agencies included were the local Departments of Human or Social Services and the Housing Authority. Similarly, 87 percent of plans indicated nonprofit participation. Private stakeholders were slightly less likely to be included, with 83 percent of plans identifying private stakeholder involvement. Hospitals and health care providers were the most common private stakeholders involved in ten-year planning.

Stakeholders least likely to be included in ten-year planning were people who were currently or formerly homeless. Only 28 percent of the first ninety

Table 15.1 Community Adoption of the Ten Year Plan Elements and Ten Essentials for Ending Homelessness

Ten Year Plan Elements	Ten Essentials for Ending Homelessness	Percent of Early Plans Adopting Strategy (n=90)
Plan for Outcomes	• Create a Plan to End Homelessness—Engaged diverse stakeholders to develop a set of strategies aimed at addressing the unique needs of the people experiencing homelessness in your community.	91
	• Create a Data System to Help End Homelessness—Develop a data management system that helps communities assess how long people have been homeless and what their needs are to evaluate programs and allocate resources appropriately.	
Close the Front Door	• Establish Emergency Prevention Programs—Emergency prevention should include rent and/or utility assistance, landlord intervention, and other strategies to help prevent eviction.	79
	• Make System Changes That Prevent Homelessness—Assure mainstream programs assess and respond to housing needs of the low-income people they are already serving and create processes for obtaining stable housing for those discharged from public institutions.	92
Open the Back Door	• Outreach to People Living on the Streets—Develop a system designed to reduce barriers and encourage people to enter housing and service programs.	79
	• Shorten the Time Spent Homeless—Reorient emergency shelter and other homeless assistance programs to prioritize minimizing the amount of time and the number of times people are homeless.	57
	• Rapidly Re-House People—Develop housing search methods to help people quickly access permanent housing.	56
Build the Infrastructure	• Create Access to Treatment and Other Services—After households are re-housed, connect people to services and mainstream programs.	94
	• Create an Adequate Supply of Permanent Affordable Housing—Develop a supply of permanent housing, both permanent supportive housing and general affordable housing, to meet the needs of all people experiencing homelessness.	92
	• Ensure People Have Incomes to Pay for Housing—Link people to employment and benefits to ensure they have sufficient income to afford rent.	81

plans completed indicated that currently or formerly homeless people contributed to the planning process. This level of engagement is disappointing because people who have or are using the system have a unique and important point of view. They can provide feedback on services that were needed, but not available; services that were available, but may or may not have been helpful; and help to identify what makes a system accessible and navigable for the people who would be using it.

Of the first ninety plans completed, M. Cunningham et al. (2006) found that 91 percent contained strategies for creating data systems. One community that was already using local data in this manner was Columbus, Ohio, where the Community Shelter Board developed a jurisdiction-wide data collection system that tracked the use of emergency homeless shelters. These data were used for a variety of reasons, including for analyzing shelter utilization trends to inform a responsive homeless assistance system and for monitoring progress. When Columbus was faced with moving two of its emergency shelters, it used the data it had collected on shelter utilization to identify those people in shelter who were experiencing chronic homelessness, and then built permanent supportive housing for them instead of moving them to a shelter in another location.

Another community, Hartford, Connecticut, also began creating a local data system in 2001 known as a Homeless Management Information System, the development of which was required by HUD. When the city released its ten-year plan in 2005, it included a goal of having 80 percent of assistance providers inputting consumer information in the data system within one year. The city planned to use the information collected in the data system to identify and provide services for people experiencing chronic homelessness.

Efforts to close the front door were also widely adopted: M. Cunningham and Henry (2006) found that 79 percent of plans addressed emergency prevention, and 92 percent outlined system prevention efforts, including discharge planning from criminal justice and health and mental health systems. The focus on system prevention in early plans to end homelessness may have been a reflection of the fact that, prior to ten-year planning processes, many communities had focused on emergency assistance to prevent homelessness and, for them, creating a systemic plan to end homelessness was a new strategy.

An example of a community already undertaking emergency prevention efforts was Hennepin county, Minnesota. The community's program was funded by the state and dedicated to families experiencing, or at risk of experiencing, homelessness. Families that had received written eviction notices, were in overcrowded housing, lived in a condemned building, were victims of domestic violence, or were unable to remain in their housing for other reasons were eligible for assistance. The program proved effective with only 3–4 percent of families entering a shelter after receiving assistance.

In a similar emergency prevention effort, Grand Rapids, Michigan's ten-year plan to end homelessness (Grand Rapids Area Housing Continuum of Care, 2004) incorporated a central intake system that included services for prevention such as a resource pool to assist with temporary rental, mortgage, and utilities arrearages, and necessary repairs to owned homes. Grand Rapids added systemic prevention in the form of a housing specialist to help those exiting institutions to avoid homelessness when they were discharged.

In addition, M. Cunningham et al. (2006) found that the vast majority of early plans also outlined strategies for opening the back door by helping people experiencing homelessness to access permanent housing: 92 percent had strategies for permanent housing, including over half of plans that proposed rapid re-housing as a permanent housing strategy despite its being a relatively new model in the field.

Likely due to the emphasis on chronic homelessness in early local ten-year plans, many communities included strategies to increase permanent supportive housing. The San Francisco plan (2004, p. 8) called for the development of 3,000 units of permanent supportive housing to respond to the needs of the estimated 3,000 chronically homeless individuals in the city. Portland and Multnomah county, Oregon, were other examples of communities that called for the development of a large number of permanent supportive housing units—2,200 units by 2015.

Another strategy for opening the back door was rapid re-housing, an intervention with the primary goal of reducing the amount of time people spend homeless by providing assistance to locate rental housing and pay rent for a time-limited period. As rapid re-housing was a lesser known and newly established permanent housing intervention when earlier plans were being developed, fewer communities included specific rapid re-housing strategies in their ten-year plans. But some innovative communities and programs were experimenting with the idea. Hennepin county's Rapid Exit program and Los Angeles's Beyond Shelter program were the best known efforts to rapidly re-house families. Beyond Shelter employed housing search staff, helped families negotiate leases, assisted with move-in funds, and helped families overcome the barriers of poor credit histories and prior evictions. In Minnesota, families were referred to the Rapid Exit program within one week of entering a shelter. A Rapid Exit caseworker was responsible for helping families find housing and connecting them with any needed follow-up services. The first ninety local ten-year plans to end homelessness ignited a flurry of creation that took place from 2004 to 2010. By 2009, nearly 250 communities across the country had developed ten-year plans to end homelessness, an impressive number considering ten-year plans were not required by any federal funding stream, and communities that undertook them did so on their own accord and at their own expense. Figure 15.1 shows the percentage of communities who completed plans by year as of 2009, the last year comprehensive data were analyzed.

Figure 15.1 Percentage of Plans Completed by Year

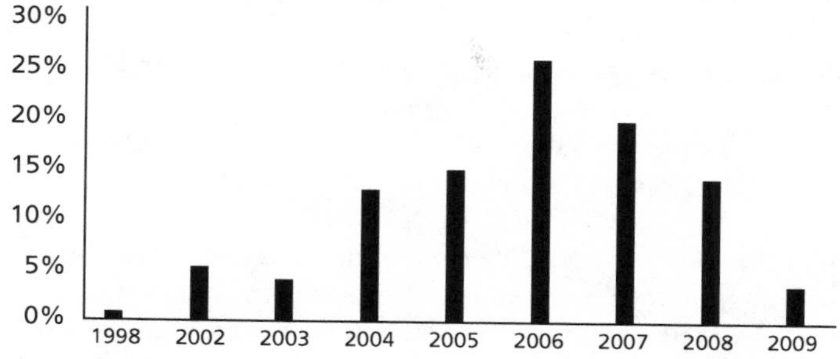

Source: National Alliance to End Homelessness, 2009.

Strategy Shifts

Significant change in the homeless assistance field was seen in the years from the late 1990s through 2010. Housing First models, those focusing on providing people with swift access to housing without preconditions, including permanent supportive housing and rapid re-housing, rose to prominence as communities and the federal government focused more on the goal of decreasing the time people spent homeless and prioritizing the most vulnerable people—those with disabilities and living on the streets or those who had been homeless for protracted periods. Paralleling the trends in homeless assistance, there were some shifts in the degree to which specific strategies were focused on plans written earlier compared with those completed closer to 2010.

M. Cunningham et al. (2006) found that, of the first ninety community plans completed, 34 percent focused exclusively on chronic homelessness, which was likely due to the federal focus on ending chronic homelessness that was initiated in 2002. As later plans were created, the Alliance (NAEH, 2009) found that chronic homelessness was not a singular priority as often seen in plans developed after 2006, with homelessness among families, youth, and other subpopulations receiving more attention than they had in earlier years.

In addition to the expansion of plans to populations beyond those experiencing chronic homelessness, the Alliance (NAEH, 2009) found shifts in the strategies that local ten-year plans prioritized. Plans written in later years, those published after 2006, focused heavily on emergency prevention approaches, including eviction prevention tactics such as paying back rent and utility assistance. This was in stark contrast to earlier plans that focused significantly more on strategies for systems prevention such as discharge planning from institutions. This shift to emergency prevention in plans completed later in the decade may have been caused by concerns in communities at the beginning of and during the housing collapse that preceded the Great Recession that started in late 2007.

Another noted difference between earlier and later plans was the emergence of rapid re-housing and shortening of the length of time people spent homeless as prominent strategies. Cunningham et al. (2006) found that 56 percent of the first ninety plans completed included rapid re-housing. The Alliance (NAEH, 2009) found that 68 percent of later plans included rapid re-housing. Similarly, of the first ninety plans, 57 percent included strategies to shorten homelessness while 69 percent of later plans included similar ways of accomplishing this. This is likely due to the fact that rapid re-housing began to be promoted more directly as a promising strategy and that, in 2009, federal funding streams for the model were established.

Implementation

The development of local ten-year plans, with their inclusion of promising strategies, was a step in the right direction for many communities. But to end homelessness, communities must have the capacity to put plans into action; unfortunately, most local ten-year plans did not include key elements that would provide the platform from which to implement the proposed strategies. M. Cunningham et al. (2006) identified several such key elements — numeric outcome goals, time lines, naming entities responsible for implementation, and identifying funding sources for strategies as mechanisms — that would increase the likelihood that the strategies outlined in the plans would be implemented. In 2009, the Alliance observed that the vast majority of plans (82 percent, $n = 234$) did not include clear, numeric outcome goals and only 8 percent of plans identified funding sources (NAEH, 2009). More communities, but still less than half, included time lines for implementation (41 percent) and identified entities responsible for that implementation (35 percent).

Impact

Despite the absence of clear paths to implementation in local ten-year plans, homelessness has decreased across the nation. Starting in 2005, HUD began publishing data from Point-in-Time counts that communities report as part of their applications for competitive federal homeless assistance funds. In 2005 before most ten-year plans were completed, HUD (2007) estimated there were 754,147 people experiencing homelessness on a given night. Since then HUD (2014a) estimated that, in 2014, homelessness on a given night in the United States decreased to 578,424 people. While it is possible that the community buy-in for and strategic investment in proven strategies included in local ten-year plans have contributed toward the decreases in homelessness observed since 2005, there is limited information on the impact of a ten-year plan on each local jurisdiction's number of homeless people. Further, there could be a number of other causes for the national decrease, including an improving economy and increased investment in permanent supportive housing and rapid re-housing by the federal government.

To our knowledge, almost no communities have rigorously evaluated the impact of their ten-year plans, which may be because many cities have not reached their plans' ten-year mark or that the ten-year plans have been eclipsed by other local efforts. The city of Chicago is an exception, and was also one of the first jurisdictions in the country to complete a local ten-year plan. In 2009, as the plan was nearing its tenth anniversary, researchers from Loyola University and the University of Chicago were engaged to conduct an evaluation of the effectiveness of the plan and where improvements could be made.

Chicago's ten-year plan, *Getting Housed, Staying Housed* (City of Chicago, 2002), focused on three core tenets: prevent homelessness whenever possible, rapidly re-house people when homelessness cannot be prevented, and provide wraparound services that promote housing stability and self-sufficiency. The evaluation of Chicago's ten-year plan (City of Chicago, 2009) found that people who were placed in permanent housing remained successfully housed. Unfortunately, relatively low numbers of people experiencing homelessness in shelters and interim housing programs moved to permanent housing programs during the study period, and people who began the period under review in shelters experienced lengthy stays. Additionally, the evaluation found that the homeless assistance system was not well coordinated and not easily accessed by those who needed help.

In 2012 using the information from that evaluation, local data on people experiencing homelessness in Chicago, and information about the local community context, the city published an updated plan to end homelessness. Chicago Plan 2.0 (2012) was built on the principles of the original ten-year plan, but incorporated important changes in federal and state policies and utilization of emerging promising practices and policies. The new plan also included clear numeric outcomes, short- and long-term action steps, and mechanisms for ongoing performance evaluation and goal setting. The city reports on progress on the plan twice a year. Chicago's updated plan and ongoing evaluation of progress are reflective of a recent shift in the federal response to homelessness toward measuring effectiveness and efficiency as well as in the way communities approach ongoing performance evaluation and goal setting as part of dynamic planning processes to end homelessness.

Shifts in Federal Policy

In 2009, the McKinney-Vento Homeless Assistance Grant programs were reauthorized with the passage of the Homeless Emergency Assistance and

Rapid Transition to Homelessness Act. The HEARTH Act was the most significant change to the program in fifteen years and greatly reflected the themes in local ten-year plans to end homelessness. Homelessness prevention was significantly expanded and new incentives were placed for permanent housing solutions, including rapid re-housing and permanent supportive housing.

Additionally, in a major shift, outcome-based strategic planning and more extensive coordination became requirements for all communities seeking federal funding for homelessness assistance. Communities were now obliged to create governance systems that included a wide variety of stakeholders. Similarly reflecting the themes seen in the Alliance's Ten Year Plan and local ten-year plans from communities across the country, communities were required to report on community-wide performance goals of reduction in the number of people becoming homeless, reduction in the length of time people are homeless, increases in the number of people exiting to permanent housing, reductions in the number of people returning to homelessness, and increases in jobs and income. Communities were also required to create coordinated entry systems to streamline access for people seeking homeless assistance, which is intended to provide quicker access to the assistance needed to exit homelessness and to help communities maximize resources.

The changes required by the HEARTH Act would take time to be implemented by the federal government and local communities, but more immediate changes were coming for communities. Almost simultaneous to the passage of the HEARTH Act, the Homelessness Prevention and Rapid Re-Housing Program was included in the American Recovery and Reinvestment Act, more commonly known as the stimulus package created in response to the Great Recession that began in 2007. HPRP represented the single largest investment in homeless assistance up until that time and, in 2009, HUD began distributing funds from the $1.5 billion program that funded rent and utility assistance, housing location assistance, and case management for both emergency homelessness prevention and rapid re-housing. The provisos attached to these funds were the clearest indication to communities to date that federal homeless assistance was focused on decreasing the number of people becoming homeless and the amount of time people spend homeless and on helping people secure permanent housing.

Following the start of HPRP and the passage of the HEARTH Act, the US Interagency Council on Homelessness released the first comprehensive federal plan to end homelessness for all populations, *Opening Doors: Federal Strategic Plan to Prevent and End Homelessness* (US Interagency Council on Homelessness, 2010). The plan was announced in 2010 with the goal of ending veteran and chronic homelessness by 2015, and family and youth homelessness by 2020. Although the core goals and, for the most part, the time frame have remained consistent, it has been amended multiple times to reflect evolving priorities and new research and best practices emerging from communities.

Evolution of Community Planning

The current federal plan to end homelessness is not a static document, just as local community planning is no longer synonymous with static ten-year plans. In many communities the ten-year plans written years ago, while serving as galvanizing documents that laid out a vision for ending homelessness in the community, are out-of-date, referencing federal, state, and local policies that no longer exist and promoting intervention models that have been found ineffective or that have significantly evolved. Today, communities are able to be, and are required to be, more dynamic and responsive in their planning efforts. Some communities, such as Chicago, have chosen to update their plans or make them living documents that are regularly revisited and modified. Other communities have moved beyond ten-year planning and rely on ongoing community evaluation and planning to move their efforts forward.

HPRP presented an opportunity for communities to begin dynamic community planning because it provided a large amount of flexible funds for limited activities, with few restrictions on how those activities were targeted or implemented. Some communities took advantage of these funds to test and evaluate innovative ways to target resources and end homelessness. Out of this sprang new models of strategic local planning and, without undertaking a massive community-wide planning and vision process, community leaders were able to use data and HPRP funds to determine the most effective way to target prevention resources, build momentum behind rapid re-housing as a permanent housing solution, and pilot coordinated entry processes.

HPRP funds could be used for both rapid re-housing and homelessness prevention, and nationally most of the funds were spent on the latter. From a research standpoint, proving the effectiveness of homelessness prevention has been elusive. Shinn et al. (2013) found that the number of people entering shelter in New York City was low, despite households having numerous risk factors for entry. How then should a community target limited available resources to prevent homelessness?

Alameda county, California, analyzed data the county had collected on people who had requested prevention assistance or entered emergency shelters. Gale (2012) found that the people who received prevention assistance entered homelessness at about the same low rate as those who were denied, and that the people receiving prevention assistance were not similar to those who entered shelter with respect to other factors such as where they were living, income, or age of head of household. These findings indicated that the county was spending prevention assistance resources on people that were not likely to ever become homeless; hence, it created a screener to more closely match those who were offered prevention assistance with those who were ultimately entering emergency shelters.

Rapid re-housing, which was a strategy that had emerged from local communities when local ten-year plans were first being developed, was the other major activity allowable under HPRP. Communities had begun to pilot and test rapid re-housing programs, but only a limited number of jurisdictions had invested in the model. Eventually, rapid re-housing emerged as a national best practice and HPRP was the first federal funding stream that expressly funded it on the national level.

In 2008, the Road Home in Salt Lake City, Utah, piloted a rapid re-housing model. It was successful in moving families out of shelters and overall, families did not return. When HPRP funds became available, the Road Home combined its HPRP funding with Temporary Assistance for Needy Families Emergency Contingency funding available through Utah's Workforce Services. Using the two funding sources, the Road Home was able to help families quickly find and move into housing in the community as well as connect families to benefits and employment services. When HPRP ended, the Road Home was convinced that rapid re-housing was the promising strategy (NAEH, 2013a) to continue funding and reallocated other resources to continue rapid re-housing families. The Workforce Investment Agency also saw the benefit and has remained a committed rapid re-housing partner, maintaining this partnership even after HPRP funds expired.

One of the few conditions associated with HPRP funds was that communities were required to establish community-wide criteria for eligibility for prevention and rapid re-housing assistance. Some communities used this as an opportunity to pilot the coordinated entry requirements in the HEARTH Act. For example, when HPRP funds were distributed in 2009, the county of Fairfax, Virginia, was early in the implementation of its local ten-year plan that was completed in 2007. It created a task group to tackle what was then referred to as "coordinated intake." This task group created and implemented a screener focused on prevention, diversion, and rapid re-housing. The screener was first used for families when HPRP started and, over time while HPRP was being implemented, the screener was revised and improved. As was revealed in a Community Snapshot (NAEH, 2011c), the community had found that the screener led to greater coordination between departments and agencies working on homeless services.

The HPRP program ended in 2012, but the community innovation spurred by it and the impending changes from the ongoing implementation of the HEARTH Act have remained. Today, communities continue to plan and implement those plans to end homelessness through ongoing dynamic processes, including building decisionmaking bodies composed of diverse stakeholders, blending funding sources, and using data to evaluate and improve performance. The ongoing planning process required by the HEARTH Act is reflective of the original local ten-year planning efforts, but mandates some of the activities wherein local ten-year plans had fallen short.

During the development of ten-year plans, the engagement of various stakeholders from the public, private, and nonprofit stakeholders built momentum and investment in the mission to end homelessness. Following the ten-year planning process, communities found ways to maintain that engagement to keep stakeholders invested. Today, communities are required to involve diverse stakeholders in community and policy decisions, including public, nonprofit, and private partners from a variety of service industries. And in a counterpoint to earlier local ten-year plans, federal regulations require that communities include currently or formerly homeless people in these decisionmaking bodies. As previously discussed, this is in contrast to the way in which homeless and formerly homeless people were frequently excluded from local ten-year planning processes.

The Road Home, which took advantage of HPRP and TANF resources, was not unique in its efforts to blend funding sources to assist people experiencing homelessness. Mercer County, New Jersey, has seen impressive decreases in family homelessness through expanding rapid re-housing and shifting how resources, specifically TANF funds, are used to help families move quickly to find housing.

Finally, communities are using data to evaluate and improve performance. An example of these efforts is Alameda county, California. In 2010, EveryOne Home, the planning body for Alameda county, began releasing reports detailing the performance of the community overall and individual programs in meeting the community's and the federal government's goals of ending homelessness as enumerated in the HEARTH Act. These reports share successes to build momentum in the community and create an environment of responsibility that encourages participation in efforts to meet federal goals. EveryOne Home worked with programs that had poor performance to identify needed changes and improvements in practice to improve outcomes.

Moving Forward

While local ten-year planning may not be the movement that it once was, the foundations of those plans — engaging diverse stakeholders, collecting and using local data, closing the front door, opening the back door, and building an infrastructure of support — remain the cornerstone of local efforts to end homelessness. And while many plans are approaching the ten-year mark without having ended homelessness in their respective communities, communities dedicated to systemically ending homelessness and not merely managing it have become the norm across the country. This philosophical shift can be attributed to ten-year planning. What started as local innovation became a country-wide movement. And today with the HEARTH Act mandating several strategies prominent in local plans, the essence of both local ten-year plans to end homelessness and the Alliance's Ten Year Plan lives on in federal statute. As community planning continues to evolve, federal and state regulations should remain flexible to encourage local innovation so that, like ten-year planning, other impactful strategies can emerge, can be widely adopted, and, ultimately, can become federal policy.

16

The Role of Funders

Anne Miskey

There can be little doubt that funding, whether public or private, plays a significant role in shaping communities' responses to homelessness. Whether people like it or not, money talks. Our experience at Funders Together to End Homelessness[1] (Funders Together) recognizes that investing in programs that serve people experiencing homelessness—without an understanding of the bigger systems at play in a community—has limited success. If used strategically, however, public and private investments can place communities on a path to ending and preventing what has, sadly, become a chronic problem in the United States.

What follows is an account of a significant shift from funding immediate needs to the more strategic systems approach now being taken by the federal government and many private funders. It will discuss private philanthropy's role in ending and preventing homelessness, specifically through a few key strategies and uses the terms *philanthropy, funder,* and *foundations* interchangeably.

Programmatic Responses

Homelessness in the United States has grown dramatically since 1980. Because the definition of homelessness and the methodology for counting it have changed significantly since that time, and because accurate figures are therefore unavailable, what we can surmise from a report by the US General Accounting Office (1985) is that between 1980 and 1983, homelessness increased by a rate of 10 percent per year, with total numbers ranging anywhere from 250,000 up to 3 million.

As evidence of this burgeoning problem grew in towns and cities across the country, advocates, nonprofit agencies, and funders realized they had to do something quickly to address the needs of those experiencing homelessness. Government and philanthropy answered this growing need by putting their resources into an emergency response, focusing primarily on the immediate needs of individuals and families and providing access to temporary food and shelter (HHS and HUD, 2007).

What resulted was an explosion of programs and agencies that focused on managing homelessness by providing temporary shelter and trying to ameliorate people's experiences while they remained homeless, with only limited attention to finding permanent housing. Programs evolved piecemeal in towns and cities across the country. While there were attempts at agencies and foundations working together to meet the growing needs of the community, and some did try to focus on long-term solutions, most programs and facilities were typically funded and operated in isolation from one another, often with rules or limitations about who they could serve. This left large portions of the population unserved or underserved (Funders Together to End Homelessness, 2012). There were few efforts by funders or others to create community-wide holistic strategies to end homelessness.

Beyond Programs

In the early 1990s, the federal government, seeing the confusion and chaos that often existed around homelessness services, attempted to ensure better local coordination by requiring communities to develop Continuums of Care, local planning bodies that would coordinate applications for US Department of Housing and Urban Development funds. While this did create a level of organization among local stakeholders, it rarely incentivized agencies to align or coordinate their services. Instead, existing programs remained largely isolated or only loosely affiliated with one another, and entities often ended up competing among themselves for increasingly limited federal funding (Funders Together to End Homelessness, 2012). Yet communities continued to struggle with homelessness and people started to turn more toward the idea of solutions as they saw the numbers of people experiencing homelessness increase with each passing year. Communities were working as hard as they could to serve as many people as possible, but they did not seem to be making a dent in the problem. Finally, in 2000 the National Alliance to End Homelessness, a nonprofit nonpartisan organization committed to preventing and ending homelessness in the United States, developed and disseminated a plan to end homelessness in ten years, marking the beginning of a major paradigm shift in how to approach the issue (HHS and HUD, 2007). This shift, from managing homelessness and responding primarily to immediate needs to developing a coherent community-wide plan for ending it, was outlined in *A Plan, Not a Dream: How to End Homelessness in Ten Years* (NAEH, 2000a). This bold and innovative blueprint outlined key strategies, including:

collecting population-specific data and developing community- and population-wide outcomes; homelessness prevention; creating or subsidizing a sufficient supply of affordable housing; and providing adequate services (from both the housing and mainstream systems such as health, education, and employment) to help those who needed it.

Community stakeholders, including government, nonprofits, and funders, followed this shift by coming together to create their own local ten-year plans. As they struggled to come to grips with the growing numbers of those experiencing homelessness, many began to realize that it was a complex issue that required more than simply creating and supporting programs that were about meeting immediate needs for food and shelter. Individual stand-alone programs were not getting to the root of the problem nor were they able to reach even a fraction of the number of affected individuals and families. Ultimately, communities began to understand as well that ending homelessness would require both safe, affordable, and available housing and the commitment of government agencies representing multiple systems (e.g., housing, health, education, employment), nonprofits, private funders, and community stakeholders to work together. This commitment meant responding, not just to the immediate needs of those experiencing homelessness, but to get them quickly and permanently housed and to provide supportive services and a framework for long-term stability. In other words, ending homelessness required housing and an approach that would get people into that housing quickly as well as providing the supports to keep them housed. Many funders, both government and private, involved in these efforts recognized that they would also have to begin to shift their funding from only the support of stand-alone programs or services to a more strategic systems and housing-based approach.

A Systems Approach

The movement by both the government and local communities to a systems approach, rather than a focus on individual programs, has been one of the most effective changes in the strategy to end homelessness in the United States. It is important, therefore, to more fully understand what is meant by a systems approach. A systems approach to ending homelessness is not just program-level collaboration, but systematic coordination to use all resources better.

1. *A systems approach shares a common vision,* that of getting people rapidly and permanently into housing and providing the services to help them maintain that housing.

2. *It sets clear goals, and has the means to measure them.* It first determines the scope of the problem (how many people are homeless and who

they are), sets clear targets for reducing the number as well as time lines (how quickly should someone move from homelessness to permanent housing) and long-term outcomes for housing stability (retention rates).

3. *It recognizes the role of each part in contributing to the results.* Each part of the system plays an important role in moving people from homelessness to housing stability. From prevention services, through dealing with immediate emergency needs, to permanent housing solutions and services, each program can be essential in helping end homelessness. For example, as much as housing is the ultimate goal, the fact is that people sometimes do require a place to sleep on a given night—and emergency shelters help ensure that people don't have to sleep on the streets. With a systems approach, however, the shelter is connected to housing services and helps move people out of the shelter into a permanent solution as quickly as possible.

4. *It holds each component accountable.* A coordinated system works toward a common vision and clearly defined goals; therefore, each component (organization or program) within the system is accountable for how it helps reach that vision and achieve those goals. For example, if one of the system's goals is to move people from homelessness to housing in a short defined period of time (say fifteen to thirty days), the shelter and housing programs become equally accountable for that outcome. The shelter must work in a coordinated fashion with other parts of the system to ensure that is happening. In a systems approach, it is the outcomes (measurement to agreed-on community and system goals of prevention and ending homelessness) rather than outputs (how many people served, how many beds filled) that are measured.

5. *It makes changes over time.* A systems approach is not an overnight solution; it takes time and resources to build relationships and coordination between the components of a system. For example, coordinated entry or assessment (NAEH, 2011b), which ensures that at whatever point in the system individuals and families enter they will receive the services they need to enable them to reach and maintain housing stability and end their homelessness, is a key element of an effective system to end homelessness. However, developing and implementing this element are complex tasks that require extensive community planning and funding and that can take a substantial amount of time to complete.

Some key elements to a systems approach are essential if it is to be successful, including the following.

Use Research to Inform Decisions and Design

To reach clearly defined goals, one must have an accurate picture of how many people are experiencing homelessness in a given community, who they are (individuals, veterans, chronically homeless, families, youth), and what are the contributing factors to their homelessness (economic, including the high cost of housing and low-paying jobs; mental or behavioral health issues;

chronic physical health issues; domestic violence; family breakdown). It is also critical to perform research to understand the present system, or lack of a system, in the community to obtain a clear overview of what services are currently available and where gaps exist and to determine the leverage points where investment can have the greatest impact. All too often, this type of systems mapping is noticeably missing, to the detriment of those experiencing homelessness.

Gather Data and Results on Impact

When there is a programmatic instead of a systems change focus, it is often outputs—how many beds were filled, how many people served—rather than outcomes that are tracked. While it gives some idea about the scope of the problem, looking at outputs does not indicate whether or not specific interventions and programs are successful. By data and outcomes—addressing such things as how long it takes to get people housed, what are the costs, what services were required and effective—one would have a better idea of what is working and what needs to change to create an effective system that moves people rapidly and permanently into safe, stable housing.

Client-based Programs

Probably one of the most important elements of creating effective systems is client-based programs. We too often create systems that work for those administering or funding them, rather than for the clients we are attempting to serve. Carefully mapping and fully understanding what those experiencing homelessness are going through to get housing (or whether they are even able to do so) will help determine how to improve the system to create a path that will move people quickly and effectively from homelessness to stable permanent housing.

Federal Strategy: The HEARTH Act and Opening Doors

In the early 2000s HUD had begun to shift the way that it funded, first with the creation of the CoCs and then with an increasing focus on housing-based interventions such as permanent supportive housing and transitional housing.[2] But a major step in this move toward a more community-based housing and systems approach was the passing of The Homeless Emergency Assistance and Rapid Transition to Housing Act in 2009. The HEARTH Act was one of the most important pieces of federal legislation on homelessness to pass in twenty years because it called for communities to move beyond a scattered collection of disconnected programs and services that were able to serve only a limited number of people to the creation of coordinated systems to end homelessness for everyone experiencing it.

The HEARTH Act affected how homeless services are funded and delivered, consolidated funding programs, increased local flexibility, and introduced new community-level performance expectations grounded in a systemswide approach. For example, it required communities to show their progress in ending homelessness through key indicators that included: reduction in the number of people experiencing homelessness, the length of time people remain homeless, and the rate at which some people exit but later return to homelessness. The act also created a shift when it began to emphasize proven cost-effective housing solutions that include permanent supportive housing, Rapid Re-Housing,[3] and homelessness prevention.

In 2010 as a result of the charge in the HEARTH Act, the first federal plan for ending homelessness was created, *Opening Doors: Federal Strategic Plan to Prevent and End Homelessness*. Opening Doors serves as a road map for ending homelessness for the nineteen US Interagency Council on Homelessness federal member agencies in cooperation with local and state partners in the public and private sectors. It set a goal of ending veterans and chronic homelessness in five years and family, youth, and all other forms of homelessness in ten years, all by providing a framework that seeks to reallocate funding and align programs centered on evidence-based practices of what works. It provided a clear vision, themes, goals, and strategies that pointed toward effective evidence-based and cost-efficient solutions to homelessness.

Federal Funding

In keeping with the commitment to the vision of Opening Doors, the federal government, under the Barack Obama administration, has kept funding targeted at homelessness programs relatively steady over the past few years, with slight increases year over year (ICH, 2015). The president's proposed 2016 budget for homeless assistance programs is nearly $5.5 billion. Of that, $2.48 billion is allocated to the CoC program and the Emergency Solutions Grants that fund such things as permanent supportive housing, rapid re-housing, and Housing First interventions. It also provides funding for community planning, data collection and analysis, and performance measurement—all things essential to a systems approach model. The remainder of the $5.5 billion is divided up among a variety of programs and federal agencies, including programs targeted at veterans experiencing homelessness, education for homeless children and youth, health care for the homeless, and the Runaway and Homeless Youth Act that provides funding for local agencies serving the youth population (ICH, 2015a). In 2010, the government spent approximately $3.7 billion dollars on targeted homelessness assistance programs (ICH, 2015a). Since then, there has been an increase in government investment in these programs that totals around $1.8 billion, if the new 2016 budget is approved (ICH, 2015a).

The approach of the federal government toward ending homelessness through a systems approach and with a focus on Housing First, permanent supportive housing, and now rapid re-housing has, for the most part, been embraced by both sides of Congress. There is increasing evidence that getting people into permanent housing as quickly as possible, while providing the supports they need to maintain housing stability, is a model that is efficient and effective (NAEH, 2007). For this reason, advocacy efforts focused on at least maintaining if not increasing federal funding for targeted homelessness assistance programs have largely been successful, and these programs have done a better job of surviving budget cuts than many other federally funded programs. One major exception to this was sequestration, the across-the-board budgetary cuts to discretionary programs enacted in 2013 when Congress and the president failed to reach an alternate agreement. These cuts included virtually all targeted homelessness and affordable housing programs, with the exclusion of veterans programs. While we have not seen the total effects of these cuts, the NAEH estimated that "hundreds of thousands of extremely vulnerable low-income families would lose their housing, and hundreds of thousands more would lose their chance to escape homelessness" (Budget Control Act of 2011: Impact on Ending Homelessness; NAEH, 2011a). The expectation is that the negative effects of these cuts would increase in succeeding years.

Philanthropic Funding

The latest figures from the Foundation Center, a leading source of data and knowledge about philanthropy, show that foundations gave over $300 million toward homelessness programs in the United States in 2012 (Foundation Center, 2012). For comparison, in 2002 total funding for homelessness was around $187 million (Foundation Center, 2002). Over that ten-year period, foundations added approximately $110 million in funds for the homeless. The 2012 philanthropic expenditures represent about 7 percent of the total federal expenditures on homelessness, and this percentage has not varied much over the years. Unfortunately, we have no data on the specific kinds of programs or interventions that this funding represents. Anecdotal evidence from many communities and funders, as well as surveys conducted with Funders Together's 160 member agencies, suggests that there has been a demonstrable shift away from a narrow focus on immediate needs to providing more support for prevention and long-term solutions to homelessness. Next, I examine some examples of funders who have moved to a systems approach to housing.

Philanthropy's Support of a Housing-based Systems Approach

By its very nature, systems change is complex, as is ensuring the availability of adequate housing. It is therefore extremely difficult to list all the various strategies that funders have utilized in their support of a systems model to end homelessness. In an attempt to educate philanthropy about the opportunities for strategic investment in both housing and systems change, Funders Together has outlined a number of key strategies that have proven successful in preventing and ending homelessness compiled from the experiences of its members as well as from national experts in housing and homelessness.

To End Homelessness, Start with a Home

Housing First is an approach that is based on the principle that, first and foremost, homelessness is a housing problem and needs to be treated as such. Programs cannot expect to successfully treat an individual's mental illness or help them find a stable job while that person is still living on the streets. Housing First prioritizes placement into housing as quickly as possible, and then provides services as needed to ensure long-term housing stability.

Program models for Housing First differ depending on the population being served, from models that include permanent supportive housing, a combination of housing and support services for the chronically homeless, to rapid re-housing of homeless families (with or without added services). Evaluation of these strategies has shown the effectiveness and efficiency of a Housing First model for individuals and families. Funders can play strategic roles in increasing the supply as well as improving access to housing.

Permanent Supportive Housing to Address Chronic Homelessness

Major funders like the Conrad N. Hilton Foundation have taken a Housing First, systems approach to solving problems such as chronic homelessness. While they have focused on a number of strategies, one of their key approaches has been to increase access to supportive housing in Los Angeles county. To date, they have invested more than $90 million to solve the problem of homelessness, nearly $65 million of that targeted to increased access to supportive housing.[4]

The Melville Charitable Trust, the largest foundation in the United States exclusively devoted to supporting solutions to prevent and end homelessness, has invested over $120 million to develop supportive housing as well as build community solutions and a stronger policy environment. The Melville Trust's investments have sparked the effort to develop over 150,000 units of permanent supportive housing for the chronically homeless across the country.[5]

Rapid Re-Housing and Family Homelessness

Rapid Re-Housing identifies homeless households and helps get them into housing in the community, whether permanently subsidized or at market rate. While this is a relatively new model, funders are beginning to provide critical resources to help agencies explore new ways of working, develop more effective strategies, and build housing capacity and the capacity of agencies to work with this new strategy (Funders Together to End Homelessness, 2012). Although there are fewer examples to date of funders working on rapid re-housing as opposed to the longer established method of permanent supportive housing, a number of funders are creating innovative funding strategies to rapidly re-house families.

The Hampton Roads Community Foundation invested money in a Housing Broker Team—housing specialists that connect with landlords to build relationships to expand rental opportunities for families and individuals. The program moves quickly, re-housing families often in a matter of days after becoming homeless. The program now has over 300 landlords who own or manage 4,500 apartments and houses, providing access to affordable housing for families and the ability to quickly leave homelessness (Funders Together to End Homelessness, 2012).

The Bill & Melinda Gates Foundation invested in building an innovative rapid re-housing model to serve survivors of domestic violence. They made significant investments in research and the capacity of providers to effectively roll out rapid re-housing for domestic violence survivors. Results of the program show high rates of stability for those served, with 86 percent retaining housing for a year or more (Bill & Melinda Gates Foundation, 2011).

Funding and Supporting Systems Change

While funders have traditionally focused their efforts on programs or capital expenses that directly serve individuals or families, there is an increased awareness of the importance of funding less immediate strategies that can have a profound long-term impact on a community's success in ending homelessness. Some of these strategies, which focus on creating and supporting systems to prevent and end homelessness, include: convening or bringing a wide variety of stakeholders together to identify gaps in service and investments and to work on shared vision and goals; building community knowledge through investment in data, research, and pilot projects; investing in building the capacity of the system, including the people (organizations), processes, and infrastructure; raising awareness of the issue and building support for effective evidence-based long-term strategies; and measuring progress and investing in continuous learning.

An excellent example of this approach is the Raikes Foundation initiative to solve youth homelessness in King county, Washington. Appropriately named *A Place to Call Home,* this initiative focuses on investing in efforts to create a more coordinated regional system that effectively responds to young people's needs.[6] This model is, to date, one of the most comprehensive plans focused on youth homelessness in the country, and it is now being used as a model by other communities.

Forging Commitments to a Systems Approach

Collaborations and partnerships are at the heart of a systems approach to preventing and ending homelessness. Funders often have the ability, more than almost any other stakeholders in a community, to build these partnerships and bring people to the table to focus on effective solutions. One of the recent approaches being taken by more and more communities is the formation of local funder networks focused on ending homelessness. These networks have been critical to bringing together all kinds of funders, including government and philanthropy, and forging commitments to a systems approach—aligning resources and strategies in a way that can fill gaps, build capacity, and move systems into more effective solutions that improve the lives of people they are trying to serve.

Funders Together presently has three active networks: Los Angeles Homeless Funders Group/Funders Together Los Angeles, Funders Together San Diego, and Funders Together Houston. Soon to launch are two new networks: Funders Together Canada and Funders Together/Florida Philanthropic Network Affinity Group on Homelessness. While each of these networks operates in different ways, with different funding models and governance structures, all of them have common elements: a shared vision and goals, continuous opportunities for learning, a focus on evidence-based practices, and the belief that funders can play a catalytic role in ending homelessness. Funder networks can also be extraordinary vehicles to create local public-private partnerships by bringing both government and private funders together to look at gaps and determine opportunities for leveraged and shared funding models.

The Los Angeles Homeless Funders Group/Funders Together Los Angeles has focused on three goals: developing standards of excellence and measuring success, homelessness data collection, and forming a funders' collaborative. With an initial challenge grant of $1 million, the funders' collaborative has gone on to leverage $18.3 million in private funds and $420 million in public funding to support Home for Good, the Los Angeles action plan to end veteran and chronic homelessness.[7]

Spearheaded by the Frees Foundation and the Simmons Foundation, Funders Together Houston supported the creation of a Homeless Outreach Team within the Houston Police Department, which was recently detailed in a documentary called *The Shepherds in Blue*. This strategic partnership between philanthropy and law enforcement enabled the police to create a specialized team comprised of police and mental health experts who are proactively engaged in street outreach to chronically homeless individuals. The initiative has already made contact with over 2,000 homeless individuals and has permanently housed 123 people experiencing homelessness.

Funders as Advocates

While foundations have traditionally feared involvement in any kind of advocacy (based on strict Internal Revenue Service restrictions on legislative activity), they are beginning to realize that it is absolutely necessary in a systems approach to ending homelessness. The harsh reality is that lack of government funding and policies that create barriers for individuals or families trying to move out of homelessness make it difficult, if not impossible, to definitively end homelessness. These barriers include such things as restrictive or punitive eligibility requirements for certain programs, lack of investment in affordable housing, lack of investment in rental subsidies, and reluctance of mainstream systems to provide services for those who are homeless or formerly homeless.

By providing general operating funds to advocacy organizations, working closely with government at the administrative level and investing in public education efforts to inform political leaders, community stakeholders, and the general public about the issues surrounding homelessness, many funders continue to effectively finance advocacy without contravening legislative regulations.

Funders can also bring together different government agencies and private funders to discuss opportunities for collaboration and shared funding or programs. This strategy raises awareness among funders of the need to remove barriers that prevent individuals and families from accessing mainstream services, such as health care and child welfare, once they become housed.

An outstanding example of this strategy is a recent meeting held in Washington, DC, called Partnerships for Opening Doors. A summit on integrating employment and housing strategies to prevent and end homelessness, it brought together communities and federal government agencies (including the US Department of Labor and HUD) to learn about promising practices and identify common misconceptions and barriers to using federal funding to support these practices. This convening was initiated and funded by the Butler Family Fund,[8] in partnership with ICH, the Department of Labor, and HUD.[9]

New Funding Models

Continuous learning is a key element of systems change, and so funders must always look for new and innovative models to address homelessness. Not all of these funding approaches will be successful or the right fit for an individual community, but funders should be open to both established best practices and new ways of investing in solutions to homelessness.

A relatively new funding model that is gaining in popularity across the country is social impact financing. Also called Pay for Success, this model offers potential public sector savings and improved social outcomes; it is used as a way of raising private investments to pay for innovative and effective interventions and programs. Investors assume the risks (instead of government), but receive a return on investment if the initiative is successful and saves money in the public sector. Payments are based on agreed-on outcomes, not on the activities of the agencies. For example, a Pay for Success program between Roca, an organization serving justice system involved youth in Chelsea, Massachusetts, and the Commonwealth of Massachusetts focuses on reducing incarceration rates among high-risk young men who were formerly involved in the justice system. It is hoped that this program will create improved social and financial outcomes by reducing crime and incarceration among these young men. Private investments are used to pay for services at the front end, which the Commonwealth will reimburse only if and when outcome benchmarks are hit. The ultimate goal is to reduce the financial burden of the public, generate long-term cost savings, and produce improved social outcomes.[10]

Homelessness is seen as a fertile field for social impact investing because the costs to the system are relatively straightforward, because research has demonstrated the effectiveness of solutions like permanent supportive housing, and because widespread implementation can positively impact the health care system, the criminal justice system, and others. The Corporation for Supportive Housing (CSH) announced the selection of six subgrantees of a 2014 Social Innovation Fund Pay for Success grant award it received from the Corporation for National and Community Service. This funding will be used to support communities working to create and evaluate innovative ways to finance effective supportive housing interventions targeted at high users of the health care and criminal justice systems. The hope is that supportive housing will produce measurable reduction in costs to these systems while improving the social outcomes for individuals and communities (CSH, 2015).

Although proponents of this model are convinced of its potential, and there has been some initial private investment, philanthropy has yet to wholeheartedly embrace this new model. The general feeling is wait and see—to determine whether there really will be cost savings and the desired results. Funders will be closely watching the outcomes of the Roca and CSH Pay for Success initiatives because of the potential for a new funding model that could reduce the need for government funding and improve both fiscal and social outcomes.

Moving Forward: The Need for Strategic Funding

While the movement toward prevention and ending homelessness by the federal government and philanthropy has been a positive step, and one that is reducing chronic veteran and family homelessness in communities across the country (HUD, 2014c), there is more to do.

Funding levels—especially from government—are still not adequate to effectively serve all those who experience homelessness. Perhaps the biggest gap lies in the availability of affordable housing. With government cutbacks, the increasing cost of housing, and the lack of rental housing subsidies and of development of affordable housing, we have reached a point of crisis in this country. The National Low Income Housing Coalition (NLIHC, 2014) has reported that in no state could a full-time minimum wage worker afford a one or two bedroom apartment. More and more people are being squeezed out of housing.

Since housing is, in the simplest terms, the solution to homelessness, Funders Together advocates on behalf of its members for better housing policies and funding, including: making rental homes affordable to more people by expanding the supply of rental housing subsidies; expanding the supply of affordable rental homes by directing low-cost capital resources to the production and preservation of decent safe rental housing; increasing access to private market and public housing rental units by people experiencing homelessness and people with disabilities; and expanding supportive housing options by increasing funding for services. Of course, there are many other areas of need for funding if we are to truly end homelessness. The majority of this money will have to come from government, and we must continue to call for increased and robust funding of both housing and services. Philanthropy does not have the resources to fund all that is needed to prevent and end homelessness, although this funding can be critical to filling in gaps that government cannot fund, building the capacity of organizations and the system as a whole, financing data and evaluation, and supporting various strategies such as coordinated entry, rapid re-housing, and support services.

While there has been a positive change in the focus of philanthropy as it addresses homelessness, there is resistance by many funders to fund in ways that will get us to the needed outcomes. Much of philanthropy continues to focus on short-term year-by-year grants, and funders are hesitant to fund things such as data and research, organizational capacity, or outcome measurement.

While there are a variety of reasons for their focus on short-term funding, many funders see their role as catalysts or seed funders—helping to launch or leverage major initiatives, programs, or even systems. They do not want, nor do they believe it is their role, to sustain programs or organizations. They feel that nonprofit organizations will somehow become complacent if they come to expect their funders to continue to fund them year over year.

While seed funding is important—and there is the hope that other funders, especially government, will step in and begin to fund proven approaches or initiatives—the fact is that if philanthropy is actually invested in systems change and long-term solutions, it must begin to understand that short-term limited funding puts added pressure on nonprofits and makes it difficult to create truly effective systems.

Over the past ten to fifteen years, philanthropy has begun to embrace the importance of research, data, and evaluation to determine needs, develop goals, and ensure the effectiveness of prevention efforts and solutions to homelessness. It has been through the understanding of the numbers of people who experience homelessness, the reasons why they are experiencing it, and what is effective in preventing or ending it that communities have moved toward successful solutions. And yet, even while believing in the importance of research, data, and evaluation—and often requiring that nonprofits use it or do it—philanthropy has been hesitant to fund these things.

It is difficult to determine the reasons for this reluctance, other than the historical focus on program funding. Programs are simpler to define, with clear parameters, time lines, outputs, and narrowly defined goals and outcomes. It is easy to get a handle on programs and understand how funding has made a difference. It is easy for program managers to report back to boards or trustees on how the funder's grant affected the program. There is a clear cause and effect—and often opportunities for celebration and pictures of the happy smiling faces of those helped by the program.

Data and research have much more intangible long-term results, but it is more difficult for funders to see how their funding has created positive outcomes—and little opportunity to celebrate. Taking your picture beside charts, graphs, and reports is not nearly as heartwarming as taking it beside young children involved in a program you funded, even if there is the understanding of the potential impact of research and data. As for evaluation, funders often expect that it is something that nonprofits should simply do, that it should be part of any program—and yet often don't understand the cost or the need to fund it.

Much of the same difficulty—and same reluctance—surrounds the need for funders to invest in capacity building and the organizational structure of nonprofits. Asking organizations to work within a systems approach—to build relationships with other organizations or systems, to coordinate and align programs, to work toward systems goals rather than program goals—requires capacity at the organizational level, and these are things that government generally does not fund. If we look to systems change, then philanthropy must begin to understand the need to develop and sustain the capacity of each part of the system—and that includes the capacity of individual nonprofit organizations and programs.

Conclusion

Ending homelessness does not mean that individuals and families will never again experience housing crises. Instead, it means that communities will have a systematic response in place that can address immediate needs, quickly move people into housing, and provide appropriate services to ensure long-term stability. Many communities that have embraced a systems approach are already reducing the numbers of people experiencing homelessness, due in large part to the coordinated efforts of government, service providers, advocates, and philanthropy. Both public and private funders continue to play a strategic role in these efforts to bring key players in the community together, to build the capacity of the system to serve those who experience homelessness, and to fund what works.

For these efforts to continue, funders need to keep investing in a permanent housing-based systems approach and to work together with other stakeholders in the community to prevent and end homelessness in the United States.

Notes

1. A national network of foundations and United Ways focused on effective evidence-based practices and a systems approach to preventing and ending homelessness.

2. According to HUD's definition, *transitional housing* is "a project that is designed to provide housing and appropriate supportive services to homeless persons to facilitate movement to independent living within 24 months, or a longer period approved by HUD," See http://definitions.uslegal.com/t/transitional-housing-hud/.

3. *Rapid re-housing* is the practice of focusing resources on helping families and individuals quickly move out of homelessness and into permanent housing, which is usually housing in the private market. Services to support rapid re-housing include housing search and landlord negotiation, short-term financial and rental assistance, and the delivery of home-based housing stabilization services, as needed. See http://usich.gov/usich_resources/solutions/explore/rapid_re_housing.

4. Conrad N. Hilton Foundation, *Ending chronic homelessness*, available at www.hiltonfoundation.org/homelessness.

5. Melville Charitable Trust, *About us*, available at www.melvilletrust.org/about-us/.

6. Raikes Foundation, *A place to call home*, available at https://d3n8a8pro7vhmx.cloudfront.net/funderstogether/pages/289/attachments/original/1426709459/Raikes_oct_strategy_brief_r109.pdf?1426709459.

7. Los Angeles's Home for Good, available at http://homeforgoodla.org/about-us/grantseekers/.

8. A Washington-based, national funder that focuses on homelessness and the criminal justice system.

9. The ICH Partnership for Opening Doors Summit took place on October 16, 2014. See http://usich.gov/partnerships-for-opening-doors-summit.

10. For more details on Roca and Pay for Success, see http://rocainc.org/what-we-do/pay-for-success/.

17

Where Do We Go from Here?

Donald W. Burnes

Are we there yet in our effort to end homelessness in the United States? Despite all our efforts, we clearly have not ended this national tragedy. The people we see on the streets and in alleyways, the individuals and families inhabiting our shelters and transitional housing facilities, and the data that the authors present throughout this volume provide overwhelming evidence that the phenomenon of homelessness is still very much with us. How is it that we seem poised to accept another generation of pervasive homelessness as a normal feature of life in virtually every US city and town? And what, if anything, can be done about it?

This volume assumes that much can be done. To the credit of the authors who contributed to this work, each envisions a future where we might move the needle forward in a national effort to end homelessness. Throughout the book, these scholars, practitioners, theorists, and program directors, and an individual who was formerly homeless, share their knowledge and experience. They offer new perspectives, provocative and ambitious policy recommendations, and rich fodder for further exploration via several themes.

Freedom from Want

Toward the end of his January 1941 "Four Freedoms" State of the Union address, President Franklin D. Roosevelt declared, "In the future days, . . . we look forward to a world founded upon four essential human freedoms." In his enumeration, "The third is *freedom from want* . . . a healthy peacetime life for [every nation's] inhabitants everywhere in the world" (emphasis added).[1] Seventy-five years later, this statement still rings true with nobility and real urgency. Yes, we all want everyone to be free from want, to no longer live under the tyranny of economic and social circumstances. But that is precisely what people experiencing homelessness are besieged with every day. We have much work to do before we realize Roosevelt's clarion call for emancipation from deprivation and destitution.

Economic Injustice

At its most basic level, homelessness confronts us with questions about economic and social injustice with which we all struggle. Debates about the social safety net stretch the US political system across a major ideological divide. While we have done much to alleviate poverty and homelessness, we have not accomplished nearly enough to keep up with a growing problem. Housing for our poorest citizens is in very short supply, and we have failed to mobilize the resources to overcome this major hurdle. People experiencing homelessness—and the very poor who are insecurely housed—fight a losing battle. Even if they are lucky enough to find housing, rent and maintenance costs consume almost all of their income. Assistance remains outside the mainstream government housing programs, thereby exacerbating the problem. Meanwhile, federal subsidies decidedly favor homeowners, especially wealthier ones. The gap in income and wealth between the richest Americans and the poorest has widened considerably, and our wealth distribution is the most unequal among Western industrialized nations, as Bristow Hardin describes in Chapter 11. The mechanics of free-market capitalism serve to benefit the rich on the backs of the poor and those who are homeless. This is truly economic and social injustice. It is also bad economic policy.

What can be done? Certainly, programs like universal health care and affordable postsecondary education are a start but, as several of the authors indicate, we must go substantially beyond those initiatives. Reducing or eliminating the mortgage interest deduction and dedicating this revenue stream to low-income housing could change the dynamics of homelessness; so too would raising the age of eligibility and means testing social security benefits and Medicare. Why, some might consider, should some of us continue to receive these benefits when we may not need them to maintain our current standards of living? Because savings in revenue from such measures would not necessarily be used to ameliorate the situation of those experiencing homelessness or the very poor, savings should be specifically targeted to strengthen our country's safety net. Even though these recommendations are controversial, they are necessary to eliminate the injustices endemic to our system. Absent reforms of this magnitude, we will never come close to ending homelessness, or making the lives of the poorest of the poor more livable.

An even more radical suggestion has been made independently by Robert Reich and Betsy Isaacson; that is, "universal basic income" (Reich, 2015, p. 214; Isaacson, p. 44). Not unlike President Richard Nixon's 1970 Family Assistance Plan that never received congressional approval, a basic income strategy would provide every adult American a minimum income that could be supplemented by earned wages. Proposals like this should be part of a national dialogue about how to address extreme poverty and homelessness.

Inadequate Housing and Economic Resources

This volume includes several chapters on housing — and for good reason: homelessness and the availability of housing can, at times, masquerade as a maddeningly simple equation. A major barrier to ending homelessness is our failure to create an adequate supply of low-income units. Currently, across the country, as indicated in Chapter 1, we need 7.5 million low-income housing units to meet present housing demands for persons experiencing homelessness and those at substantial risk of becoming homeless. Assuming there were no new people becoming homeless over the next ten years, every state would have to produce 150,000 units of low-income housing during that same period, specifically designated for those experiencing homelessness or at significant risk, to meet the demand. It's as simple, and as complicated, as that!

As Martha R. Burt, Jill Khadduri, and Sheila Crowley make clear in Chapters 4, 7, and 10, respectively, to make a serious dent in homelessness, a much more comprehensive effort must be made to provide housing and wraparound services. The recent emphasis on tiny houses and retrofitting shipping containers could prove useful, but a significant infusion of dollars on all levels is the only way to address the issue successfully. Although there have been recent increases in federal funding for this task, and even more is anticipated as the National Housing Trust Fund garners funding, we remain orders of magnitude short of what is needed.

It is not as though federal subsidies for housing are lacking. Homeowners, especially wealthier homeowners who are able to utilize itemized deductions on their tax returns, receive four times as much in federal housing subsidies as do those who rent, especially those in poverty, and those experiencing homelessness are among the poorest of those in poverty. Just as every senior qualifies for social security and Medicare, one might legitimately wonder whether all Americans shouldn't also be guaranteed some measure of housing stability. There is no moral symmetry in providing every school-age child, including the poorest of our children, access to public education and leaving those experiencing homelessness, many of whom are children, without access to reliable shelter. As US society seems poised to make health care universal, one may ponder if housing stability can one day become a civil right, just as did equal access to educational opportunity over fifty years ago. Or, in the challenging words of Pope Francis, "We see no social or moral justification, no justification whatsoever, for lack of housing."

Although some people experiencing homelessness are in fact working, they are frequently doing so in part-time low-wage jobs, in unpredictable day labor pools, or by panhandling at red lights or on busy downtown thoroughfares. Income from these activities is insufficient to rent even the cheapest housing units, forcing individuals and families to rely on an inadequate supply of shelter beds. For some, income derives only from one or another federal benefit such as TANF, SNAP, or SSI and SSDI. And funds from these sources are inadequate to provide housing and other essentials, as Crowley and Hardin document so convincingly. Very-low-income renters and homeowner families spend 85–90 percent of their total annual income on housing, leaving them with little more than $1,000 per year for every other household expense, including food, transportation, clothing, health care, and childcare, as I document in Chapter 1. Those who are homeless have even less for everyday expenses.

Because over one-third of those experiencing homelessness have some education beyond high school, we must abandon the egregious stereotype that those experiencing homelessness are all uneducated and shiftless. The demographic analyses provided by Kerri Tobin and Joseph Murphy in Chapter 3 tell us that there is a deep well of untapped human resources that we are routinely excluding from the economy. We must do a better job of helping individuals find and keep jobs through a variety of strategies such as workers' cooperatives, social enterprise businesses, job shadowing, and job coaching. Raising the minimum wage to an appropriate level is another policy change that is much needed. Only in this way will we make progress in incorporating those experiencing poverty and homelessness into the economic life of the country and a shared prosperity.

The Numbers Game and the Need for Better Data

It is complex and challenging to estimate the number of Americans experiencing homelessness, and as Burt and Tracey O'Brien suggest in Chapters 4 and 13, respectively, we are not even close to having accurate numbers. But the raw numbers, difficult though they may be to gather, are staggering. As I suggest in Chapter 1, forty-five million Americans—about 14 percent of the population—will experience homelessness at some point in their lives.

Do we, in fact, need all of the data that the Point-in-Time count and the Homelessness Management Information System generate? Might we get by, the way Congress does, with a full census count every five years or even ten years? Do we need the amount of information currently required on numbers of persons involved in various types of services, or could that level of detail also be garnered on a less-frequent schedule? Rather than worrying about whether the actual size of the decline in homelessness from year to year is satisfactory, can't we agree that the existence of even one person experiencing homelessness is one too many?

Despite all of the issues that confound the accuracy of the counts, policymakers and practitioners alike are wedded to them. But numbers themselves may obscure, rather than clarify, the challenges associated with addressing homelessness. Rather than trumpeting slight decreases in the absolute numbers, which in many cases are merely numerical anomalies, we should be focusing on the quality of programs and on whether the lives of those experiencing homelessness have actually improved.

Agency and systems impact evaluations are critical to the future of our efforts. As O'Brien points out, we need to do a substantially better job of determining which programs work and which do not. Even most of the communities that have developed ten-year planning efforts have made no effort to evaluate their effectiveness, as Samantha Batko notes in Chapter 15, despite community demands for documentation that dollars are being well spent. All of this represents an unfunded mandate; funders and the public want impact evidence, but they rarely put aside the money to gather it. In light of this, according to Anne Miskey in Chapter 16, the philanthropic sector is in a unique position to assist local Continuums of Care and service agencies in developing the capacity to undertake the kind of serious outcome evaluations that are so desperately needed. This must be an important new role for the philanthropic sector.

Program Elements

There has been a marked evolution in the types of services aimed at assisting those experiencing homelessness. Several of the authors trace this evolution from Band-Aid soup kitchens and shelters, to housing ready abstinence-based transitional housing and permanent supportive housing, to harm reduction housing first units and rapid re-housing. Throughout the evolution, the Department of Housing and Urban Development and US service providers have struggled with efforts to prevent individuals and families from becoming homeless. This evolution suggests that there are a variety of alternatives for providing housing and services and that this diversity should be encouraged as a matter of policy.

Furthermore, program developers have created very different models that have successfully addressed the needs of persons experiencing homelessness. Evaluations of Housing First projects, based on the concepts of no barriers to admission, harm reduction, and no requirements for service participation, have demonstrated high success rates in helping individuals into housing, maintaining their placement, and assisting them in achieving other important improvements in their lives, as Sam Tsemberis and Benjamin F.

Henwood document in Chapter 5. The evolution of the Alcohol and Drug Free Community at Portland's Central City Concern, described by Richard L. Harris in Chapter 6, demonstrates that a high-barrier abstinence-based environment can be equally successful in addressing the needs of some individuals and families who are homeless.

The nation's shelter system would also benefit from an injection of this increased variety. There are too many examples of mentally ill persons experiencing chronic homelessness because they find existing shelters too densely populated, too noisy, too dirty, and too crime-ridden to be acceptable as a place to lay their heads at night. For them, unfortunately, the streets and alleyways are preferable; these locations are the best among a few terrible choices. Two-parent families are often unable to remain together in shelters because of regulations that require men and women to live in separate quarters. Transgender persons find themselves uncomfortable in many of the existing shelter situations.

Given the complexity, the one-size-fits-all approach doesn't work, and yet regulations and guidance out of Washington, DC, don't always seem to appreciate this important insight. Strong encouragement from HUD focuses on Housing First as the answer to the housing needs of many. It seems as though, due to limited attention spans, federal decisionmakers grasp at quick fixes and rush to judgment about the utility of a single strategy. Rather, what is needed is a broad spectrum of shelter and housing options that permit all persons an opportunity to find comfort and empowerment in their living situation.

Other approaches to programs are equally troubling. Service agencies have historically treated individuals who are homeless as though they suffer from a moral failing. While consistent with the way that homelessness has historically been understood in US culture, this ignores structural factors that contribute significantly to it. Consider the following analogy: a first-grade student attends class and is taught how to add and subtract. Is this a treatment? Presumably, the student needs help in developing a skill. We do not normally refer to the classroom as a "treatment model," or consider six-year-olds who can't add as problems to be fixed. Resources are devoted to their empowerment. The language we use to describe the treatment models for people experiencing homelessness often sounds more like we are curing a disease than empowering human beings, as Jason Adam Wasserman and Jeffrey Michael Clair indicate in Chapter 8.

The treatment model also dictates a paternalistic relationship between the service provider and the client. Most often, treatment is viewed as it would be in a medical environment in which a professional treats a less-sophisticated and less-knowledgeable patient. "The doctor knows best." In the homelessness arena, the traditional treatment model suggests that the service provider knows best and that the service recipient should therefore accept whatever treatment is offered. In Chapter 2, Michelle McHenry-Edrington provides a perfect example of the fallacy of this unequal relationship. The person experiencing homelessness is, and should be treated as, an equal partner in determining his or her own future, and we should prefer empowerment over treatment. The person experiencing homelessness is empowered by living in a home, just as the first-grader is empowered by going to school. In the same manner that a bank might make a small business loan or a vendor might lease a machine to a construction company, service providers need to empower persons who are homeless to participate in developing strategies that allow them to become self-sufficient.

Fiscal Incentives and Paradigmatic Emphases

Although agency mission statements specifically identify reducing homelessness as a major goal, all too often in communities across the country, funders are supporting agencies that are experiencing increases in the numbers of persons served. It is easy to understand why funders wish to provide added support in cases where rising numbers of people who are homeless place added demands on an already overburdened service system. However, it seems counterintuitive not to reward those efforts that are actually reducing homelessness. Rarely does this happen. In the ever present numbers game, more clients mean more funding; fewer numbers rarely do. As a correction, HUD could demonstrate a greater depth of understanding by incorporating various incentives for reducing homelessness into its panoply of funding opportunities.

"If our agency really does a good job," a notion often heard among providers, "we all will soon be out of work." While no one expects to lose his or her job as the ultimate reward for exemplary work, the incentive structure among service providers within the homelessness industry does raise intriguing questions. There has been a precipitous growth in what Paul A. Toro and Corrissa Carlson in Chapter 14 and Wasserman and Clair in Chapter 8 refer to as the "homelessness industry." Tens of thousands of service providers are presently employed in what has effectively become a homelessness industrial complex. Regardless of the effectiveness of various programs, we have been effective in creating an employment program for service workers. We can continue to mindlessly feed the beast, or we can advocate for transformational initiatives.

It is also necessary to raise questions about the basic housing and service paradigm of our national effort. Currently, a major federal focus is on individuals who are chronically homeless. Is our central goal to reduce the number of persons experiencing homelessness, or is our goal to save money by helping the hardest to serve, the so-called chronics, move into housing and reduce their reliance on local public facilities? Could we reduce the numbers of those who are homeless by focusing more of our efforts on those easiest to serve?

While we should not ignore people experiencing chronic homelessness, we must clearly articulate policies and the rationales that inform them. Focusing on the hardest to serve is essentially a fiscally conservative approach. The driving forces behind this strategy are cost savings and cost avoidance, and the elimination of those individuals that the public associates with homelessness. Would we be better off, for example, to adopt a more deliberate triage approach and focus more on those who need less assistance and support and who stand a much better chance of becoming and staying housed? There are many more in this category than in the chronic group so, presumably for the same cost, we could actually end homelessness for a larger number. We need to be clear about what our ultimate goals are and adopt general strategies that have the greatest likelihood of success.

A corollary to the triage strategy is prevention. We have been unsuccessful in stemming the tide of homelessness; that is, our efforts at preventing people from becoming homeless have not worked sufficiently. To use an oft-quoted parable, a fisherman discovered a body floating in the water one day. He pulled out the body and laid it on the grass. Soon, a second body came floating by, and the fisherman pulled it out too. When a third body followed the first two, the fisherman exclaimed, "Let me go upstream and find out why bodies are falling into the river in the first place." Let's stop simply treating persons after they have become homeless and work with them before they become homeless. We will then be better positioned to prevent those most vulnerable from falling into the river in the first place.

Although prevention has been in the homelessness lexicon for thirty-five years, federal funding explicitly for this strategy was initiated only in 2009 and it was short lived, ending in 2012 at the end of the Homelessness Prevention and Rapid Re-Housing initiative. Part of the rationale for the demise of this funding was the difficulty that CoCs had in distinguishing who among those helped by prevention dollars was actually going to become homeless. However, in considering prevention, in a real sense, what difference does it make whether the support goes to someone who is going to become homeless in the next few weeks or the next few months? Also, given the number of persons who applied for prevention dollars, was the amount of money dedicated to each person or family enough to make a lasting difference? It is imperative that policymakers think through questions like these as they consider the future of prevention efforts.

Several intriguing strategies for focusing more dollars on prevention do exist. As Khadduri suggests, these include: the HomeBase Community Prevention program in New York City; use of the criminal justice system, the child welfare system, and the mental health system as ways to identify persons who may well become homeless; renter insurance programs; and emergency assistance low-interest loans. All of these are potentially useful ways to focus increased attention on preventing individuals and families from becoming homeless.

Expanding Rights and Responsibilities

The arena of rights and responsibilities of people who are homeless is complex. What rights do people living on the street have? Are these rights enforceable? Are the current efforts to curtail certain behaviors effectively criminalizing life without a permanent residence? In the inevitable conflict between the people living on the streets and the people making their living on those streets, it is important to realize all interested constituencies have rights and responsibilities. Just as those experiencing homelessness have the right to a safe and secure place to lay their heads, the business community has a right to undisturbed opportunities to conduct commerce and the public has a right to a safe and commodious environment.

However, along with these rights come responsibilities. Those who are homeless have the responsibility to take care of their basic needs in a way that does not despoil the environment; the business community and the public have the responsibility to provide the necessary facilities so that those experiencing homelessness can fulfill that responsibility.

We would argue that, much like the state of New York's provision, everyone should have a right to shelter. As Collin Jaquet Whelley and Kate Whelley McCabe suggest in Chapter 12, there are important clauses of various constitutional amendments that may, sometime in the future, bear directly on the rights of those experiencing homelessness. Articulating legal protections may well become the next frontier in the effort to end homelessness, just as it was some sixty years ago for the civil rights movement. What remedies our political system has not been able to provide may, in the near future, be mandated by our courts. Future generations will no doubt look at these issues very differently from the way we conceptualize them at present.

Connecting Institutional Silos

Currently, there are two parallel, but unconnected, programs of housing assistance: one targeted at those who are homeless and one for the rest, as Khadduri documents. Our failure to tie homelessness to the mainstream benefits of the social safety net has worked to the serious disadvantage of those experiencing homelessness. What is needed is to unite the mainstream system of housing assistance and the homeless housing and services system; the two systems should act in concert, not in isolation. More housing vouchers would help substantially in reducing homelessness. Simultaneously, mainstream housing programs should be targeted more toward those experiencing homelessness. The

Family Options Study, reported by Khadduri, reinforces the need for this. Increasing support through TANF, SNAP, SSI and SSDI, and VA benefits, among others, could make the lives of those experiencing homelessness measurably better. Even though they are eligible, many of the very poorest in our society are not receiving these benefits. In the spirit of voter registration drives that in the past empowered a dormant constituency and changed the national political climate, we must increase the number of eligible persons who actually receive their benefits by streamlining relevant administrative and regulatory provisions.

One of the consequences of the creation of a parallel system is the isolation of a separate homelessness political constituency; it could well be called the "single-issue homelessness interest group." This has a certain obvious appeal since it is comprised of passionate individuals committed to issues surrounding poverty and homelessness, and they bring invaluable experience to their work.

But there are two major problems. First, policymakers, service providers, and other interested and concerned stakeholders have not figured out how to harness the experience and the wisdom of those actually experiencing homelessness. Therefore, the core of the alliance, those most directly affected, is by and large absent. We all make some effort to incorporate those with direct experience into planning and strategy sessions; we ask persons experiencing homelessness to sit on boards and advisory groups, and some of us even pay attention to the comments and suggestions from those directly affected. But we have failed to enlist the wisdom and experience that is so desperately needed. The difficulties of engaging those experiencing homelessness in program development and political advocacy are challenging, but must be overcome, as McHenry-Edrington indicates so eloquently. Unless we make special efforts to include these individuals, they will continue to remain outside our sphere of influence.

The second problem is the size of this alliance. It consists of those who are directly involved in some way, either as service providers, researchers and other interested stakeholders, funders, and those who experience homelessness. The latter group doesn't vote. The other groups are relatively small in numbers. In fact, all of these groups combined constitute a small voting bloc, certainly not one that can have a substantial impact on decisions made by elected representatives or major funding decisions.

Various national organizations have failed to collaborate and join together to form a united front. There are a large number of national organizations that champion some aspect of the homelessness arena such as the National Alliance to End Homelessness, the National Coalition for the Homeless, the National Low Income Housing Coalition, Stand Up for Kids, the National Center on Family Homelessness, the National Law Center on Homelessness and Poverty, the National Coalition for Homeless Veterans, and Funders Together to End Homelessness, to name just a few. There is, however, no umbrella coalition that brings all of these groups together as one. Responding to this dearth of alliance building, a group of graduate students at my university has created the Neighbors Overcoming Poverty and Homelessness, a nascent effort to begin to address the atomized national alliance.

The National Alliance for the Mentally Ill (NAMI) has created what may be a useful organizational model. With a large and influential national office based in Washington, DC, NAMI has developed a national network of local and state affiliates, all of which are committed to furthering the cause of persons with a mental illness. Admittedly, there are many more persons with a mental illness in our midst than there are persons experiencing homelessness; however, the creation of a formal network of affiliates is not beyond the realm of possibility. It will take some real coalition building in Washington and around the country, and leadership will have to step forward if such a network is to become a reality.

Homelessness is intricately related to a web of other social problems. Persons experiencing homelessness are connected to employment systems, physical and behavioral health care systems, the criminal justice system, transportation systems, childcare programs, nutritional programs, and benefits programs, among others. Stakeholders in these other systems are natural allies in our efforts to improve the lives of the most destitute among us. A collaborative coalition of all these interested parties would yield far more influence than a single-issue homelessness group.

Public Perceptions—
The Deserving and the Undeserving Poor

We have criminalized homelessness in the United States, and living on the streets is "cruel and unusual punishment," to use David L. DiLeo's term in Chapter 9. For most of us, our brief encounters with people experiencing homelessness consist of contact with mostly unshaven, dirty, hobbling men dressed in rags and flying cardboard signs. We tend to create stereotypes based on these contacts made when the traffic light turns red, and most of us do our best to avoid interactions with these fliers. Given these interactions, it is not surprising that most of us tend to characterize the homeless as bums and hoboes, as drunks, drug addicts, and people with mental illness. Many of us argue that they choose to live that way, that they have made bad choices, or that they are lazy people who just need to get a job.

These stereotypes ignore the experiences of the vast majority of those experiencing homelessness. Most Americans experiencing homelessness do not have a clinical diagnosis, are not substance addicted, and have not chosen their lifestyle except as a better alternative to a depressing shelter. Some, of course, have made bad choices, but haven't we all? Historically, benefits in US society have accrued to citizens based on categories such as skin color, gender, or some exercise of political or economic power; they are the deserving. The moral imagination that will be required to end homelessness must call for the abandonment of this selectivity, the stereotypes, and the judgments that have informed our policies and our attitudes. Americans are attracted to the universality of rights when called to it. Our common humanity, not a narrow characteristic of it—like race, gender, or sexual orientation—should inform our public policies. Ultimately, to provide housing stability for all, rights enumerated in our national charters will need to extend to all citizens without reference to their merit as economic actors, or their sophistication as social beings. This is dignity without condition. Every single human being, by dint of being human, is deserving; no one is undeserving.

Some Encouraging Signs

There are some encouraging signs. As Batko indicates, coordinated planning is a positive sign of the increased and collaborative attention that is being paid to the issue. The increased focus of the federal government, as indicated by Opening Doors, is encouraging. Especially promising is the advancement in dealing with veteran homelessness; the effort among veterans provides an important harbinger of what can happen if the entire federal government were to identify homelessness as a national priority. The so-called 25 Cities effort will undoubtedly focus added attention on homelessness in many of our large urban areas. Efforts to target the most vulnerable are also encouraging. All these efforts do suggest that there is an increase in collective planning and that, at least in the Barack Obama administration, there is a willingness to target more resources on the problem.

Thinking Outside the Box

Although there are some positive signs, we remain far from achieving our goal. Housing units need to be built, options expanded, and a greater range of services contemplated to meet the needs of an increasingly diverse population. Funding needs to be multiplied exponentially, employment opportunities expanded, wages increased, outcome data emphasized, existing data systems reexamined, prevention prioritized, and parallel systems conjoined. In response to the major tasks that lie in front of us, these strategies should be considered imperatives, not options.

Who should head and conduct these efforts? Should helping those experiencing homelessness be the responsibility of government, or should the primary source of help be private charitable organizations? As Miskey indicates, in the recent past the federal government has provided the great bulk of the funding to support program efforts. But it can't be just the federal govern-ment or private charities that shoulder the responsibility. Collaborative efforts and joint projects are necessary. The government, private charities and foun-dations, corporations, service agencies of every stripe, faith communities, and individuals across the nation must all work together if we are to over-come the misery that affects so many of our fellow citizens.

By and large, supporters and advocates for those experiencing homeless-ness do not try to affect policy; unfortunately, we have not created enough meaningful opportunities for individuals to do that. Homelessness advocates are not sufficiently active or engaged. We must change that; we must create more chances for each of us to engage in some form of advocacy on behalf of those experiencing homelessness. Failure to do so will continue to con-sign our most destitute citizens to a life on the streets.

The single most important task confronting the advocacy community is to develop a much stronger political will to address the many issues that we have raised. This is no easy job. Social and cultural change comes about only over time, and only if there is strong leadership and a strong impetus behind it. Mustering these will require changing public attitudes. We need to build public will and develop a stronger political base. What's required is a mas-sive public relations effort, and the campaign must be appealing to both sides of the aisle.

The political will necessary to change policy and funding priorities as well as to create collaborative efforts does not currently exist. There is noth-ing on the immediate horizon to suggest that the country will miraculously shift gears and suddenly appropriate the funding to build the necessary hous-ing units, provide the necessary support services, or prevent the next genera-tion of the very poorest from becoming homeless.

To build public will, we need to determine ways to change public atti-tudes about those experiencing homelessness and to develop possible strate-gies for changing the nature of the political, economic, and social systems that maintain homelessness at such a high level in this country. We need a tsunami of change in public perceptions about and attitudes toward homelessness.

Ending homelessness will require thinking outside the box. Service providers, policymakers, marketing specialists, educators, and stakeholders of every description will all need to be part of this movement. And central to all of this, the voice of those most affected—those experiencing homeless-ness and those at risk of becoming homeless—must be marshaled. But if coalitions are to be enlarged and new stakeholders created, reconceptualiza-tions of the complex of issues leading to homelessness will be required. As a start in this direction, we made a conscious editorial decision in this vol-ume to use people-first language, preferring "people experiencing homeless-ness" to "homeless people." In doing so, we are stressing that the condition of homelessness is temporary, not a character trait; we are thus affirming the humanity of those experiencing homelessness, not their particular circumstances.

Changes in language, while prompting us to think differently, are not enough. We must act differently. Satisfaction with the isolated impact of one agency, or one department, or one voice, while critical to our efforts, is not enough. Independent entities and voices will need to behave more collaboratively if we expect to strengthen political coalitions that will be necessary to eliminate homelessness from life in the United States.

To repeat, even if there is only one person experiencing homelessness, that's one too many! This is a vision and a clarion call to all of us who work to end the misery on our streets and in our shelters.

Note

1. www.fdrlibrary.marist.edu/pdfs/fftext.pdf, p. 8.

References

Abbott, A. (2001). *Chaos of disciplines*. Chicago, IL: University of Chicago Press.

ABC News Nightline. (1990, December 19). More homeless and hungry face colder hearts. New York, NY: WABC.

Abel, J., Deitiz, R., Su, Y. (2014). Are recent college graduates finding good jobs? *Current Issues in Economics and Finance, 20*(1). New York, NY: Federal Reserve Bank of New York. Retrieved from www.newyorkfed.org/research/current_issues

An Act Concerning a Homeless Person's Bill of Rights, Pub. L. No. 13-251, Conn. (2013).

Adams, C. T. (1986). Homelessness in the post-industrial city: Views from London and Philadelphia. *Urban Affairs Quarterly* 21 (4) 527–549.

Adolino, J. R., and Blake, C. H. (2010). *Comparing public policies: Issues and choices in industrialized countries* (2nd ed.). Washington, DC: CQ Press.

Agans, R. P., Liu, G., Jones, M., Verjan, C., Silverbush, M., and Kalsbeek, W. D. (2011). *Public attitudes toward the homeless*. Unpublished manuscript, Survey Research Unit, University of North Carolina, Chapel Hill, NC.

Alker, J. (1992). Ensuring access to education: The role of advocates for homeless children and youth. In J. H. Stronge (Ed.), *Educating homeless children and adolescents: Evaluating policy and practice* (pp. 179–193). Newbury Park, CA: Sage.

Amenta, E., and Halfmann, D. (2000). Wage wars: Institutional politics, WPA wages, and the struggle for US social policy. *American Sociological Review, 65*(4), 506–528.

Amster, R. (2003). Patterns of exclusion: Sanitizing space, criminalizing homelessness. *Social Justice, 30*(1): 195–221.

Amster, R. (2008). *Lost in space: The criminalization, globalization, and urban ecology of homelessness*. New York, NY: LFB Scholarly.

Apgar, W. C. (1993). An abundance of housing for all but the poor. In G. T. Kingsley and M. A. Turner (Eds.), *Housing markets and residential mobility* (pp. 99–123). Washington, DC: Urban Institute Press.

Arnold, K. R. (2004). *Homelessness, citizenship, and identity: The uncanniness of late modernity*. Albany, NY: SUNY Press.

Aron, L., and Fitchen, J. (1996). Rural homelessness: A synopsis. In J. Bauhmol (Ed.), *Homelessness in America* (pp. 81–85). Phoenix, AZ: Oryx Press.

Aron, L. Y., and Sharkey, P. T. (2002). The 1996 SNSHAPC: A comparison of faith-based and secular non-profit programs. Washington, DC: Urban Institute.

Attanasi, K., and Yong, A. (Eds.) (2012). *Pentecostalism and prosperity: The socio-economics of the global charismatic movement.* New York, NY: Palgrave Macmillan.

Auerswald, C., and Eyre, S. (2002). Youth homelessness in San Francisco: A life cycle approach. *Social Science and Medicine, 54*(10), 1497–1512. doi:10.1016 /S0277-9536(01)00128-9

Autor, D., Dorn, D., and Hanson, G. (2013). The China syndrome: Local labor market effects of import competition in the United States. *American Economic Review, 103*(6), 2121–2168. doi: 10.1257/aer.103.6.2121

Aviles, A., and Helfrich, C. (1991). Life skill service needs. *Journal of Adolescence, 33*(4), 331–338.

Axelson, L. J., and Dail, P. W. (1988). The changing character of homelessness in the United States. *Family Relations, 37*(4), 463–469.

Bahr, H. (1971). *Disaffiliated man: Essays and bibliography on skid row, vagrancy, and outsiders.* Toronto, ON: University of Toronto Press.

Bahr, H. (1973). *Skid Row: An Introduction to Disaffiliation.* New York: Oxford University Press.

Baker, D. (2004, May/June). The housing bubble: A time bomb in low-income communities? *Shelterforce.* Retrieved from www.nhi.org/online/issues/135/bubble .html

Bannister, J., Fyfe, N., and Kearns, A. (2006). Respectable or respectful? (In) civility and the city. *Urban Studies, 43*(5–6), 919–937.

Barber, M. (2014). *Representing the preferences of donors, partisans, and voters in the U.S. Senate* (Working Paper No. X). Princeton, NJ: Princeton University. Retrieved from https://csed.byu.edu/Documents/BarberPaper2.pdf.

Baron, S., and Hartnagel, T. F. (1998). Street youth and criminal violence. *Journal of Research in Crime and Delinquency, 35*(2), 166–192.

Baron, S., Kennedy, L., and Forde, D. (2001). Male street youths' conflict: The role of background, subcultural and situational factors. *Justice Quarterly, 18*(4), 759–789.

Barrow, S., McMullin, L., Tripp, J., and Tsemberis, S. (2007). Consumer integration and self-determination in homeless research, policy, planning, and services. In D. Dennis, G. Locke, and J. Khadduri (Eds.), *Toward understanding homelessness: The 2007 National Symposium on Homeless Research* (pp. 3-1–3-55). Washington, DC: US Department of Health and Human Services and US Department of Housing and Urban Development.

Barry, P., Ensign, J., and Lippek, S. (2002). Embracing street culture: Fitting health care into the lives of street youth. *Journal of Transcultural Nursing, 13*(2), 145–152.

Bassuk, E. L. (1984, July). The homelessness problem. *Scientific American,* pp. 40–45.

Bassuk, E. L. (2010). Ending child homelessness in America. *American Journal of Orthopsychiatry, 80*(4), 496–504.

Bassuk, E. L., DeCandia, C. J., Beach, C. A., and Berman, F. (2014). *America's youngest outcasts: A report card on child homelessness.* Waltham, MA: National Center on Family Homelessness, American Institutes for Research.

Bassuk, E. L., Rubin, L., and Lauriat, A. (1984). Is homelessness a mental health problem? *American Journal of Psychiatry, 141*(12), 1546–1549.

Baum, A. S., and Burnes, D.W. (1993). *A nation in denial: The truth about homelessness.* Boulder, CO: Westview Press.

Baxter E., and Hopper, K. (1981). *Private lives/public spaces: Homeless adults on the streets of New York City.* New York, NY: Community Service Society, Institute for Social Welfare Research.

Beckett, K., and Herbert, S. (2008). Dealing with disorder: Social control in the post-industrial city. *Theoretical Criminology, 12*(1), 5–30.

Bender, K., Ferguson, K., Thompson, S., and Langenderfer, L. (2014). Mental health correlates of victimization classes among homeless youth. *Child Abuse and Neglect, 38*(10), 1628–1635.

Berg, S. (2015). Homeless assistance: McKinney-Vento homeless assistance programs. In National Low Income Housing Coalition (Ed.), *Advocates' guide 2015* (pp. 4-1–4-3). Washington, DC: National Low Income Housing Coalition.

Bernard, C., and Pope, E. (2014). *Nonprofit performance management: Using data to measure and improve programs.* Portland, ME: Idealware. Retrieved from www.issuelab.org/resource/nonprofit_performance_management_using_data_to _measure_and_improve_programs

Bickford, S. (2000). Constructing inequality: City spaces and the architecture of citizenship. *Political Theory, 28*(9), 355–376.

Bigelow, G. (2005, May). Let there be markets: The evangelical roots of economics. *Harper's Magazine,* pp. 33–40.

Biggar, H. (2001). Homeless children and education: An evaluation of the Stewart B. McKinney Homeless Assistance Act. *Children and Youth Services Review, 23*(12), 941–969.

Bill and Melinda Gates Foundation. (2011). *Ending family homelessness in Washington state.* Retrieved from https://docs.gatesfoundation.org/Documents/family -homelessness-strategy.pdf. Seattle: Author.

Bill of Rights for the Homeless Act, Pub. L. No. 098-0516, Ill. Laws, § 5 (2013).

Bipartisan Policy Center. (2013). *Housing America's future: New directions for national policy.* Washington, DC: Author.

Bivens, J. (2013). *Using standard models to benchmark the costs of globalization for American workers without a college degree* (Briefing Paper No. 354). Washington, DC: Economic Policy Institute. Retrieved from www.epi.org/publication /standard-models-benchmark-costs-globalization/

Bivens, J., Gould, E., Mishel, L., and Shierholz, H. (2014). *Raising America's pay: Why it's our central economic policy challenge* (Briefing Paper No. 378). Washington, DC: Economic Policy Institute. Retrieved from www.epi.org/publication /raising-americas-pay/

Blanch, A. K., Carling, P. J., and Ridgway, P. (1988). Normal housing with specialized supports: A psychiatric rehabilitation approach to living in the community. *Rehabilitation Psychology 33(1),* 47–55.

Blank, R., and Greenberg, M. (2008). *Improving the measurement of poverty.* Washington, DC: Brookings Institution. Retrieved from www.brookings.edu/papers /2008/12_poverty_measurement_blank.aspx

Blasi, G. (1994). And we are not seen: Ideological and political barriers to understanding homelessness. *American Behavioral Scientist, 37*(4), 563–586.

Blinder, A., and Krueger, B. (2009). *Alternative measures of offshorability: A survey approach* (Working Paper No. 15287). Cambridge, MA: National Bureau of

Economic Research. Retrieved from http://citeseerx.ist.psu.edu/viewdoc/down
load?doi=10.1.1.506.9682&rep=rep1&type=pdf

Bloom, P. (2005, December). Is God an accident? *Atlantic Monthly,* pp. 105–112.

Boesky, L., Toro, P., and Bukowski, P. (1997). Differences in psychosocial factors among older and younger homeless adolescents found in shelters. In E. Smith and J. Ferrari (Eds.), *Diversity within the homeless population: Implications for intervention* (pp. 19–36). New York, NY: Haworth Press.

Bolton, M., Bravve, E., and Crowley, S. (2014). *The Alignment Project: Aligning federal low income housing programs with housing need.* Washington, DC: National Low Income Housing Coalition.

Bolton, M., Bravve, E., Miller, E., Crowley, S., and Errico, E. (2015). *Out of reach 2005: Low wages & high rents lock renters out.* Washington, DC: National Low Income Housing Coalition.

Bopp, J., Jr., La Rue, J. E., and Kosel, E. M. (2011). The game changer: Citizens United's impact on campaign finance law in general and corporate political speech in particular. *First Amendment Law Review, 9*(251).

Bray, J. H., Milburn, N. G., Cowan, B. A., Gross, S. Z., Ponce, A. N., Schumacher, J., and Toro, P. A. (2010). *Helping people without homes: The role of psychologists and recommendations to advance training, research, practice and policy.* Washington, DC: American Psychological Association, Presidential Task Force on Psychology's Contribution to End Homelessness. Retrieved from www.apa.org/pi/ses/resources/publications/end-homelessness.aspx

Bremer, F. J. (1976). *The Puritan experiment.* New York, NY: St. Martin's Press.

Brennan, T. (1980). Mapping the diversity among runaways. *Journal of Family Issues,* 1, 189–209.

Brickner, P. (1985). Health issues in the care of the homeless. In P. Brickner, L. Scharer, B. Conanan, A. Elvy, and M. Savarese (eds.), *Health care of homeless people,* pp. 3–18. New York: Springer Publishing Company.

Brock, A., Buteau, E., and Herring, A. (2012). *Room for improvement: Foundations' support of nonprofit performance assessment.* Cambridge, MA: Center for Effective Philanthropy. Retrieved from www.effectivephilanthropy.org/wp-content/uploads/2014/01/RoomForImprovement.pdf

Brown, J., Spellman, B., Wilkins, C., and Henry, M. (2014). *Evaluation of the Conrad N. Hilton Foundation Chronic Homelessness Initiative 2014 report.* Bethesda, MD: Abt Associates.

Buchanan, D., Doblin, B., Sai, T., and Garcia, P. (2006). The effects of respite care for homeless patients: A cohort study. *American Journal of Public Health, 96*(7), 1278–1281.

Buck, P. O., and Toro, P. A. (2004). Images of homelessness in the media. In D. Levinson (Ed.), *Encyclopedia of homelessness* (pp. 301–308). Thousand Oaks, CA: Sage.

Buck, P. O., Toro, P. A., and Ramos, M. A. (2004). Media and professional interest in homelessness over 30 years (1974–2003). *Analyses of Social Issues and Public Policy, 4*(1), 151–171.

Burt, M. R. (1992). *Over the edge: The growth of homelessness in the 1980s.* New York, NY: Russell Sage Foundation; Washington, DC: Urban Institute.

Burt, M. R. (2001). *What will it take to end homelessness?* Washington, DC: Urban Institute.

Burt, M. R. (2003). Chronic homelessness: Emergence of a public policy. *Fordham Urban Law Journal, 30*(3), 1267–1279.

Burt, M. R. (2006). *Characteristics of transitional housing for homelss families.* Washington, DC: Urban Institute.

Burt, M. R. (2008) *Hilton Foundation Project to End Homelessness for People with Mental Illness in Los Angeles: Changes in homelessness, supportive housing, and tenant characteristics since 2005*. Washington, DC: Urban Institute.

Burt, M. R., Aron, L.Y., Douglas, T., Valente, J., Lee, E., and Iwen, B. (1999.) *Homelessness: Programs and the People They Serve—Summary and Technical Reports*. Findings of the 1996 National Survey of Homeless Assistance Providers and Clients. Washington, DC: Interagency Council on the Homeless.

Burt, M. R., Aron, L., and Lee, E. (2001). *Helping America's homeless: Emergency shelter or affordable housing?* Washington, DC: Urban Institute.

Burt, M. R., and Cohen, B. E. (1989). *America's homeless: Numbers, characteristics, and the programs that serve them*. Washington, DC: Urban Institute.

Burt, M. R., Pollack, D., Sosland, A., Mikelson, K. S., Drappa, E., Greenwalt, K., and Sharkey, P. (2002). *Evaluation of Continuums of Care for homeless people: Final report*. Washington, DC: Urban Institute; Fairfax, VA: ICF Consulting.

Bushman, R. (1980). *From Puritan to Yankee: Character and the social order in Connecticut, 1690–1965*. Cambridge, MA: Harvard University Press.

Carlson, C., Toro, P. A., and Buck, P. O. (2015). *Media and professional publications on homelessness over four decades (1974–2013)*. Unpublished manuscript, Department of Psychology, Wayne State University, Detroit, MI.

Carrier, S. (2015, March/April). Room for improvement. *Mother Jones*, pp. 30–39.

CBO. *See* Congressional Budget Office.

Center on Budget and Policy Priorities. (2015). *Policy basics: Federal rental assistance*. Washington, DC: Author. Retrieved from www.cbpp.org/sites/default/files/atoms/files/PolicyBasics- housing-1-25-13RA.pdf

Chicago v. Morales, 527 U.S. 41 (1999).

Chung, P., and Tran, M. (2015). *State of evaluation in Colorado's nonprofit sector*. Denver: The Colorado Trust.

Cingano, F. (2014). *Trends in income inequality and its impact on economic growth* (Social, Employment and Migration Working Papers No. 163). Paris, France: Organisation for Economic Co-operation and Development. Retrieved from http://dx.doi.org/10.1787/5jxrjncwxv6j-en

Citro, C., and Michaels, R. (Eds.) (1995). *Measuring poverty: A new approach*. Washington, DC: National Academies Press.

City of Chicago (2012). *Chicago's Plan 2.0: A Home for Everyone*. Retrieved from www.cityofchicago.org/ChicagoPlan2web082712.pdf.

City of Chicago. (2002). *Getting housed, staying housed*. Chicago, IL: Author. Retrieved from www.endhomelessness.org/library/entry/il-chicago

Civil Action for Deprivation of Rights, 42 U.S.C. § (1983).

Clark v. Community for Creative Non-Violence, 468 U.S. 288, 293–299 (U.S. 1984).

CNN Money. (2015, April 23). Retrieved from http://money.cnn.com/2015/04/23/news/economy/poor-spending

Coalition for the Homeless. (2015). *Basic facts about homelessness: New York City*. New York, NY: Author. Retrieved from www.coalitionforthehomeless.org/basic-facts-about-homelessness-new-york-city/

Collins, S. E., Clifasefi, S. L., Dana, E. A., Andrasik, M. P., Stahl, N., Kirouac, M., and Malone, D. K. (2012). Where harm reduction meets housing first: Exploring alcohol's role in a project-based housing first setting. *International Journal of Drug Policy, 23*(2), 111–119.

Collinson, R., Ellen, I. G., and Ludwig, J. (2015). *Low-income housing policy* (Working paper no. 21071). Cambridge, MA: National Bureau of Economic Research.

Congressional Budget Office. (2011). Trends in the distribution of household income between 1979 and 2007, supplemental data. Retrieved from www.cbo.gov /publication/42537

Congressional Budget Office. (2013). The distribution of major tax expenditures in the individual income tax system. Retrieved from www.cbo.gov/publication/43768

Conlon, K., and Shoichet, C. E. (2014, November 5). 90-year-old Florida man charged for feeding homeless people. CNN. Retrieved from www.cnn.com /2014/11/04/justice/florida-feeding-homeless-charges/index.html

Cooper, E., Korman, H., O'Hara, A., and Zovistoski, A. (2009). *Priced out in 2008: The housing crisis for people with disabilities.* Boston: Technical Assistance Collaborative, Inc. Retrieved from http://www.tacinc.org

Cordray, D. S., and Pion, G. M. (1991). What's behind the numbers? Definitional issues in counting the homeless. *Housing Policy Debate, 2*(3), 585–616.

Corman, H., and Mocan, N. (2005). Carrots, sticks, and broken windows. *Journal of Law and Economics, 48*(1), 235–266.

Corporation for Supportive Housing. (n.d.). *Social innovation fund pay for success.* New York, NY: Author. Retrieved from www.csh.org/pfs

Couch, L. (2015). Public housing: Moving to work demonstration program. In National Low Income Housing Coalition (Ed.), *Advocates' guide 2015* (pp. 4-17–4-20). Washington, DC: National Low Income Housing Coalition.

Cronley, C. (2010). Unraveling the social construction of homelessness. *Journal of Human Behavior in the Social Environment, 20*(2), 319–333.

Cross, F. B. (2001). The error of positive rights. *UCLA Law Review, 48* (4): 857–922.

Crouse, J. M. 1986. *The homeless transient in the Great Depression: New York state, 1929–1941.* Albany, SUNY Press. Citing results of the national study conducted in 1933 by the National Committee on Care of Transient and Homeless.

Crowley, S. (2009). HOPE VI: What went wrong? In H. G. Cisneros and L. Engdahl (Eds.), *From despair to hope: HOPE VI and the new promise of public housing in America's cities* (pp. 63–81). Washington, DC: Brookings Institution Press.

CSH. *See* Corporation for Supportive Housing.

Culhane, D. P. (2008). The costs of homelessness: A perspective from the United States. *European Journal of Homelessness 2,* 97–114.

Culhane, D. P., and Byrne, T. (2010). *Ending chronic homelessness: Cost-effective opportunities for interagency collaboration.* Working Paper. Philadephia, PA: Penn School of Social Policy and Practice. Retrieved from http://repository .upenn.edu/cgi/viewcontent.cgi?article=1151&context=spp_papers

Culhane, D. P., Dejowski, E. F., Ibanez, J., Needham, E., and Macchia, I. (1994). Public shelter admission rates in Philadelphia and New York City: The implications of turnover for sheltered population counts. *Housing Policy Debate, 5*(2), 107–140.

Culhane, D. P., Lee, C. M., and Wachter, S. M. (1996). Where the homeless come from: A study of the prior address distribution of families admitted to public shelters in New York City and Philadelphia. *Housing Policy Debate, 7*(2), 327–365.

Culhane, D. P., and Metraux, S. (2008). Rearranging the deck chairs or reallocating the lifeboats? Homelessness assistance and its alternatives. *Journal of the American Planning Association, 74*(1), 111–121.

Culhane, D. P., Metraux, S., and Byrne, T. (2011). A prevention-centered approach to homelessness assistance: A paradigm shift? *Housing Policy Debate, 21*(2), 295–315.

Culhane, D. P., Metraux, S., Byrne, T., Stino, M., and Bainbridge, J. (2013). The age structure of contemporary homelessness: Evidence and implications for public policy. *Analyses of Social Issues and Public Policy, 13*(1), 228–244.

Culhane, D. P., Metraux, S., Park, J. M., Schretzman, M., and Valente, J. (2007). Testing a typology of family homelessness based on patterns of public shelter utilization in four US jurisdictions: Implications for policy and program planning. *Housing Policy Debate, 18*(1), 1–28.

Culhane, D. P., Parker, W. D., Poppe, B., Gross, K. S., and Sykes, E. (2007). Accountability, cost-effectiveness, and program performance: Progress since 1998. In D. Dennis, G. Locke, and J. Khadduri (Eds.), *Toward understanding homelessness: The 2007 national symposium on homeless research* (pp. 12-1–12-42). Washington, DC: US Department of Health and Human Services and US Department of Housing and Urban Development.

Cunningham, C. (2003). *Trends and issues: Social and economic context.* Washington, DC: Office of Educational Research and Improvement.

Cunningham, M. B., Biess, J., and Emam, D. (2013). *Veterans Homelessness Prevention Demonstration evaluation: Interim report.* Washington, DC: US Department of Housing and Urban Development.

Cunningham, M., Burt, M. R., Scott, M., Locke, G., Burton, L., Klerman, J. . . . Stillman, L. (2015). *Homeless prevention study: Prevention programs funded by the Homelessness Prevention and Rapid Re-Housing Program.* Washington, DC: Urban Institute; Bethesda, MA: Abt Associates; and Hyattsville, MD: Cloudburst Consulting Group.

Cunningham, M., Lear, M., Schmitt, E., and Henry, M. (2006). *A new vision: What is in community plans to end homelessness.* Washington, DC: National Alliance to End Homelessness.

Cutuli, J. J., Montgomery, A. E., Evans-Chase, M., and Culhane, D. P. (2015). Childhood adversity, adult homelessness and the intergenerational transmission of risk: A population-representative study of individuals in households with children. *Child and Family Social Work.* doi: 10.1111/cfs.12207

Daskal, J. (1998). *In search of shelter: The growing shortage of affordable rental housing.* Center on Budget and Policy Priorities. Retrieved from: www.cbpp.org /archiveSite/615hous.pdf. Washington, DC: Author.

Davis, M. (2004). Planet of slums. *New Left Review, 26,* 5–34.

Davis, T. H., and Lane, T. S. (2012). *Rapid re-housing of families experiencing homelessness in Massachusetts: Maintaining housing stability.* Boston, MA: Metropolitan Boston Housing Partnership.

Decker, S. H., Spohn, C., Ortiz, N. R., and Hedberg, E. (2014). *Criminal stigma, race, gender and employment: An expanded assessment of the consequences of imprisonment for employment.* Phoenix, AZ: Arizona State University, School of Criminology and Criminal Justice and College of Public Programs. Retrieved from http://thecrimereport.s3.amazonaws.com/2/fb/e/2362/criminal_stigma_race_crime _and_unemployment.pdf

Deegan, P. E., and Drake, R. E. (2006). Shared decision making and medication management in the recovery process. *Psychiatric Services, 57*(11), 1636–1639.

Denver's Road Home. (2013). *Denver's ten-year plan to end homelessness: 2013 update-year 8-fourth revision.* Denver, CO: Author.

DeParle, J. (1998, October 20). Slamming the door. *New York Times Magazine,* pp. 52–57, 68, 94–95.

Desertrain v. City of Los Angeles, No. 11-56957, 2014 WL 2766541 (9th Cir. June 19, 2014).

Desmond, M., Gershenson, C., and Kiviat, B. (2015). Forced relocation and residential instability among urban renters. *Social Service Review, 89*(2), 227–262.

Dickey, B., Normand, S. L., Eisen, S., Hermann, R., Cleary, P., Cortes, D., et al. (2006). Associations between adherence to guidelines for antipsychotic dose and health status, side effects, and patient care experiences. *Medical Care, 44*(9), 827–834.

Dolbeare, C., and Crowley, S. (2002). *Changing priorities: The federal budget and housing assistance 1976–2007*. Washington, DC: National Low Income Housing Coalition.

Domhoff, G. W. (2015). Power in America: Wealth, income and power. Retrieved from WhoRulesAmerica, http://www2.ucsc.edu/whorulesamerica/power/wealth.html

Donley, A. M., and Wright, J. D. (2008). Cleaning up the streets: Community efforts to combat homelessness by criminalizing homeless behaviors. *Homelessness in America 3(1)*, 75–92.

Drake, R. E., and Deegan, P. E. (2008). Are assertive community treatment and recovery compatible? Commentary on "ACT and recovery: integrating evidence-based practice and recovery orientation on assertive community treatment teams." *Community Mental Health J, 44*(1), 75–77.

Drake, R., McHugo, G., Xie, H., Fox, M., Packard, J., and Helmstetter, B. (2006). Ten-year recovery outcomes for clients with co-occurring schizophrenia and substance use disorders. *Schizophrenia Bulletin, 32*(3), 464–473.

Drake, R. E., Mueser, K. T., Brunette, M. F., and McHugo, G. J. (2004). A review of treatments for people with severe mental illnesses and co-occurring substance use disorders. *Psychiatric Rehabilitation J, 27*(4), 360–374.

Drake, R. E., Osher, F. C., and Wallach, M. A. (1991). Homelessness and dual diagnosis. *American Psychologist, 46*(11), 1149–1158.

DRH. *See* Denver's Road Home.

Dunton, L., Henry, M., Kean, E., and Khadduri, J. (2013). *Study of PHAs' efforts to serve people experiencing homelessness*. Bethesda, MA: Abt Associates.

Dvorak, P. (2014, April 21). Without affordable rents, DC's rehousing program can't rescue homeless families. *Washington Post*.

Economic Policy Institute. (2014). State of Working America, updated tables. Retrieved from http://stateofworkingamerica.org/

The Economist. (2011, October 15). Why the Pruitt-Igoe housing project failed.

Ellen, I. G., and O'Flaherty, B. (Eds.). (2010). *How to house the homeless*. New York, NY: Russell Sage Foundation.

Elsby, M., Hobijn, B., and Sahin, A. (2013). The decline of the U.S. labor share. *Brookings Papers on Economic Activity*. Retrieved from www.frbsf.org /economic-research/files/wp2013-27.pdf

Eng, A. (2014). *Updated options to reform the deduction for home mortgage interest*. Washington, DC: Tax Policy Center. Retrieved from www.taxpolicycenter.org /UploadedPDF/413124-updated-options-to-reform-the-deduction-for-home -mortgage-interest.pdf

Ennett, S., Bailey, S., and Federman, E. (1999). Social network characteristics associated with risky behaviors among runaway and homeless youth. *Journal of Health and Social Behavior, 40*(1), 63–78.

EPI. *See* Economic Policy Institute.

Evans, J. (2011). Exploring the (bio)political dimensions of voluntarism and care in the city: The case of a "low barrier" emergency shelter. *Health and Place, 17*(1), 24–32.

Farrow, J., Deisher, R., Brown, R., Kulig, J., and Kipke, M. (1992). Health and health needs of homeless and runaway youth. *Journal of Adolescent Health, 13*(8), 717–726.

Federal Housing Finance Agency. (2014). *2013 Low-income housing and community development activities of the Federal Home Loan Banks*. Washington, DC: Author.

Ferrell, J. (2001). *Tearing down the streets: Adventures in urban anarchy*. New York: Palgrave Macmillan.

Finkel, M., Henry, M., Matthews, N., Spellman, B., and Culhane, D. P. (in press).

Evaluation of the Rapid Re-Housing for Homeless Families demonstration: Final report. Bethesda, MD: Abt Associates.

Fisher, B. W., Mayberry, L. S., Shinn, M., and Khadduri, J. (2014). Leaving homelessness behind: Housing decisions among families exiting shelter. *Housing Policy Debate, 24*(2), 364–386.

Fisher, G. M. (1992). The development and history of the poverty thresholds. *Social Security Bulletin, 55*(4), 3–14. Retrieved from www.ssa.gov/history/fisheron poverty.html

Fitzpatrick, S. (2005). Explaining homelessness: A critical realist perspective. *Housing, Theory and Society, 22*(1), 1–17.

Flannery, T. (2014, December). Only human: The evolution of a flawed species. *Harper's Magazine*, pp. 98–102.

Florida, R. L. (2012). The rise of the creative class: Revisited. New York, NY: Basic Books.

Fosburg, L., Locke, G., Peck, L., and Finkel, M. (1997). *National evaluation of the Shelter Plus Care program.* Cambridge, MA: Abt Associates.

Foundation Center. (2002). Foundation stats. Retrieved from http://data.foundation center.org/#/fc1000/population_group:econ_disadvantaged/nationwide/total /list/2002

Foundation Center. (2012). Foundation stats. Retrieved from http://data.foundation center.org/#/fc1000/population_group:econ_disadvantaged/nationwide/total /list/2012

Frank, K. A. (1998). Single room occupancy housing. In W. Van Vliet (Ed.), *Encyclopedia of housing* (pp. 538–540). Thousand Oaks, CA: Sage.

Frank, T. (2004). *What's the matter with Kansas: How conservatives won the heart of America.* New York, NY: Henry Holt.

Freeland, C. (2012). *Plutocrats: The rise of the new global super-rich and the fall of everyone else.* New York, NY: Penguin.

Fremstad, S. (2010). *A modern framework for measuring poverty and basic economic security.* Washington, DC: Center for Economic Policy Research.

Friedman, M. (1980). *Free to choose: A personal statement.* New York: Harcourt Brace Jovanovich.

Fulop, M. (2011, February 3). *The critical need for program accountability & evaluation.* Retrieved from http://facilitationprocess.com/the-critical-need-for-program-accountabiltiy-evaluation

Funders Together to End Homelessness. (2012). Improving housing outcomes with rapid rehousing. Retrieved from http://d3n8a8pro7vhmx.cloudfront.net/funders together/pages/261/attachments/original/13887808 81/grantmakers_toolkit_improving _housing_outcomes_rapid_rehousing.pdf?1388780881

Gale, K. (2012). *The prevention effectiveness challenge: Can we do better at preventing homelessness?* Paper presented at the Twenty-second Annual Conference on Ending Homelessness, Yakima, WA.

Gans, H. J. (1995). *The war against the poor: The underclass and antipoverty policy.* New York, NY: Basic Books.

Gargiulo, R. M. (2006). Homeless and disabled: Rights, responsibilities, and recommendations for serving young children with special needs. *Early Childhood Education Journal, 33*(5): 357–362.

Gilens, M. (2005). Inequality and democratic responsiveness. *Public Opinion Quarterly, 69*(5), 778–896.

Gilens, M. (2012). *Affluence and influence.* Princeton, NJ: Princeton University Press.

Gilens, M., and Page, B. (2014). Testing theories of American politics: Elites, interest groups, and average citizens. *Perspectives on Politics, 12*(30), 564–581.

Gilmer, T. P., Manning, W. G., and Ettner, S. L. (2009). A cost analysis of San Diego County's REACH program for homeless persons. *Psychiatric Services, 60*(4), 445–450.

Gindin, S., and Panitch, L. (2013). *The making of global capitalism: The political economy of American empire.* Cambridge, UK: Verso Books.

Gladwell, M. (2006). Million-dollar Murray. *The New Yorker, 13*, 96.

Glyn, A. (2006). *Capitalism Unleashed: Finance, Globalization, and Welfare.* Oxford, UK: Oxford University Press.

Goldman, H. H., Morrissey, J. P., Ridgely, M. S., Frank, R. G., Newman, S. J., and Kennedy, C. (1992). Lessons from the Program on Chronic Mental Illness. *Health Affairs, 11*(3), 51–68.

Goleman, D. (1986, November 4). To expert eyes, city streets are open mental wards. *New York Times,* p. C1.

Goodwin, D. K. (1994). *No ordinary time.* New York: Simon and Schuster.

Gore, A. (1992). *Earth in the balance: Ecology and the human spirit.* Boston, MA: Houghton Mifflin.

Gould, E., Wething, H., Sabadish, N., and Finio, N. (2013). *What families need to get by: The 2013 update of EPI's Family Budget Calculator* (Issue Brief No. 368). Washington, DC: Economic Policy Institute. Retrieved from www.epi.org /publication/ib368-basic-family-budgets/

Gould, T. E. (2010). Family homelessness: An investigation of structural effects. *Journal of Human Behavior in the Social Environment, 20*(2), 170–192.

Gowan, T. (2010). *Hobos, hustlers, and backsliders: Homeless in San Francisco.* Minneapolis, MN: University of Minnesota Press.

Gramlich, E. (2015). Rental assistance demonstration. In National Low Income Housing Coalition (Ed.), *Advocates' guide 2015* (pp. 4-21–4-25). Washington, DC: National Low Income Housing Coalition.

Grand Rapids Area Housing Continuum of Care. (2004). *Vision to end homelessness.* Retrieved from http://b.3cdn.net/naeh/d3f446f919cc4edeb3_n0m6bob5k.pdf

Greenberg, G. A., and Rosenheck, R. A. (2008). Homelessness in the state and federal prison population. *Criminal Behaviour and Mental Health, 18*(2), 88–103. doi: 10.1002/cbm.685

Greene, J., Ringwalt, C., and Iachan, R. (1997). Shelters for runaway and homeless youth: Capacity and occupancy. *Child Welfare, 76*(4), 549–561.

Greenwood, R. M., Schaefer-McDaniel, N. J., Winkel, G., and Tsemberis, S. J. (2005). Decreasing psychiatric symptoms by increasing choice in services for adults with histories of homelessness. *American Journal of Community Psychology, 36*(3-4), 223–238.

Gubits, D., Shinn, M., Bell, S., Wood, M., Dastrup, S., Solari, C. D., . . . Spellman, B. E. July 2015. *Family Options Study: Short-term impacts of housing and service interventions.* Bethesda, MD: Abt Associates.

Gubits, D., Spellman, B., Dunton, L., Brown, S., and Wood, M. (2013). *Family Options Study: Interim report.* Bethesda, MD: Abt Associates.

Gulcur, L., Tsemberis, S., Stefancic, A., and Greenwood, R. M. (2007). Community integration of adults with psychiatric disabilities and histories of homelessness. *Community Mental Health Journal, 43*(3), 211–228.

Gutierrez, O., and Friedman, D. H. (2005). Managing project expectations in human services information systems implementations: The case of homeless management information systems. *International Journal of Project Management, 23*(7), 513–523.

Hahn, J. A., Kushel, M. B., Bangsberg, D. R., Riley, E., and Moss, A. R. (2006). Brief report: The aging of the homeless population: Fourteen-year trends in San Francisco. *Journal of General Internal Medicine, 21*(7), 775–778.

Hallett, R. (2007). Education and homeless youth: Policy implementations. *The Navigator: Directions and Trends in Higher Education Policy, 7*(1), 1–7.

Hammer, H., Finkelhor, D., and Sedlak, A. (2002). *Runaway/thrownaway children: National estimates and characteristics* (National Incidence Studies of Missing, Abducted, Runaway, and Throwaway Children Report). Washington, DC: US Department of Justice, Office of Justice Programs, Office of Juvenile Justice and Delinquency Prevention.

Hanson, A., Brannon, I., and Hawley, Z. (2014) Rethinking tax benefits for home owners. *National Affairs, 19,* 40–54.

Harding, C. (2005). Changes in schizophrenia across time: Paradoxes, patterns, and predictors. In L. Davidson, C. Harding and L. Spaniol (Eds.), *Recovery from Severe Mental Illness: Research Evidence and Implications for Practice* (Vol. 1). Boston: Center for Psychiatric Rehabilitation.

Harvey, D. (2005). *A brief history of neoliberalism.* New York, NY: Oxford University Press.

Harvey, D. (2012). *Rebel cities: From the right to the city to the urban revolution.* New York, NY: Verso Books.

Hathaway, K. C. (2013). Job openings continue to grow in 2012, hires and separations less so. *Monthly Labor Review.* Washington, DC: US Department of Labor. Retrieved from www.bls.gov/opub/mlr/2013/article/hathaway.htm

Hawken, P. (1993). *The ecology of commerce: A declaration of sustainability.* New York, NY: HarperCollins.

Henry, M., Cortes, A., Shivji, A., and Buck. K. (2014). *The 2014 annual homeless assessment report to Congress: Part 1. Point in Time estimates of homelessness.* Washington, DC: US Department of Housing and Urban Development.

Henwood, D. (2014, April/May). The top of the world. *Bookforum.com.* Retrieved from www.bookforum.com/inprint/021_01/12987

HHS. *See* US Department of Health and Human Services.

HHS and HUD. *See* US Department of Health and Human Services and US Department of Housing and Urban Development.

Hibbs, J. R., Benner, L., Klugman, L., Spencer, R., Macchia, I., Mellinger, A. K., and Fife, D. (1994). Mortality in a cohort of homeless adults in Philadelphia. *New England Journal of Medicine, 331*(5), 304–309.

Hilbur, C. A. L., and Turner, T. M. (2013). The mortgage interest deduction and its impact on homeownership decisions. *Review of Economics and Statistics.* Retrieved from http://papers.ssrn.com/sol3/papers.cfm?abstract_id =2375853

Hinkle, J. C. (2014). Broken windows thesis. In G. Bruinsma and D. Weisburd (Eds.), *Encyclopedia of criminology and criminal justice* (pp. 213–223). New York, NY: Springer.

Hobden, K. L., Tompsett, C. J., Fales, A. K., and Toro, P. A. (2007). Comparing public opinion and prevalence of homelessness in Canada to the United States. *Canadian Journal of Urban Research, 16*(2), 76–92.

Hoch, C., and Slayton. R. (1990). *New homeless and old: Community and the skid row hotel (conflicts in urban and regional development).* Philadelphia, PA: Temple University Press.

Hoffman, L., and Coffey, B. (2008). Dignity and indignation: How people experiencing homelessness view services and providers. *Social Science Journal, 45*(2), 207–222.

Hogan, M. F., and Carling, P. J. (1992). Normal housing: a key element of a supported housing approach for people with psychiatric disabilities. *Community Mental Health J, 28*(3), 215–226.

Holland, G. (2013, December 22). No ticket, no sitting at L.A.'s Union Station. *Los Angeles Times,* p. A33.

Holtzen, H. (n.d.). *Ohio Human Services Data Warehouse: Frequently asked questions.* Retrieved from www.ohiodatawarehouse.org/documents/OHSDW_FAQs.pdf

Hombs, M. E. (2001). *American homelessness.* Santa Barbara, CA: ABC-Clio.

Hombs, M. E., and Snyder, M. (1982). *Homelessness in America: A forced march to nowhere.* Washington, DC: Community for Creative Non-Violence.

Homeless Bill of Rights, Pub. L. Ch. 356, R.I. Laws, § 2 (2012).

Homelessness Research Institute, National Alliance to End Homelessness. (2010). *Geography of homelessness.* Washington, DC: Author. Retrieved from http://b.3cdn.net/naeh/3953e7051f30801dc6_iim6banq3.pdf

Hope, M., and Young, J. (1986). *The faces of homelessness.* Lanham, MD: Rowman and Littlefield.

Hopkins, D. J. (2011). The limited local impacts of ethnic and racial diversity. *American Politics Research, 39*(2), 344–379.

Hopper, K. (1991). Homelessness old and new: The matter of definition. *Housing Policy Debate, 2*(3), 755–813.

Hopper, K. (2007). Rethinking social recovery in schizophrenia: What a capabilities approach might offer. *Social Science & Medicine 65,* 868–879.

Hopper, K., and Barrow, S. M. (2003). Two genealogies of supported housing and their implications for outcome assessment. *Psychiatric Services, 54*(1), 50–54.

Hopper, K., and Hamberg, J. (1984). *The making of America's homeless: From skid row to new poor.* New York, NY: Community Service Society of New York.

Hopper, K., Shinn, M., Laska, E., Meisner, M., and Wanderling, J. (2008). Estimating numbers of unsheltered homeless people through plant-capture and postcount survey methods. *American Journal of Public Health, 98*(8), 1438–1442.

HRI. *See* Homelessness Research Institute, National Alliance to End Homelessness.

HUD. *See* US Department of Housing and Urban Development.

Huey, L. (2012). *Invisible victims: Homelessness and the growing security gap.* Toronto, ON: University of Toronto Press.

Hughes, J. (1983). *American economic history.* Glenview, IL: Scott, Foresman.

Hunt, S. R., and Baumohl, J. (2003). Drink, drugs and disability: An introduction to the controversy. *Contemporary Drug Problems, 30*(1–2), 9–76.

Hutson, S., and Liddiard, M. (1994). *Youth homelessness: The construction of a social issue.* London, England: Macmillan.

Hwang, S. W. (2006). Homelessness and harm reduction. *Canadian Medical Association Journal, 174*(1), 50–51.

Hwang, S. W., Weaver, J., Aubry, T., and Hoch, J. S. (2011). Hospital costs and length of stay among homeless patients admitted to medical, surgical, and psychiatric services. *Medical Care, 49*(4), 350–354.

ICH. *See* US Interagency Council on Homelessness.

Ignatieff, M. (2003, January 5). The American empire: The burden. *New York Times Magazine,* pp. 2–10.

ILO. *See* International Labour Organization.

IMF. *See* International Monetary Fund.

Inciardi, J. A., and Harrison, L. D. (2000). Introduction: The concept of harm reduction. *Harm reduction: National and international perspectives,* 2–19. Rockville, MD: National Criminal Justice Reference Service.

International Labour Organization. (2015). *Global wage report 2014/2015: Wages and income inequality.* Geneva: Author. Retrieved from www.ilo.org/global/research/global-reports/global-wage-report/2014/lang—en/index.htm.

International Monetary Fund. (2014). *Fiscal policy and income inequality* (Policy Paper). Washington, DC: Author. Retrieved from www.imf.org/external/np/pp/eng/2014/012314.pdf.

Isaacson, B. (2014). Pennies from heaven and DC. *Newsweek Global,* December 26, 2014, p. 44.

Jackson, T. E. (2013). Social neuroscience, the imitative animal, and Aronofsky's black swan. *Style, 47*(4), 445–461.

Jahiel, R. (1992). Health and health care of homeless people. In M. Robertson and M. Greenblatt (Eds.), *Homelessness: A national perspective* (pp. 133–163). New York, NY: Plenum Press.

Janofsky, M. (1994, December 14). Many cities in crackdown on homeless. *New York Times,* p. 8.

JCT. *See* Joint Committee on Taxation.

Jencks, C. (1994). *The homeless.* Cambridge, MA: Harvard University Press.

Johnsen, S., and Fitzpatrick, S. (2010). Revanchist sanitization or coercive care? The use of enforcement to combat begging, street drinking and rough sleeping in England. *Urban Studies, 47*(8), 1703–1723.

Johnson, A. (1988). *Homelessness in America: A historical and contemporary assessment.* Saint Louis, MO: Washington University.

Joint Committee on Taxation. (2014). *Estimates of federal tax expenditures for fiscal year 2014–2018.* Retrieved from www.jct.gov/publications.html?func=start down&id=4663

Jones, J. M. (2007). Public: Family of four needs to earn average of $52,000 to get by. Gallup News Service. Retrieved from www.gallup.com/poll/26467/Public -Family-Four-Needs-Earn-Average-52000-Get.aspx

Jones, M. M. (2015). Creating a science of homelessness during the Reagan era. *Milbank Quarterly, 93*(1), 139–178.

Julianelle, P. F. (2007). *The educational successes of homeless youth in California: Challenges and solutions.* Sacramento, CA: California Research Bureau. Retrieved from www.library.ca.gov/crb/07/07-012.pdf

Justin v. City of Los Angeles, 2000 WL 1808426 (C.D. Cal. Dec. 5, 2000).

Karabanow, J. (2004). *Being young and homeless: Understanding how youth enter and exit street life.* New York, NY: Peter Lang.

Kertesz, S. G. (2015, April). *Making housing first happen: Organizational leadership in VA's expansion of permanent supportive housing.* Paper presented at the National Alliance to End Homelessness Research Council.

Kertesz, S. G., Crouch, K., Milby, J. B., Cusimano, R. E., and Schumacher, J. E. (2009). Housing First for homeless persons with active addiction: Are we over-reaching? *Milbank Quarterly, 87*(2), 495–534.

Kertesz, S. G., and Weiner, S. J. (2009). Housing the chronically homeless: High hopes, complex realities. *Journal of the American Medical Association 301*(17), 1822–1824.

Khadduri, J. (2008). *Housing vouchers are critical for ending family homelessness.* Washington, DC: National Alliance to End Homelessness, Homelessness Research Institute.

Khadduri, J. (2010). Rental subsidies: Reducing homelessness. In I. G. Ellen and B. O'Flaherty (Eds.), *How to house the homeless* (pp. 59–88). New York, NY: Russell Sage Foundation.

Khadduri, J. (2015). The founding and evolution of HUD: 50 years, 1965–2015. In US Department of Housing and Urban Development. *HUD at 50: Creating pathways to opportunity*

Khanna, M., Singh, N.M., Nemil, M., Best, A., and Ellis, C.R. (1992). Homeless women and their families: Characteristics, life circumstances, and needs. *Journal of Child and Family Studies, 1*(2), 155–165.

Kidd, S., and Scrimenti, K. (2004). Evaluating child and youth homelessness. *Evaluation Review, 28*(4), 325–341.

Kimball, W., and Mishel, L. (2015). *Unions' decline and the rise of the top 10 percent's share of income* (Economic Snapshot). Washington, DC: Economic Policy Institute. Retrieved from www.epi.org/publication/unions-decline-and-the-rise-of-the-top-10-percents-share-of- income/

Kincaid v. Fresno, 2006 WL 3542732 (E.D. Cal. Dec. 8, 2006).

Klein, N. (2007). *The shock doctrine: The rise of disaster capitalism.* New York, NY: Macmillan.

Kling, N., Dunn, L., and Oakley, J. (1996). Homeless families in early childhood programs: What to expect and what to do. *Dimensions of Early Childhood, 24*(1), 3–8.

Koenig, P. (1978, May 21). The problem that can't be tranquilized. *New York Times Magazine,* pp. 14–17, 44–52, 58.

Kondratas, A. (1991). Estimates and public policy: The politics of numbers. *Housing Policy Debate, 2*(3), 629–647.

Kozol, J. (1988). *Rachel and her children.* New York, NY: Three Rivers Press.

Križnik, B. (2011). Selling global Seoul: Competitive urban policy and symbolic reconstruction of cities. *Revija za sociologiju, 41*(3), 291–313.

Krugman, P. (2014, January 26). Paranoia of the plutocrats. *New York Times.* Retrieved from www.nytimes.com/2014/01/27/opinion/krugman-paranoia-of -the-plutocrats.html?_r=0

Kuhn, R., and Culhane, D. P. (1998). Applying cluster analysis to test a typology of homelessness by pattern of shelter utilization: Results from the analysis of administrative data. *American Journal of Community Psychology, 26*(2), 207–232. Retrieved from http://citeseerx.ist.psu.edu/viewdoc/download?doi= 10.1.1.453.3802&rep=rep1&type=pdf

Kushel, M. B., Hahn, J. A., Evans, J. L., Bangsberg, D. R., and Moss, A. R. (2005). Revolving doors: Imprisonment among the homeless and marginally housed population. *American Journal of Public Health, 95*(10), 1747–1752.

Kushel, M. B., Perry, S., Bangsberg, D., Clark, R., and Moss, A. R. (2002). Emergency department use among the homeless and marginally housed: Results from a community-based study. *American Journal of Public Health, 92*(5), 778–784.

Kusmer, K. (2002). *Down and out, on the road: The homeless in American history.* New York, NY: Oxford University Press.

Kyle, K. 2005. *Contextualizing homelessness: Critical theory, homelessness, and federal policy addressing the homeless.* New York, NY: Routledge.

Lapham, L. H. (2012, May). Ignorance of things past: Who wins and who loses when we forget American history. *Harper's Magazine,* pp. 26–33.

Larkin, H., and Park, J. (2012). Adverse childhood experiences (ACEs), service use, and service helpfulness among people experiencing homelessness. *Families in Society: The Journal of Contemporary Social Services, 93*(2), 85–93.

Lee, B. A., Tyler, K. A., and Wright, J. D. (2010). The new homelessness revisited. *Annual Review of Sociology, 36:* 501.

Leginski, W. (2007). Historical and contextual influences on the U.S. response to contemporary homelessness. In D. Dennis, G. Locke, and J. Khadduri (Eds.), *Toward understanding homelessness: The 2007 National Symposium on Homeless Research* (pp 1-1–1-36). Washington, DC: US Department of Health and Human Services and US Department of Housing and Urban Development.

Lehr v. Sacramento, 624 F.Supp.2d 1218 (E.D. Ca. 2009).

Lepore, J. (2010). *The whites of their eyes: The Tea Party's revolution and the battle over American history*. Princeton, NJ: Princeton University Press.

Levinson, B. M. (1963). The homeless man: A psychological enigma. *Mental Hygiene, 47*(4), 590–599.

Lind, R. A., and Danowski, J. A. (1999). The representation of the homeless in U.S. electronic media: A computational linguistic analysis. In E. Min (Ed.), *Reading the homeless: The media's image of homeless culture* (pp. 109–120). Westport, CT: Praeger.

Link, B., Phelan, J., Bresnahan, M., Stueve, A., Moore, R., and Susser, E. (1995). Lifetime and five-year prevalence of homelessness in the United States: New evidence on an old debate. *American Journal of Orthopsychiatry, 65*(3), 347–354.

Link, B., Phelan, J., Stueve, A., Moore, R., Bresnahan, M., and Struening, E. (1996). Public attitudes and beliefs about homeless people. In J. Baumohl (Ed.), *Homelessness in America* (pp. 143–148). Phoenix, AZ: Oryx Press.

Link, B. G., Schwartz, S., Moore, R., Phelan, J., Struening, E., Stueve, A., and Colten, M. E. (1995). Public knowledge, attitudes, and beliefs about homeless people: Evidence for compassion fatigue? *American Journal of Community Psychology, 23*(4), 533–555.

Link, B. G., Susser, E., Stueve, A., Phelan, J., Moore, R. E., and Struening, E. (1994). Lifetime and five-year prevalence of homelessness in the United States. *American Journal of Public Health, 84*(12), 1907–1912.

Lipstadt, Deborah. (1997, October). *Keynote address*. Presented at the National Collegiate Honor Council, Atlanta, GA.

Lobao, L., Adua, L., and Hooks, G. (2014). Privatization, business attraction, and social services across the United States: Local governments' use of market-oriented, neoliberal policies in the post-2000 period. *Social Problems, 61*(4), 644–672.

Locke, G., Khadduri, J., and O'Hara, A. (2007). Housing models. In D. Dennis, G. Locke, and J. Khadduri (Eds.), *Toward understanding homelessness: The 2007 National Symposium on Homeless Research* (pp 10-1–10-30). Washington, DC: US Department of Health and Human Services and US Department of Housing and Urban Development.

Logan, J. R., and Molotch, H. L. (2007). *Urban fortunes: The political economy of place*. Berkeley, CA: University of California Press.

Low, S. M. (2006). How private interests take over public space: Zoning, taxes, and incorporation of gated communities. In S. M. Low and N. Smith (Eds.), *The politics of public space* (pp. 81–103). New York, NY: Routledge.

Luhby, Tami. (2015, April 23). It's expensive to be poor. *CNN Money*. Retrieved from http://money.cnn.com/2015/04/23/news/economy/poor-spending/index.html

Lyon-Callo, V. (2000). Medicalizing homelessness: The production of self-blame and self-governing within homeless shelters. *Medical Anthropology Quarterly, 14*(3), 328–345.

Lyon-Callo, V. (2004). *Inequality, poverty, and neoliberal governance: Activist ethnography in the homeless sheltering industry*. Peterborough, ON: Broadview Press.

MacLean, M., Embry, L., and Cauce, A. (1999). Homeless adolescents' paths to separation from family: Comparison of family characteristics, psychological adjustment, and victimization. *Journal of Community Psychology, 27*(2), 179–187.

Mandiberg, S. F., and Harris, R. (2015). Alcohol- and drug-free housing: A key strategy in breaking the cycle of addiction and recidivism. *McGeorge Law Review, 46*(4), 843–895

Mares, A. S., Greenberg, G. A., and Rosenheck, R. A. (2007). *HUD/HHS/VA collaborative initiative to help end chronic homelessness: National performance outcomes assessment: Is system integration associated with client outcomes?* Westhaven, CT: Northeast Program Evaluation Center. Retrieved from https://www.hudexchange.info/resources/documents/CICH_SystemIntegrationAndClient Outcomes.pdf

Mathieu, A. (1993). The medicalization of homelessness and the theater of repression. *Medical Anthropology Quarterly, 7*(2), 170–184.

McAllister, W., Lennon, M. C., and Kuang, L. (2011). Rethinking research on forming typologies of homelessness. *American Journal of Public Health, 101*(4), 596–601.

McCaskill, P., Toro, P., and Wolfe, S. (1998). Homeless and matched housed adolescents: A comparative study of psychopathology. *Journal of Clinical Child and Adolescent Psychology, 27*(3), 306–319.

McChesney, K. (1990). Family homelessness: A systemic problem. *Journal of Social Issues, 46*(4), 191–205.

McChesney, K. (1992). Homeless families: Four patterns of poverty. In M. Robertson and M. Greenblatt (Eds.), *Homelessness: A national perspective* (pp. 245–256). New York, NY: Plenum Press.

McNeil, D., Binder, R., and Robinson, J. (2005). Incarceration associated with homelessness, mental illness, and co-occurring substance abuse. *Psychiatric Services, 56*(7), 840–846.

Medcalf, N. (2008). *Kidwatching in Josie's world.* Lanham, MD: University Press of America.

Melville Charitable Trust. (n.d.). *About us.* Retrieved from www.melvilletrust.org /about-us/

Memorial Hosp. v. Maricopa County, 415 U.S. 250, 258–259 (1972).

Metraux, S., and Culhane, D. P. (2004). Homeless shelter use and reincarceration following prison release. *Criminology and Public Policy, 3*(2), 139–160.

Metraux, S., Roman, C., and Cho, R. (2007, March). *Incarceration and homelessness.* Paper presented at the 2007 National Symposium on Homelessness Research, Washington, DC.

Metropolitan Denver Homeless Initiative. (2014, August). *2014 state of homelessness report, seven-county Denver metropolitan region.* Denver: Author.

Metz, D., and Weigel, L. (2015). *Perspectives on homelessness in the Denver metro area: Key findings from opinion research to guide public will-building.* Denver, CO: Denver Foundation.

Mihaly, L. K. (1991, January). *Homeless families: Failed policies and young victims.* Washington, DC: Children's Defense Fund.

Milburn, N. G., Iribarren, F. J., Rice, E., Lightfoot, M., Solorio, R., Rotheram-Borus, M. J., and Duan, N. (2012). A family intervention to reduce sexual risk behavior, substance use, and delinquency among newly homeless youth. *Journal of Adolescent Health, 50*(4), 358–364.

Miller, P. M. (2012). Families' experiences in different homeless and highly mobile settings: Implications for school and community practice. *Education and Urban Society, 47*(1), 3–32.

Miller, R. (1982). *The demolition of skid row.* Lexington, MA: DC Heath.

Miller, W. R., and Rollnick, S. (2013). *Motivational interviewing: Helping people change.* New York, NY: Guilford Press.

Mishel, L., Bivens, J., Gould, E., and Shierholz, H. (2012). *The state of working America* (12th ed.). Ithaca, NY: Cornell University Press.

Mishel, L., Gould, E., and Bivens, J. (2015, January 6). *Wage stagnation in nine charts*. Washington, DC: Economic Policy Institute. Retrieved from www.epi.org /publication/charting-wage-stagnation/

Mishel, L., Schmitt, J., and Shierholz, H. (2014, Fall). Wage inequality: A story of policy choices. *New Labor Forum*. doi:10.1177/10095796014544325

Mitchell, D. (1997). The annihilation of space by law: The roots and implications of anti-homeless laws in the United States. *Antipode, 29*(3), 303–335.

Mitchell, D. (1998). Anti-homeless laws and public space: Begging and the First Amendment. *Urban Geography, 19*(1), 6–11.

Mitchell, D. (2003). *The right to the city: Social justice and the fight for public space*. New York, NY: Guilford Press.

Mitchell, D. (2011). Homelessness, American style. *Urban Geography 32*(7), 933–957.

Mitra, S. (2006). The capability approach and disability. *Journal of Disability Policy Studies, 16*(4), 236–247.

Montgomery, A. E., Hill, L. L., Kane, V., and Culhane, D. P. (2013). Housing chronically homeless veterans: Evaluating the efficacy of a Housing First approach to HUD-VASH. *Journal of Community Psychology 41*(4), 505–514.

Moore, J. (2007). *A look at child welfare from a homeless education perspective*. Greensboro, NC: National Center for Homeless Education, SERVE.

Moore, T. L. (2000). *Portland Addictions Acupunture Center Program, final report*. Central City Concerns. August.

Morgan, E. S. (1958). *The Puritan dilemma: The story of John Winthrop*. Boston, MA: Little Brown.

Morgan, E. S. (1963). *Visible saints: The history of a Puritan idea*. Ithaca, NY: Cornell University Press.

Mossman, D. (1997). Deinstitutionalization, homelessness, and the myth of psychiatric abandonment: A structural anthropology perspective. *Social Science and Medicine, 44*(1), 71–83.

Mueser, K. T., Drake, R. E., and Wallach, M. A. (1998). Dual diagnosis: A review of etiological theories. *Addictive Behaviors, 23*(6), 717–734.

Myers, M., and Popp, P. (2003). *Unlocking potential! What educators need to know about homelessness and special education*. Williamsburg, VA: Project HOPE-Virginia and Virginia Department of Education. Retrieved from http://education.wm.edu/centers /hope/publications/infobriefs/documents/ unlockingfamilies2014.pdf

NAEH. *See* National Alliance to End Homelessness.

National Alliance to End Homelessness. (2000a). *A plan, not a dream: How to end homelessness in ten years*. Washington, DC: Author. Retrieved from http:// b.3cdn.net/naeh/b970364c18809d1e0c_aum6bnzb4.pdf

National Alliance to End Homelessness. (2000b). *Ten year plan*. Washington, DC: Author. Retrieved from www.endhomelessness.org/pages/ten-year-plan

National Alliance to End Homelessness. (2003). *Getting housed, staying housed: A collaborative plan to end homelessness*. Chicago, IL: Chicago Continuum of Care. Retrieved from www.endhomelessness.org/library/entry/il-chicago

National Alliance to End Homelessness. (2007). *Supportive housing is cost effective*. Washington, DC: Author. Retrieved from http://b.3cdn.net/naeh/470e1875afd 865aa0a_5lm6bn51c.pdf

National Alliance to End Homelessness. (2009). *A shifting focus: What's new in community plans to end homelessness?* Washington, DC: Author. Retrieved from http://b.3cdn.net/naeh/a6504d938aeba7d59c_7vm6ibuf7.pdf

National Alliance to End Homelessness. (2010). *The Columbus model: Performance measurement & evaluation*. Washington, DC: Author. Retrieved from www.end homelessness.org/library/entry/the-columbus-model-performance-measurement -evaluation

National Alliance to End Homelessness. (2011a). *Impact of "sequestration" on federal homelessness assistance*. Washington, DC: Author. Retrieved from www .housingalliancepa.org/sites/default/files/Impact%20of%20Sequestration%20on% 20Federal%20Homelessness%20Assistance%20%282%29_0.pdf

National Alliance to End Homelessness. (2011b). *One way in: The advantages of introducing system-wide coordinated entry for homeless families*. Washington, DC: Author. Retrieved from www.endhomelessness.org/library/entry/one-way -in-the-advantages-of-introducing-system-wide-coordinated-entry-for-

National Alliance to End Homelessness. (2011c). *Community snapshot: Fairfax– Falls Church, Virginia*. Washington, DC: Author. Retrieved from www.endhome lessness.org/page/-/files/3855_file_Fairfax_Falls_Church.pdf

National Alliance to End Homelessness. (2013a). *Promising strategies: Utah Workforce Services and the Road Home*. Washington, DC: Author. Retrieved from http://b.3cdn.net/naeh/3dc987b56fb1d727c2_a5m6i29ud.pdf

National Alliance to End Homelessness. (2013b). *The state of homelessness in America 2013*. Washington, DC: Author.

National Alliance to End Homelessness. (2014a). *The Workforce Investment Act: An overview and recommendations* (Solutions Brief). Washington, DC: Author.

National Alliance to End Homelessness. (2014b). *Rapid Re-Housing: A history and core components*. Washington, DC: Author. Retrieved from www.endhomelessness .org/library/entry/rapid-re-housing-a-history-and-core-components

National Alliance to End Homelessness. (2015). *The state of homelessness in America 2015*. Washington, DC: Author.

National Alliance to End Homelessness. (n.d.). *Housing First*. Washington, DC: Author. Retrieved from www.endhomelessness.org/pages/housing_first

National Association for the Education of Homeless Children and Youth. (2010). *A critical moment: Child and youth homelessness in our nation's schools*. Washington, DC: Author.

National Center on Family Homelessness. (2009). *America's youngest outcasts: State report card on child homelessness*. Newton, MA: Author.

National Center on Family Homelessness. (2014). *America's youngest outcasts: A report card on child homelessness*. Waltham, MA: National Center on Family Homelessness, American Institutes for Research.

National Center for Homeless Education. (2009). *Education for homeless children and youths program: Analysis of data*. Greensboro, NC: Author.

National Center for Homeless Education. (2012). *Education for homeless children and youth program: Data collection summary*. Greensboro, NC: Author. Retrieved from http://center.serve.org/nche/downloads/data_comp_0909-1011.pdf

National Center for Homeless Education. (2016). National overview: Consolidated state performance report. Retrieved from http://nchespp.serve.org/profile /National?residence_year=2010-11

National Coalition for Homeless Veterans. (2015). *Background and statistics*. Washington, DC: Author. Retrieved from http://nchv.org/index.php/news/media/back ground_and_statistics/

National Coalition for the Homeless. (2007). How many people experience homelessness? Retrieved from http://www.nationalhomeless.org/publications/facts/How _Many.pdf.

National Coalition for the Homeless. (2009). *Mental illness and homelessness*. Washington, DC: Author.

National Commission on Fiscal Responsibility and Reform. (2010, December). *The moment of truth: Report of the commission*. Washington, DC: White House.

National Commission on Severely Distressed Public Housing. (1992). *The final report of the National Commission on Severely Distressed Public Housing: A report to the Congress and secretary of housing and urban development.* Washington, DC: Author.

National Employment Law Project and Economic Policy Institute. (2015). It's time to raise the minimum wage. New York: Author. Retrieved from http://nelp.org/publication/time-raise-minimum-wage/.

National Human Services Data Consortium. (n.d.). *Home page.* Retrieved from www.nhsdc.org

National Law Center on Homelessness and Poverty. (2004a). *Homelessness in the United States and the human right to housing.* Washington, DC: Author.

National Law Center on Homelessness and Poverty. (2004b). *Key data concerning homeless persons in America.* Washington, DC: Author.

National Law Center on Homelessness and Poverty. (2011). *Criminalizing crisis: The criminalization of homelessness in U.S. cities.* Washington, DC: Author. Retrieved from www.nlchp.org/Criminalizing_Crisis

National Law Center on Homelessness and Poverty. (2014). *No safe place: The criminalization of homelessness in U.S. cities.* Washington, DC: Author. Retrieved from www.nlchp.org/documents/No_Safe_Place

National Low Income Housing Coalition. (2012). Who lives in federally assisted housing? *Housing Spotlight 2*(2). Washington, DC: Author.

National Low Income Housing Coalition. (2014). *Out of reach 2014.* Washington, DC: Author.

National Low Income Housing Coalition. (2015). Affordable housing is nowhere to be found for millions. *Housing Spotlight 5*(1). Washington, DC: Author.

NBER. *See* Collinson, Ellen, and Ludwig, 2015.

NCFH. *See* National Center on Family Homelessness.

NCHE. *See* National Center for Homeless Education.

Neale, J. (1997). Homelessness and theory reconsidered. *Housing Studies, 12*(1), 47–61.

Nelson, G., Aubry, T., and Lafrance, A. (2007). A review of the literature on the effectiveness of housing and support, assertive community treatment, and intensive case management interventions for persons with mental illness who have been homeless. *Journal of Orthopsychiatry, 77*(3), 350–361.

Newman, S. J. (2001). Housing attributes and serious mental illness: Implications for research and practice. *Psychiatric Services 52*(10), 1309–1317.

Newman, S. J., Reschovsky, J. D., Kaneda, K., and Hendrick, A. M. (1994). The effects of independent living on persons with chronic mental illness: An assessment of the Section 8 certificate program. *Milbank Quarterly, 72*(1), 171–198.

Ng, C. (2011, June 9). Arrested for feeding the homeless in violation of new Orlando law. *World News and ABC News.* Retrieved from http://abcnews.go.com/US/arrested-feeding-homeless-orlando/story?id=13802769

NHSDC. *See* National Human Services Data Consortium.

Nicholls, C. M. (2009). Agency, transgression and the causation of homelessness: A contextualized rational action analysis. *European Journal of Housing Policy, 9*(1), 69–84.

NLCHP. *See* National Law Center on Homelessness and Poverty.

NLIHC. *See* National Low Income Housing Coalition.

Nunez, R., and C. Fox. (1999). A snapshot of family homelessness across America. *Political Science Quarterly, 114*(2), 298–307.

O'Connell, J. J. (2005). *Premature mortality in homeless populations: A review of the literature.* Nashville, TN: National Health Care for the Homeless Council. Retrieved from http://www.nhchc.org/wp-content/uploads/2011/10/Premature-Mortality.pdf

OECD. *See* Organisation for Economic Co-operation and Development.

Office of Management and Budget. (2015). *The president's budget for fiscal year 2016*. Washington, DC: White House. Retrieved from www.whitehouse.gov/omb /budget/Analytical_Perspectives (see Supplemental Materials, Tables 14-1 to 14-4).

O'Flaherty, B. (1996). *Making room: The economics of homelessness*. Cambridge, MA: Harvard University Press.

O'Flaherty, B. (2010). Homelessness as bad luck: Implications for research and policy. In I. G. Ellen and B. O'Flaherty (Eds.), *How to house the homeless* (pp. 143–182). New York, NY: Russell Sage Foundation.

O'Flaherty, B. (2011). Rental housing assistance for the 21st century. *Cityscape, 13*(2), 127–145.

O'Hara, A. (2007). Housing for people with mental illness: Update of a report to the president's New Freedom Commission. *Psychiatric Services* (58), 7, 907–913.

Olsen-Phillips, P., Choma, R., Bryner, S., and Weber, D. (2015). *The political one percent of the one percent in 2014: Mega donors fuel rising cost of elections*. Washington, DC: Center for Responsive Politics. Retrieved from www.open secrets.org/news/2015/04/the-political-one-percent-of-the-one-percent-in-2014 -mega-donors-fuel-rising-cost-of-elections/

OMB. *See* Office of Management and Budget.

Onken, S. J., Craig, C. M., Ridgway, P., Ralph, R. O., and Cook, J. A. (2007). An analysis of the definitions and elements of recovery: a review of the literature. *Psychiatric Rehabilitation J, 31*(1), 9–22.

Organisation for Economic Co-operation and Development. (2014a). *Focus on top incomes and taxation in OECD countries: Was the crisis a game changer?* Paris, France: Author. Retrieved from www.oecd.org/social/OECD2014-FocusOnTop Incomes.pdf

Organisation for Economic Co-operation and Development. (2014b). *Focus on inequality and growth: Does income inequality hurt economic growth?* Paris, France: Author. Retrieved from www.oecd.org/els/soc/Focus-Inequality-and -Growth-2014.pdf

Organisation for Economic Co-operation and Development. (2014c). *Society at a glance 2014: OECD social indicators*. Paris: Author. Retrieved from www.oecd .org/social/societyataglance.htm

Ostry, J. D., Berg, A., and Tsangarides, C. G. (2014). *Redistribution, inequality, and growth* (Staff Discussion Note). Washington, DC: International Monetary Fund. Retrieved from www.imf.org/external/pubs/ft/sdn/2014/sdn1402.pdf

Padgett, D. K. (2007). There's no place like (a) home: Ontological security among persons with serious mental illness in the United States. *Social Science & Medicine, 64*(9), 1925–1936.

Padgett, D. K., Gulcur, L., and Tsemberis, S. (2006). Housing First services for people who are homeless with co-occurring serious mental illness and substance abuse. *Research on Social Work Practice, 16*(1), 74–83.

Padgett, D. K., Henwood, B. F., and Tsemberis, S. (2015). *Housing first: Ending homelessness, transforming systems and changing lives*. New York, NY: Oxford University Press.

Padgett, D. K., Stanhope, V., Henwood, B. F., and Stefancic, A. (2011). Substance use outcomes among homeless clients with serious mental illness: Comparing Housing First with treatment first programs. *Community Mental Health Journal, 47*(2), 227–232.

Pager, D. (2003). The mark of a criminal record. *American Journal of Sociology, 108*(5), 937–975.

Palmer, R. R. and J. Colton, *A history of the modern world*. New York: Alfred Knopf, 1984. p. 551.

Palmisano, L. W. (2014). *Post-industrial approaches to urban development in Denver, Colorado: Evaluating strategic neighborhood plans*. Denver, CO: University of Colorado at Denver.

Papachristou v. City of Jacksonville, 405 U.S. 156 (1972).

Parsell, C., and Parsell, M. (2012). Homelessness as a choice. *Housing, Theory and Society, 29*(4), 420–434.

Pastore, A. L., and Maguire, K. (Eds.). (2005). *Sourcebook of criminal justice statistics*. Hindelang Criminal Justice Research Center, University of Albany. Retrieved from www.albany.edu/sourcebook/

Pauly, B. (2008). Harm reduction through a social justice lens. *International Journal of Drug Policy, 19*(1), 4–10.

Pavetti, L. (2014). Why the 1996 Welfare Law is not a model for other safety-net programs. Washington, DC: Center on Budget and Policy Priorities. Retrieved from www.cbpp.org/blog/why-the-1996-welfare-law-is-not-a-model-for-other-safety-net-programs.

Pearson, C. L., Locke, G., Montgomery, A. E., and Buron, L. (2007). *The applicability of Housing First models to homeless persons with serious mental illness*. Washington, DC: US Department of Housing and Urban Development, Office of Policy Development Research.

Pearson, C., Montgomery, A. E., and Locke, G. (2009). Housing stability among homeless individuals with serious mental illness participating in Housing First programs. *Journal of Community Psychology, 37*(3), 404–417.

Pedone, C. (1998). *Current housing programs and possible federal responses*. Washington, DC: Congressional Budget Office.

Pelletiere, D. (2008). *Getting to the heart of housing's fundamental question: How much can a family afford?* Washington, DC: National Low Income Housing Coalition.

Pelletiere, D. (2009). *Renters in foreclosure: Defining the problem, identifying the solution*. Washington, DC: National Low Income Housing Coalition.

Pelton, L. H. (2006, July/August). Getting what we deserve. *The Humanist*, pp. 14–17.

Penuel, W., and Davey, T. (1998, April). *Meta-analysis of McKinney programs in Tennessee*. Paper presented at the meeting of the American Educational Research Association, San Diego.

Pérez-Peña, R. (2007, April 17). Revolving door for addicts adds to Medicaid cost. *The New York Times*. Retrieved from http://www.nytimes.com/2007/04/17/nyregion/17detox.html

Peroff, K. (1987). Who are the homeless and how many are there? In R. Bingham and R. E. Green (Eds.) *The homeless in contemporary society*. Newbury Park, CA: Sage, 33–45.

Pew Charitable Trusts. (2015). *The precarious state of family balance sheets*. Retrieved from www.pewtrusts.org/en/research-and-analysis/reports/2015/01/the-precarious-state-of-family-balance-sheets

Phelan, J., Link, B. G., Moore, R. E., and Stueve, A. (1997). The stigma of homelessness: The impact of the label "homeless" on attitudes toward poor persons. *Social Psychology Quarterly, 60*(4), 323–337.

Phillips, K. P. (2008). *Bad money: Reckless finance, failed politics, and the global crisis of American capitalism*. New York, NY: Viking.

Pleace, N. (2011). The ambiguities, limits and risks of housing first from a European perspective. *European Journal of Homelessness, 5*(2),113–127.

Podymow, T., Turnbull, J., Coyle, D., Yetisir, E., and Wells, G. (2006). Shelter-based managed alcohol administration to chronically homeless people addicted to alcohol. *Canadian Medical Association Journal, 174*(1), 45–49.

Polakow, V. (2003). Homeless children and their families: The discards of the post-welfare era. In S. Books (Ed.), *Invisible children in the society and its schools* (pp. 89–110). Mahwah, NJ: Erlbaum.

Pottinger v. City of Miami, 810 F. Supp. 1551 (S.D. Fla. 1992).

Pottinger v. City of Miami, 76 F.3d 1154 (11th Cir. 1996).

Poulin, S. R., Metraux, S., and Culhane, D. P. (2008). The history and future of Homeless Management Information Systems. In R. H. McNamara (Ed.), *Homelessness in America* (pp. 171–179). Westport, CT: Praeger.

President's Advisory Panel on Federal Tax Reform. (2005, November). *Simple, fair, and pro-growth: Proposals to fix America's tax system*. Washington, DC: Author.

Prochaska, J. O., DiClemente, C. C., and Norcross, J. C. (1992). In search of how people change: Applications to addictive behaviors. *American Psychologist, 47*(9), 1102–1114.

Pruijt, H. (2013). Culture wars, revanchism, moral panics and the creative city. A reconstruction of a decline of tolerant public policy: The case of Dutch anti-squatting legislation. *Urban Studies, 50*(6), 1114–1129.

Quigley, J. M., Raphael, S., and Smolensky, E. (2001). Homeless in America, homeless in California. *Review of Economics and Statistics, 83*(1), 37–51.

Rader, V. (1986). *Signal through the flames: Mitch Snyder and America's homeless*. Kansas City: Sheed and Ward.

Raikes Foundation. (n.d.). *A place to call home*. Seattle, WA: Author. Retrieved from https://d3n8a8pro7vhmx.cloudfront.net/funderstogether/pages/289 /attachments/original/1426709459/Raikes_oct_strategy_brief_r109.pdf ?1426709459

Raleigh-DuRoff, C. (2004). Factors that influence homeless adolescents to leave or stay living on the street. *Child and Adolescent Social Work Journal, 21*(6), 561–572.

Rankin, S. (2015). A homeless bill of rights (revolution). *Seton Hall Law Review*. Retrieved from http://papers.ssrn.com/sol3/papers.cfm?abstract_id=2520561

Ratnesar, R. (1999, February 8). Not gone, but forgotten? Why Americans have stopped talking about homelessness. *Time*, pp. 30–31.

Reich, R. B. (2010). *Aftershock: The next economy and America's future*. New York, NY: Knopf.

Reich, R. B. (2015). *Saving capitalism*. New York, NY: Knopf.

Rescorla, L., Parker, R., and Stolley, P. (1991). Ability, achievement, and adjustment in homeless children. *American Journal of Orthopsychiatry, 61*(2), 210–220.

Richmond, F. (n.d.). eLogic Model. Camp Hill, PA: Center for Applied Management Practices.

Ridgway, P. (2001). Re-storying psychiatric disability: Learning from first person recovery narratives. *Psychiatric Rehabilitation Journal, 24*(4), 335–343.

Ridgway, P., and Zipple, A. M. (1990). The paradigm shift in residential services: From the linear continuum to supported housing approaches. *Rehabilitation Journal, 13*(4), 11–31.

Ringwalt, C. L., Greene, J. M., and Robertson, M. (1998). Familial backgrounds and risk behaviors of youth with throwaway experiences. *Journal of Adolescence, 21*(3), 241–252.

Ringwalt, C. L., Greene, J. M., Robertson, M., and McPheeters, M. (1998). The prevalence of homelessness among adolescents in the United States. *American Journal of Public Health, 88*(9), 1325–1329.

Rioux, M. (2003). On second thought: Constructing knowledge, law, disability, and inequality. In S. Herr, L. Gostin and H. Koh (Eds.), *The human rights of persons with intellectual disabilities*. New York: Oxford University Press.

Roberts, J. J. (2014, July 21). Prioritizing homeless veterans: Are we giving up on ending all homelessness? *Huffington Post*. Retrieved from www.huffingtonpost .com/joel-john-roberts/prioritizing-chronic-home_b_5606581.html

Robertson, J. (1992). Homeless and runaway youths: A review of the literature. In M. Robertson and M. Greenblatt (Eds.), *Homelessness: A national perspective* (pp. 287–297). New York, NY: Plenum Press.

Robinson, T., (2013). *The Denver camping ban: A report from the street*. Denver, CO: Denver Homeless Out Loud. Retrieved from https://denverhomelessoutloud.files .wordpress.com/2013/05/dholcampingbanreportcolor.pdf

Roca Inc. (n.d.). *Roca and Pay for Success (PFS)*. Retrieved from http://rocainc.org /what-we-do/pay-for-success/

Rog, D. J. (2004). The evidence on supported housing. *Psychiatric Rehabilitation Journal, 27*(4), 334–344.

Rog, D. J., Holupka, S., and Patton, L. (2007). *Characteristics and dynamics of homeless families with children*. Washington, DC: US Department of Health and Human Services. Retrieved from http://aspe.hhs.gov/hsp/homelessness/improving -data08/index.htm

Rollinson, P., and Pardeck, J. (2006). *Homeless in rural America: Policy and practice*. New York, NY: Haworth Press.

Rollnick, S., Miller, W. R., and Butler, C. (2008). *Motivational interviewing in health care: Helping patients change behavior*. New York, NY: Guilford Press.

Rolston, H., Geyer, J., Locke, G., Metraux, S., and Treglia, D. (2013). *Evaluation of the Homebase Community Prevention program*. Bethesda, MD: Abt Associates; Philadelphia, PA: University of the Sciences.

Ropers, R. (1988). *The invisible homeless: A new urban ecology*. New York, NY: Human Sciences Press.

Rosenheck, R., Kasprow, W., Frisman, L., and Liu-Mares, W. (2003). Cost-effectiveness of supported housing for homeless persons with mental illness. *Archives of General Psychiatry, 60*(9), 940–951.

Rossi, P. H. (1989). *Down and out in America: The origins of homelessness*. Chicago, IL: University of Chicago Press.

Rossi, P., Fisher, G. A., and Willis, G. (1986). *The condition of the homeless in Chicago*. Amherst, MA: Social and Demographic Research Institute, University of Massachusetts; Chicago, IL: National Opinion Research Center.

Roth, D., Toomey, B., and First, R. (1992). Gender, racial and age variations among homeless persons. In M. Robertson and M. Greenblatt (Eds.), *Homelessness: A national perspective* (pp. 199–211). New York, NY: Plenum Press.

Rotheram-Borus, M. J., Mahler, K., Koopman, C., and Langabeer, K. (1996). Sexual abuse history and associated multiple risk behavior in adolescent runaways. *American Journal of Orthopsychiatry, 66*(3), 390–400.

Rothman, J. (1991). *Runaway and homeless youth: Strengthening services to families and children*. White Plains, NY: Longman.

Russell, L. (1998). *Child maltreatment and psychological distress among urban homeless youth*. New York, NY: Garland Press.

Sabatier, P. A., and Mazmanian, D. A. (1981). The implementation of public policy: A framework of analysis. In D. A. Mazmanian and P. A. Sabatier (Eds.), *Effective policy implementation* (pp. 3–35). Lexington, MA: Lexington Books.

Salamon, L. M., Geller, S. L., and Mengel, K. L. (2010). *Nonprofits, innovation, and performance measurement: Separating fact from fiction*. Baltimore, MD: Listening Post Project, Johns Hopkins University.

Salit, S. A., Kuhn, E. M., Hartz, A. J., Vu, J. M., and Mosso, A. L. (1998). Hospitalization costs associated with homelessness in New York City. *New England Journal of Medicine, 338*(24), 1734–1740.

Salyers, M. P., and Tsemberis, S. (2007). ACT and recovery: integrating evidence-based practice and recovery orientation on assertive community treatment teams. *Community Mental Health Journal, 43*(6), 619–641.

San Francisco Ten Year Planning Council. (2004). *San Francisco plan to abolish chronic homelessness*. San Francisco, CA: Author. Retrieved from http://b.3cdn.net/naeh/04aa3a679315e39aae_ham6brxgj.pdf

Sard, B. (2015). Vouchers: Project-based vouchers. In National Low Income Housing Coalition (Ed.), *Advocates' guide 2015* (pp. 4-47–4-49). Washington, DC: National Low Income Housing Coalition.

Schieman, S. (2010). Socioeconomic status and beliefs about God's influence in everyday life. *Sociology of Religion, 71*(1), 25–51.

Schmitt, J. (2015). *Failing on two fronts: The U.S. labor market since 2000*. Washington, DC: Center for Economic Policy and Research. Retrieved from www.cepr.net/search?q=john%20schmitt

Schneider, M. (2015, April). *Point-in-Time research*. Unpublished manuscript, Graduate School of Social Work, University of Denver, Denver, CO.

Schwartz, A. F. (2015). *Housing policy in the United States* (3rd ed.). New York, NY: Routledge.

Schweik, S. (2009). *The ugly laws: Disability in public*. New York, NY: New York University Press.

Scolaro, J. D. and E. Eschbach. (2002). *Poverty and the power of knowledge*. Opinion paper. Valencia, FL: Valencia Community College. Retrieved from http://files.eric.ed.gov/fulltext/ED470832.pdf.

Scott, R. E. (2012). *The China toll: Growing U.S. trade deficit with China cost more than 2.7 million jobs between 2001 and 2011, with job losses in every state* (Issue Brief No. 345). Washington, DC: Economic Policy Institute. Retrieved from www.epi.org/publication/bp345-china-growing-trade-deficit-cost/

Scott, R. E. (2015). *Fast track to lost jobs and lower wages* (Working Economics Blog). Washington, DC: Economic Policy Institute. Retrieved from www.epi.org/blog/fast-track-to- lost-jobs-and-lower-wages/

Seabrook, N., Wilk, E., and Lamb, C. (2012). Administrative law judges in fair housing enforcement: Attitudes, case facts, and political control. *Social Science Quarterly, 94*(2), 362–378.

Sennett, R. (1970). *The uses of disorder: Personal identity and city life*. New York, NY: Norton.

Shane, P. (1996). *What about America's homeless children?* Thousand Oaks, CA: Sage.

Shermer, M. (2011). *The believing brain*. New York, NY: Times Books.

Shinn, M. (1992). Homelessness: What is a psychologist to do? *American Journal of Community Psychology, 20*(1), 1–24.

Shinn, M. (2007). International homelessness: Policy, socio-cultural, and individual perspectives. *Journal of Social Issues, 63*(3), 657–677.

Shinn, M., and Greer, A. L. (2012, July). *Targeting homelessness prevention services more effectively: Introducing a screener for Homebase.* Paper presented at the Annual Conference of the National Alliance to End Homelessness, Washington, DC.

Shinn, M., Greer, A. L., Bainbridge, J., Kwon, J., and Zuiderveen, S. (2013). Efficient targeting of homelessness prevention services for families. *American Journal of Public Health, 103*(S2), S324–S330.

Shinn, M., and Weitzman, B. C. (1996). Homeless families are different. In J. Baumohl (Ed.), *Homelessness in America.* Westport, CT: Greenwood, 109–122.

Shinn, M., Weitzman, B. C., Stojanovic, D., Knickman, J. R., Jimenez, L., Duchon, L., . . . Krantz, D. H. (1998). Predictors of homelessness among families in New York City: From shelter request to housing stability. *American Journal of Public Health, 88*(11), 1651–1657.

Shlay, A., and Rossi, P. (1992). Social science research and contemporary studies of homelessness. *Annual Review of Sociology, 18,* 129–160.

Shore, M. F., and Cohen, M. D. (1990). The Robert Wood Johnson Foundation program on chronic mental illness: An overview. *Hospital and Community Psychiatry, 41*(11), 1212–1216.

Short, K. (2014). *The Supplemental Poverty Measure: 2013.* Current Population Reports, P60-251. Washington, DC: US Census Bureau.

Siegel, C. E., Samuels, J., Tang, D.-I., Berg, I., Jones, K., and Hopper, K. (2006). Tenant outcomes in supported housing and community residences in New York City. *Psychiatric Services, 57*(7), 982–991.

Siegel, F. (1997). *The future once happened here: New York, DC, LA, and the fate of America's big cities.* San Francisco, CA: Encounter Books.

Silver, C., and Moeser, J. (1995). *The separate city: Black communities in the urban South, 1940–1968.* Lexington, KY: University of Kentucky Press.

Smith, C. (1991). *The emergence of liberation theology: Radical religion and social movement theory.* Chicago, IL: University of Chicago Press

Smith, N. (1996). *The new urban frontier: Gentrification and the revanchist city.* New York, NY: Routledge.

Snow, D. A., and Anderson, L. (1993). *Down on their luck: A study of homeless street people.* Berkeley, CA: University of California Press.

Snow, D. A., Anderson, L., and Koegel, P. (1994). Distorting tendencies in research on the homeless. *American Behavioral Scientist, 37*(4), 461–475.

Song, J. (2011). Situating homelessness in South Korea during and after the Asian debt crisis. *Urban Geography, 32*(7), 972–988.

Southworth, A. (2000). The rights revolution and support structures for rights advocacy. *Law and Society Review, 34,* 1203.

Spellman, B., Khadduri, J., Sokol, B., and Leopold, J. (2010). *Costs associated with first time homelessness for families and individuals.* Bethesda, MA: Abt Associates.

Stanhope, V., and Dunn, K. (2011). The curious case of housing first: The limits of evidence based policy. *International Journal of Law and Psychiatry, 34*(4), 275–282.

Stanhope, V., and Solomon, P. (2008). Getting to the heart of recovery: Methods for studying recovery and their implications for evidence-based practice. *British Journal of Social Work, 38,* 885–899.

Starling, G. (2008). *Managing the public sector.* Belmont, CA: Cengage Learning.

Stefancic, A., and Tsemberis, S. (2007). Housing First for long-term shelter dwellers with psychiatric disabilities in a suburban county: A four-year study of housing access and retention. *Journal of Primary Prevention, 28*(3), 265–279.

Stefl, M. (1987). The new homeless: A national perspective. In R. D. Bingham, R. E. Green, and S. B. White (Eds.), *The homeless in contemporary society* (pp. 46–63). Newbury Park, CA: Sage.

Stiglitz, J. (2012). *The price of inequality.* New York, NY: Norton.

Stronge, J. (1992). The background: History and problems of schooling for the homeless. In J. H. Stronge (Ed.), *Educating homeless children and adolescents: Evaluating policy and practice* (pp. 3–25). Newbury Park, CA: Sage.

Stroul, B. A. (1989). Community support systems for persons with long-term mental illness: A conceptual framework. *Psychosocial Rehabilitation Journal, 12* (3), 9.

Substance Abuse and Mental Health Services Administration. (2007). *Pathway's Housing First program.* Retrieved from https://pathwaystohousing.org/file/482 /download?token=t2V7DjAS

Substance Abuse and Mental Health Services Administration. (2011). *Current statistics on the prevalence and characteristics of people experiencing homelessness in the United States.* Rockville, MA: Author. Retrieved from http://homeless .samhsa.gov/ResourceFiles/hrc_factsheet.pdf

Susser, E., Valencia, E., Conover, S., Felix, A., Tsai, W. Y., and Wyatt, R. J. (1997). Preventing recurrent homelessness among mentally ill men: A "critical time" intervention after discharge from a shelter. *American Journal of Public Health, 87*(2), 256–262.

Szarzynska, M. E., and Toro, P. A. (2015, June). *Preventing homelessness among youth aging out of orphanages in Poland: A quasi-experimental evaluation.* Paper presented at the Biennial Conference on Community Research and Action, Lowell, MA.

Taibbi, M. (2014). *The divide: American injustice in the age of the wealth gap.* New York, NY: Spiegel and Grau.

Tars, E. S., Johnson, H. M., Bauman, T., and Foscarinis, M. (2013). Can I get some remedy: Criminalization of homelessness and the obligation to provide an effective remedy. *Columbia Human Rights Law Review, 45,* 732–771.

Taylor, D., Lydon, J., Bougie, E., and Johannsen, K. (2004). "Street kids": Toward an understanding of their motivational context. *Canadian Journal of Behavioural Science, 36*(1), 1–16.

Taylor, I. (1984). Ultimate civilization. In R. R. Palmer and J. Colton (Eds.), *A history of the modern world.* New York, NY: McGraw-Hill. (Original work published 1860).

Thompson, B. (2014, August 28). Residents, rights groups want moratorium. *Michigan Chronicle.* Retrieved from http://michronicleonline.com/2014/08/28 /residents-rights-groups-want- moratorium/

Tierney, W., Gupton, J., and Hallett, R. (2008). *Transitions to adulthood for homeless adolescents: Education and public policy.* Los Angeles, CA: Center for Higher Education Policy Analysis.

Toder, E. (2014). Congress should phase out the mortgage interest deduction. *Cityscape: A Journal of Policy Development and Research, 16*(1), 211–214.

Tompsett, C. J., and Toro, P. A. (2004). Public opinion. In D. Levinson (Ed.), *Encyclopedia of homelessness* (pp. 469–474). Thousand Oaks, CA: Sage.

Tompsett, C. J., Toro, P. A., Guzicki, M., Manrique, M., and Zatakia, J. (2006). Homelessness in the United States: Assessing changes in prevalence and public opinion, 1993 to 2001. *American Journal of Community Psychology, 37*(1–2), 47–61.

Tompsett, C. J., Toro, P. A., Guzicki, M., Schlienz, N., Blume, M., and Lombardo, S. (2003). Homelessness in the US and Germany: A cross-national analysis. *Journal of Community and Applied Social Psychology, 13*(3), 240–257.

Toro, P. (1998). Homelessness. In A. S. Bellack and M. Herson (Eds.), N. Singh (Vol. Ed.), *Comprehensive clinical psychology: Vol. 9. Applications in diverse populations* (pp. 119–135). Oxford, England: Pergamon.

Toro, P. A., Bokszczanin, A., and Ornelas, J. (2008, June). *Prevalence of and public opinion on homelessness in 9 nations*. Paper presented at the Second International Conference on Community Psychology, Lisbon, Portugal.

Toro, P. A., Hobden, K. L., Durham, K. W., Oko-Riebau, M., and Bokszczanin, A. (2014). Comparing the characteristics of homeless adults in Poland and the United States. *American Journal of Community Psychology, 53*(1–2), 134–145.

Toro, P. A., and McDonell, D. M. (1992). Beliefs, attitudes, and knowledge about homelessness: A survey of the general public. *American Journal of Community Psychology, 20*(1), 53–80.

Toro, P. A., Rabideau, J. M. P., Bellavia, C. W., Daeschler, C. V., Wall, D. D., Thomas, D. M., and Smith, S. J. (1997). Evaluating an intervention for homeless persons: Results of a field experiment. *Journal of Consulting and Clinical Psychology, 65*(3), 476.

Toro, P. A., and Rojansky, A. (1990). Homelessness: Some thoughts from an international perspective. *Community Psychologist, 23*(4), 8–11.

Toro, P. A., Tompsett, C. J., Lombardo, S., Philippot, P., Nachtergael, H., Galand, B., . . . Harvey, K. (2007). Homelessness in Europe and North America: A comparison of prevalence and public opinion. *Journal of Social Issues, 63*(3), 505–524.

Toro, P. A., and Warren, M. G. (1991). Homelessness, psychology, and public policy: Introduction to Section Three. *American Psychologist, 46*(11), 1205.

Toro, P. A., and Warren, M. G. (1999). Homelessness in the United States: Policy considerations. *Journal of Community Psychology, 27*(2), 119–136.

Torrey, E. F. (1988). *Nowhere to go: The tragic odyssey of the homeless mentally ill.* New York, NY: Harper and Row.

Tsai, J., Rosenheck, R. A., Kasprow, W. J., and McGuire, J. F. (2014). Homelessness in a national sample of incarcerated veterans in state and federal prisons. *Administration and Policy in Mental Health and Mental Health Services Research, 41*(3), 360–367.

Tsemberis, S. (1999). From streets to homes: An innovative approach to supported housing for homeless adults with psychiatric disabilities. *Journal of Community Psychology, 27*(2), 225–241.

Tsemberis, S. (2010). *Housing First: The pathways model to end homelessness for people with mental illness and addiction manual.* Center City, MN: Hazelden.

Tsemberis, S., and Eisenberg, R. F. (2000). Pathways to housing: Supported housing for street-dwelling homeless individuals with psychiatric disabilities. *Psychiatric Services, 51*(4), 487–493.

Tsemberis, S., Gulcur, L., and Nakae, M. (2004). Housing First, consumer choice, and harm reduction for homeless individuals with a dual diagnosis. *American Journal of Public Health, 94*(4), 651–656.

Turner, R. S. (2002). The politics of design and development in the postmodern downtown. *Journal of Urban Affairs, 24*(5), 533–548.

UN Population Fund. (2013). *Linking population, poverty and development.* New York: Author. Retrieved from www.unfpa.org/pds/urbanization.htm

United Way of Greater Los Angeles. (n.d.). *Home for good.* Los Angeles: Author. Retrieved from http://homeforgoodla.org/about-us/grantseekers/

US Census Bureau. (1998). Measuring 50 years of economic change using the March Current Population Survey. *Current Population Reports* (pp. 60–203). Washington, DC: US Government Printing Office.

US Census Bureau. (2014). *American Community Survey 2013 1-year estimates.* Washington, DC: Author. Retrieved from http://factfinder.census.gov/faces/table services/jsf/pages/productview.xhtml?pid=ACS_1 3_1YR_S1101&prodType= table

US Census Bureau. (2015, January). *Residential vacancies and homeownership in the fourth quarter 2014.* Washington, DC: Author. Retrieved from www.census.gov /housing/hvs/files/qtr414/currenthvspresss.pdf

US Conference of Mayors. (various years). *A status report on hunger and homelessness in America's cities.* Washington, DC: Author.

US Congress, Joint Tax Committee. (2014). *Estimates of federal tax expenditures for fiscal years 2014–2018.* Washington, DC: Author. Retrieved from www.jct .gov/publications.html?func=select&id=5

US Department of Education. (2014). *Education for homeless children and youth consolidated state performance report data: School years 2010–11, 2011–12, and 2012–13.* Washington, DC: Author. Retrieved from http://center.serve.org /nche/downloads/data-comp-1011-1213.pdf

US Department of Health and Human Services, Administration for Children and Families, Office of Family Assistance. (2013). *Temporary Assistance for Needy Families program, tenth report to Congress.* Washington, DC: Author.

US Department of Health and Human Services and US Department of Housing and Urban Development. (2007). *Toward understanding homelessness: The 2007 National Symposium on Homelessness Research.* Washington, DC: Author. Retrieved from http://aspe.hhs.gov/hsp/homelessness/symposium07/

US Department of Housing and Urban Development. (various years). *The annual homeless assessment report (AHAR) to Congress.* Washington, DC: Author.

US Department of Housing and Urban Development. (2007a). *Defining chronic homelessness: A technical guide for HUD programs.* Washington, DC: Author.

US Department of Housing and Urban Development. (2007b). *The annual homeless assessment report to Congress.* Washington, DC: Author. Retrieved from https:// www.huduser.gov/Publications/pdf/ahar.pdf

US Department of Housing and Urban Development. (2008). *The third annual homeless assessment report to Congress.* Washington, DC: Author. Retrieved from www.hudhre.info/documents/3rdHomelessAssessmentReport.pdf

US Department of Housing and Urban Development. (2010). *The 2009 annual homeless assessment report to Congress.* Washington, DC: Author. Retrieved from https://www.hudexchange.info/resources/documents/5thHomelessAssessment Report.pdf

US Department of Housing and Urban Development, Office of Community Planning and Development. (2011). Washington, DC: Author. *The 2010 Annual homeless assessment report to Congress (AHAR).*

US Department of Housing and Urban Development. (2013a). *Housing discrimination against racial and ethnic minorities: Executive summary.* Washington, DC: Author. Retrieved from www.huduser.org/portal/Publications/pdf/HUD514 _HDS2012_execsumm.pdf

US Department of Housing and Urban Development. (2013b). *Picture of subsidized households.* Washington, DC: Author. Retrieved from www.huduser.org/portal /datasets/picture/yearlydata.html

US Department of Housing and Urban Development. (2013c). *The 2013 annual homeless assessment report (AHAR) to Congress: Part 1.* Washington, DC: US Department of Housing and Urban Development, Office of Community Planning and Development.

US Department of Housing and Urban Development. (2013d). *The 2013 annual homeless assessment report (AHAR) to Congress: Part 2*. Washington, DC: US Department of Housing and Urban Development, Office of Community Planning and Development.

US Department of Housing and Urban Development. (2014a). *The 2014 annual homeless assessment report (AHAR) to Congress*. Washington, DC: US Department of Housing and Urban Development, Office of Community Planning and Development. Retrieved from www.hudexchange.info/resources/documents /2014-AHAR-Part1.pdf

US Department of Housing and Urban Development. (2014b). *An introductory guide to the AHAR*. Washington, DC: US Department of Housing and Urban Development, Office of Community Planning and Development. Retrieved from www.hudexchange.info/resources/documents/Introductory-Guide-to-the-2014 -AHAR.pdf

US Department of Housing and Urban Development. (2014c). HUD reports homelessness in U.S. continues to decline: Significant reductions noted among veterans and those living on the streets. Washington, DC: Author. HUD No. 14-135, October 30.

US Department of Housing and Urban Development. (2015a). *The 2015 annual homeless assessment report to Congress: Part 1*. Washington, DC: Author.

US Department of Housing and Urban Development. (2015b). *The 2015 annual homeless assessment report to Congress: Part 2*. Washington, DC: Author.

US Department of Housing and Urban Development, and Culhane, D. P. (2004). Homeless Management Information Systems (HMIS); Data and technical standards final notice. *Federal Register*, p. 69.

US Department of Labor, Bureau of Labor Statistics. (2015). Union members—2014. Washington, DC: Author. Retrieved from www.bls.gov/news.release/pdf/union 2.pdf

US General Accounting Office. (1985). *Homelessness: A complex problem and the federal response*. Washington, DC: Author. Retrieved from http://archive.gao .gov/f0102/126760.pdf

US Interagency Council on Homelessness. (2008). *Innovations in 10-year plans to end chronic homelessness in your community*. Washington DC: Author.

US Interagency Council on Homelessness. (2010). *Opening Doors: Federal Strategic Plan to Prevent and End Homelessness*. Washington, DC. Retrieved from www .usich.gov/resources/uploads/asset_library/USICH_OpeningDoors_Amendment 2015_Final.pdf

US Interagency Council on Homelessness. (2012). *Searching out solutions: Constructive alternatives to criminalization of homelessness*. Washington, DC: Author. Retrieved from http://usich.gov/resources/uploads/asset_library/RPT_SoS_March 2012.pdf

US Interagency Council on Homelessness. (2013). *Ending homelessness among veterans: A report*. Washington, DC: Author.

US Interagency Council on Homelessness. (2014). *Partnership for opening doors summit*. Washington, DC: Author. Retrieved from http://usich.gov/partnerships-for-opening-doors-summit

US Interagency Council on Homelessness. (2015a). *Substance abuse*. Washington, DC: Author. Retrieved from http://usich.gov/issue/substance_abuse

US Interagency Council on Homelessness. (2015b). *The president's 2016 budget: Fact sheet on homelessness assistance*. Washington, DC: Author. Retrieved from http://usich.gov/resources/uploads/asset_library/2016_Budget_Fact_Sheet_on _Homelessness_As sistance.pdf

US Interagency Council on Homelessness. (2015c). *How to build employment programs that prevent and end homelessness*. Washington, DC: Author. Retrieved from http://usich.gov/plan_objective/pathways_to_employment/how_to_build_employment_programs_that_prevent_and_end_homelessness/

Van Eijk, G. (2010). Exclusionary policies are not just about the "neoliberal city": A critique of theories of urban revanchism and the case of Rotterdam. *International Journal of Urban and Regional Research, 34*(4), 820–834.

Vissing, Y. (2004). Prepping homeless students for school. *Education Digest: Essential Readings Condensed for Quick Review, 69*(7), 34–38.

Viveiros, J., and Sturtevant, L. (2014). *Housing landscape 2014*. Washington, DC: Center for Housing Policy, National Housing Conference. Retrieved from www.nhc.org/media/files/Landscape2014.pdf

Wade, R. (2014). The Piketty phenomenon and the future of inequality. *Real-world Economics Review, 69*, 2–17. Retrieved from www.paecon.net/PAEReview/issue69/Wade69.pdf

Waldron, J. (2000). Homelessness and community. *University of Toronto Law Journal, 50*(4), 371–406.

Wallace, S. (1965). *Skid row as a way of life*. Totowa, NJ: Bedminster Press.

Wasserman, J. A., and Clair, J. M. (2010). *At home on the street: People, poverty, and a hidden culture of homelessness*. Boulder, CO: Lynne Rienner.

Wasserman, J. A., and Clair, J. M. (2011a). The medicalization of homelessness and the sociology of the self: A grounded fractal analysis. In N. K. Denzin and T. Faust (Eds.), *Studies in symbolic interaction* (pp. 37, 29–62). Bingley, England: Emerald Group.

Wasserman, J. A., and Clair, J. M. (2011b). *American refugees: Homelessness in four movements* (Documentary Film). Birmingham, AL: Bent Rail Foundation.

Wasserman, J. A., and Clair, J. M. (2013). The insufficiency of fairness: The logics of homeless service administration and resulting gaps in service. *Culture and Organization, 19*(2), 162–183.

Wasserman, J. A., and Clair, J. M. (2011c). Housing patterns of homeless people: The ecology of the street in the era of urban renewal. *Journal of Contemporary Ethnography 40*(1): 71–101.

Weber, M. (1958). *The Protestant ethic and the spirit of capitalism*. New York, NY: Scribner's.

Weicher, J. C. (2012). *Housing policy at a crossroads: The why, how, and who of assistance programs*. Washington, DC: American Enterprise Institute.

Wells, M., and Sandhu, H. (1986). The juvenile runaway: A historical perspective. *Free Inquiry in Creative Sociology, 14*(2), 143–147.

Whelan, R. (2014, October 1). Apartment rents are rising steadily and quickly. *Wall Street Journal*. Retrieved from www.wsj.com/articles/apartment-rents-are-rising-steadily-and-quickly-1412220601

Whelley, C. J. (2013). Emerging discourse surrounding Denver's urban camping ban: Denver Homeless Out Loud, agency, and structure. *Praxis: Politics in Action, 1*(1), 1–24.

Whelley, C. J. (2014). *Anti-homeless laws in US cities: A quantitative study of three theories*. Denver, CO: University of Colorado at Denver.

Whitbeck, L. B., Hoyt, D. R., and Ackley, K. A. (1997). Abusive family backgrounds and later victimization among runaway and homeless adolescents. *Journal of Research on Adolescence, 7*(4), 375–392.

Whitman, B., Accardo, P., Boyert, M., and Kendagor, R. (1990). Homelessness and cognitive performance in children: A possible link. *Social Work, 35*(6), 516–519.

Wilkerson, I. (1991, September 2). Shift in feelings on the homeless: Empathy turns to frustration. *New York Times,* p. 1.

Wilkinson, R., and Pickett, K. (2009), *The spirit level: Why greater equality makes societies stronger.* London, England: Bloomsbury Press.

Willse, C. (2008). "Universal data elements," or the biopolitical life of homeless populations. *Surveillance and Society 5*(3): 227–251.

Wilson, E. O. (2014, September). On free will: And how the brain is like a colony of ants. *Harper's Magazine,* pp. 49–52.

Wilson, J. Q., and Kelling, G. L. (1982). Broken windows. *The Atlantic.* Retrieved from www.theatlantic.com/magazine/archive/1982/03/broken-windows/304465/

Wolfensberger, W. (1983). Social role valorization: A proposed new term for the principle of normalization. *Mental retardation, 21*(6), 234.

Wolff, E. N. (2010). *Recent trends in household wealth in the United States: Rising debt and the middle-class squeeze—An update to 2007* (Working Paper No. 589). Annandale-on-Hudson, NY: Levy Economics Institute, Bard College.

Wolin, R. (2001). The Hannah Arendt situation. *New England Review, 22*(2), 97–123.

Wong, Y. L., Filoromo, M., and Tennille, J. (2007). From principles to practice: a study of implementation of supported housing for psychiatric consumers. *Administration and Policy in Mental Health, 34*(1), 13–28.

Wong, Y.-L. I., and Stanhope, V. (2009). Conceptualizing community: A comparison of neighborhood characteristics of supportive housing for persons with psychiatric and developmental disabilities. *Social Science & Medicine, 68*(8), 1376–1387.

Wright. J., Rubin, B., and Devine, J. (1998). *Beside the golden door: Policy, politics and the homeless.* New York, NY: Aldine de Gruyter.

Wright, T. (1997). *Out of place: Homeless mobilizations, subcities, and contested landscapes.* New York, NY: SUNY Press.

Wyly, E., and Hammel, D. (2005). Mapping neo-liberal American urbanism. In R. Atkinson and G. Bridge (Eds.), *Gentrification in a global context: The new urban colonialism* (pp. 18–39). New York, NY: Routledge.

Yanos, P. T., Barrow, S. M., and Tsemberis, S. (2004). Community integration in the early phase of housing among homeless persons diagnosed with severe mental illness: Successes and challenges. *Community Mental Health Journal, 40*(2), 133–150.

Yanos, P., Felton, B. J., Tsemberis, S., and Frye, V. (2007). Exploring the role of housing type, neighborhood characteristics, and lifestyle factors in the community integration of formerly homeless persons diagnosed with mental illness. *Journal of Mental Health, 16*(6), 703–717.

Yeomans, W. (2012, October 8). How the right packed the court. *The Nation,* p. 14.

Zerger, S., Doblin, B., and Thompson, L. (2009). Medical respite care for homeless people: A growing national phenomenon. *Journal of Health Care for the Poor and Underserved, 20*(1), 36–41.

Ziesemer, C., Marcoux, L., and Marwell, B. E. (1994). Homeless children: Are they different from other low-income children? *Social Work, 39*(6), 658–668.

The Contributors

Samantha Batko is director of the Homelessness Research Institute at the National Alliance to End Homelessness.

Donald W. Burnes is chair of the Board of Directors and executive director of the Burnes Center on Poverty and Homelessness, as well as adjunct professor at the University of Denver Graduate School of Social Work.

Martha R. Burt has been conducting research and evaluation on policies and practices affecting vulnerable populations for almost four decades.

Corissa Carlson is a doctoral candidate at Wayne State University, where she is working on a dissertation describing homelessness among college undergraduates.

Jeffrey Michael Clair is director of both the Center for Social Medicine and the Applied Sociology Graduate Program at the University of Alabama, Birmingham.

Sheila Crowley has been president and chief executive officer of the National Low Income Housing Coalition since 1998.

David L. DiLeo is professor emeritus of history and humanities at Saddleback College in Mission Viejo, California.

Bristow Hardin has conducted research and advocacy on social justice–related issues for nearly four decades.

Richard L. Harris is a founding employee and former executive director of Central City Concern in Portland and director of the Division of Addictions and Mental Health of the State of Oregon.

Benjamin F. Henwood is assistant professor of social work at the University of Southern California.

Jill Khadduri is principal associate and senior fellow at Abt Associates, where she is co–principal investigator of the Annual Homeless Assessment Report and part of the team conducting the Family Options Study.

Kate Whelley McCabe is a former assistant attorney general for the state of Vermont. She is currently working in nonprofit management in Montpelier.

Michelle McHenry-Edrington is a veteran of the US Air Force. She was a researcher at the Burnes Center on Poverty and Homelessness and is currently benefits acquisition specialist at Bayaud Enterprises.

Anne Miskey is chief executive officer of the Downtown Women's Center in Los Angeles. She is the former executive director of Funders Together to End Homelessness.

Joseph Murphy is Frank W. Mayborn Chair at Vanderbilt University. His work is primarily in school improvement.

Tracey O'Brien was instrumental in the development of the Burnes Center on Poverty and Homelessness. She has nearly twenty years of experience conducting program evaluation and survey research in the areas of homelessness, poverty, and prekindergarten through twelfth-grade education.

Kerri Tobin is assistant professor of education at Marywood University.

Paul A. Toro is professor of psychology at Wayne State University in Detroit.

Sam Tsemberis is founder and chief executive officer of Pathways to Housing, Inc., the agency that developed the Housing First program. He is on the faculty of the Department of Psychiatry, Columbia University Medical Center.

Jason Adam Wasserman is assistant professor of biomedical sciences and course director for clinical bioethics and medical humanities at Oakland University William Beaumont School of Medicine, Rochester Hills, Michigan.

Collin Jaquet Whelley is currently an analyst at the Center for Social Innovation in Needham.

Index

Abt Associates, 107, 109
Academic history, 158*n*6
Academic interest, professional coverage and, 238–239
ACLU. *See* American Civil Liberties Union
ACT team. *See* Assertive community treatment team
ADA. *See* Americans with Disabilities Act
Addiction, 78, 208. *See also* Central City Concern
ADFC. *See* Alcohol and Drug Free Community
Administration for Children and Families, 117
Adua, L., 211, 213*n*6
Adults, 119*n*7, 132, 133
Advocacy, 201
Advocates, 240–242, 270–271, 289
AFDC. *See* Aid to Families with Dependent Children
Affordable Housing Program (AHP), 169
African Americans, 34, 142, 179, 180–182, 185, 187
Age, 33
Agony of uncertainty, 146
Agricultural areas, 41
AHARs. *See* Annual Homeless Assessment Reports
AHP. *See* Affordable Housing Program

Aid to Families with Dependent Children (AFDC), 53, 191
AIDS. *See* Human immunodeficiency virus/acquired immunodeficiency syndrome
Alabama, 129–130
Alameda County, California, 257–258, 259
Alcohol, 7, 54, 71, 83–99, 237–238
Alcohol and Drug Free Community (ADFC), 7, 83–99
Alliance, 286–287
Alliance to End Homelessness, 225–226
Almshouses, 125–126
American Civil Liberties Union (ACLU), 156–157
American Housing Survey, 246
American Psychological Association (APA), 240
American Recovery and Reinvestment Act (ARRA), 45, 107, 256
American Recovery and Reinvestment Act Homelessness Prevention and Rapid Re-Housing Program. *See* Homelessness Prevention and Rapid Re-Housing Program
Americans with Disabilities Act (ADA), 80
AMI. *See* Area median income
Anderson, L., 34, 35
Anderson, Ray, 157
Annual Homeless Assessment Reports

325

(AHARs), 33, 37, 38, 43–44, 55, 105; annual prevalence rates, 60; data, 66n6; on ES, 108; 2009, 67–68; on veterans, 106
Annual prevalence rates, 59–61
Antifeeding ordinances, 130
Antigenerational tyranny, 157
Antihomeless laws, 201–206, 213n2, 213n3, 213n6, 213n11
APA. *See* American Psychological Association
Area median income (AMI), 168
ARRA. *See* American Recovery and Reinvestment Act
ARRA Homelessness Prevention and Rapid Re-Housing Program. *See* Homelessness Prevention and Rapid Re-Housing Program
Assertive community treatment (ACT) team, 77–78
At Home on the Street: People, Poverty, and a Hidden Culture of Homelessness (Wasserman and Clair), 126–128
Attitudes, 1, 30–31
AuCoin, Les, 128n1

BACHIC. *See* Bay Area Counties Homeless Information Collaborative
Bassuk, E. L., 34, 37
Batko, Samantha, 281, 288
Baum, Alice, 1
Bay Area Counties Homeless Information Collaborative (BACHIC), 226
BCA. *See* Budget Control Act
Beckett, K., 203, 213n5
Begging, 198
Belief, 141–157
Best practices, 5, 230
Beyond Shelter program, 252
Bigelow, Gordon, 147
Bill & Melinda Gates Foundation, 269
Bill of Rights, 213n7
Bills of rights, 198, 199–201
Bipartisan Housing Commission, 173
Birmingham, Alabama, 129–130
Bivens, J., 188
Blacks, 34, 142, 179, 180–182, 185, 187
Bois, David, 155
Bolton, M., 168
Boots to Suits, 22–23
Boston, Massachusetts, 132

Boyer, Pascal, 144
Bravve, E., 168
Brennan, T., 38
Broken windows theory, 202–203
Brooke, Edward W., 163
Brooke Amendment, 163
Brown v. Board of Education, 155
Buck, P. O., 235, 236, 237–238, 242
Budget Control Act (BCA), 163
Burnes Institute on Poverty and Homelessness, 1, 6, 24, 217, 220, 224, 228
Burnside Consortium. *See* Central City Concern
Burt, Martha R., 31, 32, 34, 35, 37, 52, 60, 105, 246, 279, 280
Bush, George H. W., administration, 102
Bush, George W., 161; administration, 241–242, 249
Business Improvement District, 91
Businesses, 203–204, 212
Butler Family Fund, 271

California, 68–69, 150, 155, 156. *See also* Alameda County, California; Los Angeles, California; Los Angeles County, California; San Francisco, California
California Assembly Bill 2034, 69
California Department of Corrections, 44–45
Canada, 69
Capital gains, 195n7
Capitalism, 146–147, 155, 158n3
Carlson, Corissa, 237
Cars, 199
Carter, Jimmy, 21, 161
Case management, 133
Case managers, 18–19, 20, 21, 26
Case notes, 135
Castle Rock, Colorado, 12–28
Cauce, A., 39
CBO. *See* Congressional Budget Office
CCC. *See* Central City Concern
CEEN. *See* Colorado eLogic Evaluation Network
Census, 227, 228
Census Bureau, US, 48, 232, 233
Center for Effective Philanthropy, 219
Central City Concern (CCC), 7, 83–99
Central intake system, 252
Charity services, 125–128

Chelsea, Massachusetts, 272
Chicago, Illinois, 57, 104, 132, 255
Chicago Plan 2.0, 255
Childhood events, 207–208
Children, 36–37, 172, 193. *See also* Department of Education, US
China, 188
Choice, 209
Choice Neighborhood Initiative (CNI), 164
Christianity, 125–128, 146, 153
Chronic homelessness, 43–44, 106, 253, 268
Chronically homeless, 61, 68, 106, 243, 244, 283–284
Churchill, Winston, 154
Cities, 40, 205–206, 210–211, 213*n*5
Citizen advocates, 9
Citizenship, 138, 150–151
Civil rights, 156–157, 198
Clackamas County, Oregon, 97
Clair, Jeffrey, 126–128, 208
Class, 152–153, 205
Clean and Safe program, 91
Cleveland, Ohio, 58
Client-based programs, 265
Clinical services, 77–78
Clinicians, 74–75
Clinton, Bill, 33, 161, 210
Clinton administration, 210
Clinton-Gingrich welfare law, 190–191
CNI. *See* Choice Neighborhood Initiative
CNN Money, 186
Coalitions, 8, 286–287
CoCs. *See* Continuums of Care
Coffey, B., 134
Cognitive failings, 143–144
Cohen, B. E., 105
Collective planning, 288
Colorado, 2, 12–28, 222. *See also* Denver, Colorado; Metro Denver Continuum of Care
Colorado Department of Human Services, 222
Colorado eLogic Evaluation Network (CEEN), 221
Colorado Organizations Responding to AIDS (CORA), 21
Columbus, Ohio, 64, 226, 251
Common Sense Housing Investment Act, 174

Commonwealth of Massachusetts, 272
Community, 80, 216–217, 245–260, 250*tab*, 253*fig*. *See also* Stakeholders; Ten-year plans
Community for Creative Non-Violence, 102, 241
Community Shelter Board, 251
Community Volunteer Corps (CVC), 91–92
Community-based rapid re-housing, 128*n*2
Conference of Mayors, US, 43, 249
Congress, US, 54, 60, 64, 66*n*6, 110, 267; JCT of, 171; sequester relief provided by, 163. *See also* Stewart B. McKinney Homeless Assistance Act
Congressional Budget Office (CBO), 191
Connecticut, 199, 200–201, 251
Conrad N. Hilton Foundation, 268
Conscious capitalism, 155
Conservative orthodoxy, 158*n*7
Constitution, US, 158*n*8, 170, 198–199, 213*n*7
Consumer choice, 78
Consumer-driven services, 73–76
Continuums of Care (CoCs), 55, 56, 57, 60–61, 66*n*6, 66*n*7, 66*n*9, 123, 125; ADFC housing as component of, 92; in Colorado, 222; Columbus, 226; Cook County, 225–226; creation of, 210; Housing Inventory Chart, 107; HUD's vision for, 104–105, 125, 227, 239, 262; PSH emphasized by, 110; social services promoted by, 139. *See also* Homeless Management Information System
Cook County, Illinois, 225–226
Coordinated intake, 258
Coordination, 9
CORA. *See* Colorado Organizations Responding to AIDS
Cost burden, 160
Cost of Homelessness study, 107
Crack cocaine epidemic, 54
Creative space, 205
Crime, 202–203
Criminal histories, 242
Criminalization, 129–130, 151, 201–206, 213*n*2, 287
Cronley, C., 206–207

Crowley, Sheila, 168, 279, 280
Cruel and Unusual Punishment Clause, 198
Culhane, D. P., 33, 59, 71, 109, 133, 134–135, 136, 232, 248
Cultural revanchism, 206
Culture shift, 204–206
Cunningham, M., 249, 251, 252, 253, 254
CVC. *See* Community Volunteer Corps

Daskal, J., 246
Data, 9; AHAR, 66*n*6; availability of, 223–224; in Colorado, 217; gathering, 265; HMIS, 133–135; homeless services systems outcome, 95–96; need for, 280–281; overview of, 215–230, 219*fig*; programs influenced by, 220–221; sources, 222–223; ten-year plan strategies for, 251; warehousing, 222–223. *See also* Point-in-Time data; Program evaluation
Data Integration Initiative, 222
Day labor jobs, 53
Deaths, 234–235
Decisions, 264–265
Decriminalization, 83–85
Deinstitutionalization movement, 44
Democratic capitalism, 155
Democratic Party, 205
Demographics, 29–45
Denver, Colorado, 2, 5–6, 12–28, 202, 216–217, 223–224. *See also* Metro Denver area
Denver's Road Home (DRH), 5–6
Department of Education, US, 37, 65
Department of Health and Human Services, US (HHS), 102, 117
Department of Housing and Urban Development, US (HUD), 2, 32, 34, 38, 43, 49, 55, 66*n*7, 67; budget, 161; on chronically homeless, 61; CoC vision of, 104–105, 125, 227, 239, 262; Final Notice, 134–135; HMIS standards, 134; homeless estimate, 246, 254–255; on homelessness, 65, 102, 104; HOPWA program of, 97; housing assistance budget, 101–102; housing first and, 70, 282; HPRP funds distributed by, 256; McKinney

Homeless Employment Grant, 90–91, 102; PHF and, 70; PIT counts, 232; programs, 62; PSH emphasized by, 109–110; rapid re-housing funded by, 112–113; SRO program supported by, 93–94; on TH, 275*n*2; VASH program, 112; window, 57. *See also* Annual Homeless Assessment Reports; Federal housing programs; Homeless services systems; Homelessness Prevention and Rapid Re-Housing Program; Housing assistance; Section 8
Department of Treasury. *See* Low-income housing tax credits
Department of Veterans Affairs (VA), 14–15, 18–20, 21, 112
Depression, 19
Deregulation, 161, 187–188
Desert theory, 152–153
Deservedness, 206–208, 213*n*9, 213*n*10, 287–288
Design, 264–265
Detoxification, 85–87
Detroit, Michigan, 156
Deunionization, 189, 189*fig*
Developer, 168
Devine, J., 136
Devolution, 213*n*12
Dignity for All campaign, 156–157
Dirksen, Everett, 191
Disabilities, 105. *See also* Mental illness
Disaffiliated man, 123
Discouraged workers, 179
Diversity, 205–206
Doctors, 21
Domestic violence, 269
Donley, 203, 204–205
Donors, 194
DRH. *See* Denver's Road Home
Drug dependency, 54
Drugs, 22, 71, 78, 208. *See also* Central City Concern
Due Process Clause, 199
Dunn, K., 5
Dylan, Bob, 177

Earned income tax credit, 191
EBPol. *See* Evidence-based policy
Economic boom, 233
Economic growth, inequality reducing, 192

Economic inequality, 8
Economic injustice, 278–279
Economic justice, 149–150, 278–279
Economic Policy Institute, 186, 189
Economic security, 187–191, 189*fig*, 190*fig*, 193–194
Ecumenical Ministries of Oregon, 98
Education, 27, 35–36, 182
Egypt, 128
Eighth Amendment, 198
ELI households. *See* Extremely low income households
Ellison, Keith, 174
eLogic, 220–221
Embry, L., 39
Emergency departments, 131, 132
Emergency Food and Shelter Program, 52, 66*n*3, 101
Emergency loan, 117
Emergency prevention, 251–252, 253–254
Emergency shelter (ES), 107, 108, 123, 133, 246
Emergency Solutions Grant, 224
Eminent domain, 156
Emotions, 27, 28
Empathy, 145
Employment, 35–36, 90–92
Employment Access Center, 90–91
Enclosure movement, 145–146
Enforcement, 200–201
England, 145–146
ES. *See* Emergency shelter
Eschbach, E., 35
Estate Hotel, 88–89, 92, 93
Ethnicity, poverty by, 186–187, 187*tab*
Europe, 69, 122
European Jews, 141–142
Evaluation, 255, 281. *See also* Program evaluation
EveryOne Home, 259
Eviction, 160
Evidence-based policy (EBPol), 5
Experiential learning, 76
Extremely low income (ELI) households, 159–160, 162, 168, 172–173, 175*n*1

Fair Market Rents (FMR), 165
Fairfax, Virginia, 258
Families, 36–37, 61, 63, 115, 282; eviction influencing, 160; rapid re-housing and, 268–269
Family Assistance Plan, 278–279
Family Options Study, 107–108, 113, 116, 286
Family transitional housing (family TH), 109
Fannie Mae, 172, 173
Farms, 41
Fear, 204–205
Federal constitutional provisions, 198–199
Federal Emergency Management Agency (FEMA), 101
Federal funding, 266–267
Federal government, 262
Federal Home Loan Banks, 169
Federal Housing Finance Agency (FHFA), 172
Federal housing programs, 161, 162–170, 172–174, 224
Federal income tax, 170
Federal policy, 206–207, 255–257
Federal Reserve Bank, 188
Federal subsidies, 279
Federalist Papers, 213*n*7, 213*n*8
Federally Qualified Health Center (FQHC), 98
FEMA. *See* Federal Emergency Management Agency
Ferrell, J., 205
FHFA. *See* Federal Housing Finance Agency
Fields, Rhonda, 21, 23
Filtering, 160–161
Financial wealth, 184–185, 185*fig*
Finkelhor, D., 39
First, R., 42
First Amendment, 198
Fiscal incentives, 283–285
Fitzpatrick, S., 208, 209
FMR. *See* Fair Market Rents
Food Not Bombs, 130
Food pantries, 246
Food stamps, 53. *See also* Supplemental Nutrition Assistance Program
Ford, Gerald, 161
Ford administration, 209
Foreclosures, 162
Foundation Center, 267
Foundations. *See* Funders

"Four Freedoms" (Roosevelt), 277–278
Fourteenth Amendment, 199
Fourth Amendment, 198
FQHC. *See* Federally Qualified Health
  Center
Francis (pope), 177, 279
Freddie Mac, 172, 173
Free Speech Clause, 198
Free will, 156
Freedom, 143, 277–278
Frees Foundation, 270
Fremstad, S., 186
Friedman, D. H., 134
Friedman, Milton, 203
Fulop, M., 219–220
Funders, 261–275, 275n1, 283
Funders Together Houston, 270
Funders Together to End Homelessness,
  261, 267–268, 270, 273
Funding, 139–140, 239, 241–242,
  266–267, 271–272, 273; change in,
  269; program, 274; strategies, 10,
  269

Gale, K., 257–258
Gallup Poll surveys, 186
Gans, H. J., 213n9
GAO. *See* General Accounting Office
Gender, 33
General Accounting Office (GAO), 261
Gentrification, 205
Getting Housed, Staying Housed (City of
  Chicago), 255
Gilens, M., 194
Gingrich Revolution, 161
Giuliani, Rudolph, 202
Gladwell, Malcolm, 72
Globalization, 188
GNP. *See* Gross national product
God, 127, 128
Golden Age, 178–179
Golden West Hotel, 97
Good practice, 230
Google, 218
Gore, Al, 153–154
Government, 153–154
Governor's office, 23
Gowan, T., 202, 207, 213n9
Grand Rapids, Michigan, 252
Great Depression, 30, 158n12
Great Recession, 6, 54, 61, 115, 242,

254; net wealth influenced by, 184;
  unemployment rates, 180. *See also*
  American Recovery and Reinvest-
  ment Act
Greenberg, G. A., 132, 133
Greer, A. L., 63
Gross national product (GNP), 158n4
Gutierrez, O., 134

Habitat for Humanity, 21
HADIN. *See* Homeless Alcohol and
  Drug Intervention Network
Hammel, D., 205
Hammer, H., 39
Hampton Roads Community Foundation,
  269
Hands Across America, 235
Hanoi Hilton, 16–22, 27
Hardin, Bristow, 280
Harm reduction, 69, 71, 78, 137–138.
  See also Low-barrier shelters; No-
  barrier shelters
Harris County, Texas, 57–58
Hartford, Connecticut, 251
Harvey, D., 211
Health, 192–193
Health conditions, 54
HEARTH Act. *See* Homeless Emergency
  Assistance and Rapid Transition to
  Housing Act
Hennepin County, Minnesota, 251, 252
Henry, M., 249, 251, 252, 253, 254
Herbert, S., 203, 213n5
HFAs. *See* Housing Finance Agencies
HHS. *See* Department of Health and
  Human Services, US
High-probability blocks, 57–58
Hispanics, 34, 179, 180–182, 187
HIV/AIDS. *See* Human immunodefi-
  ciency virus/acquired immunodefi-
  ciency syndrome
HMIS. *See* Homeless Management In-
  formation System
Hoffman, L., 134
Holocaust denial, 141–142
Hombs, M. E., 35, 42–43
HOME Investment Partnerships Pro-
  gram, 168–169
Home visit, 75–76
Homebase, 63
Homebase Community Prevention, 115

Homeless. *See* Homelessness experiencers

Homeless Alcohol and Drug Intervention Network (HADIN), 84, 85

Homeless assistance, housing assistance kept separate from, 103–107, 114, 285–287

Homeless bills of rights, 198, 199–201

Homeless Emergency Assistance and Rapid Transition to Housing (HEARTH) Act, 104, 134, 255–256, 258–260, 265–266

Homeless Management Information System (HMIS), 55, 59–60, 66n7, 251; accessibility, 223–224; in Colorado, 217, 223–224; concerns, 134–135; data, 133–135; development of, 67, 107, 133–135; examples, 224–226; HUD standards, 134; limitations, 134–135; overview of, 133–135, 224–226; social services influenced by, 133–135. *See also* Annual Homeless Assessment Reports

Homeless Outreach Team, 270

Homeless services systems, 34, 95–96, 121–133, 123*fig*, 124*fig*, 138–139

Homelessness: barriers, 271; causes of, 31, 49–52, 50*fig*, 207–209; chronic, 43–44, 106, 253, 268; coalitions, 8; definitions of, 47–49, 64–65, 104, 231; elimination of, 2; as embraced, 141–157; estimates of, 54–55, 58–61, 231–234, 246, 254–255; example, 11–28; experience of, 39–45; factors influencing, 50*fig*; family, 61; future of, 277–290; HHS on, 102; history of, 47–65; HUD on, 65, 102, 104; industrial complex, 237, 239, 283; as literal, 115; 1980s and, 52–54, 101–102, 122, 123, 233–237, 235*fig*, 245–246, 261–262; 1970s and, 122, 123, 160–161, 233–237, 235*fig*, 246; overview of, 1–10, 13*fig*, 47–65, 50*fig*; prevalence of, 231–234; as problem, 30–31; roots of, 122, 177–194, 180*tab*, 181*fig*, 182*fig*, 183*fig*, 185*fig*, 187*tab*, 199*fig*, 200*fig*; scope of, 122; size of, 122; ten-year plans influencing, 254–255; unsheltered, 61–62; in US, 52–54

Homelessness Prevention and Rapid Re-Housing Program (HPRP), 45, 114–115, 256, 257–258, 259

Homeowners, 3, 170–172, 175

Homeownership, 161

Homes, 156

Homophobia, 155

Hooks, G., 211, 213n6

Hooper Memorial Detoxification Center, 84, 85–87

HOPE VI program, 164

Hopkins, D. J., 205

Hopper, K., 34

HOPWA. *See* Housing Opportunities for Persons with AIDS

Hospitals, 131–133

Household composition, 32–33

Housing, 2, 71, 80, 234, 252, 269; as affordable, 159–162, 273; clinical services and, 77–78; costs, 3*fig*, 72–73, 160; disappearance of, 53; as inadequate, 279–280; integrated health care filled by, 98; Inventory Chart, 107; overview of, 159–175; poverty influencing, 68; ready, 135–138; segmentation, 105–107; Wage, 160. *See also* Alcohol and Drug Free Community; Homeless services systems; Housing Choice Vouchers; Low-income rental housing; Permanent housing; Permanent supportive housing; Rapid rehousing; Rental housing; Section 8; Subsidies; Transitional housing

Housing Act, US, 162

Housing and Community Development Act, 161, 165

Housing and Economic Recovery Act, 172

Housing assistance, 101–118, 167, 285–287

Housing Authority of Portland, 93–94, 97

Housing Choice Vouchers, 107, 112, 113

Housing Finance Agencies (HFAs), 167

Housing first, 7, 45, 109, 119n6, 281–282; housing ready's debate with, 135–138; overview of, 67–81, 111–112, 136–138, 268; S+C shifting to, 112; in ten-year plan, 247–248, 253; VA embracing, 112. *See also* Pathways' Housing First

Housing Opportunities for Persons with
    AIDS (HOPWA), 97, 169
Housing subsidy programs. *See* Subsi-
    dies
Housing vouchers, 116, 165–166, 168
Housing-based systems, 267–268
Houston, Texas, 12, 24, 57–58, 228, 270
Houston Police Department, 270
HPRP. *See* Homelessness Prevention and
    Rapid Re-Housing Program
HUD. *See* Department of Housing and
    Urban Development, US
Human immunodeficiency virus/ac-
    quired immunodeficiency syndrome
    (HIV/AIDS), 96–97, 169
Humanity, 141–143
Hypertrophy, 144

ICH. *See* Interagency Council on Home-
    lessness, US
ICM team. *See* Intensive case manage-
    ment team
Identification, 115–116
Ideology, 8, 63–64, 153, 158n7
Ignatieff, Michael, 148
IICA. *See* Iowa Institute for Community
    Alliances
Illinois, 157, 199, 200–201, 225–226.
    See also Chicago, Illinois
IMF. *See* International Monetary Fund
Incarceration, 43, 44–45, 132–133, 203
Incident Command System, 228
Income inequality, 148, 177–178, 189,
    192–193, 233
Incomes, 8, 35–36, 158n4, 170, 180,
    195n7; growth in, 182–183, 183*fig*;
    by quintile, 183, 183*fig*; real after-
    tax, 182, 183, 183*fig*
Individualism, 213n9
Individualized coordinated care, 85
Individuals, 51, 206–208, 209, 213n7,
    213n11
Industrial economy, 122
Inequality, 8, 184, 187–193, 189*fig*,
    190*fig*. *See also* Income inequality
Information system, 64
Infrastructure, 248–249
Initiative to Help End Chronic Home-
    lessness, 70
Inmates, 132
Institutional silos, 285–287

Integrated health care, 98
Integrated Services for the Homeless
    Mentally Ill, 69
Intensive case management (ICM) team,
    78
Interagency Council on Homelessness,
    US (ICH), 70, 102, 242, 249; creation
    of, 67; plan released by, 256–257,
    266
International Monetary Fund (IMF), 192
Interventions, 38, 85. *See also* Central
    City Concern
Involuntary residential mobility, 160
Iowa Institute for Community Alliances
    (IICA), 225
Isaacson, Betsy, 278–279

Jails, 132
JCT. *See* Joint Committee on Taxation
Jesus Christ, 127, 147
Jews, 141–142, 195n9
Job seeker/job opening ratio, 179
Job Stimulus Bill, 52
Johns Hopkins University, 229–230
Joint Committee on Taxation (JCT), 171
Joke, 158n3
Jones, M. M., 239, 241
Justice, 126, 128, 149–151, 278–279

Kelling, G. L., 202–203
Kemp, Jack, 103
Kennedy, Patrick, 21
Kentucky, 58
Keynesian model, 158n4, 158n12
Khadduri, Jill, 279, 284–285, 286
King, Martin Luther, 177
King County, Washington, 269
Koch brothers, 153
Kozol, J., 32
Križnik, B., 203
Kuhn, R., 248
Kusmer, K., 30

Labels, 145–146
Labor market, 178–183, 180*tab*, 181*fig*,
    182*fig*, 183*fig*, 188–189
Lakewood Church, 24
Landlords, 269
Language, 289–290
Lapham, Lewis, 153
Latinos, wealth of, 185

Laws, 122, 157; antihomeless, 201–206, 213*n*2, 213*n*3, 213*n*6, 213*n*11; homeless threat influencing, 202–206; responsibilities under, 197–201; rights under, 197–201. *See also* Ordinances
Learning, experiential, 76
Leaseholding, 119*n*7
Lee, B. A., 205
Leginski, W., 134
Legislators, 194
Letty Owings treatment program, 97
Liberation theology, 128
LIHTCs. *See* Low-income housing tax credits
Lincoln, Abraham, 155, 158*n*10
Link, B. G., 203, 204
Lipstadt, Deborah, 141–142
Listening Post Project, 229–230
Literal homeless, 42–43, 49
Literal homelessness, 115
Lobao, L., 211, 213*n*6
Location, 40–42
Loitering, 198, 199
Long-term homeless, 60
Long-term unemployed, 179
Los Angeles, California, 45, 56, 57, 111, 252, 270
Los Angeles County, California, 57, 268
Los Angeles Homeless Funders Group/Funders Together Los Angeles, 270
Low-barrier shelters, 135–138
Low-income housing tax credits (LIHTCs), 94, 104–105, 111, 167–168
Low-income rental housing, 3, 8, 159–162, 246, 279
Low-probability blocks, 57–58
Loyola University, 255
Luther, Martin, 213*n*9
Lyon-Callo, V., 213*n*11

MacLean, M., 39
Madison, James, 213*n*7
Mainstream housing assistance programs, 103–104
Mangano, Philip, 249
Maraccini, Karla, 23
Marital status, 33
Marriage equality, 155
Marshall, Thurgood, 155
Martha Washington Apartments, 97

Massachusetts, 132, 272
McCaskill, P., 38
McDonell, D. M., 242
McHenry-Edrington, Michelle, 286
McKinney Act. *See* Stewart B. McKinney Homeless Assistance Act
McKinney Homeless Employment Grant, 90–91, 102
McKinney-Vento homeless assistance programs, 169–170, 224
MDHI. *See* Metropolitan Denver Homeless Initiative
MDW. *See* Michigan's data warehouse
Meals on Wheels, 12–13
Means testing, 206–207
Media, 231, 234–238, 235*fig*, 239–244
Medicaid, 53
Medicalization, 213*n*11
Meek, 126
Melville Charitable Trust, 268
Men, 181–182, 213*n*10
Mental health, in treatment model, 125
Mental Health Services West, 97
Mental hospitals, 53
Mental illness, 43, 44, 53–54, 68, 282, 287; community integration, 80; costs, 72; public estimating, 242; recovery orientation, 78–79; special needs housing for, 97. *See also* Pathways' Housing First; Robert Wood Johnson Foundation
Mercer County, New Jersey, 259
Metraux, S., 133, 134, 136
Metro Denver area, 221, 227, 228–229
Metro Denver Continuum of Care, 216–217
Metropolitan Denver Homeless Initiative (MDHI), 228–229
Meyer, Joyce, 15, 24, 127
Michigan, 53, 156, 252
Michigan Statewide Homeless Management Information System (MSHMIS), 225
Michigan's data warehouse (MDW), 222–223
MID. *See* Mortgage interest deduction
Middle Ages, 122
Midwest, 41
Milburn, N. G., 34
Military industrial complex, 149
"Million Dollar Murray" (Gladwell), 72

Minimum wage, 188–189
Minnesota, 251, 252
Minorities. *See* Racial minorities
Mishel, L., 189
Miskey, Anne, 281, 288–289
Missouri, 163
Mitchell, 202, 204, 205, 206, 213*n*3, 213*n*9
"A Model of Charity" (Winthrop), 157*n*1
Moore, J., 37
Moore, Thomas, 95–96
Moral panic, 204–206
Mortgage industry, 161
Mortgage interest deduction (MID), 3, 170–172, 173–174, 278
Moses, 128
Mothers, 36
Moving to Work (MTW) program, 164
MSHMIS. *See* Michigan Statewide Homeless Management Information System
MTW program. *See* Moving to Work program
Multnomah County, Oregon, 252. *See also* Central City Concern
Murphy, Joseph, 280

NAEH. *See* National Alliance to End Homelessness
NAMI. *See* National Alliance for the Mentally Ill
A Nation in Denial: The Truth About Homelessness (Baum and Burnes), 1
National Affordable Housing Act, 168
National Alliance for the Mentally Ill (NAMI), 287
National Alliance to End Homelessness (NAEH), 2–3, 68, 226, 241, 242. *See also A Plan, Not a Dream: How to End Homelessness in Ten Years*; Ten-year plans
National Association for the Education of Homeless Children and Youth, 37
National Bureau of Economic Research, 3
National Center for Homeless Education (NCHE), 37
National Center on Family Homelessness, 32–33
National Coalition for the Homeless, 33
National Commission on Severely Dis-

tressed Public Housing, 163–164
National Employment Law Project, 189
National Housing Trust Fund (NHTF), 172–173, 174, 279
National Human Services Data Consortium (NHSDC), 216, 224
National Institute of Mental Health (NIMH), 80, 102
National Institute on Alcohol Abuse and Alcoholism (NIAAA), 84, 85
National Law Center on Homelessness and Poverty (NLCHP), 32, 34, 199
National Low Income Housing Coalition (NLIHC), 2, 273
National Survey of Homeless Assistance Providers and Clients (NSHAPC), 34, 60, 64, 105, 246
Nazi attacks, 195*n*9
NCHE. *See* National Center for Homeless Education
Neale, J., 208
Neglect, 142–143
Neighbors Overcoming Poverty and Homelessness, 287
Neoliberalism, 203–204, 210–211, 213*n*6
Net imputed rental income, 171
Net wealth, 184
Net worth, 184–185
Nevada, 72
New Deal, 140*n*1, 209
New England, 146
New homeless, 32–39, 235
New Jersey, 259
New York, 285
New York City (NYC), 33, 56–57, 59–60, 63, 66*n*8, 104, 233; homeless children in, 172; PIT survey, 228; prevention assistance, 114, 117; shelter bed costs, 71; shelters, 257
New York Times, 235
Ngram Viewer, 218
NHSDC. *See* National Human Services Data Consortium
NHTF. *See* National Housing Trust Fund
NIAAA. *See* National Institute on Alcohol Abuse and Alcoholism
Nicholls, C. M., 208, 209
Niemala, Dana, 22
NIMH. *See* National Institute of Mental Health

1981-1982 recession, 52, 54, 55
Nixon, Richard, 278–279
Nixon administration, 209
NLCHP. *See* National Law Center on Homelessness and Poverty
NLIHC. *See* National Low Income Housing Coalition
No-barrier shelters, 135–138
Nonprofits, 274
Northeast, 41
NSHAPC. *See* National Survey of Homeless Assistance Providers and Clients

Obama, Barack, 125, 164, 288
Obama administration, 125, 164, 169, 266
O'Brien, Tracy, 24, 280, 281
Occupy Movement, 152
OECD. *See* Organisation for Economic Co-operation and Development
Office of Management and Budget (OMB), 168, 170, 171
Office of Special Needs Programs, 103
Offshoring, 188
O'Flaherty, B., 114, 115
Ohio, 223. *See also* Cleveland, Ohio; Columbus, Ohio
Old Town Clinic, 98
Older people, 36
Olmstead Supreme Court decision, 80, 111
Olsen, Theodore, 155
OMB. *See* Office of Management and Budget
One-night blitz, 56
Opening Doors, 288
Opening Doors: Federal Strategic Plan to Prevent and End Homelessness (ICH), 266
Ordinances, 129, 130
Oregon, 252. *See also* Portland, Oregon
Organisation for Economic Co-operation and Development (OECD), 177, 192
Originalist views, 158*n*8
Osteen, Joel, 24, 127
Others, 142–143, 213*n*8
Outcome evaluation, 218, 219*fig*, 265
Outpatient treatment, with special needs housing, 95–96
Outputs, 218, 219*fig*

PAAC. *See* Portland Addictions Acupuncture Center
Paradigmatic emphases, 283–285
Parker, R., 32, 71
Parolees, 45, 133
Parsell, C., 208, 209
Parsell, M., 208, 209
Partnerships for Opening Doors, 271
Pathways' Housing First (PHF), 7, 68–81
Pathways to Housing program, 137
Pauly, B., 137–138
Pavetti, L., 191
Pay for Success, 271–272
PBRA. *See* Project-based rent assistance
Peasant class, 122
Peer services, 78
Pelton, Leroy, H., 152
Pennsylvania. *See* Philadelphia, Pennsylvania
People experiencing homelessness, 3–10; age, 33; chronic, 61, 68, 106, 243, 244, 283–284; counting, 31–32; gender, 33; household composition, 32–33; identification, 115–116; increase, 66*n*4; literal, 42–43, 49; location, 40–42; long-term, 60; marital status, 33; new, 32–39, 235; numbers, 31–32; as others, 142–143, 213*n*8; populations, 33–39, 55, 105–107; race, 33–34; segmenting, 105–107; stereotypes, 280, 287–288; threat, 202–206; time spent as, 39–40; veterans, 33. *See also* Children; Families; Point-in-Time (PIT) data
Perceptions, 154–155, 287–288
Perkins, Tom, 195*n*9
Permanent housing, 54, 92, 96–97, 128*n*5, 252
Permanent SHP. *See* Permanent Supportive Housing Program
Permanent subsidies, 128*n*2
Permanent supportive housing (PSH), 61–62, 103, 105, 107, 248, 268; CoCs emphasizing, 110; HUD emphasizing, 109–110; overview of, 109–114; sources of, 110–111; in ten-year plans, 252. *See also* Housing first
Permanent Supportive Housing Program (SHP), 103
Personal Responsibility and Work Op-

portunity Reconciliation Act
(PRWORA), 33, 210
Pew Charitable Trusts, 185, 186
PHAs. *See* Public Housing Agencies
PHF. *See* Pathways' Housing First
Philadelphia, Pennsylvania, 59–60, 66*n*8,
104, 115
Philanthropy, 10, 198, 267–269,
273–274, 281. *See also* Funders
Pickett, K., 192–193
PIT data. *See* Point-in-Time data
A Place to Call Home (Raikes Founda-
tion), 269
*A Plan, Not a Dream: How to End
Homelessness in Ten Years* (NAEH),
9, 245, 262–263
Plans, 245–260, 250*tab*, 253*fig*, 266,
269, 288. *See also* Ten-year plans
Plant-capture method, 228
Pleace, N., 125
Point-in-Time (PIT) data, 39–40, 43,
54–58, 60–61, 66*n*9, 232; definition
of, 226; limitations, 227; overview
of, 226–229
Police, 21–22
Policies, 1–2, 5–6, 51–52, 209–211,
239–240, 289; economic security im-
proved by, 193–194; federal,
206–207, 255–257; PSH, 61–62. *See
also* Evidence-based policy
Politicians, 239–242
Politics, 152–153, 231, 239–242
Polls, 2, 174, 186
Poor people, 146, 147, 152, 158*n*5; de-
servedness of, 206–208, 213*n*9,
213*n*10, 287–289; economic justice,
149–150
Population, 33–39, 55. *See also* Point-in-
Time (PIT) data
Portland, Oregon, 7, 128*n*1, 252. *See
also* Central City Concern
Portland Addictions Acupuncture Center
(PAAC), 95–97
Positive good theory, 142
Post-traumatic stress disorder (PTSD),
13, 15–16, 22
Poulin, S. R., 134
Poverty, 34, 63–64, 65, 68, 151; of
blacks, 187, 187*tab*; estimates,
186–187, 187*tab*; of Hispanics, 187,
187*tab*; measurement, 186–187,

187*tab*, 204*n*4; by race and ethnicity,
186–187, 187*tab*; of whites, 187,
187*tab*
Poverty-level wages, 181–182
Practice, policy as separated from, 5–6
Prejudices, 145–146
Presidential Task Force on Psychology's
Contribution to End Homelessness,
240
Prevention, 114–117, 251–252, 253–254,
257, 284–285
Prisons, 131–133
Private property, 213*n*7
Private stakeholders, 249
Process/implementation evaluation, 218
Professional coverage, 234–239, 235*fig*
Professionals, 9, 234–238, 235*fig*,
240–242, 244
Program evaluation, 215–230, 219*fig*,
274
Programs, 9, 27, 45; on Chronic Mental
Illness, 102; as client-based, 265;
data influencing, 220–221; elements,
281–283; federal housing, 161; fund-
ing, 274; HUD, 62; as limited, 246;
Outcome Plan, 226; primary, 246;
public assistance, 33; responses,
261–262; systems approach,
263–265. *See also* Annual Homeless
Assessment Reports; Housing first;
Ten-year plans
Project-based rent assistance (PBRA),
166
Project-based transitional housing,
128*n*2
Project-basing, 165–166
Proposition 8, 155
Protestant work ethic, 146
Pruitt-Igoe development, 163
PRWORA. *See* Personal Responsibility
and Work Opportunity Reconciliation
Act
PSH. *See* Permanent supportive housing
PsycINFO database, 236–237
PTSD. *See* Post-traumatic stress disorder
(PTSD)
Public: assistance programs, 33; housing,
163–164; inebriation, 83–85; opinion,
231, 242–244, 287–288; policies,
51–52, 209–211; relations, 289; space,
129–130; spending, 205; will, 289

Public Housing Agencies (PHAs), 104–105, 163–164, 165
Puerto Rico, 199–200
Puritans, 63–64, 146, 147, 157*n*2

Qualified Action Plan (QAP), 167

Race, 33–34; discrimination, 161; poverty by, 186–187, 187*tab*; segregation, 155, 163, 165
Racial minorities, 34. *See also* Blacks; Hispanics
Racism, 34, 204–205
RAD. *See* Rental Assistance Demonstration
Raikes Foundation, 269
Ramos, M. A., 235, 236, 237–238, 242
Rankin, S., 201
Rapid Exit program, 252
Rapid re-housing, 45, 107, 119*n*6, 125, 248; community-based, 128*n*2; definition of, 275*n*3; family homelessness and, 268–269; HUD funding, 112–113; overview of, 112–114, 170, 268–269, 275*n*3; Road Home piloting, 258; in ten-year plans, 252, 254
Rates of disability, 105
Reagan, Ronald, 33, 209–210, 231, 236, 240
Reagan administration, 53, 101–102, 161, 209, 234
Reaganville, 241
Real after-tax income, 182, 183, 183*fig*
Real wages, 182, 182*fig*
Recession, 52. *See also* Great Recession; 1981-1982 recession
Recovery self-sufficiency, 90–92
Regulation, 129–130, 187–188
Reich, Robert, 278–279
Religions, 125–128, 213*n*9
Reno, Nevada, 72
Rent subsidies, 97. *See also* Homelessness Prevention and Rapid Re-Housing Program
Rental Assistance Demonstration (RAD), 166
Rental housing, 2, 162, 169. *See also* Low-income rental housing
Renters insurance, 116–117
Rents, 163, 168, 170
Rescorla, L., 32

Research, 264–265
Research support, 216–217
Residency, 42–43
Respite shelters, 132
Responsibilities, 197–212, 285
Revanchism, 204, 206, 213*n*4
Rhode Island, 199, 200–201
Rich Hotel, 93
Richmond, California, 156
Richmond, Fred, 221
Rights, 9, 156–157, 197–212, 213*n*1, 213*n*7, 285
Rights for the Homeless Act, 157
Road Home, 258, 259
Robert Wood Johnson Foundation, 102, 103
Roberts, Joel, 2
Roca, 272
Rocky Mountain Cares, 18
Roosevelt, Franklin, 140*n*1, 277–278
Ropers, R., 32, 35
Rosenheck, R. A., 132, 133
Rossi, Peter, 29, 36, 57
Roth, D., 42
Rubin, B., 136
Runaways, 38
Rural areas, 40–41

Saint Louis, Missouri, 163
Sally McCracken building, 92
Salt Lake City, Utah, 158*n*11, 258
San Clemente, California, 150
San Diego, California, 150
San Francisco, California, 45, 202, 207, 252
Sandrock, Richard, 23
Scatter-site apartment model, 80, 97–98
Schmitt, J., 189
Schneider, Monika, 228–229
Schwartz, S., 203, 204
Scolaro, J. D., 35
Scott, R. E., 188
Section 8, 93–94, 102, 128*n*1, 161, 165, 166
Section 811, 104, 166
Section 202, 104, 166
Sedlak, A., 39
Seed funding, 273
Segregation, 155, 163, 165
Self-sufficiency, 90–92, 283
Sennett, R., 205, 213*n*8

Sequestration, 163, 267
Service agencies, 282–284
Service organization, 27
Services, 85, 155, 243
Severely housing challenged, 2–3
Shane, P., 36
Shared assets, 149
Shaw, George Bernard, 64
Shelter beds, 71, 131, 280
Shelter Plus Care (S+C), 103, 105, 112
Shelters, 15–22, 34, 54, 282; example, 59; families reentering, 63; hospitals as, 131–133; as law domains, 157; low- or no-barrier, 135–138; NYC, 257; prisons as, 131–133; respite, 132; right to, 285; segmentation, 105–107; as unintentional, 131–133; urban camps position of, 129–130; use of, 114. *See also* Annual Homeless Assessment Reports; Emergency shelter; Housing first
The Shepherds in Blue, 270
Shermer, Michael, 143
Shierholz, H., 189
Shinn, M., 31, 42, 63, 238, 257
Shlay, A., 29, 36
SHP. *See* Permanent Supportive Housing Program
Sick-talk, 207–208
Siegel, Fred, 202
Simmons Foundation, 270
Single-issue homelessness interest group, 286–287
Single-room-occupancy (SRO) hotels, 53, 84, 93–94
Sinners approach, 126–127
Sin-talk, 207
Sixteenth Amendment, 170
Skid row, 30, 41–42, 237–238
Slavery, 142, 158n10
Smith, Adam, 148–149
Smith, N., 204
SNAP. *See* Supplemental Nutrition Assistance Program
Snow, D. A., 34, 35
Snyder, Mitch, 234–235, 241
Sober housing. *See* Alcohol and Drug Free Community
Sobriety, 85–87
Social cognition, 144
Social contract, 151

Social Darwinism, 63–64
Social impact financing, 271–272
Social justice, 126, 128, 149–150
Social mobility, 193
Social policy, 239–240
Social problems, 287
Social Security Act, 191
Social Security Disability Insurance (SSDI), 53, 54
Social services, 7–8, 121–140, 123*fig*, 124*fig*, 206–207
Social welfare ideology, 63–64
Soup kitchens, 125–126
South Korea, 213n10
Southall, Shannon, 18
Spaces, 203–204, 205, 213n3
Special needs, 96–97
Special needs housing, 83–99
Spending policies, 190–191, 190*fig*
SRO hotels. *See* Single-room-occupancy hotels
SSDI. *See* Social Security Disability Insurance
SSI. *See* Supplemental Security Income
Stability, 42, 279
Staff members, 27
Stakeholders, 149, 247, 249, 251, 263
Stanhope, V., 5
Status, 152–153
Stayers, 42
Stereotypes, 280, 287–288
Stewart B. McKinney Homeless Assistance Act, 48, 66n3, 102, 236, 239, 240
Stimulus package. *See* American Recovery and Reinvestment Act
Stolley, P., 32
Street culture, 205
Street kids, 39
Street outreach, 270
Structural factors, 51
Structure plus, 208–209
Subprime crisis. *See* Great Recession
Subsidies, 3, 7, 54, 65, 97, 113–114; federal, 279; for homeowners, 170–172, 175; as permanent, 128n2; permanent housing, 128n5; tax, 170–172, 175. *See also* Federal housing programs; Homelessness Prevention and Rapid Re-Housing Program; Housing vouchers
Substance abuse, 43, 44, 54, 68, 125

Substance use, 69, 71
Supplemental Nutrition Assistance Program (SNAP), 116
Supplemental Poverty Measure, 186
Supplemental Security Income (SSI), 53, 54
Supported employment model, 90–91
Supported housing, 80
Supportive Services for Veteran Families, 224
Supreme Court, US, 199
Surface teams, 228
Surveillance, 135
Surveys, 55–58, 59, 60–61, 232, 233; American Housing, 246; Gallup Poll, 186; in Metro Denver area, 227. *See also* National Survey of Homeless Assistance Providers and Clients; Point-in-Time data
Swift, Jonathan, 157, 158*n*13
Systems approach, 263–265, 269–270, 274–275, 275*n*1
Systems impact evaluations, 281
Systems youth, 38–39
System-talk, 207, 208

TANF. *See* Temporary Assistance for Needy Families
Tax credits, 174, 195*n*7
Tax deductions, 174, 195*n*7
Tax expenditures, 171, 191, 195*n*8
Tax increment financing (TIF), 94
Tax policies, 190–191, 190*fig*
Tax reduction, 209–210
Tax subsidies, 170–172, 175
Taylor's Relics of Barbarism, 158*n*9
TBRA. *See* Tenant-based rent assistance
Tea Party, 153
Teaming, 78
Temporary Assistance for Needy Families (TANF), 117, 191, 257–258, 259
Tenant-based rent assistance (TBRA), 165–166, 169. *See also* Housing vouchers
Ten-year plans, 9, 245–257, 250*tab*, 253*fig*, 259–260
Texas, 12, 19, 57–58. *See also* Houston, Texas
Texas de Brazil, 25
TH. *See* Transitional housing
Thatcher, Margaret, 177–178

Thormodsgaard, Jeff, 21
Throwaways, 38
TIF. *See* Tax increment financing
Tobin, Kerri, 280
Tompsett, C. J., 233
Toomey, B., 42
Toro, Paul A., 35, 38, 231, 232, 235, 236, 237–238, 242
Total net worth, 184
Tragedy of commons, 149
Training, 155
Transaction, 158*n*3
Transference, 27
Transfers, 195*n*5
Transgender persons, 282
Transitional housing (TH), 43, 107; definition of, 275*n*2; family, 109; HUD on, 275*n*2; origins of, 102–103; overview of, 108–109; project-based, 128*n*2; as special needs option, 96–97. *See also* Annual Homeless Assessment Reports
Travel, right to, 199
Treatment model, 125, 282–283
Triage strategy, 284
Tsai, J., 132–133
Tsemberis, Sam, 281–282
Turner, R. S., 211
25 Cities effort, 288
Two-parent families, 282
2009 Annual Homeless Assessment Report (AHAR), 67–68
Two-tiered citizenship, 150–151
Tyler, K. A., 205

UCD. *See* University of Colorado Denver
UFH. *See* United for Homes
Umbrella coalition, 286–287
Unaccompanied youth, 36–39, 106
Underemployment, 179–180, 180*tab*
Undocumented people, 227
Unemployment, 179–180, 180*tab*
UNICEF. *See* United Nations Children's Fund
Unintentional shelters, 131–133
Union density, 189
United for Homes (UFH), 173–174
United Nations Charter, 156
United Nations Children's Fund (UNICEF), 193

United States (US), 52–54, 158*n*4, 192–193
United Ways, 275*n*1
Universal basic income, 278–279
University of Chicago, 255
University of Colorado Denver (UCD), 12–13
University of Denver, 24
University of Edinburgh, 188
Unsheltered homelessness, 61–62
Unstable housing, 49
Urban camps, 129–130
Urban Institute, 32, 246
Urban neoliberalism, 210–211
Urban renewal funds, 94
Utah, 158*n*11, 258

VA. *See* Department of Veterans Affairs
Vagrancy laws, 122
VASH program. *See* Veterans Affairs Supportive Housing program
Veterans, 29, 33, 35, 288; AHAR data, 106; as incarcerated, 132–133; in media, 238; services for, 243; sub-population, 106–107. *See also* Department of Veterans Affairs
Veterans Affairs Supportive Housing (VASH) program, 112
Veterans of Foreign Wars (VFW), 22
Veterans Student Center, 19–20, 22
VFW. *See* Veterans of Foreign Wars
Victim blaming, 141–143, 156
Virginia, 258
Visibility, 30

Wade, R., 187–188
Wages, 8, 180–182, 181*fig*
Wait lists, 87, 92
Warren, M. G., 231, 232
Washington, 269

Wasserman, Jason, 126–128, 208
Water, 156
Wealth, 8, 146–148, 177, 183–186, 185*fig*, 203–204
Weitzman, B. C., 31, 42
Welfare systems, 206, 210
Well-being, 192–193
the West, 41
Whites, 179, 180–182, 181*fig*, 185, 187, 187*tab*
Wilkinson, R., 192–193
Willse, C., 135
Wilson, Edward O., 156
Wilson, J. Q., 202–203
Window taxes, 157*n*2
Winthrop, John, 157*n*1
Wolfe, S., 38
Women, 29–30, 33, 36, 181–182, 193
Work, 90–92, 178
Workers, 187–191, 189*fig*, 190*fig*, 193–194
Workforce Investment Agency, 257–258
Workforce Services, 257–258
World Trade Organization (WTO), 188
World War II (WWII), 158*n*12
Worst-case housing needs, 49
Wright, J. D., 136, 203, 204–205
Wright, T., 202, 204
WTO. *See* World Trade Organization
Wyly, E., 205

Youth, 36–39, 106, 119*n*7, 269

About the Book

Despite billions of government dollars spent in the attempt, we are no closer than we were three decades ago to solving the problem of homelessness. Why?

Tackling this question, the authors of Ending Homelessness explore the complicated and often dysfunctional relationship between efforts to address homelessness and the realities on the street. Their book, addressing a range of practical, cultural, and economic issues, brings into sharp focus the barriers to and opportunities for overcoming this persistent social challenge.

Donald W. Burnes is executive director of the Burnes Institute on Poverty and Homelessness. **David L. DiLeo** is professor emeritus of history and humanities at Saddleback College.